JOURNAL FOR THE STUDY OF THE NEW TESTAMENT
SUPPLEMENT SERIES
126

Executive Editor
Stanley E. Porter

Sheffield Academic Press

The Cursed Christ

Mediterranean Expulsion Rituals and Pauline Soteriology

B. Hudson McLean

Journal for the Study of the New Testament
Supplement Series 126

To Bill

Copyright © 1996 Sheffield Academic Press

Published by Sheffield Academic Press Ltd
Mansion House
19 Kingfield Road
Sheffield S11 9AS
England

Printed on acid-free paper in Great Britain
by Bookcraft Ltd
Midsomer Norton, Bath

British Library Cataloguing in Publication Data

A catalogue record for this book is available
from the British Library

ISBN 1-85075-589-2

CONTENTS

PREFACE

This book began as a doctoral dissertation under the direction of Heinz O. Guenther of Emmanuel College, University of Toronto. It was presented to the Toronto School of Theology and successfully defended in 1989. This present work is a revised, expanded and rewritten version of the original thesis. It incorporates studies in a broad range of Pauline thought and attempts to situate this thought in the broader canvas of first-century Christianity.

It is my pleasant duty to give sincere thanks to those who have helped to make this work possible. Heinz Guenther, my thesis director, provided much helpful criticism during the preparation of the dissertation. I am also tremendously greatful to John Hurd who served as my mystagogue, initiating me into the intricacies of Pauline method. I would like to express my appreciation to my friend and colleague, Terence Donaldson, for his helpful comments, criticisms and suggestions. Finally, I should like to express my gratitude to staff of the Sheffield Academic Press for their careful preparation of the final manuscript.

I have dedicated this book to my dear friend William F. Blissett, Professor Emeritus of English at the University of Toronto. He not only taught me by example the true vocation of the scholar, but also inspired this research by his grasp of the true inwardness of the Levitical scapegoat ritual.

B. Hudson McLean
June 30 1995
St John's College
University of Manitoba

ABBREVIATIONS

AAWM	Abhandlungen der Akademie der Wissenschaften in Mainz
AB	Anchor Bible Series
ANRW	*Aufstieg und Niedergang der römischen Welt*
ARW	*Archiv für Religionswissenschaft*
BAGD	W. Bauer, W.F. Arndt, F.W. Gingrich and F.W. Danker, *Greek–English Lexicon of the New Testament*
BDB	F. Brown, S.R. Driver and C.A. Briggs, *Hebrew and English Lexicon of the Old Testament*
BE	Bulletin Epigraphique, in Revue des Etudes Grecques
BEvT	Beiträge zur evangelischen Theologie
BFCT	Beiträge zur Förderung christlicher Theologie
BHT	Beiträge zur historischen Theologie
Bib	*Biblica*
BJRL	*Bulletin of the John Rylands University Library of Manchester*
BZ	*Biblische Zeitschrift*
BZNW	Beihefte zur *ZNW*
CBQ	*Catholic Biblical Quarterly*
CD	Damascus Rule
CECNT	Critical and Exegetical Commentary on the NT
CIG	*Corpus inscriptionum graecarum*
CJT	*Canadian Journal of Theology*
CNT	Commentaire du Nouveau Testament
CTH	*Catalogue des Textes Hittites*, Emmanuel Laroche
CTM	*Concordia Theological Monthly*
ClQ	*Classical Quarterly*
EGT	Expositor's Greek Testament
EKKNT	Evangelisch-Katholischer Kommentar zum Neuen Testament
EncJud.	*Encyclopedia Judaica*
EncRel.	*Encylopedia of Religion*
EvT	*Evangelische Theologie*
ExpTim	*Expository Times*
F. Delphes	Fouilles de Delphes
FFNT	Foundations and Facets: New Testament
F.Gr.Hist.	Die Fragmente der griechischen Historiker, F. Jacoby
FRLANT	Forschungen zur Religion und Literatur des Alten und Neuen Testaments

GIBM	Ancient Greek Inscriptions in the British Museum
GRBS	*Greek, Roman and Byzantine Studies*
Greg	*Gregorianum*
GTA	Göttinger Theologische Arbeiten
GThT	Gereformeerd Theologisch Tijdschrift
HJP	Schürer, *History of the Jewish People*
HKNT	Handkommentar zum Neuen Testament
HNT	Handbuch zum Neuen Testament
HR	*History of Religions*
HSCP	*Harvard Studies in Classical Philology*
HSNT	Die Heilige Schrift Neuen Testaments
HTR	*Harvard Theological Review*
HUCA	*Hebrew Union College Anuual*
IB	*Interpreter's Bible*
ICC	International Critical Commentary
IDB	G.A. Buttrick (ed.), *Interpreter's Dictionary of the Bible*
IDBSup	*IDB*, Supplementary Volume
IEJ	*Israel Exploration Journal*
I. Eph.	Die Inscriften von Ephesos, hrsg. von H. Wankel, R. Merkelbach et alii, Band I-VII (Bonn 1979–81)
IG	Inscriptiones Graecae (Berlin 1873–1972)
IGR	Inscriptiones Graecae ad res Romanas pertinentes (Paris 1911–27)
I. Perg.	M. Fraenkel, *Die Inschriften von Pergamon* (2 vols.; Berlin 1890–95)
JAAR	*Journal of the American Academy of Religion*
JAOS	*Journal of the American Oriental Society*
JBL	*Journal of Biblical Literature*
JDAI	Jahrbuch des Deutschen archäologischen Instituts
JHÖAI	Jahreshefte des Österreichischen Archäologischen Instituts
JHS	*Journal of Hellenic Studies*
JJS	*Journal of Jewish Studies*
JQR	*Jewish Quarterly Review*
JR	*Journal of Religion*
JSNTSup	*Journal for the Study of the New Testament*, Supplement Series
JSOT	*Journal for the Study of the Old Testament*
JSS	*Journal of Semitic Studies*
JTS	*Journal of Theological Studies*
KAT	Kommentar zum Alten Testament
KBo	*Keilschrifttexte aus Bogahazköi*
KNT	Kommentar zum Neuen Testament
KUB	*Keilschrifturkunden aus Boghazhoi*
LCL	Loeb Classical Library
LGS	I. von Pratt and L. Ziehen, *Leges Graecorum sacrae e titulis collectae* (Leipzig 1896–1906)

LSAM	F. Sokolowski, *Lois sacrés de l'Asie Mineure*
LSCG	F. Sokolowski, *Lois sacrées des cités greques* (Paris 1969)
LSJ	Liddell–Scott–Jones, *Greek–English Lexicon*
MNTC	Moffat NT Commentary
NA²⁶	*The Greek New Testament*, Nestle/Aland, 26th edn
NCB	New Century Bible
NICNT	New International Commentary on the New Testament
NTS	*New Testament Studies*
OBO	Orbis biblicus et orientalis
OCP	*Orientalia Christiana Periodica*
OGIS	*Orientis Graeci Inscriptiones Selectae*, ed. W. Dittenberger
PW	Paulys-Wissowa, *Realencyclopädie der classischen Altertumswissenschaft*
PWSup	Supplement to PW
RB	*Revue Biblique*
REG	*Revue des études grecques*
REL	*Revue des Etudes Latines*
RevQ	*Revue de Qumran*
RIDA	Revue internationale des droits de l'Antiquité
RGG	*Religion in Geschichte und Gegenwart*
RHR	*Revue de l'histoire des religions*
RVV	Religionsgeschichtliche Versuche und Vorarbeiten
SANT	Studien zum Alten und Neuen Testament
SBL	Society of Biblical Literature
SBLDS	SBL Dissertation Series
SBT	Studies in Biblical Theology
SCHNT	Studia ad Corpus Hellenisticum Novi Testamenti
SEÅ	Svensk exegetisk årsbok
SIG³	*Sylloge Inscriptionum Graecarum*, ed. Wm. Dittenberger.
SJT	*Scottish Journal of Theology*
SMSR	Studi e materiali di storia delle religioni
SNTSMS	Society for New Testament Studies Monograph Series
SPAW	Sitzungsberichte der preussischen Akademie der Wissenschaften
SR	*Studies in Religion/Sciences religieuses*
Str–B	[H. Strack and] P. Billerbeck, *Kommentar zum Neuen Testament aus Talmud und Midrasch*
Thayer	J.H. Thayer, *A Greek–English Lexicon of the NT*
TDNT	G. Kittel and G. Friedrich (eds.), *Theological Dictionary of the New Testament*
Theod.	Greek recension of Theodotia
THKNT	Theologischer Handkommentar zum Neuen Testament
TLZ	*Theologische Literaturzeitung*
TynBul	*Tyndale Bulletin*
TZ	*Theologische Zeitschrift*

UBSGNT	United Bible Societies' *Greek New Testament*
USQR	*Union Seminary Quarterly Review*
VT	*Vestus Testamentum*
VTSup	*Vestus Testamentum*, Supplement
WBC	Word Biblical Commentary
WMANT	Wissenschaftliche Monographien zum Alten und Neuen Testament
WUNT	Wissenschaftliche Untersuchungen zum Neuen Testament
ZAS	Zeitschrift für ägyptische Sprache und Altertumskunde
ZAW	*Zeitschrift für die alttestamentliche Wissenschaft*
ZKT	*Zeitschrift für Katholische Theologie*
ZNW	*Zeitschrift für neutestamentliche Wissenschaft*
ZTK	*Zeitschrift für Theologie und Kirche*

INTRODUCTION

When Paul states that 'Christ became a curse' (Gal. 3.13), was 'made to be sin' (2 Cor. 5.21), and was 'sent in the likeness of sinful flesh' (Rom. 8.3), he is not making an historical statement about Jesus' death, but rather interpreting the meaning of Christ's death for first century Christians. These statements reflect Paul's attempt to interpret Christ's death in relation to the problem of human sin. Each is clothed in language and ideas which extend deeply into the Hellenistic culture of Paul's time. This culture, a kind of 'hinterland' of Paul's thought, orientated Paul's perception of the problems implicit in human existence, and his belief in means of atonement accomplished in the person of Jesus Christ.

Since the time of Paul, the doctrine of the atonement has become such an intrinsic part of western religious thought and culture, that one might fail to appreciate the startling nature of Paul's assertion. How indeed could the death of one man—even of a *divine* man—atone for the sins of others? The traditional answer construes Paul's language of atonement as sacrificial language. However, as I shall argue below, Paul's concept of atonement is not rooted in a sacrificial paradigm.

Yet, Paul's concept of atonement was not a creation *ex nihilo*. The language, cosmology and anthropology of Paul were in many ways a common possession of the ancient Near Eastern religious consciousness. On this basis, one can reasonably inquire into the cultural background implicit in Paul's idea of the cursed and sinful Christ. Unless this idea is to be emptied of its fundamental meaning, it must be admitted that the idea of a cursed and sinful saviour cannot be confused with any conception which does not include this as an integral feature. This idea will provide an important principle of discernment and selection for exploring the conceptual background of Paul's atonement theology.

The principal purpose of this book is to compare Paul's theology of the atonement to analogous concepts in Jewish and Graeco-Roman religions. This brings us to a consideration of the methodological underpinnings of this comparative study.

The comparison of Christianity with Judaism and Graeco-Roman religions has traditionally been conceived of either in terms of analogy or genealogy. The concept of analogy pertains to parallel phenomena which share common characteristics. On the other hand, the concept of genealogy posits a relationship of dependency. Genealogical inferences are based upon the identification of linear relationships between phenomena, asserting that 'B' is similar to 'A' because 'B' has been influenced by 'A', or borrowed from 'A'.

In his book, *Drudgery Divine*, Jonathan Z. Smith has chronicled how such comparisons have been employed to further covert apologetic agendas.[1] For example, some scholars have portrayed 'apostolic Christianity' as being essentially Protestant in character, while the so-called Mystery Religions were depicted as resembling Catholicism. The use of 'apostolic Christianity' and the Mystery Religions as ciphers for Protestantism and Roman Catholicism provided weaponry for a Protestant assault upon Roman Catholicism. It was asserted that Protestantism was superior to Catholicism on the basis of the purported superiority of apostolic Christianity to the Mystery Religions.[2]

Putting such denominational polemics aside, other ideologically motivated issues have also been pursued under the guise of genealogy. Genealogical comparison has been an effective tool for arguing that early Christianity was superior to both the Mystery Religions and Judaism. It was argued that 'apostolic Christianity' was superior to the Mystery Religions because it preceded them and shared a closer genealogical relationship to Judaism. Then, through some intellectual mischief, the reverse argument was also applied: namely, that early Christianity was superior to Judaism because it superseded and fulfilled Judaism. Thus, Judaism was used in two contrary ways, both as an insulating devise against paganism, and as an ancestor which had been transcended.[3] Clearly, the idea that early Christianity was unsurpassed in superiority to both the Mystery Religions and Judaism was not a conclusion derived at through careful study (if research could ever prove such a value-weighted conclusion), but a guiding conviction which propelled the comparison and predetermined its conclusions.

---

1.   J.Z. Smith, *Drudgery Divine: On the Comparison of Early Christianities and the Religions of Late Antiquity* (Jordan Lectures in Comparative Religion, 14; Chicago: University of Chicago Press, 1990).

2.   Smith, *Drudgery Divine*, pp. 36-53.

3.   Smith, *Drudgery Divine*, p. 117.

The above examples share one thing in common: they are fuelled by the conviction that Christianity is of incomparable superiority, *sui generis*, or, in other words, is ontologically unique.[4] The very notion of ontological uniqueness excludes the possibility of comparison at the outset for it implies that there are no significant points of comparison with other phenomena. However, the task of comparing early Christianity to anything depends upon the prior recognition that Christianity is *not* ontologically unique.

Early Christianity is *taxonomically* unique in that its characteristics *in toto* permit it to be distinguished from other religious phenomena. Christianity, like all religions, manifests taxonomic or relative uniqueness, but this should not be confused with an assertion of ontological or absolute uniqueness. The notion of taxonomical uniqueness belongs to the category of history, whereas ontological uniqueness is an ahistorical concept. Smith describes how the belief in the taxonomical uniqueness of the so-called 'Christ-event' has often been confused with the notion of its ontological uniqueness:

> The uniqueness of the 'Christ-event', which usually encodes the death and resurrection of Jesus, is a double claim. On the ontological level, it is a statement of the absolutely alien nature of the divine protagonist (*monogenes*) and the unprecedented (and paradoxical) character of his self-disclosure; on the historical level, it is an assertion of the radical incomparability of the Christian 'proclamation' with respect to the 'environment'. For many scholars of early Christianity, the latter claim is often combined with the former, so as to transfer the (proper, though problematic) theological affirmation of absolute uniqueness to an historical statement that, standing alone, could never assert more than relative uniqueness, that is to say, a quite ordinary postulation of difference. It is this illicit transfer from the ontological to the historical that raises the question of the comparison of early Christianity and the religions of Late Antiquity.[5]

4. Cf. B.F. Mack, *Mark and Christian Origins: A Myth of Innocence* (Philadelphia: Fortress Press, 1988), pp. 1-9. Similarly, Robert Oden has noted how scholars have portrayed Israelite history as being divinely guided, thereby rendering the religion of Israel 'absolute' and placing it 'beyond any meaningful comparison'. Thus, Israelite religion is always found to be superior to those of its ancient neighbours while claims are made of objective analysis. He calls this the process of 'absolutization' under the aegis of objectivity (*The Bible Without Theology: The Theological Tradition and Alternatives to It* [San Francisco: Harper & Row, 1987]).

5. Smith, *Drudgery Divine*, p. 39; cf. J.C. Meagher, 'The Implications for Theology of a Shift from the K.L. Schmidt Hypothesis of Literary Uniqueness for the Gospels', in B. Corley (ed.), *Colloquy on New Testament Studies: A Time for*

This study takes as its starting point the premise that early Christianity, its proclamation, and the 'Christ-event' itself, are unique only in a taxonomical sense. For this reason, they are all amenable to comparison with other religious phenomena. This being the case, what method should one adopt in comparing early Christianity with the religions of Late Antiquity? To what end is the comparison made? How does one formulate accurate conclusions concerning such comparisons? Though it is clear that correlations between the religious ideas in two different cultures do not prove dependency in and of themselves, can one argue that a genealogical relationship exists if significant parallels are found to exist between two religious ideas arising in the same geographical area, in overlapping cultural contexts, and in the same time period. If all three of these criteria can be met, can it be concluded that a genealogical relationship exists between 'A' and 'B'?

The logic of this kind of comparison conceals assumptions which must be identified and critically examined. First among these is the presupposition that it is indeed possible to compare two things without specifying a conceptual framework. In fact, it is illogical to state that 'B' resembles 'A' unless a third referent is specified. Phenomena cannot be compared *in toto*—but only with respect to specified characteristics. In other words, one must argue that 'B' resembles 'A' with respect to 'C'. Thus, comparison by its very nature is triadic, not dyadic, in that it is always 'with respect to' a third referent.[6] In the words of F.J.P. Poole:

> The comparability of phenomena always depends both on the purpose of comparison and on a theoretically informed analysis. Neither phenomenologically whole entities nor their local meanings are preserved in comparison. What matters in comparison are certain variables that are posited by and cohere in theories and that are aligned with aspects of the phenomena to be compared through some set of correspondence rules.[7]

If a third referent is necessary in any comparison, who or what determines this referent? Here, one must squarely face the fact that it is the

Reappraisal and Fresh Approaches (Macon, GA: Mercer University Press, 1983), pp. 203-233.

6.   Smith, *Drudgery Divine*, p. 53; Single words cannot be employed as a third reference in any comparison since words in isolation lack clarity and fixity. Their meanings are mediated indirectly through larger literary complexes (J. Barr, *The Semantics of Biblical Language* [London: Oxford University Press, 1961], pp. 269-70; cf. pp. 249-50).

7.   F.J.P. Poole, 'Metaphors and Maps: Towards Comparison in the Anthropology of Religion', *JAAR* 54 (1986), pp. 411-57, esp. p. 415.

scholar who decides what this third referent will be. Referents are not predetermined by the data. Scholars decide what is of intellectual significance to themselves. Clearly, the choice as to which referent is of intellectual interest is a subjective decision which will vary according to the personal interests and questions of the researcher. Yet it is this very choice which will determine the nature of the comparison and, what is more, the conclusions of the research.

Therefore, it is essential that researchers be conscious of their role in the act of comparing. The researcher is not a passive 'reader' of the data supplied by antiquity, nor is a comparison a statement of how things *are*. Comparison is a creative and intellectual exercise within a scholar's mind whose aim is to envision one way in which the relationship between two things might be described. In the words of Smith:[8]

> A comparison is a disciplined exaggeration in the service of knowledge. It lifts out and strongly marks certain features within difference as being of possible intellectual significance, expressed in the rhetoric of their being 'like' in some stipulated fashion. Comparison provides the means by which *we* 're-vision' phenomena as *our* data in order to solve *our* theoretical problems.[9]

Comparison then is an inventive analytical exercise who purpose is to fulfil the intellectual intent of the scholar. It is not a matter of discovering something which has been 'hiding' in the data and 'waiting' to be discovered.[10] The notion of similarity and difference between two things is an intellectual construct created by the scholar, not a property of the data. The scholar alone imagines their cohabitation.

Since the statement 'B' is similar to 'A' with respect to 'C' is an intellectual construct, not an innate property of the 'A' or 'B', this argument cannot be used to prove that 'B' is dependent on 'A' in a historical and causal sense. This form of argument demonstrates analogy, but not genealogy. This is not to deny that causal relationships can and do occur, but rather to assert that the above argument cannot demonstrate such relationships.

8. Smith, *Drudgery Divine*, p. 52.
9. Emphasis Smith's (*Drudgery Divine*, p. 52).
10. As Smith describes it,

> comparison... is an active, and at times even a playful, enterprise of deconstruction and reconstruction which, kaleidoscope-like, gives the scholar a shifting set of characteristics with which to negotiate the relations between his or her theoretical interests and the data stipulated as exemplary' (*Drudgery Divine*, p. 53).

Accordingly, this monograph is not a study in genealogy. I will not argue that Paul's soteriology is historically and causally dependent upon particular religious phenomena. This study will proceed on the basis of three principles. First, Paul's soteriology is taxonomically unique, and therefore can be profitably compared with other religious concepts. In particular, this study will compare it with the concepts implicit in Mediterranean apotropaeic rituals; that is, rituals used in averting evil, curses and defilement, the best known example being the Levitical scapegoat ritual.

Secondly, before any such comparison is possible, it is necessary to identify the third referent in the comparison. Paul's soteriology and Mediterranean apotropaeic rituals will be compared with reference to clearly specified points of comparison (e.g., the idea of a cursed or ritually defiled victim, internal logic of the ritual, social needs addressed by the ritual). Thirdly, the outcome of this inquiry will be a statement of analogy, not genealogy; I will argue that Paul's concept of the cursed and sinful Christ is analogous to the concept implicit within apotropaeic rituals and therefore, that they draw upon a shared paradigm.

Starting from the desiderata contained in these three principles, I will attempt a fresh analysis of those elements in Paul's soteriology and apotropaeic rituals which I consider to be analogous. The outline of this argument can be summarised as follows. After demonstrating the inadequacy of the sacrificial paradigm as a means of accounting for Paul's theology of the atonement (ch. 1), this study will outline a so-called 'apotropaeic paradigm' which was pervasive in particular rituals throughout the Mediterranean basin in the ancient world (ch. 2).

I will then compare Paul's idea of the sinful and cursed Christ with the victims of these apotropaeic rituals. Though a few scholars have tentatively suggested that 2 Cor. 5.21 and Gal. 3.13 may be based on the Levitical scapegoat ritual, their proposals have been far from decisive, each author offering at best a few sentences on the subject.[11] On the

---

11. Re: 2 Cor. 5.21: J.H. Bernard, *The Second Epistle to the Corinthians* (EGT, 3; ed. W. Robertson Nicoll; New York: George H. Doran & Co., 1903), p. 73; A. Plummer, *A Critical and Exegetical Commentary on the Second Epistle of St Paul to the Corinthians* (ICC; Edinburgh: T. & T. Clark, 1915), p. 187; H. Windisch, *Der zweite Korintherbrief*, (Kritisch-exegetischer Kommentar über das NT, 6; Göttingen: Vandenhoeck & Ruprecht, 9th edn, 1924), p. 198; J. Héring, *La Seconde Epître de Saint Paul aux Corinthiens* (Neuchatel: Delachaux; Paris: Niestlé, 1958), p. 54; H. Thyen, *Studien zur Sündenvergebung im Neuen Testament und seinen alttestamentlichen und jüdischen Voraussetzungen* (FRLANT, 96; Göttingen:

basis of this comparison, I shall argue that an analogy exists between Paul's theology of atonement and these apotropaeic rituals in that they share a common paradigm. Therefore, Paul's idea of atonement can be profitably interpreted in the light of this broader ritual context (ch. 3).

After this has been established, I will attempt to situate Paul's apotropaeic soteriology within the overall development of his theology (chs. 4–6). This will involve the examination of his letters in order of composition, and a consideration of the local factors which contributed towards this theological development. The dominant picture which emerges is as follows. In his early career, Paul's theology centred, first on Christ's expected parousia, and subsequently upon Christ's resurrection, which he understood principally in apocalyptic terms. After the inordinate delay of the parousia and Paul's 'affliction in Asia', Paul developed the apotropaeic paradigm wherein Christ is laden with humanity's sin and curse. In this same period, Paul's theology of the resurrection underwent two striking developments: first, Christ's resurrection is related to the gradual transformation of believers beginning at baptism; secondly, Paul explains this concept of the transformation in terms of the believer's mystical participation in the resurrected Christ.

Finally, I shall argue that Paul's resurrection and apotropaeic paradigms are complementary in nature. The resurrection paradigm, was unable to account for the means by which Christ removed human sin and its curse, though it did provide a basis for understanding the resurrection of believers. The apotropaeic paradigm, on the other hand, addressed the vital issue of atonement, though it was unsuited to furnish a conceptual framework for individual resurrection.

Vandenhoeck & Ruprecht, 1970), p. 188; J.-F. Collange, *Enigmes de la Deuxième Epître de Paul aux Corinthiens: Étude Exegetique de 2 Cor 2.14–7.14* (Cambridge: Cambridge Univerisity Press, 1972), p. 276.

Re: Gal. 3.13: J.B. Lightfoot, *Saint Paul's Epistle to the Galatians* (London: Macmillan, 1865), p. 139; A.W.F. Blunt, *The Epistle of Paul to the Galatians* (Oxford: Clarendon Press, 1925), p. 97; E.B. Allo, *Seconde Epître aux Corinthiens* (Paris: Gabalda, 1937), p. 172; Thyen, *Sündenvergebung*, p. 189; F.E. Vokes, *The Riddle of the Didache* (London: SPCK, 1938), pp. 23, 27; B.F. Westcott, *St Paul and Justification* (London: Macmillan, 1913), p. 54.

Part I

A COMPARATIVE STUDY OF PAUL'S CONCEPT OF ATONEMENT

Chapter 1

PAUL AND SACRIFICE

In the past, the presupposition of many scholars has been that Paul's concept of Christ's atoning death is first and foremost a Jewish sacrificial idea. The American sociologist Alvin Gouldner has termed such presuppositions 'domain assumptions'. They could be characterised as 'the key or master conceptual frames of reference which affect the kinds of models and hypotheses that are imaginable—and therefore possible...in a circle of scholarship'.[1] Samuel Sandmel is highly critical of tendencies in New Testament scholarship which reflect ingrained domain assumptions: 'The fact must be faced that value judgments on Judaism, as distinct from a detached description of it, constitute an ongoing reality in much of modern New Testament scholarship.'[2] The hidden and unargued nature of many domain assumptions is such that they can impede the advancement of scholarship into new and potentially fruitful areas of inquiry.

The dominance of the sacrificial interpretation of Pauline soteriology, at least in traditional scholarship, is one such example. In my opinion, the comparison of key Pauline texts with Jewish sacrificial theology is of intellectual interest, not because of their analogy, but precisely on account of their differences.

At the very outset of this inquiry, the scholar is faced with two problems. The first is that the average reader has many misconceptions with regard to the practice and meaning of sacrifice which invite misleading

1. With these words, Norman Gottwald has paraphrased Gouldner's definition of 'domain assumptions' and adapted it to the field of biblical studies ('Domain Assumptions and Societal Models in the Study of Pre-Monarchic Israel', VTSup 28 [1974], pp. 89-100, esp. p. 89; cf. A.W. Gouldner, *The Coming Crisis of Western Sociology* [New York: Basic Books, 1970]).

2. S. Sandmel, *The First Christian Century in Judaism and Christianity: Certainties and Uncertainties* (New York: Oxford University Press, 1969), p. 166.

comparisons. This is especially true if the reader is familiar with the liturgical space of a church and its related sacramental and liturgical theology. Within this frame of reference, the Jewish sanctuary might be thought of, by analogy, as a kind of 'church', and the sanctuary altar, the altar of the Mass...a kind of table upon which the victim is ritually slaughtered.

However, the temple sanctuary was in no way a 'church' for it was rarely used, and even then, principally by the high priest: all Jewish commoners were prohibited from entering the sanctuary. It was not the place were hymns were sung, nor prayers said. Nor for that matter was it a place of animal sacrifice.[3] The sacrifices were conducted in the open air *in front of* the sanctuary. The sacrificial altar which stood in front of the sanctuary was not a table upon which animals were slaughtered, but was comparable to a pyre.[4] Its surface consisted of a grate under which a fire of burning faggots was kept perpetually alight for the burning of animal flesh. Of particular importance were the bronze corners on the altar, the so-called 'horns' (cf. Lev. 4.30-34). These were especially connected with the idea of holiness. Blood was rubbed on these horns in the course of purification and reparation sacrifices in order to effect purification.[5] Blood was also splashed onto the sides of the altar and poured around its circumference such that the whole area became bloodied in order to return the life of the animal back to the Lord.

A second issue concerns the problem posed in comparing Paul's *ideas* with Jewish cultic *rituals*. Clearly, such a comparison is impossible unless

3.   Cf. S. Safrai, 'The Temple', in *The Jewish People in the First Century: Historical Geography, Political History, Social, Cultural and Religious Life and Institutions* (2 vols.; S. Safrai and M. Stern [eds.]; Assen: Van Gorcum, 1976), II, pp. 865-907.

4.   See photos of reconstructed altars in J. Milgrom, *Leviticus 1–16: A New Translation with Introduction and Commentary* (AB, 3; New York: Doubleday, 1991), p. 235. There is no biblical information about the construction of the second temple altar unless 2 Chron. 4.1 can be interpreted as what the Chronicler saw in the second temple period. The second temple altar probably resembled Solomon's altar in construction, being made of planks of acacia wood, overlaid with bronze plates; overtop was fitted a bronze grating (cf. Exod. 27.1-8; 38.1-7). It was modelled on an altar in Damascus which had steps or a ramp (2 Kgs 16.10-16). According to Pseudo-Hecataeus (c. 200 BCE), it measured 20 cubits by 20 cubits by 10 cubits high and had a ramp (in Jos. *Ag. Ap.* 1.198). These measurements are confirmed by 2 Chron. 4.1.

5.   E.g., Exod. 29.12; 30.10; Lev. 8.15; 9.9; 14.14-17; 16.18; Ezek. 43.20.

the cultic rituals are reduced to a set of constituent ideas. Westerners are so accustomed to thinking of sacrifice metaphorically, that sacrifice itself has tended to be perceived primarily as a set of ideas. In other words, the theological significance of sacrifice has been given much more attention than the rituals themselves, such that the act and experience of animal sacrifice is totally ignored as if it had no relevance to the under-standing of sacrifice itself. The hidden assumption here is that praxis did not inform theory. However, in a living culture where sacrifice is prac-ticed, what is done tends to take priority over what is meant. Sacrifice is first and foremost something one does—not a way one thinks. The very act of sacrifice informs the participant's understanding of the event.

The danger of reducing the practice of sacrifice too quickly to a set of beliefs is illustrated by certain Protestant biblical scholars who have interpreted the Levitical sacrifice with an implicit anti-liturgical bias. For example, in Ludwig Köhler's book *Old Testament Theology*, one can hear the protestations of Martin Luther: he declares that Levitical sacrifice 'is begun, continued and accomplished by man; it is works, not grace; an act of self-help, not a piece of God's salvation...Salvation is the way of the world...this cult deserves only very limited discussion within a theology of the Old Testament'.[6] Likewise, Walther Eichrodt remarks that there is 'a tendency of the [Levitical] sacrificial system to make the forgiveness of sins a mechanical process'.[7]

Rather than beginning with a discussion of the meaning of sacrifice, we shall find ourselves on a much firmer footing if we begin by des-cribing the event itself. What can be said about the experience of partici-pating in a sacrifice? What did it look like? Who performed it? Only then shall the meanings of sacrifice be adduced for comparison with Pauline theology.

The Problem of Sources

The code of sacrifice outlined in the Torah describes sacrifice in the context of the Tent of Meeting and the Tabernacle (cf. Exod. 33.11, Num. 12.8). Here one must recognise that these terms are used as ciphers for the Jewish temple. In this way, the Torah projects the Post-

6.   L. Köhler, *Old Testament Theology* (trans. A.S. Todd; London: Lutterworth Press, 1936–1957), pp. 181-82.

7.   W. Eichrodt, *Theology of the Old Testament* (trans. J.A. Baker; Philadelphia: Westminster Press, 1961), I, p. 168.

exilic cult back onto Israel's idealized epic past.[8] This explains why the proportions of the Tent of Meeting are exactly half the proportions of the temple sanctuary, since the latter is its model (cf. Exod. 26). Thus, from the point of view of the redacted Torah, references to the rituals of the Tent of Meeting and Tabernacle should be understood as the rituals of the post-exilic temple in Jerusalem.

Though an understanding of sacrifice in the post-exilic period will provide an invaluable foundation upon which to build, its usefulness for this study will be greatly increased if it is augmented with information from Jewish sources contemporaneous with Paul. Any discussion of first-century Jewish sacrifice must first address the problem of sources. The three principle sources of information about sacrifice in the first century are Josephus, Philo of Alexandria and the Mishnah.

Josephus is by far the best authority since he was familiar with the day to day practice of sacrifice from his boyhood through to the time that he himself became a priest. When Josephus furnishes information beyond that found in the Pentateuch it can be assumed that he is relating what he has learned as a priest. Unfortunately, Josephus informs the reader much more about the practice of sacrifice than its purpose. Therefore, the data supplied by Josephus must be supplemented by other sources.

Philo had limited first-hand acquaintance with the temple. Though he had visited the temple, his discussion of sacrifice is much more theoretical and seems intellectually removed from the temple cult. Moreover, at important points, he depends upon the Septuagint for information. Though Philo may also have been familiar with the Palestinian Halakah, this point should not be overemphasized. On the one hand, Samuel Belkin asserts that the Palestinian Oral Law 'which originated in Palestine was not limited to Palestine, and that Philo's Halakah is based upon the Palestinian Oral Law as it was known in Alexandria'.[9] However, taking a more cautious position, Samuel Sandmel remarks:

---

8. R. de Vaux, *Ancient Israel: Its Life and Institutions* (trans. J. McHugh; New York: McGraw–Hill, 1961), p. 415; J. Bright, *A History of Israel* (Philadelphia: Westminster Press, 3rd edn, 1959), p. 170; Eichrodt, *Theology of the Old Testament*, p. 130.

9. For further discussion of this point, and Jewish witnesses for and against, see S. Belkin, *Philo and the Oral Law: The Philonic Interpretation of Biblical Law in Relation to the Palestinian Halakah* (Cambridge, MA: Harvard University Press, 1940), pp. 55-56.

A prudent set of conclusions, gleaned from the views of scholars, would be the following. There are overlaps in halacha between Philo and the Rabbis. Communication between Alexandria and Palestine need not be denied. Overlaps, however do not prove the dependency of Philo on the Rabbis.[10]

In regard to the use of the Mishnah, we are immediately faced with the problems associated with the use of Rabbinic texts for the reconstruction of pre-70 Judaism. George Foot Moore once maintained that Rabbinic Judaism could be taken as normative for Pharisaism in the first century CE, in contrast to apocalyptic Judaism, mystic (or gnostic) Judaism and Philonic Judaism, which he considered to be aberrations of Judaism.[11] This simple equation of Rabbinic Judaism with first-century Pharisaism has since been rejected by scholars.[12] Louis Finkelstein argues that substantial portions of Rabbinic literature, when handled sensitively, may be used to establish normative first-century Pharisaism.[13] However, this process is not without its difficulties for, as E.P. Sanders points out, 'the rabbis continued to debate rules of sacrifice long after living memory of how it had been done had vanished. Consequently, in reading the Mishnah one is sometimes reading second-century theory'.[14] Indeed, as Sanders demonstrates, 'second century rabbis were quite willing to vote against practice in discussing the behaviour of the priests and the rules they followed'.[15] It is now recognised that some tractates of the Mishnah are more reliable than others. For example, both Sanders and Aaron Rothkoff agree that *Tamid* and *Zebahim 5* provide reliable information about second temple practice.[16] With regard to the Day of Atonement ritual, Jacob Milgrom thinks that the Priestly account in the Mishnah still

10. Sandmel, *First Christian Century*, p. 166.

11. G. Moore, *Judaism in the First Three Centuries of the Christian Era* (3 vols.; Cambridge, MA: Harvard University Press, 1927–30), III, pp. v-vi.

12. Cf. E. Goodenough, *Jewish Symbols in the Greco-Roman Period* (12 vols.; New York: Pantheon Books, 1953–65), XII, p. 6; J. Neusner, *Rabbinic Traditions about the Pharisees Before 70* (3 vols.; Leiden: J.C.B. Mohr, 1971), III, p. 359.

13. L. Finkelstein, *The Pharisees: The Sociological Background of Their Faith* (2 vols.; Philadelphia: Jewish Publication Society, 3rd edn, 1962).

14. E.P. Sanders, *Judaism: Practice and Belief 63 BCE–66 CE* (Philadelphia: Trinity Press, 1992), p. 103.

15. Sanders, *Judaism*, p. 104.

16. A. Rothkoff, 'Semikah', *EncJud*, XIV, 1140-41; Sanders, *Judaism*, pp. 506-507, nn. 1, 6, 16.

preserves the essential Levitical understanding despite its expansion and interpretation of the ritual.[17]

As a way of proceeding, the argument shall begin with a discussion of the practice and purpose of sacrifice as it is outlined in the Torah. Next, the testimony of Josephus, Philo and the Mishnah will be considered. The purpose of this exercise is to document, to the extent possible, both continuity and change in the practice and theory of sacrifice in the time of Paul.

The Practice and Purpose of Jewish Sacrifice

Jewish sacrifice involved the slaughter and often consumption of a domesticanimal for the Jewish god, Yahweh. The most honourable sacrifice was the ox, especially the bull, and next, the ram. The most common sacrifices involved sheep, goats, lambs and kids. The sacrifice of poultry (pigeons and turtle doves), and even wheat flour, was also common, especially among the poor.

Since there are three general types of sacrifice, and the execution and purpose of each is in some measure peculiar to itself, the terms of reference must be more precise for fruitful discussion. The three fundamental categories of Levitical sacrifice are the 'whole-offering', the 'thank-offering', and lastly, the 'purification' and 'reparation-offering'.[18] Of these three categories of sacrifice, only the last was used for purification. In the case of both the purification and reparation-offering, it is clearly specified that such a sacrifice was reserved for 'inadvertent' (*shegagha*) sins (Lev. 4.2, 22, 27; 5.15, 18; 22.14; Num. 15.24-29; 35.11, 15; Josh. 20.3, 9). This three-fold division of sacrifice continued on into the first century; Josephus, Philo and Clement of Rome all enumerate these three categories.[19]

---

17. J. Milgrom, 'Day of Atonement', *EncJud* V, pp. 1384-86.

18. The 'purification-offering' (*hatta't*) is often translated 'sin-offering'. For the reasons given below, I consider this translation to be misleading (cf. B.H. McLean, 'The Interpretation of the Levitical Sin Offering and the Scapegoat', *SR* 20/3 [1991], pp. 345-56).

19. Josephus, *Ant.* 3.226, 228, 230; Philo *Spec.* 1.247; Clement of Rome, *First Letter to the Corinthians* 41.2; Philo discusses each type at length individually (*Spec. Leg.* 1.198-211; 212-25; 226-46).

The Whole-offering

A whole-offering, or as it is sometimes called, a 'holocaust sacrifice',[20] is one which is completely consumed by fire: none of the meat is held back to be consumed by the offerer or the priests.[21] The animals offered were to be without blemish (Lev. 1.3). According to Philo, the priests would inspect the animals before they were allowed to be slaughtered.[22] To offer a blemished animal would not only invalidate the sacrifice, but the act of sacrifice itself would be counted as a transgression (Philo, *Spec. Leg.* 1.166-67). For this reason, animals were bought in or near the temple precincts in order to avoid them being injured in transit.

The offerer would present the victim for sacrifice by laying a single hand upon its head (Lev. 1.4). The imposition of a single hand did not imply that the offerer's sins were transferred to the victim but only that a particular animal was being offered by a particular person (or group), and that it was being sacrificed for his benefit.[23] Thus, the victim was not a substitutionary victim. No confession of sin was made over a purification victim because the intention was not to transfer sin. The laying on of a single hand was a gesture of sacralisation: it designated the animal as inviolate and similarly identified the beneficiary of the sacrifice. As Roland de Vaux explains:

> This action [of ritual hand-laying on a purification-offering] is not...a symbolic action implying that the victim is a substitute for the man, whose sins are thereby transferred to the victim for expiation...rather it is a solemn attestation that this victim comes from this particular individual who is laying his hands on it, that the sacrifice which is going to be presented to God by the priest is offered in his name, and that the fruits of this sacrifice shall be his.[24]

---

20.   Hebrew *'olah*, lit. 'that which goes up to heaven' (LXX: τὸ ὁλοκαύτωμα). It is also translated 'whole burnt-offering'. Besides *'olah*, the whole-offering is sometimes called *kalil* (1 Sam. 7.9; Deut. 33.10; Ps. 51.21), *qorban* (Lev. 1.2, 10, 14) and *'ishesh* (Lev. 1.9, 13, 17).

21.   Though the animal skin was given to the priest (e.g, Lev. 1; Jos. *Ant.* 3.226).

22.   Josephus prescribes a male ox, lamb or kid (*Ant.* 3.226); cf. Philo who substitutes a calf for the ox (*Spec. Leg.* 1.198).

23.   R. Péter, 'L'imposition des mains dans l'Ancien Testament', *VT* 27 (1977), pp. 48-55, esp. pp. 51-52; D.P. Wright, 'The Gesture of Hand Placement in the Hebrew Bible and in Hittite Literature', *JAOS* 106 (1986), pp. 433-46, n. 118; H.W. Robinson, 'Hebrew Sacrifice and Prophetic Symbolism', in *JTS* 48 (1942), pp. 129-39, esp. p. 131; Milgrom, 'Sacrifices', p. 765.

24.   de Vaux, *Ancient Israel*, p. 416, cf. p. 449; cf. R. de Vaux, *Studies in Old Testament Sacrifice* (Cardiff: University of Wales Press, 1964), pp. 28-29.

Unfortunately, Josephus does not describe the hand laying ritual. Philo's description of the hand-laying begins with the statement that the offerer should first wash his hands (for one can hardly wash one without the other). As a result of this preliminary statement, the number of hands used in the actual hand-laying is ambiguous in the Greek text (*Spec. Leg.* 1.199).[25] The Mishnah prescribes the use of two hands for sacrificial hand-laying (e.g., *m. Men.* 9.7-8).[26] It is regrettable that the Mishnah does not explain the purpose of this hand-laying.

Immediately following the hand-laying, the offerer would slaughter his own animal—a familiar task of domestic life of which every male would have experience. Priests and Levites only slaughtered the victims of public sacrifices (2 Chron. 29.22, 24, 34, Ezek. 44.11).[27] According to the rabbinic view, any Jew, if pure, was permitted to slay his own sacrificial animal (*m. Zeb.* 3.3). The offerer was probably permitted to enter the Court of the Priests in order that the priests might assist in slaughtering the animal. This was permitted according to the Mishnah: 'The Court of the Priests is still more holy, for Israelites may not enter therein save only when they must perform the laying on of hands, slaughtering, and waving [the breast of the offering]' (*m. Kel.* 1.8).

One priest would hold the animal down, a second would pull the head back, thereby exposing the neck, while a third would stand at the ready with a bowl to collect the blood. E.P. Sanders describes the technique of slaying the animal:

> In Jewish slaughter, because of the prohibition of consuming blood, one had to be especially careful to slit the throat in such a way that the animal lost most of its blood; that is, the windpipe was not to be cut through, lest the animal choke on its own blood. A deft stroke would sever the carotid arteries relatively painlessly, the blood would gush out, and the animal would soon lose consciousness.[28]

25. ἔπειτα δ' ἀπονιψάμενος ὁ προσάγων τὰς χεῖρας ἐπιφερέτω τῇ τοῦ ἱερείον κεφαλῇ (*Spec. Leg.* 1.199). F.H. Colson and G.H. Whitaker gloss this passage and translate 'two hands' (*Philo in Ten Volumes* [LCL; Cambridge: Cambridge University Press, 1930], 7.213). E.P. Sanders seems to be unaware of the distinction between one and two hands. He switches between referring to one hand and two hands without explanation (*Judaism*, pp. 107, 109).

26. 'Both hands must be laid upon the head; and in the place where they lay on the hands there they slaughter the beast and the slaughtering straightaway follows the laying on of hands' (*m. Men.* 9.8); cf. A. Rothkoff, 'Semikah'.

27. According to Philo, it was the priest, not the offerer who slew the animal. Josephus does not specify who killed the animal.

28. Sanders, *Judaism*, p. 107.

It is indeed surprising that this act of slaying is not described in the Hebrew Bible, nor in other ancient sources. This would suggest that this act was of little importance in itself, but merely served to prepare the victim for the ritual which followed. The slaying of the animal was not the emotional climax as it was in Greek sacrifice where the act of slaughter was accompanied by the shrill screams of women.

According to Leviticus, the blood was collected and splashed against the sides of the altar (Lev. 1.5, 15). Josephus states that the blood was poured around the base of the altar (*Ant.* 3.227). This blood was splashed or poured out, not in order to purify the altar, but simply to return the blood to the Lord since, in the Jewish mind, life was in the blood and it belonged to Yahweh (Lev. 17.14; Gen. 9.4; Deut. 12.23). The victim was then skinned, butchered into four quarters, washed, and all (except the skin) was burnt on the altar (Lev. 1.1-13). Josephus describes the ritual in the first century CE:

> An individual who offers a whole-offering kills an ox, a lamb, and a kid, these last being a year old; the slain ox may be older than this; but all victims for these whole-offerings must be males. The beasts being slaughtered, the priests drench with blood the circuit of the altar,[29] and then, after cleansing them [the animal parts], dismember them, sprinkle them with salt,[30] and lay them upon the altar, already laden with wood and alight. The feet and inwards of the victims are carefully cleansed before being placed with the other portions for consecration in the flames; the skins are taken by the priests.[31] (*Ant.* 3.226-27)

In the latest form of this ritual, the offering was accompanied by flour, oil, and a libation of wine poured around the altar (Sir. 50.15). The most solemn example of whole-offering is the Tamid, the daily sacrifice in the temple as prescribed in Exod. 29.38-46 and Num. 28.1-8.[32] Two male yearling lambs were offered each day. One lamb was sacrificed in the

---

29. Cf. Lev. 1.5.
30. Cf. Lev. 2.13.
31. Lev. 1.6 mentions the flaying of the larger animal only.
32. The performance of the Tamid sacrifice is described in detail in *m. Tam.* 4.1–7.4; cf. Josephus *Ant.* 3.237-40; Philo *Spec. Leg.* 1.169. The Tamid was paid for by the temple tax of a half-shekel levied on every adult male Jews both in Israel and throughout the Diaspora (cf. Neh. 10.32-33 where the tax is only one-third shekel). Strangely, Philo calls the Tamid a thank-offering, not a whole-offering. He states that it serves to thank God 'for benefactions of the day-time, the other for the night, given to the human race ceaselessly and constantly by the bounty of God' (*Spec. Leg.* 1.169).

morning to commence the temple service, the second in the evening just before its conclusion. The wine was poured around the altar as a libation. The flour and oil were mixed together and burned. On the Sabbath, the offering was doubled to four lambs. At each new moon additional sacrifices were made: two oxen, seven yearling lambs, a ram and a kid. Additional whole-offerings were required on other major festivals and on the annual fast, the Day of Atonement.

Having described the practice of the whole-offering, what can be said about its purpose. In pre-exilic times, prior to the use of the more specific purification and reparation sacrifices for atonement, the whole-offering was used as an expiatory sacrifice of general character (Lev. 1.4; 2 Sam. 24.25; cf. Job 1.5; 42.8). However, the whole-offering was by no means restricted to this purpose. Rather, it was all-encompassing in its function, serving as the customary offering for petition (1 Sam. 13.13) and thanksgiving (Lev. 22.17-19; Num. 15.1-16).[33] In post-exilic and Hellenistic times, the expiatory feature of the whole-offering was taken over by the purification-offering and reparation-offering.

According to Josephus' view, the whole-offering was offered 'for the well-being of the people' (*Ant.* 11.137; cf. 11.110; 15.419). The Jews offered the whole-offering in the belief that good things arise from devout acts. So it is that when Moses honoured the Lord with a whole-offering, Yahweh appeared to him in the night 'and bade him choose what gifts he [Yahweh] should confer upon him in return for his piety' (*Ant.* 8.22). Josephus relates how the whole-offering was sometimes used to appease God's wrath. When king David offered a whole-offering and peace-offering, 'the Deity was appeased and once more became gracious' (*Ant.* 7.333; cf. 2 Sam. 24.8-25). Thus, according to Josephus, the whole-offering was used to secure God's favour and to turn away his disfavour. He did not consider its purpose to be atonement.[34]

Similarly, Philo and the Mishnah[35] did not recognise the whole-offering to have any atoning significance: however, unlike Josephus, Philo thought

---

33. de Vaux, *Ancient Israel*, pp. 451-53; Milgrom, 'Sacrifices', pp. 763-71, esp. p. 769; W.B. Stephenson, 'Hebrew 'Olah and Zebach Sacrifices', in W. Baumgartner (ed.), *Festschrift Alfred Bertholet* (Tübingen: Mohr, 1950), pp. 488-97; J. Dan, 'Sacrifice', *EncJud*, XIV, 599-616.

34. Josephus points out that it was only the kid offered at new moons and festivals that was atoning (*Ant.* 3.238, 246, 247, 249, 253).

35. 'The blood of the *hatta't* (purification) offering precedes the blood of the whole-offering since it [the former] makes atonement' (*m. Zeb.* 10.2).

that the whole-offering was devoid of any element of self-interest; it was simply used to honour God (*Spec. Leg.* 1.195-97; *Abr.* 128).[36] Thus, neither Josephus nor Philo considered the whole-offering to be an atoning sacrifice, though they disagree as to whether it was offered with some motive of self-interest.

The Thank-offering

The characteristic feature of the thank-offering (Heb. *zebah sh^elamin*) is that the victim is shared between God, the priest, the offerer and his family (cf. Lev. 3; 7).[37] The thank-offering could be made as a freewill offering, or in fulfilment of a vow (Lev. 22.17, 21). The ritual commenced, as in the case of the whole-offering, with the laying on of a single hand (Lev. 3.2, 8, 13), the cutting of the throat, and the splashing of blood on the four sides of the altar (Lev. 3.2, 8, 13; cf. Josephus, *Ant.* 3.228). Animal fat and some of the vital organs, like the blood, were reserved for Yahweh (Lev. 3.16-17; cf. 7.22-24; Josephus, *Ant.* 3.228). The priest received the breast and right thigh; he boiled it in cooking vessels (Lev. 6.28) in the Priest's Court and then ate it (Lev. 7.28-34; 10.14-15; Num. 18.11; Josephus, *Ant.* 3.229). The remainder of the animal was eaten by the offerer, his family and guests. All partakers were required to be in a state of ritual purity before partaking of the sacrifice. Josephus is in agreement with this general procedure though his description is less detailed.[38]

The common purpose shared by all kinds of thank-offerings is the

---

36. For further discussion of this point, and Jewish witnesses for and against, see: Belkin, *Philo and the Oral Law*, pp. 55-56.

37. Besides *zebah shelamim*, the thank-offering is also termed *zebah* without qualification, or simply *shelamim* (always pl. except once *shelem* [Amos 5.22]). It is also translated 'communion-sacrifice' and 'covenant-sacrifice'. The translation 'peace-offering', is inspired by the LXX (for σωτήριον can mean either 'welfare' or 'peace') and by false analogy with *shalom* (the plural of *shalom* is spelt differently— with a *waw hôlem*). Josephus translates *zebah shelamim* correctly as 'thank-offering' (χαριστηρίος θυσία; [*Ant.* 3.9.2]). Philo adopts the LXX term 'welfare-offering' (σωτήριον) (*Spec. Leg.* 1.212, 224). The Passover sacrifice, votive-offering and freewill-offering are kinds of thank-offerings.

38. 'Having slain these, they stain the altar with their blood; the kidneys, the caul, all the fat along with the lobe of the liver, as also the lamb's tail, they then lay upon the altar. But the breast and right leg are offered to the priests, and for two days they feast upon the remainder of the flesh, all that is left over being burnt up.' (*Ant.* 3.228-29)

element of thanksgiving and the fortification (or establishment) of a covenant between the worshippers and Yahweh through the sharing of a common meal:[39] 'You shall sacrifice these *shelamim* and eat them, rejoicing before the Lord your God' (Deut. 27.7). In the Levitical mind, the thank-offering was not an atoning sacrifice. The blood was poured around the altar simply as a way of returning it back to the Lord. Indeed, the thanksgiving sacrifice cannot have been expiatory in function since all who partook of the victim's flesh were required to be in a state of ritual purity (Lev. 7.19-21).[40] The offering of a thanksgiving sacrifice was not a penitential occasion, as was the purification sacrifice. Roland de Vaux describes it as 'a joyful sacrifice in which the two ideas of gift and thanksgiving were both included; the offering was made by man, and it achieved its effect in maintaining friendship with God'.[41]

According to Josephus the thank-offering was 'performed with the intention of providing a feast for those who have offered it' (*Ant.* 3.225). Similarly, Philo, states that the thanksgiving sacrifice was shared as a feast with friends and family (*Spec. Leg.* 1.221); its purpose was to thank God 'with hymns and benedictions and prayers and sacrifices and other expressions of gratitude...All these connected and summed up have obtained the single name of praise' (*Spec. Leg.* 1.224). Philo states that there were three factors which distinguished the thank-offering from the purification-offering: the place, the time and the partakers (*Spec. Leg.* 1.220-21). Thus, the thanksgiving sacrifice was really a feast in which

39. de Vaux, *Ancient Israel*, pp. 451-53; Milgrom, 'Sacrifices', p. 769; Stephenson, 'Hebrew *'Olah*', pp. 488-97; Dan, 'Sacrifice'. The *minḥah* ('tribute-offering') was a cereal-offering which served as an inexpensive *'olah* for the poor (cf. Lev. 2; *m. Men.* 13.11).

40. On this point, it should be observed that the thank-offering described in Lev. 17.11 was not an atoning sacrifice in the normal sense of the term: 'For the life of the flesh is the blood and I have assigned it to you upon the altar to purify for your lives, for it is the blood as life that purifies' (Lev. 17.11). According to the Priestly doctrine of Creation, humans were intended to be vegetarian (Gen. 1.29). However, from the time of Noah onward, God conceded that humans may eat animal flesh so long as they do not eat the blood. The blood must be returned to its Creator (Gen. 9.3-4; Lev. 17.3-4, 13-14; cf. 19.2; 20.26). Thus, he who sacrifices animals is a murderer unless he returns the animal's blood to God as a ransom for the animal's life thereby 'purifying' his act (J. Milgrom, 'Atonement in the OT', *IDBSup*, pp. 78-82, esp. p. 80; Milgrom, 'Sacrifices', p. 770; also H.C. Brichto, 'On Slaughter and Sacrifice, Blood and Atonement', *HUCA* 47 [1976], pp. 19-55).

41. de Vaux, *Ancient Israel*, p. 453, cf. pp. 417-18.

the sacrifice provided the meat course. Though appropriate pious obser-
vances were kept, the event was as much an occasion for feasting as a
religious observance.

Likewise, the Passover sacrifice, itself a type of thank-offering, was
not understood to be an atoning sacrifice, nor was the blood considered
to have had a purgative significance.[42] The Law prescribes no forms of
humiliation or contrition. The Jews regarded the Passover as a divinely
appointed feast for the purpose of bringing to remembrance their
deliverance by God from Egyptian bondage: 'You shall tell your son on
that [Passover] day: "It is because of what the Lord did for me when I
came out of Egypt"' (Exod. 13.8). The Passover blood was interpreted
as a reminder of the sparing of the first born in Egypt who had been
protected by the blood on the door lintel (Exod. 12.29; 13.1-2, 11-16;
Num. 8.17; 3.4). This same understanding of the Passover is preserved
in the Mishnah:

> In every generation a man must so regard himself as if he came forth him-
> self out of Egypt, for it is written, 'And you shall tell your son in that day
> saying "It is because of that which the Lord did for me when I came forth
> out of Egypt"'. Therefore we are bound to give thanks, to praise, to
> glorify, to honour, to exalt, to extol, and to bless him who wrought all these
> wonders for our fathers and for us. (*m. Pes.* 10.5)

Philo did not understand the Passover sacrifice to be atoning in nature.
He calls this feast a 'symbol of light' reasoning that light is the symbol
of the soul in the training of philosophy (*Leg. All.* 3.167), virtue (*Sacr.*
63) and thanksgiving (*Migr. Abr.* 25). He says that blood was applied to
the door lintels in order 'to show confidence in the greatness and abun-
dance of God's gracious acts' (*Quaest in Exod.* 1.12).

Walther Eichrodt illustrates the modern tendency to interpret the
Passover sacrifice in terms of atonement. After he correctly states that
the Passover recalls 'the forbearance of Yahweh in "passing over" the
Israelite' and 'Yahweh's fundamental act of deliverance', he refers to
the Passover as 'the solemn spring festival of *expiation*' and likens it to
the Day of Atonement![43] Similarly, Robert Daly concludes that 'the
Passover and the sin [purification] offering were two rites which the

---

42. It is difficult for the modern to imagine the carnage and profusion of blood
which would attended sacrifice of animals during the high festivals. For example,
Josephus records that on one Passover alone, over two hundred and fifty-five thousand
lambs were slaughtered in the inner temple court in a three hour period (*JW* 6.423-25).

43. Eichrodt, *Theology*, p. 130.

Jews of New Testament times associated most closely with redemption and forgiveness of sin'.[44] Comments such as these misrepresent the nature and function of the Passover sacrifice.

The Purification- and Reparation-offering

The term *hatta't* (LXX ἁμαρτία) names both the sin and the purification sacrifice which does away with the effects of sin. It is sometimes translated 'sin-offering' or 'expiation offering' but for reasons given below, I shall translate it 'purification-offering'. Likewise the term *'asham* (LXX πλεμμέλεια) designates both guilt and the offering which does away with guilt. It is customarily translated 'reparation-offering' or 'guilt-offering'. Originally the reparation-offering included the idea of making some sort of material compensation or repayment for injury or damage, usually by repaying an additional one fifth of the cost (Lev. 6). However, the last redactors of the Pentateuch did not clearly understand the distinction between *hatta't* and *'asham* and consequently often confused these terms or used them synonymously.[45]

The ritual. After the offerer presented the animal by laying a single hand upon its head, he would slaughter it by slitting its throat. Priests then collected in basins the blood from the animal's throat. Depending upon the severity of the impurity, purification was effected by either daubing the horns of the altar of holocausts, or by spattering the blood in the sanctuary or in the Holy of Holies. The remainder of the blood was poured around the base of the altar. In all purification-offerings, the fat around the intestines, the kidneys and the liver reverted to Yahweh by burning upon the altar of holocausts.

The function. According to Leviticus, the Temple acquired impurity whenever a human will revolted against the divine command (cf. Lev. 4.1–5.13; Num. 5.2).[46] In the words of Milgrom: 'sin is a miasma that,

44. R.J. Daly, *Christian Sacrifice* (Washington: Catholic University of America Press, 1978), p. 240, cf. p. 237.

45. W.O.E. Oesterly, *Sacrifices in Ancient Israel: Origin, Purposes and Development* (London: Hodder & Stoughton, 1937), p. 77; de Vaux, *Ancient Israel*, pp. 420-21; P.P. Saydon, 'Sin-Offering and Trespass-Offering', *CBQ* 8 (1946), pp. 393-99, esp. p. 393. For an attempt to distinguish *hatta't* and *'asham* see: J. Milgrom, 'The Cultic *shegagah* and its influence in Psalms and Job', *JQR* 58 [1967], pp. 115-25, esp. pp. 116-17.

46. Sins such as the failure to purify oneself from corpse contamination (Num.

wherever committed, is attracted magnet-like to the sanctuary. There it adheres and amasses until God will no longer abide in the sanctuary.'[47] The severity of this Temple impurity varied in proportion to the severity of the offence. There were three successive degrees to which the Temple could become contaminated by the sins of the people. In each case, the remedy varied in proportion to the degree of contamination. When an individual (Lev. 4.27-35) or a ruler (Lev. 4.22-26) committed an inadvertent transgression, or had become a carrier of impurity (Lev. 12–15), only the Temple's inner court was thought to become polluted. Purification was effected by daubing with blood the horns of the altar of holocausts located in the inner court. The remainder of the blood was poured around its base (Lev. 4.25, 30, 34). Only the daubing of the altar had purificatory significance. The act of pouring the blood around the base of the altar returned the life of the victim to the Lord. In this case, the remainder of the animal reverted to the priests for their own consumption. The priests were permitted to consume the purification-offering because 'it is most holy' (Lev. 6.24, 29; 7.1, 6).

The sin of the high priest (Lev. 4.3-12) or the whole community (Lev. 4.13-21) penetrated more deeply to pollute the Holy Place, the area in the sanctuary before the curtain of the Holy of Holies. Hence the blood was not daubed outside the sanctuary on the altar of holocausts, but taken *inside* for two purification rites (Lev. 4.5, 16). First, the priest would dip his finger into the blood, and spatter the floor seven times before the curtain (Lev. 4.6, 17). Next, he would apply the blood to the horns of the altar of perfumes which stood in front of the curtain. The animal organs were offered to God as before, while the animal remains were carried outside the sanctuary 'to a clean place' and burned (Lev. 4.11-12).

Premeditated sins penetrated most deeply and polluted the Temple to its very core, piercing through the curtain to contaminate even the Holy of Holies and the gold lid (*kappôret*) of the Ark of the Covenant. Thus, despite the fact that Israelites had no access to the Holy of Holies (Exod. 30.26-29; 40.9-11), this area still needed to be purged 'of the impurities

19.13, 20), certain sexual impurities (if prescriptions are not observed; Lev. 15.31), and the offering of children to Molech (Lev. 20.3) are explicitly described as defiling the sanctuary.

47. Milgrom, 'Atonement in the OT', cf. Milgrom, 'Sacrifices', p. 767; J. Milgrom, 'Israel's Sanctuary: The Priestly "Picture of Dorian Gray"', *RB* 83 (1976), pp. 390-99, esp. p. 395.

of the Israelites' (Lev. 16.16). Such contamination could only be removed once a year on the Day of Atonement. Only the blood of the purification goat, the so-called 'inside goat' (as opposed to the scapegoat which was the 'outside goat'), could accomplish this deep cleansing (Lev. 16.15-19).

Jacob Milgrom perhaps more than any other contemporary scholar is responsible for overturning many conclusions concerning the purpose and theology of *hatta't* sacrifice. At one time, scholars held that the purification-offering was employed in order to atone for personal sin. Buchanan Gray is representative of this view. In his own words, a purification-offering is 'the means of which the sins of men who offered them were removed'.[48]

Milgrom has argued strongly against this interpretation. In his view, the verb *kipper* in the context of *hatta't* sacrifice means 'to cleanse', not 'to make atonement'.[49] The function of the *hatta't* was to cleanse the sanctuary—not the offerer—of the contamination conferred upon it by the sin or impurity of the offerer.[50] In his own words, the blood of the *hatta't* offering was 'the ritual detergent employed by the priest to purge the sanctuary of the impurities inflicted upon it by the offerer of the sacrifice'.[51]

---

48. B. Gray, *Sacrifice in the Old Testament: Its Theory and Practice* (Oxford: Clarendon Press, 1925), p. 60.

49. Philologists have been divided on the etymology of *kipper*. Evidence from Semitic cognates can be cited in support of the translation 'to cover' (Arabic) and 'to wipe' (Akkadian). However, both notions seem to go back to a common idea since a substance can be either rubbed on (i.e., covered) or rubbed off (uncovered). Milgrom argues that the translation of the verb *kipper* (*piel*) as 'to atone' or 'to expiate' is usually incorrect. In ritual contexts, its normative meaning is 'to rub off' or 'to purge'.

50. Milgrom, 'Israel's Sanctuary', pp. 390-99; Milgrom, 'Sacrifices', pp. 763-71, esp. pp. 766-67; J. Milgrom, 'The Day of Atonement', *EncJud*, V, 1375-87, esp. 1384-85; J. Milgrom, 'Sin-offering, or Purification-offering?', *VT* 21 (1971), pp. 237-39; J. Milgrom, 'The Function of *hatta't* Sacrifice', *Tarbiz* 40 (1970), pp. 1-8, esp. pp. 1-3; Milgrom, *Leviticus 1–16*, pp. 254-69; also: B.A. Levine, 'Leviticus', *EncJud*, XI, 138-47, esp. p. 139; opposed by N. Kiuchi, *The Purification Offering in the Priestly Literature: Its Meaning and Function* (JSOTSup, 56; Sheffield: JSOT Press, 1987), pp. 35-37; also the new proposal of A. Marx, ('Sacrifice pour les péchés ou rites de passage? Quelques réflexion sur la fonction du *hatta't*', *RB* 96 [1986], pp. 27-48) and Milgrom's response (*Leviticus 1–16*, pp. 289-92).

51. Milgrom, 'Israel's Sanctuary', p. 392, cf. p. 391; cf. Milgrom, 'Sacrifices', p. 766. Noam Zohar has sought to refute Milgrom's thesis, arguing that the sin-

Milgrom's thesis is reducible to two principal arguments. First, though the active purging element is the blood from the *hatta't*, this blood is never applied to a person. Its use is confined to the sanctuary, the sanctuary furniture, and the altar of holocausts (e.g., Lev. 8.15). For this reason, the verb *kipper* ('to cleanse') never takes a person as a direct object, but only inanimate objects such as the altar and temple. In the latter case, *kipper* can take both a direct object and a prepositional object: when it takes a direct object, it indicates that which is purged; when it takes a prepositional object (with '*al* or *b^e*), it indicates that 'upon which' or 'in which' purification takes place.[52] Therefore, the temple cleansing (*kipper*) should be understood literally: it takes place 'on' ('*al*) the floor before the curtain, 'on' the altar of perfumes, 'on' the lid (*kappôret*) of the Ark, and 'inside' (*b^e*) the Holy of Holies such that on the Day of Atonement the entire room is '*kipper*-ed' (e.g., Exod. 30.10; Lev. 6.23; 16.14, 18-19). When *kipper* is used with a person, it always requires the preposition '*al* (e.g., Lev. 16.24, 30, 33; Num. 8.12, 21) or sometimes *b^e* '*ad* (e.g., Lev. 16.6) signifying agency ('on behalf of'). In other words, the offerer has the purification of the temple accomplished *on his behalf.*

Secondly, sacrifice was not required for personal atonement. In the case of physical impurity, it was removed by water ablutions (Lev. 15.8; cf. 12.6-7, 8; 14.9, 20). In the case of the spiritual impurity resulting from inadvertent sins (*shegagah* sins), no ablutions were required, nor was blood applied to the sinner. The use of blood was reserved for the temple and temple furniture alone (cf. Lev. 4.20, 25-26, 31). Atonement of sins was accomplished through repentance alone.[53]

The Witness of Philo of Alexandria

In turning to our attention to Philo, one finds that he affirms these two essential characteristics: (1) the purification-offering cleansed the temple,

offering accomplishes personal atonement as well as purifying the sanctuary ('Repentance and Purification: The Significance and Semantics of *hatta't* in the Pentateuch', *JBL* 107/4 [1988], pp. 609-618; see my rejoinder: B.H. McLean, 'The Interpretation of the Levitical Sin Offering', pp. 345-56; and that of J. Milgrom: 'The *Modus Operandi of Hatta't*: A Rejoinder', *JBL* 109/1 (1990), pp. 111-13.

52. Milgrom, 'Israel's Sanctuary', p. 391. This conclusion is also confirmed by the synonyms of *kipper*, *hitte'* and *tihar* which are used with *kipper* in Ezek. 43.20 and 43.26 respectively.

53. On inadvertent sin, see: Milgrom, 'Cultic *shegagah*', pp. 115-25. On repentance: J. Milgrom, *Cult and Conscience: The Asham and the Priestly Doctrine of Repentance* (Leiden: Brill, 1976), pp. 3-12.

not the individual; (2) repentance atoned for individual sin. The two key texts are *Spec. Leg.* 1.233 and 234-38. The function of the purification-offering in *Spec. Leg.* 1.233 can easily be misinterpreted. Philo stipulates that a ruler was required to offer a he-goat for purifications (*Spec. Leg.* 1.233). But what is the object of this purification, the temple or the ruler? F.H. Colson translates the passage: 'But if a trespass is committed by a ruler, *he purges himself* with a he-goat (χιμάρῳ ποιεῖται τὴν κάθαρσιν)'.[54] I suggest that the force of the middle voice of ποιεῖται in this passage is not reflexive but indicates the he performs the act for his own benefit or in his own interest. In other words, the passage should be translated, 'he performs purifications *for himself* with a he-goat', which is to say, he purifies the temple of the impurity conferred upon it by his own transgressions.

This interpretation is supported by Philo's discussion of the repara tion sacrifice (*Spec. Leg.* 1.234-38). First, he makes it clear that it is repentance—not sacrifice—which is of importance for the atonement of personal sins. The transgressor should feel 'convicted inwardly by conscience', confess his guilt, request pardon from the offended party, and finally make good the loss suffered by the injured party, by adding an additional one-fifth of its value.

Only after this process has been completed, and the offender has atoned for his transgression is he required offer a sacrifice. The purpose of this sacrifice was to cleanse the temple and its furniture:

> ...besides the regulations already stated for dealing with involuntary offences against men, Moses lays down that *in the case of the holy things* [the temple furniture] the reparation sacrifice (κάθαρσιν ἱλάσκεσθαι) should be made with a ram, the offenders having first made full compensation for the subject of the tresspass with the addition of a fifth part of its proper value (*Spec. Leg.* 1.234).

Philo's emphasis on repentance as the key to personal atonement is reiterated in *On Special Laws* where he states that the priests were permitted to consume the flesh of the purification and reparation-offerings in order to 'secure them [the offerers] in the belief that the graciousness of God extends to those who feel remorse for their sin' (*Spec. Leg.* 1.242).

---

54. Philo, *Spec. Leg.*, 1.233.

The Paradox of Holiness

In the case of all purification-offerings, it was the blood—and whole
animal by association—which effected purification by absorbing impurity.
Despite its absorption of impurity, the blood and meat remained very
'holy' and the priests were permitted to consume the meat of the
purification sacrifice because 'it is most holy' (Lev. 6.24, 29; 7.1, 6).
Furthermore, this meat must be eaten in a 'holy place', in the temple
court (Lev. 6.26; 7.6). In these texts, the blood and meat were deemed
to be 'holy', not in an ethical sense, but 'holy' in the ritual sense of
having been consecrated or removed from the public domain. In other
words, the purification offering was set apart from public use and public
access.

The Priestly writers stressed the holiness of the blood and the carcass
because these had the capacity to transmit impurity through contact.
Thus, a garment accidently sprinkled with the blood of a *hatta't* victim
became 'holy', and therefore required washing because it could then
transmit impurity (Lev. 6.27; 16.28). On the same principle, an earthen
vessel used to boil the purification meat for the priests, though holy,
must be smashed, and a bronze vessel scoured and rinsed with water
(Lev. 7.28). Anyone who touched the flesh or blood of the sacrificed
victim likewise became 'holy' in the sense of being set apart (Lev. 6.27).
The same is true of the purification sacrifice offered on behalf of the
community or high priest: the carcass must be burned in a 'clean place'
because it is 'holy'; yet it must be burned *outside* the camp because it
can infect others with its impurity through physical contact (Lev. 4.12;
cf. 4.21; 7.30).

There is a remarkable paradox in this conception of holiness: despite
its absorption of impurity and its ability to transmit this impurity by
contact, priests were permitted to consume the *hatta't* meat because 'it
is most holy' (Lev. 6.24, 29; 7.1, 6) and this meat was to be eaten in a
'holy place'. From these texts it would appear that the meat had become
a carrier of impurity without itself becoming defiled. In the words of J.
Milgrom, the victim becomes 'a most-sacred yet impurity-bearing
sacrifice'.[55] The purification sacrifice contaminates that which is pure,
while remaining pure itself.

This paradox is most evident in the sacrifice of the red heifer (Num.
15.1-22). This rite originally had nothing to do with sacrifice but was
reconstructed in accordance with the practice of Levitical purification

55. Milgrom, 'Sacrifices', p. 767.

sacrifice (cf. Num. 19.4-5) such that even the term *hatta't* is applied to it (Num. 19.17). In this rite, the carcass of the red heifer is burnt after being used to purify the temple. Despite the fact that these ashes can confer impurity by contact (Num. 19.7-9), the ashes are stored in a 'clean place' (Num. 19.9), and can be mixed with water to be reused for purifying those who have come into contact with a corpse (Num. 19.11-19).

There is no consensus in the first century CE regarding the import-ance of this paradox nor even any recognition of it. In his discussion of the sacrifice of the red heifer (*Spec. Leg.* 1.261-62, 268), Philo para-phrases the entire text of Num. 19.1-22 with the exception of every passage which refers to the ability of the holy carcass to confer impurity. In so doing, he deliberately omits its most puzzling aspect.[56] The fact that Philo passed over this paradox suggests that he believed that the purification sacrifice remained pure and undefiled, perhaps by analogy with the Greek Olympian sacrifice.[57]

Though it is difficult to understand fully the subtle logic of the purification ritual, one point is clear: even though a purification sacrifice had the capacity to transmit impurity, the priestly writers were very careful to avoid giving the impression that its substance became defiled by this contamination. In contrast, no such paradox attended the final state of the Levitical scapegoat. This goat, being thoroughly contami-nated by the imposition of human sin, was not holy, and therefore was ritually expelled to the wilderness. It is precisely because the scapegoat was loaded with sin that it was regarded unworthy for sacrifice to Yahweh.

Paul and Jewish Sacrifice

In the context of Pauline scholarship, the sacrificial interpretation of Paul's soteriology persists as a central domain model. For example, James Dunn argues that Paul had a 'fully thought-out theology of

---

56. R.D. Hecht, 'Preliminary Issues in the Analysis of Philo's *De Specialibus Legibus*', in *Studia philonica* 5 (1978), pp. 1-55, esp. pp. 17-20.

57. In contrast to this, the Rabbis considered this paradoxical element to be the most important part of the sacrifice of the red heifer. Joseph Blau states that the frequent Rabbinic attestations 'should be understood in terms of the endless capacity of the human mind to be fascinated with the insoluble problem' (J. Blau, 'The Red Heifer: A Biblical Purification Rite in Rabbinic Literature', *Numen* 14 [1967], pp. 70-78, esp. p. 78).

sacrifice'. He substantiates this view with the following explanation: 'In brief, Paul's view seems to be that Christ's death was effective in dealing with human sins because he represented the sinners and by his death he destroyed their sins (cf. Rom. 8.3; 2 Cor. 5.21).'[58]

It is immediately apparent that Dunn's explanation of Paul's 'theology of sacrifice' bears little resemblance to Jewish sacrificial theology. First, a sacrificial victim did not 'represent' the offerer as his substitute, nor did it bear human sin. Hence, by killing the victim, 'human sins' were not 'destroyed'. Secondly, as we have seen, it was not the death of the animal, but the application of the blood which accomplished the purification. Finally, the purpose of Jewish sacrifice was not to atone for 'human sins', but to purify the temple. If Dunn is correct in concluding that Paul has a theology of sacrifice, then it follows that Paul has so transformed the Jewish understanding of sacrifice, that he has created something substantially different.

This is not to suggest that Christ's death was never interpreted by Christians in sacrificial terms. For example, the sacrificially correct notion of Christ's blood being employed as cleansing agent by spattering it, occurs in a number of non-Pauline passages.[59] These passages present Christ's blood as a purifying agent, albeit with regard to personal sin rather than temple cleansing. This is evidence for the adaptation or mis-interpretation of Jewish sacrificial theology among Christians, perhaps under the influence of Greek sacrifice. Christians who were in regular contact with the sacrificial cult of Graeco-Roman religions, and geographically removed from Jerusalem, may have interpreted Jewish sacrifice from the vantage point of the sphagion sacrifice which, unlike the Jewish purification sacrifice, was used to purify individuals.

However, my starting-point for interpreting Paul's atonement language should be the Jewish sacrificial theology of the first century CE, not the adaptation and misinterpretation of this theology in later Christian writers. The fact that the key features of the Levitical understanding of

58. J. Dunn, *Romans 1–8* (Dallas: Word Books, 1988), p. 181. According to Martin Hengel, the earliest interpretation of the death of Jesus was as a vicarious sacrifice (*The Atonement: Origins of the Doctrine in the New Testament* [Philadelphia: Fortress Press, 1981]). Joel B. Green tests Hengel's conclusion and concludes that the pre-canonical passion narrative was not dominated by a single theological perspective, and that the last and least of these motifs is the atoning significance of Jesus' death (J.B. Green, *The Death of Jesus: Tradition and Interpretation in the Passion Narrative* [WUNT, 2.33; Tübingen: Mohr (Siebeck), 1988]).

59. Heb. 9.12-14, 22, 25-26; 12.24; 1 Pet. 1.2; 1 Jn 1.7; Rev. 7.14.

sacrifice was preserved intact in the first century makes it dubious whether Paul, a Pharisee (Phil. 3.5) who was 'extremely zealous' for the traditions of Judaism (Gal. 1.14) could have been so confused about the fundamental ideas of Jewish sacrifice.

This is not to suggest that there is no explicit sacrificial terminology in Paul's letters. Paul occasionally does employ sacrificial language, but never with reference to atonement. The verb θύειν ('to sacrifice') occurs only in Paul's letters in connection with Christ's death. In 1 Cor. 5.7 Paul employs this verb in a passover metaphor: 'For Christ, our paschal lamb, has been sacrificed'.[60] I have demonstrated above that at no stage in the evolution of the Passover was the paschal sacrifice ever understood to be atoning in nature, nor for that matter was the blood considered to have had a purgative significance. This solitary reference in 1 Cor. 5.7 to Christ being sacrificed cannot be interpreted as an atoning sacrifice. Rather, Paul is alluding to the freedom purchased for Christians by the slaughter of Christ, God's passover lamb.

Another term which is sometimes interpreted in terms of sacrifice is ἱλαστήριον (Rom. 3.25). This term is not, as some have suggested, the Greek translation equivalent for the golden lid (*kappôret*) of the Ark of the Covenant. Neither the translators of the Septuagint nor Philo use the term ἱλαστήριον to designate the actual *kappôret*. For example, in 1 Chron. 28.11, the phrase 'house of *kappôret*' is interpreted in Greek as ὁ οἶκος τοῦ ἐξιλασμοῦ ('house of atonement'), not ὁ οἶκος τοῦ ἱλαστήριου.[61] Similarly, Philo refers to the lid of the Ark of the Covenant, not as a ἱλαστήριον, but as the ἐπίθεμα τῆς κιβωτοῦ ('lid of the Ark'), adding that this 'lid' is known as a ἱλαστήριον. In *De Vita Mosis*, Philo indicates to the reader that the term ἱλαστήριον is a specialised descriptor of the term 'lid' (ἐπίθεμα) by positioning this term at the end of the sentence as if it were in quotation marks: 'The

60. καὶ γὰρ τὸ πάσχα ἡμῶν ἐτύθη Χριστός. Other passover allusions in the New Testament include Jn 1.29, 36; 19.36; 1 Pet. 1.19; Rev. 5.6, 9, 12; 12.11. Jn 1.29, 36 may also allude to the apocalyptic lamb of Rev. 4.1–5.14 (C.K. Barrett, *A Commentary on the Epistle to the Romans* [Black's New Testament Commentaries; London: A. & C. Black, 1957], or the Suffering Servant lamb (Isa. 53.7) (R. de Vaux, *Ancient Israel*).

61. In Exod 26.34, the translators of the LXX did not read *kappôret*, but *parôket* ('curtain'), and translated it as καταπέτασμα: 'And you shall hide from view with the (Temple) curtain the Ark of the Testimony in the Holy of Holies' (καὶ κατακαλύψεις τῷ καταπετάσματι τὴν κιβωτὸν τοῦ μαρτυρίου ἐν τῷ ἁγίῳ τῶν ἁγίων).

Ark...which was covered with a sort of lid (ἐπίθεμα) which is called in the sacred books a 'hilasterion' (ἡ δὲ κιβωτὸς..., ἢ ἐπίθεμα ὡσανεὶ πῶμα τὸ λεγόμενον ἐν ἱεραῖς βίβλοις ἱλαστήριον' (*Vit. Mos.* 2.95). This same usage is found in *De Fugaet Inventione* which states that 'the lid of the Ark' is called a 'hilasterion (τὸ ἐπίθεμα τῆς κιβωτοῦ, καλεῖ δὲ αὐτὸ ἱλαστήριον)'.[62] Note that in each case, the term ἱλαστήριον is used with a definite article.

If ἱλαστήριον does not mean *kappôret*, what does it mean? The two most common answers to this question are 'means of atonement' or 'place of atonement'.[63] Since my principal concern is the meaning of ἱλαστήριον in Rom. 3.25, I shall suspend consideration of this question for a moment.

Does the term *hilasterion* in Rom. 3.25 refer to a sacrificial victim, as some have suggested?[64] Does the use of this term in Rom. 3.25 draw

---

62. *Fug.* 100; cf. G.A. Deissmann, *Bibelstudient: Beitrage, zumeist aus den Papyri und Inschriften, zur Geschichte der Sprache, des Schriftums und der Religion des helenistischen Judentums und des Urchristentums* (Hildesheim: Georg Olms, 1977), pp. 120-32, esp. p. 124.

63. E.g., Gottfried Fitzer interprets it as the *place* of atonement:

> The *hilasterion* is not an atonement victim, nor a means of atonement, neither in the LXX, nor in Philo, but it is the place of God's *presence*, of God's mercy where, through manipulation of the priests, namely the healing rituals of the cult, where God's mercy becomes reality. In the expression ὃν προέθετο ὁ θεὸς ἱλαστήριον (Rom. 3.25) Jesus is not compared in this passage to the manipulations of the priests, but he himself represents the place of God's mercy and presence ('Der Ort der Versöhnung nach Paulus: Zu Frage des *Sühnopfers Jesus*', *TZ* 22 [1966], pp. 161-83, esp. p. 171).

Daniel Bailey has brought the following work to my attention after the manuscript was completed: J.W. van Henten, 'The Tradition-historical Background of Rom. 3.25: A Search for Pagan and Jewish Parallels', in M.C. De Boer (ed.), *Jesus to John: Essays on Jesus and New Testament Christology in Honour of Marinus de Jonge* (JSNTSup 84; Sheffield: JSOT Press, 1993), pp. 101-28.

64. Some have suggested that ἱλαστήριον is an atonement victim according to the analogy of σωτήριον, χαριστήριον, καθάριον and others. For example, C.K. Barrett translates this term by the phrase 'bloody sacrificial death' arguing that the 'shedding of blood implies sacrifice' (*Romans*, p. 73). This translation seems forced in the light of Barrett's own comments in which he interprets ἱλαστήριον as the place and means of atonement:

> there is much to be said for the traditional view that Paul represented Christ as the true 'mercy-seat' What else to a Jew represented at once the place and the means of atonement?...But we can go with certainty no further than the translation: God set for Christ as a means of dealing with sin' (Barrett, *Romans*, p. 74).

upon the image of the lid of the Ark of the Covenant as a means or place of atonement? The lack of clarity regarding the meaning of ἱλαστήριον in Rom. 3.25 is due to the narrow semantic field considered by most New Testament scholars, restricted principally to the use of ἱλαστήριον in connection with *kappôret*. This argument relies upon the questionable premise that Christians were more familiar with the use of ἱλαστήριον in the Pentateuch than its use in their own time and culture.[65] This presupposition seems unlikely. Moreover, the context of Rom. 3.25 suggests that Paul did *not* have the *kappôret* in mind when he used the term ἱλαστήριον. As Adolf Deissmann observes, this interpretation would contradict Paul's own theology:

> Christ, *the end of the law*, Christ of whom Paul has said is the revealer of δικαιοσύνη θεοῦ χωρὶς νόμου [God's righteousness apart from the law] would hardly at the same time be called by Paul the lid [*kappôret*] of the Ark of the Covenant containing the law. That picture would be as un-Pauline as possible.[66]

The term ἱλαστήριον was also employed in inscriptions dating from the time of the principate to designate a gift (e.g., a statue) which was dedicated to a god in order to curry favour with, or appease, him. Such gifts were known as ἱλαστήρια μνήατα or simply as ἱλαστήρια. For example, an inscription from Cos inscribed on a statue base reads as follows: 'The People (erected) this *gift* (ἱλαστήριον) to the gods for the welfare (σωτηρίας) of the Emperor Caesar Augustus, son of God, Saviour.'[67] The term ἱλαστήριον is employed in this same sense in

The term ἱλαστήριον cannot be verified in the sense of a sacrificial victim. G.B. Winer, *Grammatik des neutestamentlichen Sprachidioms* (Rev. W. Schmiedel; 2 vols.; Göttingen: Vandenhoeck & Ruprecht, 8th edn, 1894-98) only points to Byzantius Theophanes Continuatus. Moreover, as Adolf Deissmann notes, in the context of Rom. 3.25, 'it cannot be said about a victim that God προέθετο ["displayed publically"] it' (*Bibelstudient*, p. 126).

65. The use of the term ἱλαστήριον 'means/place of atonement' in Heb. 9.5 has probably contributed towards this assessment.

66. Deissmann, *Bibelstudient*, p. 126. Moreover, one would not expect Paul to designate Christ with name of an inanimate object. As Deissmann argues: 'If the cross was to be called that [ἱλαστήριον = *kappôret*], it would be an understandable picture; used of a person, it is neither appropriate or comprehensible' (*Bibelstudient*, p. 126).

67. ὁ δᾶμος ὑπὲρ τᾶς αὐτοκράτορος | Καίσαρος | Θεοῦ υἱοῦ Σεβαστοῦ σωτηρίας | Θεοῖς ἱλαστήριον (W.R. Paton and E.L. Hicks, *The Inscriptions of Cos* [Oxford:1891], p. 126, no. 81); the term appears in a second inscription from

Josephus, Dio Chrysostom and others. Josephus states that King Herod built a lavish memorial of white marble at the entrance of the tomb of David 'as a gift (ἱλαστήριον) to curry favour with (or appease) God'.[68]

Paul, and indeed all Christians who were in daily contact with the Graeco-Roman cults, would have been more familiar with the use of ἱλαστήριον in this context than in association with the Hebrew term *kappôret*. The interpretation of ἱλαστήριον as a gift to God fits the context of Rom. 3.25. It is also well-suited to the use of the verb προέθετο since one would 'publicly display' a gift such as a statue. In the words of Deissmann, 'God has *displayed publicly* the crucified Christ in his blood before the cosmos...Christ crucified is the gift of God's love for the good of the people'.[69] Paul is saying that God provided the *hilasterion* for himself and thus fulfilled the requirement which humanity could not fulfil; 'God is doing everything in Christ'.[70] Thus, the term ἱλαστήριον in Rom. 3.25 does not refer to a sacrificial victim.

Another phrase which has been interpreted in terms of sacrifice is περὶ ἁμαρτίας in Rom. 8.3. Though this phrase is sometimes used in the Septuagint with reference to the purification-offering (*hatta't*), it is always accompanied by the definite article, unlike Rom. 8.3.[71] Since I shall discuss this passage in detail in Chapter 3, it will suffice to say that περὶ ἁμαρτίας in Rom. 8.3 simply means 'to deal with sin', not 'for a sin-offering'. As C.K. Barrett, remarks, 'on the whole it seems more probable that Paul means here nothing more precise than in Gal. 1.4'[72] (ὑπὲρ τῶν ἁμαρτιῶν). In other words, God sent his own son 'to deal with sin'.[73]

The sacrificial terms θυσία ('sacrifice') and φρασφορά ('offering')

Cos on a column fragment, also dating from the principate: [ὁ δᾶμος ὁ Ἀλεντίων] [---Σε]βαῖσ[τ]σῷ Διῒ Σ[τ]ρατίῳ ἱλασΙτήριον δαμαρχεῦνΙτος Γαίου Νωρι βανοῦ Μοσχίω[ν]ο[ς φι]λοκαίσαΙρος (Paton and Hicks, *Inscriptions of Cos*, pp. 225-26, no. 347).

68. περίφοβος δ'αὐτὸς ἐξῄει, καὶ τοῦ δέους ἱλαστήριον μνῆμα λευκῆς πέτρας ἐπὶ τῷ στομίῳ κατεσκευάσατο πολυτελεστάτῃ δαπάνῃ (*Ant.* 16.182); Dio Chrysostom, *Discourses*: καταλείψειν γὰρ αὐτοὺς ἀνάθημα κάλλιστον καὶ μέγιστον τῇ Ἀθηνᾷ καὶ ἐπιγράψειν· ἱλαστήριον Ἀχαιοὶ τῇ Ἰλιάδι 11.121).

69. Deissmann, *Bibelstudient*, p. 130.

70. Deissmann, *Bibelstudient*, p. 130.

71. E.g., πάντα τὰ περὶ τῆς ἁμαρτίας (Lev. 14.9).

72. Barrett, *Romans*, p. 147.

73. Barrett, *Romans*, p. 147.

are applied to Christ in Eph. 5.2: 'Walk in love, as Christ loved us and gave himself up for us, a fragrant offering and sacrifice to God'. The great majority of scholars reject the authenticity of Ephesians, making this text irrelevant to a consideration of Pauline soteriology. Even those who do accept its genuineness consider it to be one Paul's latest letters, containing theological ideas which are not found in his undisputed letters. All of this aside, though Eph. 5.2 refers to Christ's death as a sacrifice, there is no hint that the author is alluding to a sacrifice which is *atoning* in nature.

In view of this total absence of explicit sacrificial terminology concerning the atonement in Paul, one question remains: are there significant similarities between references to Christ's blood in Paul's letters and references to blood in purification sacrifices? Blood was of course vital in the operation of the atoning sacrifices because it functioned as the active purging element. Hence it is necessary to apply the blood to the horns of the altar, the temple floor and the *kappôret*. Paul, on the other hand, generally uses the term 'blood' as a synonym for Christ's life[74] or his death[75] just as it is used elsewhere as a synonym for the life[76] and death[77] of ordinary people. Paul also employs the term 'blood' in combination with the term 'flesh' ('flesh and blood') as a synonym for 'human life'.[78]

One cannot argue that Paul's eucharistic texts concern atonement by analogy with either the Passover sacrifice or the thanksgiving sacrifice, since neither were employed for atonement. The Jewish understanding of the thank-offering as an offering which strengthened the human-divine relationship corresponds to Paul's own theology of the eucharist. Paul contrasts the cup and table of the Lord with the sacrificial meals of the Graeco-Roman cults; just as the latter made the devotee a partner with demons, so the Lord's supper brings about partnership with the Christ (1 Cor. 10.16-21). The term 'blood' in the phrase κοινωνία τοῦ αἵματου τοὺς χριστοῦ (1 Cor. 10.16) does not specify the physical substance, but is employed as a synonym for the 'covenant'. This is made clear in 1 Cor. 11.25 where the two terms occur together

74. E.g., 1 Cor. 10.16; 11.25.
75. E.g., Rom. 3.25; 5.9; cf. Eph. 1.7; 2.13; Col. 1.20; 1 Pet. 1.18; Rev. 1.5.
76. Mt. 27.4; Acts 20.26.
77. Mt. 23.29, 35; 27.6, 24, 25; Lk. 11.20; Acts 5.28; 18.6.
78. E.g., 1 Cor. 15.50; Gal. 1.16; cf. Eph. 6.12; Mt. 16.17. In Heb. 2.14 the expression 'flesh and blood' is used of both Christ and other people.

in the phrase 'the blood of the covenant'.[79]

There is yet another sharp contrast between Paul's portrayal of Christ's death and Jewish sacrifice. The fact that Jesus suffered physical agony on the cross is a historical fact, regardless of its theological significance for Paul. Crucified prisoners typically survived a number of days through a slow agonising process of suffocation, hence the custom of breaking of legs in order to speed up the process of death (cf. Jn 19.31-32). However, Paul's writings are not motivated by biographical interest, much less a concern for historical authenticity. When Paul refers to Christ's suffering on the cross, he is making a *theological* statement.

Paul connects the saving work of Christ with his suffering and insists that believers who share his sufferings will also be glorified.[80] Yet, Paul's emphasis on Christ's suffering is irreconcilable with the fast, painless death of a sacrificial animal. Sacrificial animals were killed quickly and efficiently by cutting their throat with a sharp knife. A carelessly performed, and therefore painful, slaying would risk having the animal swallow its own blood, thereby jeopardising the worthiness of the animal for sacrifice. Horace Bushnell recognized the unsuitability of a theology of suffering in the context of sacrifice; he comments that 'there was no pain in the dead victim'.[81]

Moreover, the slaughter of a victim was not considered to be part of the actual sacrificial ritual but merely a preliminary act which prepared the carcass for the sacrificial ritual to follow. Royden Yerkes has commented upon the lack of importance attached to act of slaying in Jewish sacrifice: 'slaying for sacrifice was naturally performed with solemnity proper for the occasion, but no significance was ever attached to the fact that the animal had died. We never hear of death *qua* death effecting

---

79. R. Bultmann, *Theology of the New Testament* (ET; trans. K. Grobel; New York: Charles Scribner's Sons, 1955 [1951]), p. 148; cf. H. Conzelmann, *1 Corinthians* (ET; Philadelphia: Fortress Press, 1975 [1969]), p. 199. Rudolf Bultmann has recognized that one cannot demonstrate atonement theology in the eucharist based on the theology of the Levitical thank-offering. In an effort to resolve this dilemma he proposed that in the eucharist, the idea of the thank-offering has been merged with the conception of Jesus' death as an atoning sacrifice (*Theology*, p. 296). Bultmann's proposal falls short of solving the problem since neither thanksgiving nor purification sacrifice atone for sins. How then could they have merged to form the conception of personal atonement?

80. E.g., Rom. 8.17; 2 Cor. 1.5; Phil. 3.10; cf. Col. 1.24.

81. H. Bushnell, *The Vicarious Sacrifice* (London: Richard D. Dickenson, 1880), pp. 393-94.

anything.'[82] For example, in the case of the Tamid, the high-point of the ritual occurred when the flesh was cast onto the burning altar. The fact of the death was incidental. This explains why the act of slaying is never described in any detail. If the animal's death had no significance in the ritual, then Christ's death could have no significance if interpreted in terms of sacrifice.

In a curious comment, Hans Schoeps remarks, 'the conception of vicarious suffering is very ancient and has its roots in the Biblical institution of sacrifice'.[83] After making this statement, Schoeps quotes no passage, nor describes any sacrificial ritual where such an idea can be found. Instead of citing Levitical text, Schoeps discusses sacrifice in Paul from the perspective of three traditions, the Suffering Servant, the righteous martyrs and the sacrifice of Isaac.[84] The fourth Suffering Servant Song (Isa. 52.13–53.12) is the only text in the whole of the Hebrew Bible where suffering and death could be interpreted as having expiatory significance for others. The concept of atonement in this passage is so foreign to anything else in the Hebrew Bible that Martin Hengel describes it as being 'at best on the very periphery of the Old Testament'.[85] As a rule, the Hebrew Bible rejects the concept of vicarious atonement on the grounds that 'a person may die only for his own sins' (Deut. 24.16; cf. 2 Kgs 14.6; 2 Chron. 25.4).[86] Hence, Moses' request that he might offer his own life as ransom in the place of his people is denied by God (Exod. 32.30-33).[87]

For the moment, it is sufficient to note that Paul quotes only twice from the fourth Servant Song. Strangely, he does not quote any verse

82. R. Yerkes, *Sacrifice in Greek and Roman Religions and Early Judaism* (New York: Charles Scribner's Sons, 1952), p. 5.

83. Schoeps, *Paul*, p. 129. Similarly, Henry W. Robinson comments on Isa. 53 saying that it 'uniquely illustrates the *sacrificial* principle as applied to the interpretation of human suffering' (*Suffering, Human and Divine* (New York: Macmillan, 1939), pp. 43-44.

84. Schoeps, *Paul*, pp. 127-49.

85. Hengel, *Atonement*, 8; Klaus Koch describes it as an 'erratic block misunderstood to lie at the heart of the New Testament period' ('Sühne und Sündenvergebung um die Wende von der exilischen zur nach exilischen Zeit', *EvT* 26 [1966], pp. 217-39, esp. p. 237).

86. K. Wengst, *Christologische Formeln und Lieder des Urchristentums* (Gütersloh: Gütersloh Verlagshaus, 1973), pp. 65-66.

87. H. Gese, *Essays on Biblical Theology* (trans. K. Crim; Minneapolis: Augsburg, 1981 [1977]), p. 96.

which could be interpreted in the light of crucifixion or atonement.
Rather he quotes Isa. 52.15 (= Rom. 15.21) and Isa. 53.12 (=Rom.
10.16) in order to convince the Romans of the value of his planned
mission to Spain. It is remarkable that in all of Paul's letters there does
not exist a single clear allusion (let alone quotation) to any verse of Isa.
52.13–53.12 having to do with suffering, humiliation or atonement. In
view of the unrepresentative nature of this passage with respect to the
Hebrew Bible, and Paul's evident lack of interest in it, it can be set aside.

Rabbinic texts are sometimes cited in order to demonstrate the
concept of vicarious atonement in the first century CE. The texts cited in
support of this theory are sparse and scattered and belong to the second
century or later (e.g., *m. Sanh.* 6.2; *s. Num.* 112; *t. Sanh.* 9.5). Special
attention has been given to the *Aqedah Yishak* ('the binding of Isaac'
[cf. Gen. 22.42]) which is interpreted in second century rabbinic texts as
having atoning significance.[88] It is also suggested that texts such as *Jub.*
18.7, 13 and Rom. 8.32 show that there are traces of this belief in the
first century CE.[89] The question of whether Isaac was portrayed this way
in first-century sources is still disputed.[90] Though this cannot be ruled
out, its late attestation raises serious questions as to whether this theology
ever really became widespread in the first century. G.F. Moore comments on the painstaking search by New Testament scholars for evidence
of a suffering Messiah in the works of ancient Jewish interpreters.

> It would be neither strange nor especially significant, if among the many
> and diverse homiletic applications of scripture to the Messiah, something
> of a similar kind should have been said about him. Such applications
> would, however, be no evidence that the Jews had a doctrine of a suffering
> Messiah.[91]

---

88. Goodenough, *Jewish Symbols*, IV, pp. 183-84; S. Spiegel, *The Last Trial:
On the Legends and Lore of the Command to Abraham to Offer Isaac as a Sacrifice:
The Akedah* (New York: Pantheon, 1967); G. Vermes, *Scripture and Tradition in
Judaism* (Leiden: Brill, 3rd edn, 1973 [1961]), pp. 193-227; R.J. Daly, 'The
Soteriological Significance of the Sacrifice of Isaac', *CBQ* 39 (1977), pp. 45-75; P.R.
Davies and B.D. Chilton, 'The *Aquedah*: A Revised Tradition of History', *CBQ* 40
(1978), pp. 514-46.

89. Hans Schoeps thinks that this tradition 'provided the very model for the elaboration of Pauline soteriology' (*Paul*, p. 141; cf. M. Hengel, *Atonement*, pp. 61-62).

90. For recent discussion of this question see: B.D. Chilton, *Targumic
Approaches to the Gospels* (Lanham, MD: University Press of America, 1986),
pp. 39-49, cf. pp. 25-37.

91. Moore, *Judaism*, I, p. 551.

Moreover, none of these text adduce a theology of vicarious atonement in which the protagonist becomes sinful and accursed. Hence, by definition, they cannot have had a major contributory role in the formation of Paul's conception of atonement.

Finally, nothing is more clearly stated, nor more strongly insisted upon in Gal. 3.13 than the fact of Christ's cursedness (see ch. 3). Paul's startling statement, 'Christ became a curse in our place' (Gal. 3.13) cannot be side-stepped in any analysis. The fact that the purification-offering was not cursed or used as a substitutionary victim strongly suggests that Paul is not employing sacrificial concepts in this text. Indeed, there is no text in the Jewish tradition which contains a teaching that a righteous man can vicariously atone for the sin of others by becoming accursed and sinful.[92]

92. According to Seeley, the main interpretation of Jesus' death can be traced to the 'noble death' motif, especially as it appears in the Jewish Hellenistic martyrology of 2 and *4 Macc.* For example, he argues that *4 Macc.* employs language of atonement (17.22, ἱλαστήριον), purification (1.11; 6.29; 17.21) and ransom (6.29; 17.21, ἀντίψυχον). Seeley identifies four aspects of what he calls the 'noble death' in 2 and *4 Macc.* (1) vicariousness; (2) obedience; (3) military context; (4) overcoming physical vulnerability. In *4 Macc.* he identifies a fifth aspect, the application of sacrificial metaphors. In turning to Paul, he finds all five aspects, though the fifth is of secondary importance (D. Seeley, *The Noble Death: Graeco-Roman Martyrology and Paul's Concept of Salvation* [JSNTSup, 28; Sheffield: JSOT Press, 1990]). Sam Williams, publishing prior to Seeley, argues that these two texts do not refer to the atonement of the Jews by means of the death of the righteous martyr. He gives the following reasons to substantiate his conclusion: (1) there is no reference to forgiveness in *4 Macc.* (2) it is not the people who are purifed but the 'land' (cf. 17.21-22); (3) the purification is accomplished by courage and steadfastness, rather than by death; (4) the author does not intend to argue that the deaths of the nine martyrs specifically reversed the political situation; the 'nine martyr story' is representative of all steadfast Jews (*Jesus' Death as Saving Event: The Background and Origin of a Concept* [Harvard Dissertations in Religion, 2; Missoula: Scholars Press, 1975], pp. 169-83). Marinus de Jonge, who argues in favour of interpreting 2 and *4 Macc.* in terms of vicarious atonement, explains why the understanding of these passages is difficult:

> The terms employed to express the vicarious nature and the atoning effect of these deaths are much more developed than those in the earlier documents. Yet in the overall picture of the book, more emphasis is laid on the exemplary nature of their [the righteous martyrs'] devotion and on the divine reward granted to them and to all true children of Abraham' (*Christology in Context: The Earliest Christian Response to Jesus* [Philadelphia: Westminster Press, 1988], p. 183).

Whether or not *4 Macc.* teaches vicarious atonement, it should be pointed out that this text can at best supply a partial analogy to Paul's soteriology as it appears in Gal.

To sum up: When Paul's theology is compared with Jewish sacrifice, it is the contrasts—not the similarities—which abound. According to Cilliers Breytenbach 'speculation about sacrifice (*Opfergedanke*) plays no role' in Paul's theology of atonement.[93] Modern biblical scholars who read the purification sacrifice into Paul's atonement theology prove uninformed about Jewish sacrificial practices and theory. As Roberston Smith observes: 'Christian theologians, looking on the sacrifices of the Old Testament as a type of the sacrifice on the cross...have undoubtedly over-estimated the ethical lessons embodied in the Jewish sacrificial system.'[94] In my view, there is no theological or textual justification to describe Paul's cursed and sinful Christ as sacrificial.

Paul and Greek Sacrifice

If the analogy between Paul's theology of atonement and Jewish sacrifice is unconvincing, the possibility exists that the analogy with Graeco-Roman sacrifice is stronger. After all, Paul travelled widely throughout the Hellenistic world where sacrifice was as central to Graeco-Roman religion as it was to pre-70 Judaism. Though the Greeks and Romans found Jewish Sabbath and dietary laws strange, the importance of sacrifice in Judaism was self-evident to them and required no explanation. So vital was sacrifice to Greek religion that Plato has Socrates define piety as 'knowledge of sacrificing and praying'.[95] The most important distinction in Greek sacrifice is between sacrifices consumed by the worshippers, the Olympian sacrifice, and whole-offerings which were either entirely burnt, or simply slaughtered and abandoned.[96]

3.13, 2 Cor. 5.21 and Rom. 8.3, since there is no suggestion here that the righteous martyrs became cursed or sinful in their deaths.

93. C. Breytenbach, *Versöhnung: Eine Studie zur paulinischen Soteriologie* (WMANT, 60; Neukirchen–Vluyn: Neukirchener Verlag, 1989), p. 221. David Seeley concludes that though Paul was familiar with the temple cultus, allusions to it are not cultic in nature, but concern Jesus' death as a turning point between and the old and new aeon. According to Seeley, the pattern of Paul's thought is cosmic, not cultic (*Noble Death*, ch. 1).

94. W. Roberston Smith, *Religion of the Semites: The Fundamental Institutions* (New York: Meridian Books, 1889), p. 424.

95. Plato, *Euthyrphr*. 14c.

96. This distinction became the starting point for Karl Meuli's theory of the origin of sacrifice based on hunting cultures, recently revived by Walter Burkert. See, W. Burkert, 'Greek Tragedy and Sacrificial Ritual', *GRBS* 7 (1966), pp. 87-121, esp.

The Olympian Sacrifice

> No man shall approach the holy ground with unclean hands.
> Yet there stands the priest himself, wallowing in gore...
> Lucian, *On Sacrifices* 13.

The typical sacrifice offered by a city or a voluntary religious association was the Olympian sacrifice, a bloody sacrifice of the alimentary type. It consisted of the killing and consumption of an animal for a god or goddess. As in the case of Jewish sacrifice, the Olympian sacrifice embraced butchery, religion and cooking. The only extant piece of connected prose describing the practice of sacrifice in the Hellenistic period is that of Dionysios of Halicarnassus in his *Roman Antiquities* (1 BCE).[97] The information provided by inscriptions is somewhat fragmentary since inscriptions tend to discuss only what was open to doubt, not what was taken for granted. However, the epigraphical evidence does demonstrate that the practice of sacrifice was complex and highly differentiated. The general remarks which follow are made with the understanding that sacrificial ritual varied somewhat from location to location and cult to cult.

The Place of Sacrifice
Temples were normally located in a temenos (τεμένος), a plot of land dedicated to a particular god which was cut off from the surrounding profane space. That this temenos was also known as a 'sanctuary' (ἱερόν) is an assertion of its sacred character. This sacred space was usually marked out by 'pillars' (ὅροι)[98] or a continuous boundary wall

pp. 105-113; W. Burkert, *Homo Necans: The Anthropology of Ancient Greek Sacrificial Ritual and Myth* (trans. P. Bing; Berkeley: University of Califoria Press, 1983 [1972]), pp. 12-22; W. Burkert, 'The Problem of Ritual Killing', in R.G. Hamerton-Kelly (ed.), *Violent Origins: Walter Burkert, René Girard, and Jonathan Z. Smith on Ritual Killing and Cultural Formation* (Stanford, CA: Stanford University Press, 1987), pp. 149-76, esp. pp. 164-68.

97. Dionysios of Halicarnussus, *Rom. Ant.* 7.72.15-18; cf. Marcus Terentius Varro on Roman public rites, Bk. 3 (47–45 BCE); Philo, *Leg. Gai.*, §§349-67, esp. §357. For the best modern descriptions of Greek sacrifice see: Walter Burkert, *Greek Religion* (trans. J. Raffan; Harvard University Press, 1985), pp. 54-82; Burkert, *Homo Necans*, pp. 8-20; M. Detienne, 'Culinary Practices and the Spirit of Sacrifice', in *The Cuisine of Sacrifice among the Greeks* (ed. M. Detienne and J.-P. Vernant; trans. P. Wissing; Chicago: University of Chicago Press, 1979), pp. 1-20.

98. '(This) boundary stone (marks the) sacred asylum of (the temple precincts) of Dionysos Bacchus; do not harm the one who seeks asylum (beyond this point) nor

(περίβολος). Personal purity was compulsory for admittance into a temenos. Basins of lustral water were set up at the entrance for people to purify themselves before entering. The purity of the sanctuary was also protected by sacred laws posted at its entrance prohibiting polluting acts and forbidding impure persons from entering.[99]

The temple (ναός) within this temenos was not a building in which people would assemble for worship. Its principal function was to house and protect the cult statue of the god[100] and the god's property.[101] For the security of both, temples were equipped with metal screens, doors and locks, which prevented public access for most of the year. Limited access to the temple was given on chief festivals of the god, but even in these cases, temples did not serve as a place of assembly and worship. On such occasions, individuals might have the opportunity to touch the statue, to clothe it in special garments, and sometimes to temporarily remove it and carry it in a public procession (e.g., Artemis in Ephesos).[102]

The place for cultic activity was not the temple but the altar. Altars were not located *inside* temples, but in front of them.[103] Here, wor-

---

may he who has been wronged keep close watch on him/her; and if he does, he and his children will be utterly destroyed' (*LSAM*, 75, ll. 8-12).

99. Consider for example the statutes concerning the cult of Dionysos Bromios in Smyrna (2 BCE):

> You, as many as pass through the *temenos* and shrines of (Dionysos) Bromios, let (a period of) forty days be observed after the exposure of a new-born child, lest then there be blood-guilt, and likewise (observe) as many days for a woman's abortion; and if death and fate should cover someone belonging to (your) household, the sacrifice required on the third day after the funeral shall be performed outside the entrance during that month, and if perhaps some kind of defilement should come from other households (besides your own), let him stay away from the decaying corpse for three days (before entering here)...' (*LSAM*, 84; Georg Petzl [ed.], *Die Inschriften von Smyrna*, Inschriften griechischer Städte aus Kleinasien, vols. 23–24/1–2, [Bonn: Rudolf Habelt, 1982–90], p. 227, no. 728).

100. The statue was usually made of wood and painted, sometimes sheathed in gold and ivory (chryselaphantine).

101. Especially votive-offerings; the parthenon of Athens also housed the state treasury.

102. Cf. G.M. Rogers, *The Sacred Identity of Ephesos: Foundation Myths of a Roman City* (London: Routledge & Kegan Paul, 1991).

103. Aeschylus, *Septem contra Thebas*, p. 275; the reasons for this can be guessed. First, in most temples there was insufficient room for large groups of people to congregate around an altar; moreover, such frequent access would compromise the security of the valuables. Lastly, the smoke produced by repeated burning of sacrifices would discolour the interior of the building and the cult statue.

shippers would form a circle (or semi-circle) around the altar, with the priest(ess) standing with his or her back to the temple facade. Thus, the cultic activity was focused on the altar not on the temple. Pavement around the altar served to connect it with the temple of the god to whom it belonged.

An altar was a raised stone platform upon which a fire was lit.[104] Its purpose was to burn animal sacrifices. Some altars had a depression on the upper surface for the fire. The top surface (or depression) on which the fire was burned was called the hearth (θυμέλη). With the exception of the household hearth, the fire of the altar did not burn continuously, but rather was kindled afresh for each sacrificial ritual. Animals were not slain or butchered on altars. They were killed near the altar and then butchered on a chopping block (ἐπίξηνον) set up beside the altar.

The act of sacrifice can be divided into five steps: selection, consecration, slaughter, butchering and lastly, burning and sharing. The verb 'to sacrifice' (θύειν) includes this entire sequence of rituals from consecration to sharing, not just the act of slaughtering.[105]

The Selection
Sacrificial victims were restricted principally to domesticated animals, especially oxen, bulls, sheep, goats and pigs.[106] In the Greek mind, the

---

104. βωμός (*altare*): altar dedicated to a major deity; ἐσχάρα (*ara*): low altar with shallow depression in top dedicated to a lesser deity; ἑστία (*focus*): domestic altar. The use of these terms were not kept rigidly separate. See M.P. Nilsson, *Opuscula selecta linguis Anglica, Francogallica, Germanica conscripta*, Svenska institutet i Athen. Skrifter. Acta. Series altera, II (3 vols.; Lund: C.W.K. Gleerup, 1951–60), I, p. 211, n. 124 (= Nilsson, *JHÖAI* 31 [1916], p. 337, n. 4); F. Robert, *Thymélè: Recherches sur la signification et la destination des monuments circulaires dans l'architecture réligieuse de la Grèce* (Paris: E. de Boccard, 1939), pp. 260-68; G.S.F. Gow, 'On the Meaning of the Word ΘΥΜΕΛΗ', *JHS*, 32 (1912), pp. 213-38. The altar was often set up on a square stone base called a socle (*soculus*). These were often equipped with horns on the four upper corners, or bolsters on the sides. Greeks preferred round altars, and Romans four-sided altars. Sacrifices to chthonic deities were made in pits (βόθροι). The tops of altars might be of four general styles: flat top, flat with horns on the corners, flat with bolsters on the sides, and shallow depression (sometimes with horns for bolsters).

105. J. Casabona, *Recherches sur le vocabulaire des sacrifices en Grec, des origines à la fin de l'époque classique* (Publication des Annales de la Faculté des lettres, nouv. ser. 59; Aix-en-Provence: Editions Ophrys, 1966), pp. 77, 86.

106. Except for poultry, the sacrifice of other birds such as geese and pigeons was rare; fish were also rarely sacrificed (Burkert, *Greek Religion*, p. 368, nn. 3, 4).

animal kingdom was divided into two groups, those which should be hunted because they posed a threat to humans, and those which ought to be protected because of their benefit to society.[107] Only the latter were fit for sacrifice. It was the priest's responsibility to assure that each animal met the criteria of purity prescribed in the cultic regulations.

Consecration

The ritual began with a procession, the purpose of which was to escort the sacrificial animal to the altar. This was a festive occasion for the participants. Clean clothes were required, and often a garland of woven twigs for the head.[108] The procession was led by the priest, and in the case of public sacrifices, the civic officials who would offer the sacrifice in the name of the city. Following them were others participating in the sacrifice, one of whom carried a tricorn reed-basket of barley in which was hidden the sacrificial knife.[109] A second person carried a water-jug, a third, an incense burner. The procession was often accompanied by musicians, especially an *aultete*. Having reached the altar, the participants formed a circle or semi-circle marked out by the carrying of the

---

107. M. Detienne, *Dionysus mis á mort* (Paris: Gallimard, 1977), pp. 140-42; U. Dietauer, *Tier und Mensch im Denken der Antike* (Amsterdam: Gruner, 1977), pp. 100-161.

108. J. Köchling, *De coronarum apud antiquos vi atque usu* (Giessen: Töpelmann, 1914); K. Baus, *Der Kranz in Antike und Christentum, eine religionsgeschichtliche Untersuchung mit besonderer Berucksichtigung Tertullians* (Bonn: P. Hanstein, 1940); cf. Plutarch, *Consol. ad Apoll.* 119a; Diogenes Laertius, 2.54. Sacrifice without a garland seems to require an explanation (cf. Apollodoros, 3.210 on the Charites cult of Paros).

109. κάνεον (κανοῦν Attic contraction); J. Rudhardt, *Notions fondamentales de la pensée religieuse et actes constitutifs du culte dans la Grèce classique* (Geneva: E. Droz, 1958), pp. 259-61; J. Schelp, *Das Kanoûn: Der griechische Opferkorb* (Wurzburg: K. Triltsch, 1975), pp. 23-25; F. Humborg, κανοῦν, PWSup, 4 (1924), pp. 867-75. According to Burkert, this role was performed by a blameless maiden. Lewis Farnell and F. Sokolowski agree, arguing that only a few cults excluded women from sacrifice. Marcel Detienne asserts that women customarily were excluded both from sacrificial ritual and from the consumption of sacrificial meat ('The Violence of Wellborn Ladies: Women in the Thesmophoria', in *A History of Women*. I. *From Ancient Goddesses to Christian Saints* (eds. G. Duby and M. Perrot; Cambridge, MA: Belknap Press of Harvard University Press, 1992), pp. 338-76, esp. pp. 338-39. In response, Robin Osborne has argued that women were indeed permitted to consume sacrificial meat (R. Osborne, 'Women and Sacrifice in Classical Greece', *CQ* 43/2 [1993], pp. 392-405).

water-jug. Then, while the priest recited prayers, water was poured over the hands of the participants, and over the head of the victim.[110] This latter act was intended to elicit the victim's assent by a nod of the head (ὑπόκυπτειν).[111] The priest and each of the participants then took a handful of oats from the reed-basket and raised their arms in the air. The priest recited a prayer, invocation, petition and vow, and all who looked on signified their 'Amen' by hurling the grain at the animal.[112] Thus, though only one person wielded the knife, this ritual of assent made the immolation a corporate act. According to Marcel Detienne, the slaughterer 'is no more than an instrument by which the sacrificers can ritually kill their victim'.[113] Some hairs were then cut from the animal's forehead, thereby marking the animal as inviolate.[114]

Slaying

The act of slaughter could be performed by the priest but was often delegated to some other person, usually a *mageiros* (μαγείρος). However, a priestess was *required* to delegate the act of slaughtering.[115] The appointed slaughterer (βουτύπος) then proceeded to slay the animal, first by striking it on the forehead with an axe, then by cutting its throat with a knife. At the precise moment of slaying, the women in attendance would cry out in a high shrill wail (ὀλολυγή) thereby invoking the god.[116] Cutting the throat required pulling the animal's head upwards so

110. *Rom. Ant.* 7.72.15; R. Ginouvès, *Balaneutikè: Recherches sur le bain dans l'antiquité* (Paris: E. de Boccard, 1962), pp. 309-310; Homer attributes the practice to Priam (*Iliad*, 24.302-6).

111. *Rom. Ant.* 7.72.15. The Greeks seemed to have been much more concerned than the Jews about the compliance of the animal in this affair. The Delphic oracle permitted the sacrifice of an animal 'which willingly nods at the washing of hands' (Porphyrios, *De Abstintentia*, 2.9). In a sacred law from Cos, the victim for Hestia is sacrificed only if it nodded its assent by lowering its head (*LSCG*, no. 151, pp. 252-61); cf. Plutarch, *Quaest. con.* p. 729; Burkert, 'Greek Tragedy', p. 107, n. 43.

112. *Rom. Ant.* 7.72.15. Sometimes stones, not barley, were thrown (Burkert, *Homo Necans*, p. 9, n. 16).

113. Detienne, 'Culinary Practices', p. 12.

114. S. Eitrem, *Opferritus und Voropfer der Griechen und Römer* (Kristiania: Jacob Dybwad, 1915), pp. 344-72; Burkert, *Homo Necans*, p. 5.

115. E.g., the priestess of Athena Polias did not slaughter the victims consumed at the Panathenaia (J. Martha, *Les sacerdoces athéniens* [Paris: E. Leroux, 1882], p. 81).

116. In the words of Burkert, 'life screams over death' (*Greek Religion*, p. 56). *Rom. Ant.* 7.72.15; Aeschylus, *Septem contra Thebas*, p. 269. However, as noted above, some scholars argue that women had no role whatsoever in sacrifice (cf.

that the blood might spurt out.[117] The blood was collected in a vase and poured over the altar and against its sides. It was considered to be a pious duty to bloody the altar.[118] Altars on vase paintings are often depicted as being splashed with blood. However, the Greeks had none of the blood taboos of the Jews. In most cases, the blood ritual is simply a prelude to the meal; it is not a means of returning the life of the victim back to the god as in Jewish sacrifice.

Butchering

The act of butchering was performed by a cook or *mageiros* (μαγείρος).[119] The carcass was butchered on a chopping block (ἐπίξηνον) with a butcher's knife (κόπις). The thorax was opened and the viscera (σπλάγχνα, consisting of the lungs, heart, liver, kidneys, spleen) and the entrails (ἔντερον, the digestive system) were removed, and the animal was then skinned.[120] The entrails were later eaten as sausages and black pudding. After the removal of the organs, the carcase was cut up in three stages: first, the thigh bones (μηρία) and pelvis with tail (ὀσφύς) were removed. Secondly, the viscera—considered to be the most precious part of the victim—were cut up into smaller pieces and put on spits (ὀβελοί). Finally, the remainder of the meat was cut up into strips.

Burning and Sharing

There were two steps to the burning. First, the portion for the god was burned. This consisted of the inedible parts, namely the thigh-bones, pelvis and tail. These were symbolically assembled on the altar into a

n. 109), with the exception of the priestess.

117. The British Museum has several fine examples of sculpture depicting Athena Nike pulling back the head of a bull in order to cut its neck (*BM Cat. Sculpture*, 1699, 1700; *BM Cat. Terracotta*, D 569).

118. The bloodying of the altar was an important aspect of Greek sacrifice (Aeschylus, *Septem contra Thebas*, p. 275; Theocritos, *Epigrammata* 1; Porphyrios, *De Abstintentia*, 1.25; P. Stengel, *Opferbrüche der Griechen* [Leipzig: Teubner, 1910], pp. 18-19).

119. Cf. G. Berthiaume, *Les rôles du mágeiros: étude sur la boucherie, la cuisine et le sacrifice dans la Grèce ancienne* (Montréal: Les Presses de l'Université de Montréal, 1982).

120. In private sacrifices, the skin reverted to the priest; in civic sacrificies it was sold for the benefit of the sacred treasury of the polis.

kind of skeleton.[121] To this was added the gall bladder, a libation of diluted wine and some incense. After this was burnt, the spitted viscera were roasted and shared among all the worshippers for consumption (*Rom. Ant.* 7.72.15). The Greeks marvelled at the custom of the Jews' whole-offering in which no meat reverted to the people.[122] It was a privilege and duty of the participants to taste immediately these blood engorged organs.[123] Once the viscera had been consumed, the meat was either boiled immediately in cauldrons (λέβητες)[124] and eaten or, more usually, distributed on the basis of social status. One portion of this meat, euphemisticially known as the 'god's portion' (θευμορίη), was reserved for the priest or high-ranking civic officials.

Table Offerings
In addition to the bloody offerings, there were also bloodless offerings such as bread, cakes, fruits, vegetables, cooked dishes and spices. Offerings of this kind are known as *trapezomata* (τραπεζώματα) or 'table-offerings' because they were set out and offered to the god on offering-tables (τράπεζαι).[125] Table-offerings could either be offered in

121. Hesiod, *Theogony*, 541; Burkert, *Homo Necans*, p. 6 n. 24. K. Meuli, 'Griechische Opferbräuche', in *Phyllobolia Festschift P. Von der Mühll*, (Basel: B. Schwabe, 1946), pp. 185-288, esp. pp. 218, 256, 262.

122. Theophrastos in the work of Porphyrios, *Abst.* 2.26; cf. Philo *Leg. Gai.* 356.

123. Marcel Detienne argues that women were not only excluded from sharing the meat, they were also excluded from participating in sacrificial ritual (cf. n. 109).

124. The viscera were distinguished from the entrails—the stomach and intestines (cf. Berthiaume, *Viandes grecques*; J.-L. Durand, 'Greek Animals: Toward a Topology of Edible Bodies', in *The Cuisine of Sacrifice among the Greeks* [ed. M. Detienne and J.-P. Vernant], pp. 87-118, esp. pp. 100-104). The rule that roasting must preceed the boiling (stewing) followed the logic of 'the worse to the better' in culinary history: the knowledge of how to grill meat preceeded the knowledge of stewing meat (Detienne, *Dionysus mis á mort*, pp. 174-82). It is this firm practice which is challenged in the Orphic account of Dionysus who was boiled and *then* roasted (O. Kernt, *Orphicorum Fragmenta* [Berlin: Weidmannos, 1922], pp. 34-36, pp. 209-214).

125. Compare for example the offering-table used by an Athenian voluntary association (*koinon*) in the early fourth century BCE consisting of three compartments (ἐσξάραι) framed with the inscribed names of the members of the society, one of whom is a priest (*IG* II2 2343; C. Michel, *Recueil d'inscriptions grecques* [Paris: Polleunis & Centerick, 1900], no. 1547; cf. F. Poland, *Geschichte des griechischen Vereinswesens* [Leipzig: B.G. Teubner, 1909], p. 19).

conjunction with bloody sacrifices or separately.[126] No altar was needed for these offerings because they were not burnt.

Greek Olympian and Jewish Sacrifice

It is clear from the above that in neither Greek Olympian nor in any form of Jewish sacrifice did the victim become accursed or polluted. However, there were important differences between the two. These can be summarised as follows. In the Greek ritual:

more of the animal reverted to the offerers for consumption

more importance is attached to the slaying of the victim

concern is shown for the willingness of the animal

care is taken to share the responsibility for the slaying amongst the entire group

unlike Jewish sacrifice, the ritual began with a procession

unlike the Jews who had only one temple in the Roman period and sacrifice was permitted only in that temple, the Greeks and Romans had innumerable temples and sacrifice was permitted even where no temple existed.[127]

The Meaning of Olympian Sacrifice

The practice of sacrifice as described above can be interpreted at several levels. Understood pragmatically, sacrifice provided most, if not all, of the meat required for domestic consumption.[128] Interpreted anthropologically, the Olympian sacrifice can be thought of as a meal offered in thanksgiving to a deity, hence Dio Chysostom's exclamation 'What sacrifice is pleasing to the gods without the fellow banqueters?' (*Or.* 3.97). The obvious irony in this case is that the god received virtually

126. For example, on Delos, apart from the altar of Apollo on which a hundred head of cattle were sacrificed, there was a table reserved for *trapezomata* on which it was forbidden to kindle a fire or offer bloody sacrifices.

127. The last temple to be constructed outside Jerusalem was the Zadokite temple in Leontopolis, Egypt (*HJP*, III, pp. 145-47).

128. Marcel Detienne thinks that the only meat available for consumption was sacrificial meat. Accordingly, butcher shops were not permitted to sell meat from from non-sacrificed animals, much less, animals unfit for sacrifice ('Culinary practices', p. 3). However, he also argues that killing animals in a butcher shops was also considered to be a sacrifice. Guy Berthiaume argues that some meat sold in butcher shops was from animals who were not slaughtered at an altar, or even slaughtered in a ritual way (*Les rôles de mageiros*, pp. 62-70, 89).

none of the sacrifice since the best parts of the animal were returned to the participants and wider community.

This peculiar state of affairs found its justification in the myth of Prometheus who, at the first sacrifice, set the meat and entrails of a bull on one side, and covered them with the hide and stomach. On the other side, he set the bones and animal fat and covered them also. When asked to pick one pile on behalf of the gods, Zeus chose the latter. Whether Zeus was duped or made the choice deliberately (as Hesiod would have it), the myth became the justification for the established practice of apportioning out the sacrifice.[129]

Perhaps the meagerness of portions allotted to the gods should not be overemphasised since it may have been the smoke, more than the meat, which enacted the communion between the worshippers and their god. The aroma from the burnt bones, fat and incense was thought to delight the gods.[130] Whatever the case, the Greeks hoped that, by pleasing the deity with sacrifice, their god's benefaction towards them would continue, though realising that fulfilment of this hope was beyond their control.[131]

Sacrifice also had a sociological dimension in that it formed the basis of community (κοινωνία). The very act of offering sacrifice served to reinforce the social bonds that united people together into a community. According to Marcel Detienne, sacrifice was the way in which the community ate together: the congruence of the roles of the sacrificial slaughterer and cook (*mageiros*) 'indicates to what extent the offering of a sacrificial victim is regarded and enacted as a way of eating together'.[132] Walter Burkert attributes the uniting and reinforcing effects of sacrifice to the mutually shared guilt associated with the slaying of the victim. The Olympian sacrifice is

129. Regardless, this ironic state of affairs became a common theme in comedy (M.L. West, *Hesiod: Theogony, edited with Prolegomena and Commentary* [Oxford: Clarendon, 1966], p. 321; Burkert, *Homo Necans*, p. 6, n. 24, p. 7, n. 30). This explains why the Greeks marvelled at whole-offerings of the Jews in which no meat reverted to the people. See also, Theophrastos (in Porphyrios, *De Abstinentia*, 2.26); Philo, *Leg. Gai.*, p. 356.

130. L.B. Zaidman and P.S. Pantel, *Religion in the Ancient Greek City* (ET; trans. P. Cartledge; Cambridge: Cambridge University Press, 1994 [1989]), p. 36.

131. Burkert, *Greek Religion*, p. 55.

132. Detienne, 'Culinary Practices', p. 11. Foreigners were forbidden to participate in sacrifice except through the mediation of a citizen. Similarly, in founding a new political colony, it was necessary to bring a pot containing fire for future sacrifices (Aristophanes, *Birds*, pp. 43-45, 356-60, 387-91).

the communally enacted and shared guilt [of sacrifice] which creates solidarity...The order of life, a social order, is constituted in the sacrifice through irrevocable acts; religion and everyday existence interpenetrate so completely that every community, every order must be founded through a sacrifice.[133]

The Whole Offering

Though far less common, whole-offerings (ὁλοκαυτώματα) were also made to the gods,[134] especially to the chthonic deities.[135] In the category of whole-offerings, the most widely practiced was the *sphagion* (σφάγιον) ritual in which the entire carcass was given over to the deity, usually by burning. *Sphagia* (pl.) were used in three contexts, for purifications, at burials and before battle. At the burial of the dead, blood was poured on the ground which then worked its way down to the deceased and restored life to them.[136] The blood of animals shed as sacrifices before battle served to anticipate in a controlled context the slaughter and perils which awaited the warriors.[137]

The *sphagion* for purification finds a partial analogy with the Jewish purification-offering.[138] In this sacrifice, the blood was used to purify

133. Burkert, *Greek Religion*, pp. 58-59.

134. According to Pausanius, the worship of Artemis Laphria in Patrae included burning wild animals alive (*Description of Greece*, 7.18.8-13). There are also whole-offerings for Zeus (*LSCG* no. 18, Γ23, Δ21, E13; *LSCG*, no. 151, A 29-36).

135. Burning was seen as characteristic of chthonic sacrifices; inscriptional references to cthonic deities include: Ζεύς Χθόνιος (*LSCG* 96.25); Ζεύς Μειλίχος (*LSCG* 1 A.4; 18 A.40; 75.4-8); Χθόνιοι θεοί (156 A.9); Χθόνια Δημήτηρ (BE no. 65, p. 263); Χθόνιος 'Ερμῆς (BE no. 31, p. 220; no. 58, p. 111; no. 67, p. 350); cf. P. Stengel, *Die griechischen Kultusaltertümer* (Munich: C.H. Beck, 2nd edn, 1920), pp. 105, 124; cf. E. Rohde, *Psyche: Seelencult und Unsterblichkeitsglaube der Griechen* (Freiburg: J.C.B. Mohr, 1894), pp. 148-52; F. Pfister, *Der Reliquienkult im Altertum* (2 vols.; Giessen: Töpelmann, 1920 [1909]), p. 477; J.E. Harrison, *Prolegommena to the Study of Greek Religion* (Cambridge: Cambridge University Press, 2nd edn, 1908), pp. 1-31.

136. Burkert, *Greek Religion*, p. 60; Burkert, *Homo Necans*, p. 53.

137. W.K. Pritchett, *The Greek State at War*. III. *Religion* (Berkeley, CA: University of California Press, 1979), pp. 83-90; A. Henrichs, 'Human Sacrifice in Greek Religion: Three Case Studies', in *Le sacrifice dans l'antiquité* (Entretiens Fondation Hardt, 27; ed. J.-P. Vernant; Geneva: Entretiens Fondation Hardt, 1981), pp. 195-235, esp. 208-224.

138. E.g., *LSAM* 88.5; BE no. 39, p. 393; σφαφίαζω (SIG³ 685.25); Cf. Stengel, *Opferbrüche*, pp. 92-102; L. Ziehen, *PW* III A 1669-79; Casabona, *Vocabulaire des sacrifices en Grec*, pp. 180-93; S. Eitrem, 'Mantis und sphagia', *Symbolae Osloenses*

people and places of impurity.[139] For example, certain socially taboo acts such as murder were thought to defile the transgressor with an almost physical pollution. The *sphagion* was used to remove this defilement.[140] Blood from *sphagion* sacrifices was used to purify, not only people, but also places. For example, designated officials would delineate the square of the Athenian Assembly by encircling it with pigs in their arms. The pig's throats were then cut and their blood sprayed all over the seats of the assembly.[141] This ritual served to purify the area in anticipation of the rekindling of the hearth and the resumption of normal sacrifices and prayers.[142]

Paul and Greek Sacrifice

The Olympian sacrifice, as in the case of the Jewish thank-offering, lacks significant features for comparison with Paul's concept of the cursed Christ. It was not an atoning sacrifice, nor was it employed to purify people or places from sin, curses or any other form of defilement. In contrast, the blood of the *sphagion* was employed for purifying people and places, and provides a partial analogy to the concept of sacrifice in specific New Testament text in which Christ's blood is said to cleanse people of their sins (e.g., Heb. 9.12-14, 22, 25-26; 12.24; 1 Pet. 1.2; 1 Jn 1.7; Rev. 7.14). Many Christians in the first and second century lived far removed from the sacrificial cult of Jerusalem, and/or after the demise of the Jewish cult in 70 CE. They undoubtedly had far more opportunity to learn about the purposes of Greek sacrifice than its Jewish counterpart. Hence, they would naturally have interpreted the Levitical purification-offering and thank-offering in the Septuagint in terms of the Greek *sphagion* and Olympian sacrifices respectively.

Whether or not this is the case, the *sphagion* provides a very poor

18 (1938), pp. 9-30; Harrison, *Prolegomena*, pp. 64-65.

139. The use of blood for purification is mocked by Heraclitus: 'They purify themselves by defiling themselves with other blood, as if someone in mud should try to wash himself with mud' (Heraclitus B 5).

140. Burkert, *Greek Religion*, p. 81.

141. The pigs were then castrated and genitals discarded (Jacoby, *F. Gr. Hist.* 334 F 16).

142. Burkert, *Greek Religion*, pp. 81-82. Similarly, the Mantineans purified their land by leading animals set aside for *sphagia* around the land and then slaughtering them (Polyb. 4.21; cf. Paus. 2.34.2). A variant of this practice involved purifying an army before battle by decapitating a dog, and having the army march between the bloody halves (Liv. 40.6).

analogy for Paul's concept of the cursed and sinful Christ. Whereas a central feature of the *sphagion* sacrifice is the blood ritual, blood has no function (nor is it even mentioned) in Gal. 3.13, 2 Cor. 5.21 and Rom. 8.3. Moreover, there is no evidence that the *sphagion* victim became defiled or accursed in the course of this ritual. Therefore, neither Greek nor Jewish sacrifice can provide an adequate analogy for interpreting Paul's theory of atonement.

Chapter 2

MEDITERRANEAN APOTROPAEIC RITUALS

The popular meaning of the term 'scapegoat' has contemporary connotations which are foreign to its technical meaning. The scapegoat concept is often confused with misplaced guilt, ritual sacrifice, orgiastic violence, evasive defence mechanisms, violent political tactics and the victimization of minorities. For this reason, several issues must be addressed if misunderstanding and ambiguity are to be avoided.

The term 'scapegoat'[1] was coined by William Tyndale for his translation of the Bible (1530): 'And Aaron cast lottes over the gootes: one lotte for the Lorde and another for a scape goote.'[2] Since the time of Tyndale, his term 'scapegoat' has been employed as a technical term for the goat which was expelled on the Day of Atonement. Besides the book of Leviticus there are scapegoat traditions in many other Jewish and Christian writings.[3] The 'scapegoat concept' has also been employed in connection with primordial religion (James Frazer), Greek myth and ritual (Walter Burkert), literature (John Vickery), family therapy (Eric Berman), violence and religion (René Girard) and Jungian psychology

---

1.   Literally, 'escapegoat'; German: *Sündenbock*; French: *bouc émissaire*.
2.   The Revised Version (1884) included this term in the margin, but translated the Hebrew proper name correctly as *Azaz'el*.
3.   The range of sources for this rite are complex: in addition to the book of Leviticus (16.7-10, 20-22), there are scapegoat traditions in the book of *Jubilees* (34.18-19), the Qumran Temple Scroll (*11QTemple* col. 25-27), Philo of Alexandria (*Spec. Leg.* 1.188; *Leg. All.* 2.51-52; *Plant.* 60-61; *Rer. Div. Her.* 179), a Qumran targum to Leviticus (R. de Vaux and J.T. Milik, *Discoveries in the Judean Desert*. VI. *Qumran Grotte 4* [Oxford: Clarendon Press, 1977], II, p. 156 [Pl. 28], pp. 86-88; appendix, pp. 92-93), the *Mishnah* (*Yom.* 3.8; 4.1; 6.1-8; 8.8-9; *Šebu.* 1.6-7; *Men.* 3.6; 9.7) and the *Sifra* (60.1.2-3; 181.2.9; 186.2.2-3, 5). There are also several early Christian sources such as the *Epistle of Barnabas* (7.4-7), Justin Martyr (*Dial.* 40.4; 95.2), Tertullian (*Adv. Marc.* 7.7-8), Origen (*Homilies on Lev.* 10.1-2) and Clement of Alexandria (*Strom.* 7.33).

(Sylvia Perera). This secondary usage probably stems from the writings of Sir James Frazer. His use of the term 'scapegoat' for one volume of his *Golden Bough* (3rd edn, 1913) has been decisive for general and learned usage alike. This usage continues in the works of modern scholars such as Walter Burkert. The following quotation demonstrates how the term 'scapegoat' has become dissociated from its Jewish roots to such an extent that Burkert must take pains to inform his readers of its original connection:

> The common pattern emerging from Hittite, Greek, and Roman ritual and myth is of course a familiar one, that of the 'scapegoat', a term which has become so familiar that some may not even remember that it goes back indeed to a ritual, described in the Old Testament, of *Yom Kippur*, the Day of Atonement.[4]

This practice of classifying a collective group of rituals by the name of one of that group's constitutive members (the Levitical scapegoat ritual) is both confusing and imprecise for it presumes common features between the Levitical scapegoat and these other rituals without ever specifying them or demonstrating the cogency of the parallel. For example, many authors refer to Oedipus Rex as a 'scapegoat' when they actually mean to say that he resembles a *pharmakos* victim.[5] This results from the confusing practice of translating the term '*pharmakos*' as 'scapegoat'.

'Scapegoat Rituals': The Theories of Frazer and Girard

The overgeneralization of the term 'scapegoat' is further complicated by the fact that the contemporary understanding of what it means to be a 'scapegoat' has many connotations which are contrary to its proper sense. For example, Frazer's *Scapegoat* volume is the supreme example of 'parallelomania' taken to its logical conclusion.[6] 'Parallelomania'

---

4.   W. Burkert, *Structure and History in Greek Mythology and Ritual* (Sather Classical Lectures, 47; Berkeley, CA: University of California Press, 1979), p. 65.

5.   E.g., Burkert, *Structure and History*, p. 65; J.E. Harrison, *Epilegomena to the Study of Greek Religion* (Cambridge: Cambridge University Press, 1921), p. xli, p. 25; J.P. Vernant, *Tragedy and Myth in Ancient Greece* (Brighton: Harvester Press, 1973), pp. 114-131; René Girard, *The Scapegoat* (ET; trans. Y. Freccero; Baltimore: Johns Hopkins University, 1986 [1982]), pp. 89-91.

6.   J.G. Frazer, *The Golden Bough*. IV. *The Scapegoat* (London: Macmillan, 3rd edn, 1911–15), pp. 229-73.

describes the questionable practice of picking out and comparing elements from different religious systems without first understanding them in the original contexts in which they functioned. Under the general classification 'scapegoat', Frazer included countless instances of irrational mass violence against individuals from all periods of history and innumerable countries. In contrast to this, it must be noted that the Levitical scapegoat was *not* a victim of mob feeling, but was carefully and dispassionately selected by casting lots. The ritual was deliberate, disciplined and limited in scope, not a spontaneous, uncontrolled act of mass aggression.

Since scholars of the nineteenth century were less methodologically self-conscious than scholars are today, we should not judge Frazer 'the stereotypical armchair anthropologist' too harshly. As Robert Ackerman observes, Frazer's egregious ethnocentrism and outright racism, his uncompromising rationalism and his staunch atheism, were conventional tenets of his time, so that to find fault with them is to court presentism.[7] Frazer's peculiar equation of the scapegoat with victims of indiscriminate mass violence was intended to serve his overarching purpose of proving that primitive religions were founded on magic, which he considered to be the lowest form of religion. According to Frazer, 'magical religion' evolved naturally over time into 'ethical religion' such as found in the prophets of the Old Testament. Frazer presumed all ritual to be magic—empty form grounded in superstition.[8] Mary Douglas has lampooned Frazer's portrayal of primitive religion: 'Magic was carefully separated [by Frazer] from other ceremonial, as if primitive tribes were populations of Ali Babas and Aladdins, uttering their magic words and rubbing their magic lamps.'[9]

Frazer's reconstruction of the 'primitive mind' with his bias towards

7.   R. Ackerman, *J. G. Frazer: His Life and World* (Cambridge: Cambridge University Press, 1987), pp. 99-101.

8.   Frazer's distinction between myth and religion arises in the second edition (1900) and is then softened in the third (1911–15) (Ackerman, *Frazer*, pp. 109-110, 165).

9.   M. Douglas, *Purity and Danger: An Analysis of Concepts of Pollution and Taboo* (New York: Praeger, 1966), pp. 58-59. In correction of this oversimplification Douglas remarks that the primitive concept of 'magic' should be rendered in modern terminology as 'miracle'. Though primitive cultures believed that the possibility for miracles was always present, it is not under automatic control, nor did it necessarily depend on a rite; 'The power of miraculous intervention was believed to exist, but there was no way of harnessing it' (*Purity and Danger*, p. 59).

ethics over magic is based on anthropological models which have long been dismissed.[10] His version of comparativism severs phenomena from their contexts. His rigid division of magic and religion is no longer tenable. Despite these facts, Frazer's interpretation of the scapegoat has had a decisive influence on subsequent research on this subject. The inaccuracy which characterised Frazer's use of the term 'scapegoat' continues to the present day.

The scapegoat concept has been thrust into renewed prominence by Walter Burkert and René Girard who both develop the thesis that violence lies at the heart of religion.[11] While Burkert focuses specifically on ritual sacrifice, Girard considers a much broader range of human violence and its religious implications. According to Girard, human learning is almost entirely based on imitation. This inevitably led to serious conflict in primitive societies when successful imitators challenged the authority of those whom they imitate. According to Girard, the survival of the human species depended upon the invention of social structures to solve this mimetic crisis. Girard theorises that sometime in the remote past a random altercation broke out between two rivals. In the course of the conflict, the spectators came to project their own inner hostilities onto the weaker individual, the 'scapegoat', such that he was blamed for whatever conflicts and troubles were threatening the integrity of the community. Hence a 'scapegoat' was substituted in place of their true social rivals, and as a result he aroused both fear and the promise of salvation through his destruction. The temptation to imitate the blind rage of the assailant grew in the spectators until ultimately all members of the community joined together in an act of unified violence against the 'scapegoat'. At this moment, by 'unanimous victimage', all the confused aggressions of the group were focused on that one victim.

10. E. Evans-Pritchard, *A History of Anthropological Thought* (New York: Basic Books, 1981), pp. 132-52; M. Harris, *The Rise of Anthropological Theory* (New York: Harper & Row, 1968), pp. 204-208; E. Leach, 'On the Founding Fathers', *Current Anthropology* 7 (1966), pp. 560-67; E.J. Sharpe, *Comparative Religion* (New York: Charles Scribner's Sons, 1975), pp. 87-94; J.Z. Smith, 'When the Bough Breaks', *HR* 12 (1973), pp. 342-71; Burkert, *Structure and History*, pp. 35-36, 99-122.

11. Burkert, *Homo Necans*; R. Girard, *Violence and the Sacred* (trans. P. Gregory; Baltimore: The Johns Hopkins University Press, 1977). Girard's theory is elaborated in *The Scapegoat* and *Things Hidden Since the Foundation of the World* (Girard with J.-M. Oughourlian and G. Lefort; Stanford, CA: Stanford University Press, 1987); cf. R.G. Hamerton-Kelly (ed.), *Violent Origins*.

By means of this consolidated act of violence against an artificial antagonist, a metamorphosis took place within the community. By the redirection of all angry passions onto a 'scapegoat', the community purged itself of all its social aggressions and rivalries, achieving peace and unification. The community instinctively attributed this newly realized peace to the collective act of killing the 'scapegoat'. The blessings of peace which resulted from this murder were real—though not bestowed by a deity—because the vicious circle of interpersonal aggression had been broken. Through this 'scapegoat mechanism' inter-societal violence was resolved.[12]

For Girard, the power of 'scapegoating' lies precisely in its absence from conscious thought. Having achieved peace once by this process, societies institutionalize it, repeating it again and again in a ritualized form, in unconscious imitation of the original event in order to deflect new aggressions. This served to stabilize community life and provide a model for human culture. Here, says Girard, is the origin of sacrifice. Sacrifice is the ritualized mimetic expression of the scapegoat mechanism:

> If the unanimous violence directed against the surrogate victim succeeds in bringing this crisis to an end, clearly this violence must be at the origin of a new sacrificial system. If the surrogate victim can interrupt the destructive process, it must be at the origin of structure.[13]

Hence, while sacrificial ritual is in itself a controlled rational observance, it is rooted, according to Girard, in the irrational spontaneous violence against an innocent victim. Through such mob violence against an innocent victim, social harmony is restored. Girard finds evidence for this generative principle everywhere he looks. His theory is universal in scope. He describes how in myth, ritual, literature and history, innocent victims are presented as guilty in order to legitimate collective violence.

The extreme uniformity of Girard's conclusions depends upon his single interpretive key which he systematically applies to all data. Violence is certainly *a* common denominator in all societies, but it is not the only one, nor is it self-evident that it is the *key* common denominator for the interpretation of all religions and rituals. For example, Emile Durkheim (1858–1917) thought that totemism was the founding form of religion; Edward B. Tylor (1832–1917) posited animism as the starting point; James Frazer argued for magic as the origin (1854–1941);

12. Girard, *The Scapegoat*, pp. 39-41; Girard, *Things Hidden*, pp. 26-27.
13. Girard, *Violence and the Sacred*, p. 93.

Sigmund Freud (1856–1939) believed that a suppressed libido was at the heart of religion.

Girard's universalist theory may simplify the data but it does not necessarily clarify it. Burkert rejects Girard's 'generative principle' from which all subsequent sacrificial ritual is to be derived, and criticises Girard for failing to distinguish the scapegoat pattern from ritual sacrifice, which is derived from Paleolithic hunting according to Burkert.[14] To these criticisms, I would add that Girard's choice of the term 'scapegoat' to describe the origin of *sacrifice* is most unhelpful since (as I shall argue below) the scapegoat concept is actually opposite to the concept of sacrifice.

All this being said, some generic terminology is needed to describe the 'scapegoat paradigm'.[15] For the purpose of the following analysis, I shall employ the term 'apotropaeic paradigm' and 'apotropaeic ritual' in place of 'scapegoat paradigm' and 'scapegoat ritual'. The use of this term has two advantages. First, it diminishes the temptation to colour the analysis of diverse rituals by association with the Jewish scapegoat ritual. Secondly, it is free of the confused and value oriented connotations which scholars such as Frazer and Girard have attached to the term 'scapegoat'.

Apotropaeic Rituals

If one is to understand apotropaeic rituals, it is necessary to know something of the interior belief which inspired them.[16] Life in the ancient world was governed by taboos and sacred laws, many of which were connected with issues of purity and defilement, to duties owing to the gods (εὐσέβεια) and to the consequences of neglecting these duties. In

---

14.   Burkert, following the theory of Karl Meuli's theory (Burkert, 'Greek Tragedy', esp. pp. 105-13; Burkert, *Homo Necas*, pp. 12-22. Jonathan Z. Smith is also critical of Girard's historical foundationalism, and rejects 'the notion that religion was formed at some point in time' (in Hamerton-Kelly [ed.], *Violent Origins*, p. 235).

15.   B.H. McLean, 'On the Revision of Scapegoat Terminology', *Numen* 37/2 (1990), pp. 168-73.

16.   For the most recent general discussion of these human expulsion rituals see: Burkert, *Structure and History*, pp. 59-77; Burkert, *Greek Religion*, pp. 82-84; J. Bremmer, 'Scapegoat Rituals in Ancient Greece', *HSCP* 87 (1983), pp. 299-320; D. Hughes, *Human Sacrifice in Greece* (London: Routledge & Kegan Paul, 1991), pp. 139-65; cf. V. Gebhard, *Die Pharmakoi in Ionien und die Sybakchoi in Athen* (Diss.; Amberg: H. Böes Söhne, 1926).

some cases, contact with defilement was unavoidable (e.g., family burial, menstruation). In other cases, defilement resulted from willful transgression of a taboo or sacred law. These defilements could manifest themselves in the form of curses. In the words of Robert Parker, a curse was 'a spontaneous and automatic product of transgression';[17] Robertson Smith remarks that they were used 'to stamp an offender with the guilt of impiety and bring him under the direct judgment of the supernatural powers'.[18]

According to Mary Douglas, this fear of defilement, which is so characteristic of the ancient world, is a product of the need for order, structure and defined rules and norms in society.[19] Similarly, R.C.T. Parker interprets this persistent concern over purification as a desire for order and as a kind of science of division.[20] From this point of view, defilement can be defined as a disturbance of the system of classification which determines two distinct worlds: the inner world of society, order and culture; and the outer world of chaos, wilderness and natural forces. Defilement poses a real danger in society because it threatens to damage the border between these two worlds such that society is overtaken by chaos and its deadly natural forces.[21]

The apotropaeic rituals were used to maintain and restore these borders. They reflect a shared belief in the reality of defilement from the outer world of chaos. Once unleashed in society, there was a very real possibility of physical contagion and social disruption. This contagion or curse will work itself out on society unless a substitute victim is provided upon whom it might be discharged. This belief, so foreign to modern sensibility, is explained by A.E. Crawley: 'good and evil in all but the higher stages of thought are constantly "embodied", either by analogy, personification, or the much more normal and prevalent mode of mere

17.   R. Parker, *Miasmus: Pollution and Purification in Early Greek Religion* (Oxford: Clarendon Press, 1983), p. 191. In the words of William Robertson Smith, curses were used 'to stamp an offender with the guilt of impiety and bring him under the direct judgment of supernatural powers' (*Religion of the Semites*, p. 163).

18.   Smith, *Religion of the Semites*, p. 163.

19.   Douglas, *Purity and Danger*; Douglas, *Implicit Meanings: Essays in Anthropology* (London: Routledge & Kegan Paul, 1975); for critical reactions see Parker, *Miasma*, p. 61, n. 101; Douglas replied in *Natural Symbols* (Harmondsworth: Penguin Books, 2nd edn, 1973).

20.   Parker, *Miasma*, p. 31.

21.   Cf. H.S. Versnel, *Transition and Reversal in Myth and Ritual* (Inconsistencies in Greek and Roman Religion, II; Leiden: Brill, 1993), pp. 309-310.

mental objectification.'[22] Similarly Jane Harrison remarks, 'the notion, so foreign to our scientific habit of thought, so familiar to the ancients, was that evil of all kinds was a physical infection that could be caught and transferred'.[23] Diogenes Laertius illustrates this causal relationship between transgression and the resulting curse which threatened severe social disruption through pestilence. According to Diogenes, a pestilence which infected Athens was in fact the manifestation of a *curse* (ἄγος) resulting from the transgression of one named Cylon. The citizens of Athens resorted to an apotropaeic ritual in order to purify the city of this curse, thereby restoring social order.[24] Apotropaeic rituals take advantage of this very feature of transferability by selecting a victim upon whom this physical infection could be transferred, and by expelling the victim, the curse is also expelled.

Particular mythic tales are helpful in explaining the framework of belief behind apotropaeic rituals. Comparisons between ritual and myth can be very illuminating since, as Burkert demonstrates, myths often arise in order to interpret the meaning of ritual and can be enacted by ritual.[25] According to Burkert, 'ideas and beliefs are produced by ritual, rather than vice versa'.[26] Consider, for example, the myth of king Oedipus, whom many consider to be a mythic apotropaeic (*pharmakos*) victim.[27] On the occasion of a prolonged plague in Thebes, Oedipus consulted an oracle only to discover that the plague was caused by a curse resulting from transgression: one of the citizens of Thebes was

22. A.E. Crawley, 'Cursing and Blessing', PW, IV, pp. 367-74, esp. 368.

23. Harrison, *Prolegomena*, p. 103, cf. p. 105.

24. 'When the Athenians were attacked by pestilence, and the Pythian priestess bade them purify the city…According to some writers Nicias declared the plague to have been caused by the pollution (ἄγος) which Cylon brought on the city and showed them how to remove it. In consequence two young men, Cratinus and Ctesibus, were put to death and the city was delivered from the scourge (λυθῆναι τὴν συμφοράν)' (R.D. Hicks, [ed. and trans.], *Diogenes Laertius: Lives of Eminent Philosophers* [2 vols.; LCL; London: Wm. Heinemann, 1959], I, p. 110).

25. Burkert, *Greek Religion*, p. 8, cf. p. 9.

26. Burkert, *Homo Necans*, p. 156. This is succinctly stated by Jan Bremmer: 'the myth clarified the meaning of the ritual' (Bremmer, 'Scapegoat Rituals', p. 318). The practice of tracing myths to rituals, which began with W. Mannhardt, H. Usan, A. Dietrich and M. Nilsson, was continued by the Cambridge Ritualists, Jane Harrison, Gilbert Murray, Franci Macdonald Cornford (Burkert, *Greek Religion*, pp. 2-3).

27. In Athens, the victim of an apotropaeic ritual was termed as '*pharmakos*'; cf. Burkert, *Structure and History*, p. 65; Girard, *Scapegoat*, pp. 84-91; Vernant, *Tragedy and Myth*, pp. 114-31; Harrison, *Epilegomena*, p. xli, p. 25.

responsible for the assassination of king Laïus. At the outset of his investigation, Oedipus prays that this curse may be transferred to the guilty party. Finally, when it comes to light that Oedipus himself had killed Laïus, he blinds himself and banishes himself from the city 'bearing the curse' in order to save the city (Sophocles, *O. Rex.* 1290-93).

The myth of Oedipus Rex—and the myths of Thersites, Aesop, Codrus and Pentheus[28]—testifies to the belief in curses which result from transgression, and the devastation which such pollutions could wreak upon society; only when the threatening curse was removed, could society's health and order be restored. For this, a substitutionary victim was needed upon whom the curse might be transferred. Walter Burkert describes these rituals as a reflex of communal instincts for self-preservation.[29] From an anthropological point of view, they maintain and restore the boundaries between the 'two worlds'. They can root out the chaotic forces which intrude upon society and threaten its order and culture.

The Apotropaeic Paradigm
The act of performing an apotropaeic ritual can be divided into five steps: selection, consecration, investiture, transference and finally expulsion (sometimes followed by execution).

Selection
The purification of a menacing curse, and the reinstatement of boundaries, necessitated the use of a victim which would substitute for the community and bear this curse in its place. The range of victims selected for this purpose included animals (e.g., goats, steers, pigs) and humans (e.g., slaves, criminals, the poor). The victims sometimes offered themselves voluntarily (Petronius, *fr.* 1; Jon. 1.12), though there is also mention of 'rewards'[30] and the offering of money (Callimachus, *fr.* 90). In times of drought the provision of food would have proved a strong incentive, especially for the poorer classes.[31] Of the varieties of human beings chosen for this ritual, those who were marginalized from society

28. For bibliography see: Hughes, *Human Sacrifice*, p. 242, n. 5.
29. Burkert, *Structure and History*, pp. 70-72; Burkert, *Greek Religion*, pp. 83-84.
30. E.g., *proliciebatur praemiis* in Lactarntius Placidi on Statius, *Theb.*, X, p. 793.
31. E.g., Lactarntius Placidi on Statius, *Theb.* X, p. 793; Callimachus, I, pp. 32-33; scholiast, Aristophanes, *Eq.* 1136; Petronius, *fr.* 1.

were deemed the most suitable subjects for taking evil away from a community.[32] The goat is likewise a marginal animal, being neither fully domesticated nor fully wild.[33]

Consecration

The victim, once selected, was consecrated (set apart) as a substitute for the group by a rite of investiture. Such rites serve to mark the victim's transformation from a previously 'normal' state to a new status, that of a consecrated substitutionary victim. These victims were made to be holy, and therefore became social outsiders or outcasts. In the words of Versnel, the consecration 'entails that they become social pariahs, comparable to those persons who have transgressed the *lex sacrata*, but, in this case, without being guilty'.[34] Thus, they can truly be described as innocent transgressors.

Investiture

To mark their separation from their community, victims were sometimes fed on special foods and clothed in sacred garments or wreathed in figs.[35] There are instances of ceremonial whippings with leaves and branches of special plants to render the victim suitable to bear the evil of the society.[36] Some plants with strong smells and purgative qualities were regarded as especially suitable for expelling evil and restoring purity.

Transference

Following the investiture, the evil or curse which threatened the people was ritually transferred to the victim; the imposition constituted the removal of the curse from the group. Hence from another point of view, these rituals might be termed 'reversal rituals' in that the circumstances of the community and victim were reversed: the accursed community became saved while the victim became accursed.

32. E.g., slaves (Callimachus [*fr*. 90] 1.30; Plutarch, *M*. 693-694); criminals (Strabo, *NH* X, 2.9; cf. Lysias, *c. Andok.* 53); the poor (Petronius, *fr*. 1).

33. Cf. B.H. McLean, 'A Christian Sculpture in Old Corinth', *OCP* 57 (1991), pp. 199-205.

34. Versnel, *Transition and Reversal*, pp. 309, 311.

35. Special food: Hipponax, *fr*. 7; Tzetzes, *H*. 732; Petronius, *fr*. 1; Callimachus [*fr*. 90] 1.32-33; Lactantius Placidi on Statius, *Theb*., X, 793; holy garments: Petronius *fr*. 1; wreath of figs: Helladius in Photius, *Bibl*. 534a.

36. E.g., Hipponax *fr*. 4, 5, 8, 9; Tzetzes, *H*. 733-734; Plutarch, *M*. 693-694; Servius on Virgil, *Aen*. 7.188.

Expulsion or Execution
Once laden with this infectious and dangerous curse, the victim must be expelled from the community so as to put the curse at a distance. In some cases, this was followed by the execution of the victim. Execution assured the permanency of the transfer by preventing the victim's return to the society.

Apotropaeic Rituals versus Sacrifice
Having described the inner logic and progression of the apotropaeic ritual, it is essential to understand from the outset the fundamental distinction between this ritual and sacrificial ritual. This distinction is easily missed since the writings of later Antiquity use the term *thusia* ('sacrifice') generally of any ritual.[37]

A sacrificial victim of the Jewish or Greek Olympian type was not offered as a substitute for the community, nor did it bear their defilement, curses or sin. Rather, this sacrifice was a pure, undefiled offering, and as such, it represents human goodness and purity. It is on account of this fact that it was an appropriate gift for the deity.

Apotropaeic rituals are the reverse of this. The victim stood as a substitute for an endangered group. By the imposition of society's evil, it became desecrated and therefore unsuitable to be offered to the deity. Such victims did not represent human goodness and purity, but human defilement and cursedness. The victim, polluted by the imposition of this impurity, must either be banished or destroyed in order to prevent its return.[38] This essential distinction is recognised by Jane Harrison: 'the two ceremonies of sacrifice and riddance express widely different conditions

---

37. Cf. Gebhard, *Die Pharmakoi*, pp. 3-5, 47-48.
38. I am grateful to William Blissett for pointing this distinction out to me. Dennis Hughes acknowledges that though scholars frequently refer to Athenian *pharmakos* victims as 'human *sacrifices*', only the very latest ancient writers (twelfth century CE or later) apply the verb 'to sacrifice' (θυεῖν) to such killings (Hughes, *Human Sacrifice*, p. 11, cf. pp. 3-4). Many other scholars have drawn the distinction between human 'sacrifices' which are offered to a deity and the 'slaying' of humans without reference to any cult or deity (A. Brelich, 'Symbol of a Symbol', in J.M. Kitagawa and C.H. Long [eds.], *Myths and Symbols: Studies in Honor of Mircea Eliade* [Chicago: University of Chicago Press, 1969], pp. 195-207, esp. p. 200, n. 7; F. Schwenn, *Die Menschenopfer bei den Griechen und Römern*, RVV, 15.3, [Giessen, Töpelmann, 1915], p. 9; J. Heninger, 'Menschenopfer bei den Arabern', *Anthropos* 53 [1958], pp. 721-805, esp. pp. 797-98).

and sentiments in the mind of the worshipper'.[39] The vectors of these two paradigms extend in different directions. Sacrifice is vertically oriented; it is offered *up* to the deity. In contrast, apotropaeic rituals are oriented horizontally; victims are pushed *out* of society to the no-man's-land beyond the borders of society, and then either abandoned or executed.

In the following pages, I intend to give an account of various apotropaeic rituals including their methods, probable purposes and geographical locations. It is important that a broad sample of rituals be illustrated. Otherwise the impression might be conceived that such rituals were extraordinary or exceptional. On the contrary, I will demonstrate that the apotropaeic paradigm was geographically and chronologically pervasive, and deeply embedded in popular folklore and imagination. This analysis will also serve to map out a territory for analogical comparison with Paul's thought. By showing that the apotropaeic paradigm was a prevalent way of dealing with the problem of dangers and curses associated with the transgression of law, I will argue that Paul has employed this same paradigm in dealing with the issues of sin, curse and law in his congregations.

The scholarly research bearing on these many rituals is extensive and the range of sources complex. Exploring them sometimes involves the reconstruction and restoration of fragmentary and conflicting sources. Since scholarly conclusions are frequently provisional, the same provisional character will attend to some of my observations. I shall begin with the best known instance of an apotropaeic ritual, namely the Levitical scapegoat ritual, followed by other instances of animals used as apotropaeic victims. Next follow instances in which human beings are employed in these rituals. The chapter will conclude with examples of apotropaeic rituals in the Hebrew Bible and New Testament besides that of the Levitical scapegoat. The original texts for some of the most important (but less accessible) sources are provided at the end of this book. These texts are referred to throughout this chapter as Text 1, 2, 3 and so on.

The Levitical Scapegoat Ritual

Though no sacrifice was necessary for the atonement of *inadvertent* sin, the scapegoat ritual was necessary to purify those who had committed

---

39. Harrison, *Prolegomena*, p. 109.

deliberate sins (literally sins committed 'with a high hand' [Num. 15.30-31]). This point is illustrated by Lev. 16.15-23 which contrasts the functions of the two goats used on the Day of Atonement. The first goat was used to purify the temple. The second goat, the 'scapegoat', was used to purify the community of deliberate sins:[40]

> [15]He [Aaron] shall then slaughter the people's goat of purification-offering, bring its blood inside the curtain, and manipulate its blood as he did with the blood of the bull; he shall sprinkle it upon the *kapporet* and before the *kappôret*. [16]Thus he shall purge the adytum [Holy of Holies] of the pollution and transgressions of the Israelites…[20]And when he has finished purging the adytum, the Tent of the Meeting, and the altar, he shall bring forward the live [scape]goat. [21]Aaron shall lean both his hands upon the head of the live goat and confess over it all the iniquities and transgressions of the Israelites, including all their sins, and put them on the head of the goat; and it shall be sent off to the wilderness by a man in waiting. [22]Thus the goat shall carry upon it all of their iniquities to an inaccessible region. (Lev. 16.20-22)[41]

This text makes it clear that the goat offered as a purification-offering was used to purify the temple precincts alone. Only when the purification ritual was complete, did the atonement ritual begin with the scapegoat. Thus, the Atonement Day ritual was actually a combination of two distinct rituals for the removal of two different kinds of evil. The first goat purged the temple of 'uncleanness' (Lev. 16.16), while the second goat (scapegoat), carried away the deliberate 'transgressions' of the people (Lev. 16.21).

The scapegoat ritual embodies the belief that once sin had blighted the people, it would work itself out upon them unless a substitute could be provided upon whom it might be discharged. The Lord's people required repeated purifications in order to continue to be God's *holy* people (cf. Lev. 11.44; 19.2; 20.26). There was also the related danger of the people contaminating the temple—the very dwelling place of the Lord—after its purification, rendering it unfit for his presence (cf. Num. 5.3). On account of the contagiousness of the impurity associated with personal sin, the need was felt to perform a thorough cleansing of the entire congregation each year in conjunction with the annual purification

---

40.   That the Day of Atonement is concerned with deliberate sins is indicated by the term *ps'* (Lev. 16.16, 21). This word was borrowed by P from political terminology denoting rebellion or revolt (e.g., 2 Kgs 3.5; Ezek. 20.38). In the context of Leviticus 16, it specifies deliberate rebellion against the ordinances of God.

41.   ET: Milgrom, *Leviticus 1–16*, p. 1010.

of the temple. Hence, the scapegoat ritual was adopted into the Jerusalem cult. In all likelihood the scapegoat ritual was not instituted before the time of Ezra (c. 397 BCE) since there is no mention of this feast in any pre-exilic text.[42]

The scapegoat ritual began by the casting of lots in order to determine which goat would be set apart for the purification of the temple, and which would be employed for the ridding of personal sin.[43] The two lots were inscribed respectively '[intended] for YHWH [Yahweh]' and '[intended] for Azaz'el'. The opinion of the majority of scholars is that since the inscription on the first lot specified a proper name (Yahweh), the parallel construction of Lev. 16.8 demands that the term *Azaz'el* on the second lot should also specify a proper name.[44] Most scholars agree that Azaz'el was *originally* understood as a proper name of a desert demon.

> [7]And he [Aaron] shall take two he-goats and set them before the Lord at the entrance of the Tent of the Meeting. [8]Aaron shall place lots upon the two goats, one marked 'for YHWH' and the other 'for Azazel'. [9]Aaron shall bring forward the goat designated by lot 'for YHWH' to sacrifice it as

---

42.   Though the intention of Ezek. 45.18-20 is the same as the Day of Atonement, it was observed on a different day (on the 1st and 7th day of the first month, not the 10th day of the 7th month) and it does not mention the scapegoat ritual. The feast is also mentioned in Lev. 23.26-32, but this text is a late addition to the Law of Holiness (Oesterly, *Sacrifices*, p. 226; de Vaux, *Ancient Israel*, pp. 509-510; cf. pp. 461-64). There is wide-ranging consensus that the scapegoat ritual was borrowed from outside Judaism. For instance, W.O.E. Oesterly says that 'there can be no doubt that an extremely ancient rite has been adopted to the worship of Yahweh' (*Sacrifices*, pp. 230-31). Yehezkel Kaufmann remarks, 'Of all purifications the most pagan-like seems to be the rite of the scapegoat' (Y. Kaufmann, *The Religion of Israel: From Its Beginnings to the Babylonian Exile* [Chicago: University of Chicago Press, 1960], p. 114; cf. M. Noth, *Leviticus: A Commentary* [trans. J.E. Anderson; Philadelphia: Westminster Press, 1962–1965], p. 124; de Vaux, *Ancient Israel*, pp. 507-508).

43.   Probably sacred stones known as Urim and Thummin (cf. Deut. 33.8; Exod. 28.30; Lev. 8.3).

44.   de Vaux, *Ancient Israel*, p. 509; T. Gaster, 'Demon, Demonology', *IDB* (1962), I, pp. 817-24; Kaufmann, *Religion*, VI, pp. 506-507; H. Tawil, 'Azazel, The Prince of the Steepe [*sic*]: A Comparative Study', *ZAW* 92 (1980), pp. 43-59, esp. pp. 58-59; M. Delcor, 'Le mythe de la chute des anges', *RHR* 190 (1976), pp. 3-53, esp. pp. 35-37. Against this deduction, Godfrey Driver argues that the choice was between 'for the Lord' and 'for [the] Rugged Rocks' taken as a proper name, and that the scapegoat was driven over the rocks in order to assure its death (G. Driver, 'Three Technical Terms in the Pentateuch', *JSS* [1956], pp. 97-105, esp. p. 98).

a purification-offering; [10]while the goat designated by lot 'for Azazel' shall be stationed alive before YHWH to perform expiation upon it by sending it off into the wilderness to Azazel.[45]

Following the selection of the scapegoat by lots and the purification of the temple with the purification goat (Lev. 16.16, 20), the high priest would lay both hands upon the head of the scapegoat and, by means of a confession, transfer all the sins of Israel onto the goat (Lev. 16.21; cf. *m. Yom.* 6.2). By this act, the scapegoat was designated to serve as a 'substitute for the corporate personality of Israel'.[46]

It is important to observe that two hands were employed in the ritual hand-laying, not one. In contrast to this, a *single* hand was used for purification victims.[47] In those texts which specify the laying on of *two* hands, the gesture marks the transfer of something such as authority (Deut. 34.9) or sin (Lev. 16.21; cf. 24.14-15) from one *nephesh* ('life') to another:

> Aaron shall *lay both his hands* upon the head of the live [scape]goat, and confess over him all the iniquities of the people of Israel, and all their deliberate transgressions, all their sins; and *he shall put them upon the head of the [scape]goat* (Lev. 16.21).

Since it was not known which goat would be sacrificed to Yahweh and which would be employed for the ridding of personal sin prior to the casting of lots, both goats must have been spotless. Therefore, from a ritual perspective, both goats can be said to have had identical natures prior to the laying on of hands. However, each had a fundamentally distinct character imputed to it by the laying on of one or two hands: the purification-goat received a beneficiary character, the scapegoat a substitutionary character.

Following the transfer of sin from the community to the scapegoat, a messenger would lead the goat away from Jerusalem into the desert where it was abandoned to Azaz'el. Though the original author of Leviticus 16 probably thought of Azaz'el as a demonic being, it is unlikely that the priestly redactors would have interpreted this text so

45. ET: Milgrom, *Leviticus 1–16*, p. 1009.
46. S.H. Hooke, The Theory and Practice of Substitution', *VT* 2 (1952), pp. 2-17, esp. pp. 8-9. In the words of D.Z. Hoffmann, 'the goat is a representation of the sinner' (*The Book of Leviticus* [2 vols.; Jerusalem: Mossad Harav Kook, 1953], I, p. 305; cf. C. Lattey, 'Vicarious Solidarity in the Old Testament', *VT* 1 [1951], pp. 267-74, esp. pp. 272-74).
47. E.g., Lev. 1.4; 3.2, 8, 13; 4.4, 24, 29, 33 (cf. ch. 1).

concretely. Demons are devalued in the priestly tradition to such an extent that they have no active role whatsoever. Apart from Leviticus 16, the warning against the offering of sacrifices to demons (*se'irim*) in Lev. 17.7, is the only other text which suggests priestly belief in demons. In the latter text the term *se'irim* seems to be used in a pejorative sense to designate concrete idolatrous objects rather than demonic beings (cf. 2 Chron. 11.15).[48] Moreover, Leviticus 16 in particular is silent regarding the personality and role of Azaz'el. In the priestly mind, Azaz'el represents only the place or goal for the disposition of sins, not an active demonic personality.[49] In the words of Yehezekel Kaufmann, 'Azaz'el of Leviticus 16 is not conceived of either as being among the people or as the source of danger or harm; he plays no active role at all...He is merely a passive symbol of impurity—sin returns to its like'.[50]

Thus, the scapegoat is *not* a sacrifice offered to Azaz'el: the scapegoat, having become a carrier of sin, is no longer suitable for sacrifice.[51] As explained by Roland de Vaux: 'In the ceremony of the scapegoat (Lev. 16.21), the sins of the people are transferred to the goat...but precisely because the scapegoat is thereby loaded with the sins of the people, it is

48. D. Hillers, 'Demons, Demonology', *EncJud*, V, p. 1523. According to A. Weiser, the disparaging references to demons in texts such as Deut. 32.17 and Ps. 106.37 reveal not an active belief in demons, but merely a caricature of sins of idolatry as a means of criticising the efficacy of such sacrifices (*The Psalms. A Commentary* [OTL; trans. Herbert Hartwell; Philadelphia: Westminster Press, 1962], p. 678). Priestly prohibitions against idolatry include Lev. 17.3-9; 18.21; 19.4; 20.2-5; 26.1.

49. Gaster, 'Demon', p. 821; T.H. Gaster, 'Azazel', *IDB*, 1.326.

50. Kaufmann, *Religion*, pp. 114-15. According to David Wright, Azaz'el is 'simply a ritual 'place holder', denoting the goal of impurity' (D.P. Wright, *The Disposal of Impurity: Elimination Rites in the Bible and in Hittite and Mesopotamian Literature* [SBLDS, 101; Atlanta: Scholars Press, 1987], p. 30). The following work came to my attention after the manuscript was completed: B. Janowski and G. Wilhelm, 'Der Bock, der die Sünden hinausträgt: Zur Religionsgeschichte des Azazel-Ritus Lev 16, 10.21f.', in *Religionsgeschichtliche Beziehungen zwischen kleinasien, Nordsyrian und dem Alten Testament* (OBO, 129; Freiburg: Universtätsuerlag; Göttingen: Vandenhoeck & Ruprecht, 1993), pp. 109-69.

51. Kaufmann comments, 'It [the scapegoat] is not conceived of as an offering but as a vehicle for carrying off sin. What the community sends to Azazel is not so much the goat as the sin it bears' (Kaufmann, *Religion*, pp. 113, 114; cf. E. Kautzsch, *Biblische Theologie des Alten Testaments* [Tübingen: Mohr, 1911], pp. 344-45; E. König, *Theologie des Alten Testaments* [Stuttgart: Belser, 1923], pp. 290-91; Robinson, 'Hebrew Sacrifice', p. 131; Péter, 'L'Imposition des Mains', p. 51.

regarded as defiled, and unworthy to be sacrificed.'[52] The goat was expelled simply to exclude it from populated areas so that it would not spread its highly contagious impurity. The crucial fact is that the desert is unpopulated (cf. Jer. 17.6; Job 38.26; Jer. 22.6; 51.43). In the words of Douglas Davies, the scapegoat was sent 'from the holiness of the tabernacle into the chaos, into the symbolic nothingness which obtained [prevailed] outside the community of God's people'.[53]

The Scapegoat Ritual in the First Century CE
By the first century CE, the scapegoat ritual had become more elaborate than its counterpart in Leviticus 16. This signifies its growing import-ance in the cult. Perhaps the most noteworthy change is that the ceremony ended with the execution of the goat following its expulsion. Ten booths were constructed between Jerusalem and a steep precipice overlooking a particular ravine, seven and a half miles away. The scape-goat was sent off from Jerusalem with the prayer 'Bear [our sins] and be gone! Bear [our sins] and be gone!' (*m. Yom.* 6.4; cf. 6.2, 8). 'Certain of the eminent folk of Jerusalem' would then accompany the scapegoat to the first booth.[54] Common people (named 'Babylonians'?) would pull the hair of the goat as he was led away (*m. Yom.* 6.4). At each succes-sive booth, the goat was provided with food and water by the messenger (*m. Yom.* 6.4-5, 8). Sentinel stations were also set up so that a relay signal of flags would communicate to Jerusalem the moment when the goat had reached the precipice of the ravine (*m. Yom.* 6.8).

Once the appointed place had been reached, the messenger would tie a thread of scarlet wool around the horns of the scapegoat (*m. Yom.* 6.6; cf. *Barn.* 7.8). A second crimson thread was tied to the door of the temple sanctuary. Then 'the messenger pushed the [scape]goat from behind; and it went rolling down, and before it had reached half the way down the hill the [scape]goat had broken into pieces' (*m. Yom.* 6.6). According to tradition, 'when the he-goat reached the wilderness [and

52. de Vaux, *Ancient Israel*, p. 416.

53. Douglas Davies, 'An Interpretation of Sacrifice in Leviticus', *ZAW* 89 (1977), pp. 387-99, esp. pp. 394-95; also Milgrom, *Leviticus 1–16*, p. 1021.

54. Peter Richardson has observed on the temple mount the remains of a gate across from Robinson's gate. Beyond this gate is a virtual precipice overlooking the Kidron valley. As such, it would have been very difficult to construct a staircase and was probably not be used for large groups of people. He suggests that this gate and pathway may have been used by the messenger who led the scapegoat into the wilderness.

had been pushed down the cliff] the thread [tied to the sanctuary door] turned white; for it is written, "Though your sins be as scarlet, they shall be as white as snow (Isa 1.18)"' (*m. Yom.* 6.8). The Targum Pseudo-Jonathan theologises the death of the scapegoat by making it a supernatural event: 'And the goat will go up on the mountains of Beth-hadurey, and a tempest wind from the presence of the Lord will carry him away, and he will die'.[55]

The custom of killing the scapegoat may have arisen because the scapegoat did, on occasion, find its way back to Jerusalem, perhaps in search of food and water. Such an event would be considered dangerous, threatening to undo all that the Day of Atonement had accomplished. This scenario could be prevented by assuring killing the goat after its expulsion.

In view of the many changes in the observance of the scapegoat ritual, it is noteworthy that the Levitical understanding of the distinct functions of the purification-goat and scapegoat are preserved in the Mishnah:

> For uncleanness that befalls the temple and its Hallowed Things through wantonness, purification is made by the [purification] goat whose blood is sprinkled within [the Holy of Holies] and by the Day of Atonement; for all other transgressions spoken of in the Torah, minor or grave, wanton or unwitting, conscious or unconscious, sins of omission or of commission, sins punishable by extirpation or by death at the hands of the court, the scapegoat makes atonement for (*m. Šeb.* 1.6; cf. *m. Yom.* 4.2).[56]

Philo of Alexandria described the sins borne by the people as curses which were transferred to the scapegoat on the Day of Atonement:

---

55. J. W. Etheridge (trans.), *The Targums of Onkelos and Jonathan ben Uzziel on the Pentateuch with Fragments of the Jerusalem Targum* (New York: Ktav, 1968), p. 198; Lev. 16.21-22.

56. The recognition of the distinctive roles of the two goats is also found in the *Sifra* (181.2.9):

9.A. 'The [scape]goat shall bear all their iniquities upon him.'

B. 'Upon him' he bears sins, and the other [*hatta't*] goats are not with him.

C. Then for what does the other [i.e. the *hatta't*] goat-offering atone?

D. For imparting uncleaness to the sanctuary and its holy things.

E. And what is that uncleaness to the sanctuary on its holy things that the other [i.e. the *hatta't*] goat-offering atones for?

F. Those acts of deliberate contamination of the sanctuary and the holy things—lo, they are purified by the [*hatta't*] goat that is offered inside (J. Neusner, *Sifra: An Analytical Translation* [3 vols.; Brown Judaic Studies; Atlanta: Scholars Press, 1988]), pp. 138-140.

The one on whom the lot fell [i.e. the purification goat] was sacrificed to God, the other was sent out into a trackless and desolate wilderness *bearing on its back the curses which had been laid upon the transgressors* (*Spec. Leg.* 1.188 [Text 1]).

In this passage, Philo equates the 'crooked deeds', 'rebellions' and 'sins' of Lev. 16.21 with 'curses'. This is consistent with Jewish biblical theology in which the immediate consequence of transgression is often said to be a curse (e.g., Deut. 27.15-26). For an illustration of this belief in Judaism, consider Zech. 5.1-4 where God's curse is described as flying through the air in the form of a scroll, alighting upon all who transgress the divine law:

Again I lifted my eyes and saw, and behold, a flying scroll! And the Lord said to me, 'What do you see?' I answered, 'A flying scroll'…Then he said to me, 'This is the curse that goes out over the face of the whole land; for everyone who steals shall be cut off henceforth according to it. I will send it forth says the Lord of hosts, and it shall enter the house of the thief, and the house of him who swears falsely by my name; and it shall abide in his house and consume it, both timber and stones'.

This passage illustrates how a curse, like sin, was perceived as being communicable. Gen. 27.12-13 also provides a clue as to how the transfer of this curse was understood: Rebeccah offers herself to bear the curse which properly belongs to Jacob. In so doing, she saved Jacob by exhausting the strength of the curse in her own person. When Jacob says 'Perhaps my father will feel me, and I shall seem to be mocking him, and bring a curse upon myself and not a blessing' Rebeccah replies, '*Upon me be your curse, my son*; only obey my word, and go, fetch two kids to me'.

The portrayal of the scapegoat as a curse-bearer is not unique to Philo. In both the Epistle of Barnabas and Tertullian the corporate sin of the people is described as a curse, the force of which was dissipated by its transfer to the scapegoat. In the case of the Epistle of Barnabas, the author is quoting an unidentified source regarding the cursedness of the scapegoat and compares this goat with Christ:

[6]How then does he state the commandment? Pay attention: 'Take two goats, unblemished and alike, and offer them, and let the priest take the one for a whole-offering for sins'. [7]But what are they to do with the other? 'The other [i.e. the scapegoat]', he [an unidentified source] says, 'is accursed (ἐπικατάρατος)'. Observe how the type of Jesus is manifested. [8]'And you shall all spit on the scapegoat and prick it, and bind the scarlet wool around its head, and so let it be cast out into the desert.' And when

this has been done, he who takes the goat into the desert drives it out, and takes the wool and places it upon a shrub which is called *rache*...[9] What does this mean? Listen: 'the first [purification] goat is for the altar, but the other [the scapegoat] is accursed (ἐπικατάρατος)', and note that the one that is accursed (ἐπικατάρατος) is crowned, because then 'he will see him on that day wearing the long scarlet robe down to the feet, on his body, and they shall say, "Is not this he whom we once crucified and ridiculed and spat upon? Truly this was he, who then said he was the Son of God".[10] For how is he like the goat? For this reason: the goats shall be "alike", "beautiful", and a pair, in order than when they see him come at that time they may be astounded at the likeness of the goat. See then the type of Jesus destined to suffer' (*Barn.* 7.6-10 [Text 2]).

While it is difficult to date precisely the scapegoat tradition in *Barnabas* 7, the reliability of this source is evinced by the fact that it includes three points of information which are corroborated in the Mishnah but are absent in Leviticus 16, namely the mistreatment of the goat (*m. Yom.* 6.4), the scarlet thread around the scapegoat's horns (*m. Yom.* 6.6), and the emphasis on the equality of the two goats (*m. Yom.* 6.1).[57] Tertullian likewise refers to the scapegoat as 'cursed' and interprets both the scapegoat and the purification goat as types of Christ:

If also I am to submit an interpretation of the two goats which were offered at the Fast [on the Day of Atonement], are not these also figures of Christ's two activities? They are indeed of the same age and appearance because the Lord's is one and the same aspect: because he will return in no other form, seeing he has to be recognised by those of whom he has suffered injury. One of them [i.e., of the two goats] however, surrounded with scarlet, *cursed* and spit upon and pulled about and pierced, was by the people driven out of the city into perdition, marked with manifest tokens of our Lord's passion' (*Adv. Marc.* 7.7 [Text 3]).

Other Apotropaeic Rituals with Animals as Victims

The use of animals in apotropaeic rituals in not unique to the Day of Atonement ritual. Examples can be multiplied from various periods and localities including Egypt, Asia Minor, Assyria and the Decapolis.[58]

57.　*Barnabas* also passes on the Mishnaic tradition that the purification ('inside') goat was eaten by the priests (*m. Men.* 11.7).

58.　According to Robert Rogers, a similar ritual to that of the scapegoat is found in Assyria where sheep were slain for the purification of the temple and then the body cast into the river (R. Rogers, *Cuneiform Parallels to the Old Testament* [New York: Easton & Mains, 1912], p. 196).

The central myth for the interpretation of the Egyptian apotropaeic ritual is the story of the conflict of Isis and Horus with Set ('Typhon' in Greek religion).[59] According to Egyptian religion, all that is good comes from Osiris and his son Horus. On the other hand, Set, the enemy of Osiris and Horus, is responsible for all the evil in the world such as infertility, impurity, the arid desert, storms, earthquakes and floods.[60]

In the Egyptian cult, victims were identified with Set so that the slaying of a victim signified the destruction of Set,[61] and the head of a victim was regarded as the head of Set or as a trophy of victory over Set.[62] Hence ritual had an important role in combating Set and the

---

59. According to this myth, the god Set killed the god Osiris, husband to Isis, by locking him in a chest and throwing it in the Nile river. Isis having recovered the body, managed partially to revive Osiris. But when Set discovered this, he hacked the body to pieces and scattered it far and wide. Isis retrieved the pieces and restored Osiris to life. From that time onward, Osiris dwelt in the underworld as the judge of the dead. Horus, the sun god and son of Isis and Osiris, avenged his father and reclaimed his father's power from Set. The Egyptian king was considered to occupy the place of Horus, and the succession of a new king was celebrated as the replacement of Osiris by Horus.

60. E.A. Wallis Budge, *From Fetish to God in Ancient Egypt* (Oxford: Oxford University Press, 1949), p. 140; S. Mercer, *The Religion of Ancient Egypt* (London: Luzac, 1949), p. 51. By the twenty-second dynasty, Set had become a kind of devil and the enemy of all gods. In an earlier period, Set was regarded as one of the greater gods, especially in Upper Egypt. The *Pyramid Text* (204) calls him 'the Lord of the South'. He enjoyed his greatest popularity during the period of the Hyksos pharaohs of the 19th dynasty. Gradually from the 22–26 dynasties his reputation declined, becoming known as the cruel murderer of Osiris and the incarnation of evil (S. Mercer, *Religion*, pp. 59-61).

61. H. Bonnet, *Reallexikon der ägyptischen Religionsgeschichte* (Berlin: De Gruyter, 1952), pp. 124-27, 549-51; H. Junker, 'Die Schlacht- und Brandopfer und ihre Sybolik im Tempelkult der Spätzeit', *ZAS* 48 (1910), pp. 69-77; E. Otto, *Beiträge zur Geschichte der Stierkulte in Aegypten* (Hildesheim: G. Olms, 1964), pp. 5-7; H.W. Helck and O. Ebehard, *Kleines Wörterbuch der Aegyptologie* (Wiesbaden: O. Harrassowitz, 1956), p. 255; H. Kees, *Bemerkungen zum Tieropfer der Ägypter und seiner Symbolik* (Nachrichten der Akademie der Wissenschatten; Göttingen: Vandenhoeck & Ruprecht, 1942), pp. 71-73; M. Alliot, *Le Culte d'Horus á Edfou au temps des Ptolemees* (Cairo: Impr. de l'Institut français d'Archeologie orientale, 1946), II, pp. 524-27; K.H. Sethe, *Übersetzung und Kommentar zu den Pyramidentexten* (6 vols.; Glückstadt: J.J. Augustin, 1935–1962), 1543-1549.

62. K.H. Sethe, *Dramatische Texte in altaegyptischen Mysterienspielen* (Hildesheim: G. Olms, 1964), pp. 153-55; K.H. Sethe, *Urkunden der 18. Dynastie* (Urkunden des ägyptischen Altertums, 6; Leipzig: J.C. Hinrichs, 1935), pp. 14-15.

hostile forces associated with him. Herodotus has recorded the observance of a ritual involving the head of a steer which depicts this struggle
against the forces of Set:

> ...having slaughtered [the steer], they cut off its head. They next skin
> the animal's body, and *having pronounced many curses* (πολλὰ
> καταρησάμενοι) upon its head, those who have a market-square, and
> among whom many Greek merchants reside, carry it to that market, and
> accordingly dispose of it:[63] those that have no Greeks resident among
> them cast the head into the river.[64] The curses (καταρέονται) they pro-
> nounce on the heads are in these words: 'Whatever evil is about to fall on
> the slayer himself, or on the whole of Egypt, may it be diverted upon this
> head.'[65] These practices, the curses upon the heads, and the libations of
> wine, prevail all over Egypt, and extend to victims of all sorts; and in con-
> sequence of this custom, no Egyptian will ever taste of the head of any
> animal. (Herodotus, *Hist.*, II, 39.1-4 [Text 4])

The references in Herodotus to the calling down of curses (κατα-
ρησάμενοι/καταρῶνται) pertain to the *oral* rite which would have
accompanied the manual liturgical act of presenting the steer head.[66] In

Hence the ritual of the Osiris temple at Abydos contains a curse against the enemies
of Osiris while animals are sacrificed who are regarded as extensions of Set himself
(Sethe, *Urkunden*, pp. 48-51). This explains why the representations of decapitated
steer heads as offerings are legion in Egyptian art. For example, see the illustrations
in: N. de Garis Davies, *Archeological Survey of Egypt*. XXI. *Five Theban Tombs* (ed.
F.L. Griffith; London: Egyptian Exploration Fund, 1913), pl. 7-8 (Tomb of
Mentuherkhepeshef); cf. E.H. Naville, *The Temple of Deir el Bahari* (6 vols.;
London: Egyptian Exploration Fund, 1895–1908), IV, pl. 109-110; VI, pl. 155;
A.B. Kamal, *Stèles: Ptolemaiques et Romaines* (2 vols.; Cairo: Impr. de l'Institut
français d'Archeologie orientale, 1905), pl. 56.

63.   Cf. Deut. 14.21.

64.   Though the actual words are 'thrown into the river', there is convincing
evidence that the statement implies crocodile feeding (G. Wilkinson, *The Manners
and Customs of the Ancient Egyptians Including Their Private Life, Government,
Laws, Arts, Manufactures, Religion, Agriculture, and Early History* [5 vols.;
London: John Murray, 3rd edn, 1847], II, p. 379; cf. n. 68 below).

65.   εἴ τι μέλλοι ἢ σφίσι τοῖσι θύουσι ἢ Αἰγύπτῳ τῇ συναπάσῃ κακὸν
γενέσθαι, ἐς κεφαλὴν ταύτην τραπέσθαι. Adolf Erman thinks that this custom of
cursing the head was borrowed from another culture (A. Erman, *A Handbook of
Egyptian Religion* [trans. A.S. Griffith; London: A. Constable, 1907–1934], pp. 179-
80) but Alan Lloyd disagrees (A. Lloyd, *Herodotus: Book 2* [2 vols.; Leiden: Brill,
1976], II, p. 178. ET = J.E. Powell (trans.), *Herodotus: History* [2 vols.; Oxford:
Clarendon Press, 1947], II, p. 39).

66.   Lloyd, *Herodotus*, II, p. 177.

other words, the steer head was cursed when it was offered as a representation of Set. The explicit intention of this cursing was to transfer the evil experienced by 'the slayer or the whole of Egypt' to this substitutionary steer head. This evil was then permanently removed by selling the head to foreign merchants or by feeding it to the crocodiles.

The worship of Isis and Horus, of all the Egyptian gods, was the most popular amongst the Greeks and Romans. The mention of 'Greek merchants' (ἔμποροι) in Herodotus places this ritual within the Hellenistic period. The fact that Hellenistic Greeks were familiar with this ritual is confirmed by other classical sources including Plutarch:

> The Egyptians, because of their belief that Typhon (Set) was of a red complexion,[67] also dedicate to sacrifice such of their cattle as are of red colour...*For this reason, they invoke curses on the head of the victim* [διὸ τῇ μὲν κεφαλῇ τοῦ ἱερείου καταρασάμενοι] and cut it off, and in earlier times they used to throw it into the river, but now they sell it to the aliens (*M.* 363b).[68]

The chief components of this ritual are the selection of a substitutionary victim (a steer head), the imposition of a curse upon the head, and finally the act of expulsion of the head from society in order to remove the evils associated with Set. Scholars have long recognized the intrinsic similarity between this apotropaeic ritual and that of the Levitical scapegoat. Alan Lloyd describes this ritual as 'a striking parallel to the Hebrew concept of the scapegoat (cf. Lev. 16.6, 21)'.[69] As in the case of

67. The Egyptians associated the colour red with evil, and so all red things were hated. Hence Set (Typhon) was also thought to be red in complexion with red eyes: 'The Egyptians, in fact, have a tradition...that Typhon was red in complexion' (Plutarch, *M.* 359e). 'The name Typhon the wise priests give to all that is dry, fiery, and arid, in general, and antagonistic to moisture. Therefore, because they believe that Typhon was personally of a reddish sallow colour, they are not eager to meet men of such complexion, nor do they associate with them' (F.C. Babbitt [trans.], *Plutarch's Moralia* [LCL; 16 vols.; London: Wm. Heinemann, 1969], §346a).

68. Babbitt, *Plutarch's Moralia*, 363b (my emphasis). This same ritual is described by Aelian (c. 170–232 CE): 'The people [of Egypt] bring crocodiles the heads of animals which they sacrifice—they themselves will never touch that part— and throw them in, and the crocodiles come leaping round them' (A.F. Scholfield, *Aelian: On the Characteristics of Animals* [LCL; 3 vols.; London: Wm. Heinemann, 1971], X, p. 21).

69. Lloyd, *Herodotus*, II, p. 178. Gardiner Wilkinson and Joseph Lightfoot also comment on the close similarity between this rite and that of the scapegoat (Wilkinson, *Manners and Customs*, II, p. 378; Lightfoot, *Galatians*, p. 139).

the scapegoat, it is not the death of the animal which is of importance, but the transference of the curse, followed by permanent expulsion.

A similar apotropaeic ritual is attested amongst the Hittites of central Anatolia in the Bronze Age. Three texts have survived from Hittite culture attesting apotropaeic rites for the removal of an epidemic.[70] In the ritual of Ashella against an epidemic in the army, each military commander was instructed to select for himself a ram, while a woman was chosen to represent the king (CTH 394). Around the neck of each ram was tied a strand of coloured wool, a necklace, a ring and a precious stone; the woman was finely dressed. The next day, the rams and the woman were driven away on the frontier leading to the enemy. This expulsion was accompanied by the following curse:

> Whatever illness there was among men, oxen, sheep, horses, mules and donkeys in this camp, these rams and this woman have carried it away from the camp. And the country that finds them shall take over this evil pestilence.[71]

Here again is repeated the ritual pattern of investiture, transferring a polluting evil to substitutionary victims, followed by expulsion which simultaneously accomplished the expulsion of the evil.

Apotropaeic Rituals with Humans as Victims

In Athens, the apotropaeic victim was called a 'pharmakos' (φαρμακός [φάρμακος]). In other contexts this term can mean 'magic man', while the word φάρμακον means 'drug' or 'medicine'. Hence, the term φαρμακός has associations with disease and medical cures, and probably

---

70.   CTH 394 (=KUB IX 32); CTH 407 (=KBo XV 1); CTH 410 (=KUB IX 31 II 43–III 13). The fragments are numbered according to CTH (= Emmanuel Laroche, *Catalogue des Textes Hittites* [Etudes et Commentaires, 75; Paris: Edition Klinksiek, 1971]) while the numbering of KUB (= *Keilschrifturkunden aus Boghazhoi* [Berlin: Akademie-Verlag, 1921–1944]) and KBo (= *Keilschrifttexte aus Bogahazkäi* [Berlin: Gebr. Mann Verlag, 1916–1987]) is supplied in brackets (cf. O.R. Gurney, *Some Aspects of Hittite Religion* [Oxford: Oxford University Press, 1977], pp. 47-52, esp. 49). The similarity of this rite to the *pharmakos* ritual is pointed out by both Walter Burkert (*Greek Religion*, pp. 60-61) and Bremmer ('Scapegoat Rituals', pp. 305-306).

71.   Original translation: J. Friedrich, *Aus dem hethitischen Schrifttum* (Der Alte Orient, 24; 2 vols.; Leipzig: J.C. Hinrichs, 1925), II, pp. 11-13 (ET = Gurney, *Hittite Religion*, p. 49).

has the meaning 'one who heals the people'.[72] Lewis Farnell describes the Athenian *pharmakos* as an 'abject sin-carrier'.[73]

When Athens was ravaged by a plague, the citizens were accustomed to expel two such *pharmakoi* (pl.). This ritual is recorded in the writings of Helladios (third century CE) as preserved in Photius:

> It was the custom at Athens to lead in procession two pharmakoi with a view to purification (καθαρμός); one for the men, one for the women. The pharmakos for the men had black figs round his neck, the other had white ones, and he [Helladios] says they were called *Subachoi*. This purification was of the nature of an apotropaeic ceremony to avert pestilential diseases, and it took its rise from Androglos the Cretan, when at Athens the Athenians suffered abnormally from a pestilential disease, the custom was observed of constantly purifying the city by pharmakoi (Text 5).[74]

A scholiast on Aristophanes (*Eq.* 1136) testifies that certain people were kept for this ritual at public expense. Though the scholiast is certainly in error concerning the meaning of the term *demosioi*,[75] he does provide

72. In Aristophanes the term is also used as one of abuse and contempt (e.g. *Ran.* 532, 734; *Eq.* 1405). It is unclear whether Aristophanes himself employs '*pharmakos*' as a term of abuse with this ritual meaning in mind. Jane Harrison, W.B. Stanford and Robert Neil think he is alluding to the ritual (Harrison, *Prolegomena*, p. 97; W.B. Stanford, *Aristophanes: The Frogs* [London: Macmillan, 1958], p. 135; R. Neil, *The Knights of Aristophanes* [Hildesheim: Georg Olms, 1966], p. 152, n. 1135; p. 183, nn. 1404-1405), but Lewis Farnell disagrees (*Cults*, IV, p. 271).

73. Farnell, *Cults*, p. 280. He describes the inner logic of the ritual as follows:

> More primitive and more akin to animistic demonology than to religion is the idea that one's sins, like one's diseases, might be taken from one's own person and, by certain ritual, planted in some other living being, animal or man, and if this creature by magical or higher ritual could be charged with all the sins of the community and could be safely put away, here was a literal and almost mechanical expulsion of sin, and there is hardly any need for a high god in the matter (p. 280).

74. Helladios in Photius *Bibl.* 534a.

75. Here the scholiast is commenting on the lemma ὥσπερ δημοσίους in Aristophanes' *Eq.* 1135-1140. The scholiast presents three possible explanations of the meaning of this term. Either they were cows or bulls or 'some other sacrificial victim', or 'those called pharmakoi who cleanse the cities with their own blood', or 'those fed at public expense'. Lewis Farnell is probably correct in concluding that Aristophanes uses the term δημόσιοι to mean animal victims that were fattened at public expense rather than *pharmakos* victims (*Cults*, p. 271, n. *a*; following: A. Mommsen, *Feste der Stadt Athen im Altertum, geordnet nach attischen Kalender* [Leipzig: B.G. Teubner, 2nd edn, 1898], p. 475, n. 3); cf. Hughes, *Human Sacrifice*, p. 150.

additional information concerning the *pharmakos* ritual itself:[76]

> The *demosioi* (δημοσίοι) are those who were called pharmakoi and these
> pharmakoi purified cities by their slaughter...for the Athenians maintained
> certain very ignoble and useless persons, and on the occasion of any
> calamity befalling the city, I mean a pestilence or anything of that sort, they
> slay these persons with a view to purification from pollution and they
> called them purifications (καθάρματα) (Text 6).[77]

Lysias alludes to the *pharmakos* ritual when he expresses the desire that
his enemy, Andokides, might share the same fate as a *pharmakos* victim.
Andokides, having been cursed by the high priests and debarred from
the city, later returned and committed sacrilegious acts in the temple precincts. According to Lysias, by expelling this '*pharmakos*', the citizens
were 'cleansing the city' and 'solemnly purifying it from pollution':[78]

> You should, therefore, consider that today, in punishing Andokides and in
> ridding yourselves of him, you are cleansing the city, you are solemnly
> purifying it from pollution, you solemnly expel (ἀποπέμπειν)[79] a
> pharmakos, you are getting rid of a criminal; for this man is all of them in
> one (*c. Andok.* 53) (Text 7).

The Athenians were also accustomed to expel annually two *pharmakoi*
during the spring pre-harvest festival of Thargelia. The Thargelia, held in
the latter part of May or the beginning of June, was both an agricultural
feast dedicated to Apollo and an occasion for the national renewal of the
people. As an agricultural festival, it was the occasion when the still
ripening barley and other first fruits of harvest were offered to Apollo.

76. All scholia on Aristophanes are indebted to Didymus (80–10 BCE), who
himself was dependent on earlier (now lost) scholia. Hughes argues against the use of
this tradition (*Human Sacrifice*, p. 150).

77. Scholiast on Aristophanes *Eq.* 1136; cf. *Ran.* p. 734: 'Any chance man that
we come across, not fit in the old days for a pharmakos, these we use and these we
choose [to become state officials], the veriest scum, the mere refuse'; *Eq.* 1404-5: 'I
bid you take the seat in the Prytaneum where this pharmakos was wont to sit';
Aristophanes *fr.* 532: 'Your kinsman! How and whence, you pharmakos.'

78. Lysias, *c. Andok.* 53 (Text 7). Though perhaps not written by Lysias, it was
at least written by a contemporary (cf. Hughes, *Human Sacrifice*, p. 151).

79. Lysias describes the explusion of the *pharmakoi* using the verb ἀποπέμπειν.
The LXX translation of Lev. 16.8, 10 uses the substantive form of this verb,
ἀποπομπαῖος ('for dismissal'), in its mistranslation of the Hebrew proper name
Azaz'el to specify the goat 'for expulsion'. Philo of Alexandria uses the same word
to describe the scapegoat, both in his own writing (e.g. *Rer. Div. Her.*, p. 179; *Leg.
All.* 2.52) and in quoting of the LXX (*Leg. All.* 2.52; *Plant.*, p. 61).

On the first day, a ram was sacrificed to Demeter Chloe, followed by the expulsion of two *pharmakoi*. On the second day, Apollo was offered a pot filled with different kinds of seeds. There were also choral competitions, and the *eiresiônê* (a branch of olive or laurel wound round with wool and hung with fruits) was dedicated to Apollo and borne by singing boys from door to door.[80]

The ritual is attested in Diogenes Laertius (fl. 200–250 CE): 'Socrates was born on the sixth day of Thargelion, the day when Athenians purify the city' (Diogenes Laertius 2.44 [Text 8]). The significance of the expulsion of two *pharmakoi* on the 6th of Thargelion has been a matter of some debate. Wilhelm Mannhardt thought the *pharmakoi* represented the vegetation spirit, who being freed from harmful influences by whipping, was imbued with procreative powers for the coming a agricultural year.[81] Similarly, James Frazer argued that they originally embodied the 'god of vegetation' who was slain and born anew with reinvigorated powers, though Frazer recognizes that they developed over time into 'public scapegoats'.[82] Deubner, on the other hand, denied this association with fertility rites and stressed their purificatory function.[83]

Why were the *pharmakoi* expelled during the Thargelia festival? The sixth and seventh days of the month of Thargelion were perhaps the two most celebrated days in the Athenian calendar: Socrates and Alexander were born on the sixth, Apollo and Plato on the seventh. Moreover, the greatest victories of the Persian war were commemorated on the sixth of Thargelion (Artemisium, Plataea, Mycale), and also the death of Alexander the Great. The fact that the *pharmakos* ritual overlapped with the celebrations of the sixth and seventh of Thargelion suggests that the ritual had more to do with national renewal than agricultural prosperity. According to Robert Parker, a concentration on the harvest dimension of the Thargelia 'obscures the more general sense in which the Thargelia

---

80. L. Deubner, *Attische Feste* (Berlin: Akademie Verlag, 1932), pp. 179-98; Parker, *Miasma*, pp. 146-47; Bremmer, 'Scapegoat Rituals', pp. 318-20.

81. W. Mannhardt, *Mythologische Forschungen* (Quellen und Forschungen zur Sprach- und Culturgeschichte der germanischen Volker, 51; Strassburg: Karl J. Trübner, 1884), pp. 129-38.

82. Frazer, *Golden Bough*. VI. *The Scapegoat*, pp. 252-74.

83. Deubner, *Attische Feste*, pp. 193-98. Walter Burkert interprets the ritual from a sociological point of view, as a ritual of self-preservation in times of severe crises which provided an outlet of aggression against one member of the community (*Structure and History*, pp. 70-72; Burkert, *Greek Religion*, pp. 83-84).

was for Athenians a festival of purification and renewal'.[84] In any case, it is probable that the use of the ritual in the context of the Thargelia was a secondary development since the earliest sources for this ritual describe its purpose as 'to cleanse the city'.[85] In all likelihood, the Athenians adopted this annual cleansing of the polis during the Thargelia in order to rid the city of defilements which had the potential to threaten the harvest with drought, famine or pestilence.

The early sources agree that the *pharmakoi* were expelled (Helladios, Lysius), not slaughtered as some late sources attest (e.g., scholiast on Aristophanes *Eq.*).[86] This expulsion was a vital step in assuring the removal of the defilement. As Jane Ellen Harrison observes, 'the gist of the [*pharmakos*] ceremony is magical riddance; it is essential that the "scapegoat", whatever form he takes, should never return'.[87]

A ritual very similar to the Athenian *pharmakos* expulsion was performed in the Ionian colonies such as Ephesos and Colophon. The earliest source of information is the poet Hipponax, a native of Ephesos who was later expelled to nearby Claxomenae. Only a few fragments of Hipponax have been preserved concerning this ritual, chiefly in *The Thousand Histories (= Chiliades)* of Byzantine grammarian John Tzetzes.[88]

84.   Parker, *Miasma*, p. 25. Similarly, Versnel remarks, 'the expulsion of the pharmakos has often been explained as a fertility-ritual. Rather it is the articulation of the caesura in the (agricultural) year when good comes in and bad things are driven away' (Versnel, *Transition and Reversal*, p. 300, n. 37). However, it does not necessarily follow that the pharmakos ritual had no bearing on the agricultural festival whatsoever (cf. M. Nilsson, *Griechische Feste von religiöser Bedeutung mit Ausschluss derattischen* [Darmstadt: Wissenschaftliche Buchgesellschaft, 1906], pp. 113-15; Deubner, *Attische Feste*, pp. 192-93).

85.   Hughes, *Human Sacrifice*, p. 140, cf. n. 47.

86.   Hughes, *Human Sacrifice*, pp. 141-55.

87.   Harrison, *Prolegomena*, p. 104.

88.   There are seven fragments of Hipponax which are relevant to this study. These fragments have been numbered above according to Theodor Bergk (*Poetae Lyrici Graec* [Leipzig: B G. Teubner, 4th edn, 1882]) while equivalent numbering of A.D. Knox is indicated in square brackets (*fr.* 4 [= 47], 5 [= 48], 6 [= 49], 7 [= 50], 8 [= 51], 9 [= 52], 11 [= 53]) (Knox, 'Fragments of Hipponax', in *Herodes, Cercidas and the Greek Choliambic Poets* [LCL; London: Wm. Heinemann, 1929], pp. 15-65). Most recently, the text has been published by: P.A.M. Leone (ed. and trans.), *Tzetzes: Historiae* (Naples: Libreria Scientifica Editrice, 1968), V, p. 37); H. Degani, *Hipponactis testimonia et fragmenta* (Bibliotheca scriptorum Graecorum et Romanorum Teubneriana; Leipzig: B.G. Teubner, 1983 [with exhaustive apparatus]);

In his poem, Hipponax does not set out to describe the *pharmakos* ritual in particular, but to insult his enemy Boupalos and threaten him with the same fate as a *pharmakos*. In this context, the fragment calling for Boupalos to be cursed should likewise be taken as a reference to the *pharmakos* ritual. Hipponax states that the purpose of the ritual was 'to purify the city' (πόλιν καθαίρειν, *fr.* 4). The *pharmakos* was given a meal of figs, cakes and cheese (*fr.* 7), and flagellated (apparently on the penis [θυμῷ], *fr.* 5, 9). After the *pharmakos* was flagellated, he was then expelled while curses were imprecated upon him (*fr.* 11):[89]

> [4] to purify the city and be struck with fig branches
> [5] striking him [?] in winter and thrashing him [?] with fig branches and squills like a pharmakos[90]
> [6] and it is necessary to make him into [?] a pharmakos
> [7] and in the hand to furnish dried figs and cake and cheese, such as pharmakoi feed
> [8] for they have long awaited them gaping, holding fig branches in their hands, as they hold for pharmakoi
> [9] (that?) he be dried out with hunger; and on his member (penis?),[91] led a pharmakos, may be seven times be thrashed.
> [11] they uttered curses against that abomination Boupalos (Text 9).

Besides handing down some fragments of Hipponax, Tzetzes supplies his own account of the ritual. According to Tzetzes, the victim was 'an expiation (κάθαρμα) and *pharmakos* (φαρμακός) of the diseased city' (*H.* 730). Tzetzes describes the *pharmakos* ritual in the following way:

> [726] The *pharmakos*, the *katharma* in old times was as follows: [727] Did misfortune, by the wrath of heaven, overtake a city, [728] whether famine or plague or other mischief, [729] they led out as to sacrifice the ugliest of all the citizens [730] to be an expiation and pharmakos (εἰς καθαρμόν καὶ φαρμακὸν) of the diseased city. [731] And having set the sacrifice at such a spot as seemed fit [732] they placed in his hand cheese and barley-cake and

M.L. West, *Iambi et Elegi Graeci* (2 vols.; Oxford: Clarendon Press, 1971), I, pp. 109-71.

89. The translation is that of Dennis Hughes (*Human Sacrifice*, p. 141) who relies on the texts of West (*Iambi et Elegi Graeci*) and Degani (*Hipponactis*).

90. Cf. Hesychius, *Lexicon* 915, κραδίης νόμος: 'The song of the branches is a measure that they play on the flute when the pharmakoi are expelled, they being beaten with branches and fig sprigs' (Text 12).

91. Cf. Degani, *Hipponactis*, on his *fr.* 30; Bremmer thinks that this is not a detail of the actual ritual but stems from the 'malicious imagination' of Hipponax ('Scapegoat Rituals', p. 300, n. 8).

dried figs. [733]For after beating him seven times on the penis [734]with leeks and [rods of] wild fig and other wild trees [735]they finally burnt him on a fire of timber of such trees...Hipponax describes the custom best...(Tzetzes *H.* 726 [Text 10])

It is immediately apparent that Tzetzes includes material unattested in the fragments of Hipponax. According to Tzetzes:

the *pharmakos* was chosen from among the ugliest of citizens

he was finally burnt on a pyre

his ashes were scattered on the sea

that the ritual was observed when the city was beset with famine, plague or other calamity

In these instances it is not clear whether Tzetzes is describing the ritual of the Ionian colonies, or recalling information about the *pharmakos* ritual practised in another location.[92] Denis Hughes argues that Tzetzes is incorrect in his assertion that the *pharmakoi* were killed. He thinks that Tzetzes derived this idea, not from Hipponax, but from late sources describing the Athenian *pharmakos* ritual.[93]

Given the general purpose of this study, a judgment on this particular problem is not necessary. It will suffice to relate Tzetzes' own remarks on the understanding that any information which is uncollaborated by other witnesses must be used with the utmost caution. In this regard, it should be noted that Tzetzes' statement that the *pharmakoi* were 'sacrificed' (v. 731) is unexpected and unconventional in this context. No literary source prior to him used the term 'to sacrifice' (θυεῖν) or indeed any other sacrificial term to describe the death of the *pharmakoi*.[94]

92. Jane Harrison thinks that his description may be a paraphrase of fragments of Hipponax which he does not quote:

> the words of Hipponax correspond so closely in every detail with his own that we are justified in supposing that his account of the end of the ceremonial, the burning and scattering of the ashes, is also borrowed; but the evidence of this from Hipponax he omits (Harrison, *Prolegomena*, p. 99).

Taking the opposite view, Lewis Farnell argues that Tzetzes is offering a second witness, independent from Hipponax, and is speaking about the expulsion at Athens rather than Ionia. He says of Tzetzes' writing that it 'is anthropologically far too good to be a mere fiction; it must be drawn from some early and detailed account of the festival, other than that given by Istros' (*Cults*, pp. 271-72, n. *a*).

93. Hughes, *Human Sacrifice*, pp. 142-49. Hughes also argues the Ionian *pharmakos* ritual was performed at the Thargelia, not in times of famine and plague (*Human Sacrifice*, pp. 139-65, esp. 140-43).

94. Hughes, *Human Sacrifice*, p. 145. θυεῖν and θυσία are first used by Tzetzes

Tzetzes, typical of Byzantine authors, does not use sacrificial terminology with the specificity of earlier writers.

Both Hipponax and Tzetzes emphasize the whipping of the *pharmakos*. This flagellation was a sort of medical treatment intended to render the victim suitable to bear the impurity of the society. Plants with strong smells such as leeks, and plants regarded as purgative (e.g., fig branches) were deemed to be suitable medicine to purify the city.[95] As Harrison explains, 'You beat a bush, a bird escapes; you beat a garment, the dust comes out; you beat a man, the evil, whatever it be, will surely emerge. We associate beating with moral stimulus, but the first notion is clearly expulsive'.[96]

Speculation has arisen that this practice may be grounded in the belief that the *pharmakos* represented a god who was beaten in order to expel evil influences and improve his ability to care for his people.[97] For instance, Pan is beaten with leeks by worshippers when he did not produce sufficient game during a hunting party.[98] However, Walter Burkert

---

(*H.* 5.731, 733, 759; scholiast on Aristophanes, *Plut.* 454b) and then picked up by later scholiasts (Hughes, *Human Sacrifice*, pp. 243-44, nn. 15, 25).

95. According to Pythagoras, a leek hung over the doorway prevented the entrance of evil (Pliny, *NH* 20.9, 39). The same belief is found in Dioscorides, *De Maleria Medica* (2.202). Before Menippus was allowed to consult the oracle of the dead he reveals that he had been 'purged', 'cleansed' and 'consecrated...with torches and *leeks*' (A.M. Harmon, 'Decent into Hades', [= Necyomantia] in *Lucian* [LCL; 8 vols.; London: Heinemann, 1969], IV, pp. 72-109, sect. 7).

96. Harrison, *Prolegommena*, p. 100, cf. p. 101. Speculation has arisen that this practice may be grounded in the belief that the *pharmakos* represented a god who was beaten in order to expel evil influences and improve his ability to care for his people.

97. E.g., Mannhardt, *Mythologische Forschungen*, pp. 124-38; Harrison, *Prolegomena*, p. 101. For the bearing of the *pharmakos* ritual on the agricultural festival see: Nilsson, *Geschichte Feste*, pp. 113-15; Deubner, *Attische Feste*, pp. 192-93. Similarly, Victor Gebhard thinks that the *pharmakos* was beaten with lucky plants in order to drive bad magic out and good magic in, making him a kind of temporary god (*Die Pharmakoi*, p. 60). This same interpretation has been made of the *pharmakos* rituals at the Thargelia in Athens (e.g., Farnell, *Cults*, p. 281), Leukas (e.g., Farnell, *Cults*, p. 282), and in Rome (Frazer, *Golden Bough*. VI. *The Scapegoat*, p. 299).

98.
   Dear Pan, if this my prayer may granted be
   Then never shall the boys of Arcady
   Flog thee on back and flank with leeks and sting
   When scanty meat is left for offering;
   If not, thy skin with nails be flayed and torn,

warns that 'speculations about the Vegetarian Spirit have tended to obscure the simple and terrifying character of this drama'.[99]

The account of Harpocration (2 CE), once thought to be citing Istros on the Athenian *pharmakos* ritual, is now reckoned to describe the Ionian ritual.[100] Harpocration briefly describes the ritual and concludes with an etiological myth which supplies more information about the ritual itself:

> At Athens they drove out two men to be purifications (καθάρσια) for the city; it was the Thargelia, one was for the men and the other for the women. 'Pharmakos' is the proper name for a man [named Pharmakos] who stole a sacred libation cup dedicated to Apollo, and was stoned to death by the companions of Achilles, and the ceremonies done at Thargelia are imitations of these things (Harpocration, Φαρμακός [Text 11]).

Apotropaeic rituals similar to the *pharmakos* rituals of Athens and Ionia were performed through the Mediterranean basin. In the Greek colony of Massilia (Marseilles), an apotropaeic ritual was performed in which the victim was selected from amongst the poorest of the city. The primary sources for this ritual are Petronius (d. 66 CE) and Lactantius (d. 325 CE). Petronius is quoted by the Roman grammarian Servius (fl. 350–400 CE) in his commentary on the lemma, 'the sacred hunger for gold' in Virgil's *Aeneid*. According to this source, the rite was observed when a plague ravaged the city. This plague was the result of a curse, whose polluting character was thought to be contagious; it could spread from person to person leaving an epidemic in its wake. This curse was transferred to the *pharmakos* by an imprecation.[101]

> 'The sacred hunger for gold.' 'Sacred' means 'accursed'. This expression is derived from a Gallic custom. For whenever the inhabitants of Massilia

And amid nettles mayst thou couch till morn.
(Theodotia, *Id.* 7.106-109)

99. Burkert, *Greek Religion*, p. 83.

100. Farnell, *Cults*, 4.281; Gebhard, *Die Pharmakoi*, pp. 17-18; Deubner, *Attische Feste*, p. 181; Hughes, *Human Sacrifice*, p. 153.

101. This custom is rooted in the ancient belief that there was a close association between a spoken wish and its fulfilment. Oedipus is a good example of the power of a curse unleashed by the spoken word. He pronounced a curse against the as yet unknown killer of King Laius. When Oedipus discovered that it was he who had committed the murder, he cried out: 'God help me! I much fear that I have wrought a curse on mine own head, and knew it not' (Sophocles, *O. Rex.* 744-55; cf. pp. 235-45; 1380-84).

were burdened with a plague, one of the poor would offer himself to be kept at public expense and fed on food of special purity. After this period he would be decked with sacred herbs and clad in holy garments, and led about through the whole city *while people cursed him*, in order that the sufferings of the whole city might fall upon him, and so would be cast out. This account has been given us in Petronius (Text 13).[102]

According to the scholia (V-VI) on Statius' *Thebais*, the ritual purification of the city was an annual event, and not reserved for times of plague:

> To purify the community with a human victim is a Gallic custom. For someone of the most needy was enticed by rewards to sell himself for the purpose. And he was fed during the whole year at public expense on especially pure foods; and finally on a specific and solemn day he was led through the whole community (*per totam civitatem*) out of the city beyond the boundaries, and he was killed with stones by the people (Text 14).[103]

There are several conflicts between the testimony of Petronius and that of Lactantius especially as to whether the *pharmakos* was simply expelled or expelled and then stoned outside the walls.[104] Dennis Hughes thinks that Statius misunderstood the purpose of the stoning: it was used to chase the victim out of the city, not to kill him. Despite the contradictions between the two passages, Hughes argues that they are both derived from Petronius and states that the Massilienses were Greek, not Gallic. He thinks that the ritual described in the first century by Petronius was actually Ionian in origin.[105]

The city of Abdera (Thrace) was a Greek city located about fifty-two kilometres east of Philippi. Its *pharmakos* ritual is mentioned briefly in a fragment of the poet Callimachus (d. 240 BCE). In this fragment, a slave appears to be speaking: 'There, Abdera, where now…leads (me) a pharmakos'.[106]

The *Diegesis* provides detailed commentary on this fragment.[107] It

---

102. Petronius in Servius, on Virgil, *Aen.* 3.57 (= Petr. *fr.* 1). Servius greatly relied upon the work of a contemporary rival named Aelius Donatus who himself was dependent on the Virgil commentator Aemilius Asper (late second century CE).

103. Lactantius Placidi on 'Lustralemne' in Statius *Theb.* X, 793 (ET = Hughes, *Human Sacrifice*, p. 158).

104. Cf. attempt of Hughes to work out the original account (*Human Sacrifice*, p. 159).

105. Hughes, *Human Sacrifice*, pp. 158-59.

106. Callimachus, *fr.* 90: Ἔνθ', Ἄβδηρ', οὗ νῦν [--]λεω φαρμακὸν ἀγινεῖ (Rudolf Pfeiffer [ed.], *Callimachus* [2 vols.; Oxford: Clarendon Press, 1949], I, p. 97).

107. The *Diegeseis* which have come to light are said by Thomas Gelzer to be 'of

states that the *pharmakos* was processed around the city streets 'purifying in his own person the city' and finally stoned, not in order to kill him, but to drive him out of the city:

> In Abdera a slave, bought in the market, is used to purify the city. Standing on a block of grey stone, he enjoys a rich banquet, and so fed to the full he is led to the gates call Prurides. Then he goes round the walls in a circle purifying in his own person the city and the basileus, and then others throw stones at him until he is driven beyond the boundaries (Text 15).[108]

This extended procession around the city had purificatory significance, as indicated by the expression, 'to purify all around' (κύκλῳ περικαθαίρειν [1.34-36].[109] Dio Chrysostom (first–second century CE) seems to allude to this ritual during a visit to the Isthmian games: 'Or do you think those potbellies [athletes!] are good for anything? Creatures whom sensible people ought to lead around, subject to the ceremony of purification, and then thrust beyond the borders'.[110] The procession of the *pharmakos* seems to have begun at the public hearth (in the *prytaneion*; cf. Plutarch, *M.* 693e).[111] In other words, the purification of the city began at its centre.

The same ritual is recorded in a scholiast on Ovid. According to this source, a freemen was excommunicated for six days, and afterward stoned to death 'in order that he alone might bear the sins of all the people'.[112] The scholiast incorrectly interprets the purpose of the stoning,

---

inestimable value for the knowledge of the subjects Callimachus treated in his poetry' (T. Gelzer [notes] and C. Witman [trans.], *Callimachus* [LCL; Cambridge, MA: Wm. Heinemann, 1965], p. xiv). Three have survived, all deriving from a common source.

108. Scholiast on Callimachus, 1.97 (ET = Gelzer and Witman [trans.], *Callimachus*).

109. Cf. Hesychius, φαρμακοί (Text 17); 1 Cor. 4.13. This term is remarkably similar to the term περικάθαρμα in 1 Cor. 4.13, the latter being an intensive form of κάθαρμα, which is one of the two most common terms for a human apotropaeic victim: e.g., Photius, φαρμακός 640; Λευκάτης (Text 20); scholiast on Aristophanes *Plut.* 454; scholiast on Aristophanes *Eq.* 1133; *Eq*; scholiast on Aristophanes *Ran.* 742, φαρμακοῖσι; Suidas, καθάρματα (Text 23); Tzetes *H.* 726; Strabo, 10, 2.9; see also: Amp. 8.4.

110. J.W. Cohoon, *Dio Chrysostom* (LCL; 5 vols.; Cambridge, MA: Harvard University Press, 1961–1971), 8.14; cf. Hughes, *Human Sacrifice*, p. 153.

111. M. Nilsson, 'Die Prozessionstypen im griechischen Kult', in *Jahrbuch des Deutschen archäologischen Instituts* 13 (1916), pp. 319-20.

112. This is attested in the *locus classicus* on Ovid's phrase, 'Aut te devoveat' (scholiast on Ovid, *Ibis*, 467) (Text 16). Ovid's poem *Ibis* (c. 11 CE) is a curse

perhaps because of a confusion of Ovid's term *devovere*.[113]

An apotropaeic ritual was performed in the town of Leukas located on the Leucadian peninsula, north-west coast of the Peloponnese. It was observed at the time of the annual festival of Apollo. The Leucadians sought to 'avert evil' for the coming year by hurling a criminal into the sea from a white bluff at the southern end of the island. Men, waiting in a flotilla of boats at the base of the bluff, would retrieve the outcast and escort him away from the island. The earliest witness to this ritual is found in Strabo (BCE 64/3–21 CE):[114]

> It was the ancestral custom among the Leucadians, every year at the sacrifice performed in honour of Apollo, for some criminal to be flung from this rocky look-out for the sake of averting evil (ὄντων ἀποτροπῆς χάριν), wings and birds of all kinds being fastened to him, since by their fluttering they could lighten the leap, and also for a number of men, stationed all around below the rock in small fishing boats, to take the victim in, and when he had been taken on board, to do all in their power to get him safely outside their borders (Text 18).

For my last two examples, I turn to Roman religion and culture. At the beginning of each growing season, the Romans believed that agricultural fertility could be enhanced by chasing out the old tired vegetation deity from the previous growing season, along with the accumulated impurity of the people, thereby preparing the way for an invigorated, youthful deity.[115] Every year, on the day preceding the first full moon of the old

directed at an unnamed enemy of Ovid. In this poem, Ovid prays that his enemy 'may be sacrificed at the holy alter as a victim to Phoebus...or that Abdera on certain solemn days might devote him to death (*aut te devoteat*), and that a shower of stones thicker than hail might fall upon him' (R. Ellis, *P. Ovid Ovidii Nasonis Ibis* [Oxford: Clarendon Press, 1881], pp. 465-67).

113. Hughes, *Human Sacrifice*, p. 157.

114. Strabo, 10, 2.9 (Text 18) (ET = H.L. Jones [trans. and ed.], *The Geography of Strabo* [LCL; 8 vols.; London: Wm. Heinemann, 1917]). In addition to Photius' lexical entry on this rite, he also reports how a young man was annually hurled into the sea with the prayer, 'Become our *offscouring* (περίψημα)!' (Photius, περίψημα [Text 19]). Though this account does not specify any location, it has been connected with the Leucadian observance by Martin Nilsson (*Geschichte Feste*, pp. 109-110); cf. Photius, Λευκάτης (Text 20); cf. Ampelius 8.4 (Text 21); Suidas, καθάρματα (Text 23); cf. 1 Cor. 4.13: ὡς περικαθάρματα τοῦ κόσμου ἐγενήθημεν, πάντων περίψημα ἕως ἄρτι.

115. The central text is Lydus, *De mens.* 4.36. For earlier times two texts may be relevant (Servius on Virgil *Aen.* 7.188; Min. Felix, *Oct.* 24.3), though their relevance is contested; cf. A. Illuminati, 'Mamurius Veturius', *SMSR* 32 (1961), p. 41; J. Loicq,

Roman year, a man was selected to impersonate—or perhaps embody—the agricultural deity of the previous growing season. He was named *Mamurius Veturius*, 'the Old Mars'. After being clad in animal skins he was ceremonially whipped by the priests and driven away.

Our final example is an apotropaeic ritual used by the Roman army. The menacing danger in this case was the imminent defeat of the Roman army in battle. This was interpreted as the manifestation of a curse. When such circumstances arose, the consul would choose one of his soldiers to be an apotropaeic victim. The soldier was dressed in a ceremonial purple toga. He would then recite a prayer of devotion (*devotio*) by which he offered himself for the good of the army and asked that his life might 'expiate all anger of the gods, and turn aside destruction from his people and bring it on their adversaries'.[116] The best attestations to this ritual are found in the writings of Livy:

> On going down into the field of battle he had ordered Marcus Livius the pontifex not to leave his side. He now commanded this man [Decius] to recite before him the words which he proposed to devote himself... and having added to the usual prayers that... the wrath of the gods celestial and gods infernal should blight with a *curse* the standards, weapons and armour of the enemy, and that one and the same place should witness his own destruction and that of the Gauls and Samnites,—having uttered, I say, these *curses* upon himself and the enemy, he spurred his charger against the Gallic lines, where he saw that they were thickest, and hurling himself against the weapons of the enemy met his death. From that moment the battle seemed scarce to depend on human efforts (Text 22).[117]

'Mamurius Veturius et l'ancienne représentation de l'année', in M. Renard and R. Schilling (eds.), *Hommages à Jean Bayet* (Bruxelles: Latomus, 1964), pp. 401-26; W. Fauth, 'Römische Religion im Spiegel der 'Fasti' des Ovid', in *ANRW*, II, 16, 1 (1978), pp. 104-182, esp. pp. 150-55; F. Bömer, *P. Ovidius Naso: Die Fasten* (2 vols.; Heidelberg: C. Winter, 1957–58), *Fast.* 3, pp. 259-62; Frazer, *Golden Bough*. VI. *The Scapegoat*, pp. 229-31; for Mamurius in pictures: H. Stern, 'Notes sur deux images du mois de Mars', *REL* 52 (1974), pp. 70-74; H. Stern, 'Les calendriers romains illustrés', in *ANRW* II, 12 (1981), pp. 432-75, esp. pp. 436-39.

116. B.O. Foster (trans.), *Livy* (LCL; 13 vols.; London: Wm. Heinemann, 1926), 8.9.9-10. He made this prayer while unarmed, stepping on a spear, with veiled head, touching his chin with his hand. On this posture, W. Burkert comments, that it 'is evidently the opposite of a normal soldier's pose—armed, fiercely staring, aggressively stretching forth his chin, brandishing arms' (*Greek Religion*, p. 63).

117. *Livy*, 10.28.14–29.1 (my emphasis).

Apotropaeic Rituals in the Hebrew Bible and New Testament

There are other biblical text besides that of the Levitical scapegoat which bear the marks of an apotropaeic ritual. I will discuss three such stories, the sons of Saul, the tale of Jonah, and the healing of the Gedarene demoniac.

According to the story of the sons of Saul, a famine had ravaged Israel for three long years (2 Sam. 21.1-9). Finally, King David consulted an oracle ('enquired of the Lord') to determine its cause, after the same manner as Oedipus.[118] He received the same answer: the famine which was menacing his kingdom was brought on by blood guilt in the city. Previously, Israel had made an oath with the Gibeonites swearing that it would not kill them. However, Saul had transgressed this oath by attempting to wipe them out. The famine was a physical manifestation of the pollution brought on by this transgression. In order to avert this famine, David selected seven of Saul's offspring as apotropaeic victims. They were expelled from Israel and handed over to the Gibeonites who killed them and gibbeted their corpses. Upon completion of this deed the drought came to an end.

As the story of Jonah opens, the Lord comes to Jonah and commands him to travel at once to the wicked city of Ninevah to preach repentance. Jonah does not heed the Lord's request, and instead gets on a ship bound for Tarshish. When a great storm arises which threatens to break up the ship, the sailors realise that this peril was the consequence of one man's transgression. In order to achieve safety, this curse had to be transferred to a victim, who would then be thrown overboard. Lots were cast in order to determine who should be the substitutionary victim (cf. Lev. 16.8). The lot fell to Jonah (Jon. 1.7), and he accepted the outcome and volunteered himself, requesting that he be thrown into the sea so that the others might be saved (Jon. 1.12). The sailors prayed that they might not be held responsible for Jonah's 'innocent blood' (Jon. 1.14). When Jonah was flung into the sea and carried off by a great fish, the sea immediately ceased to rage (Jon. 1.15). In this story it is evident that when the author set out to narrate the calming of a raging sea by sailors, he drew upon his personal familiarity of apotropaeic rituals, casting Jonah in the image of the ritual victim.

118. Burkert comments on the close resemblance between this story and *Oedipus Rex* (*Greek Religion*, p. 66).

My last example is the story of the healing of the Gedarene demoniac drawn from the synoptic gospels (Mk 5.1-14/Mt. 8.28-34/Lk. 8.26-39). It begins with Jesus and his disciples crossing the sea of Galilee and landing on the opposite side in the country of the Gedarenes. Here they encounter a man with an unclean spirit who lived in the nearby tombs. The gospel accounts emphasize that numerous attempts had been made at imprisoning the demoniac: 'Many a time the demon had seized him; he was kept under guard and bound with chains and fetters, but he broke the bonds and was driven by the demon into the desert' (Lk. 8.29). According to Mark, 'he had often been bound with fetters and chains, but the chains he wrenched apart, and the fetters he broke in pieces; and no one had strength to subdue him' (Mk 5.4).[119] From the vantage point of apotropaeic rituals, the vital point is the social disruption and fear which this illness evoked in people, and the kind of ritual which was expected to produce a cure.

The healing which Jesus performed was probably based upon the author's personal knowledge of apotropaeic rituals. Jesus selects substitutionary victims, namely a local herd of two thousand swine. It seems that a legion of swine is required for a legion of demons. Next, the menacing evil—demons—is transferred from the demoniac to the swine. Finally, the permanent removal of the evil is accomplished when the herd rushes down a steep bank into the sea and drowns. This story is evidence of the application of the apotropaeic paradigm to Christian stories about Jesus. This obvious example in the miracle tradition raises

---

119. In ancient times, people suffering from medical conditions such as epilepsy and manic schizophrenia were thought to be under the influence of demonic spirits. The baleful influences of the moon in particular (itself a demonic force) was thought to be responsible for epilepsy. Hence, the verb 'to be brought under the influence of the moon', σεληνιάζεσθαι (from the nominal 'moon', σελήνη) is customarily translated 'to be epileptic'; cf. σεληνόβλητος, 'epileptic' (scholiast on Aristophanes, *Clouds*, 387). Whatever basis in history the meeting of Jesus and the Gadarene demoniac may have, the *description* of the demoniac does convey some of the medical symptoms associated with epilepsy: the unclean spirit had 'seized' the Gadarene many times (Lk. 8.29) such that he bruised himself with stones (perhaps by falling in convulsions) and could not be bound (Mk 5.3, 5) and would cry out. These symptoms resemble those of another synoptic miracle story where a father pleads with Jesus: 'Sir, have mercy on my son for he is an 'epileptic' and he suffers terribly and falls into the fire, and often into the water' (Mt.17.5). It is no accident that in Matthew's list of those cured by Jesus, demoniacs and 'those who were moonstruck' (i.e. epileptics) occur side by side.

the possibility of similar applications elsewhere in the kerygma of Jesus Christ.

Conclusion

This discussion has demonstrated that apotropaeic rituals were practised throughout a wide geographical sphere, as far east and west as Jerusalem and Marseilles. This is justification for naming them 'Mediterranean' apotropaeic rituals. Examples named have included cities known by Paul, such as Athens, Ephesos and Rome, and other cities such as Abdera near Philippi and Leukas near Corinth. If the apotropaeic paradigm was extensive geographically, it was also extensive chronologically in the Classical, Hellenistic and Roman periods. First-century witnesses include Plutarch (Chaeronea), Strabo (Leukas), Ovid (Abdera) and Petronius (Marseilles). There are also witnesses in the second (Harpocration [Thargelia]) and early third centuries (Philostratos [Ephesos]).[120]

Apotropaeic rituals of one sort or another continued through the Hellenistic period and Roman periods.[121] A case in point is the expulsion of *Hunger* (βούλιμος) from Chaeronea near Athens, in the first century CE.[122] This ritual was performed by the chief magistrate and by each house owner. Plutarch himself (fl. 50 CE) presided over this ceremony when he served as *archon* (*M*. 693-94). A slave was selected from each household, and one additional slave to represent the whole town. Each of these slaves was ceremonially flagellated and driven out of doors to the words, 'Out with Hunger, in with Wealth and Health!' (*M*. 693e-f). This ritual was performed in the expectation that the threat of hunger would be averted for coming year.[123] The slave was probably permitted

120. Apollonius of Tyana was clearly following an established custom when he made the people of Ephesos stone an old beggar who was the 'plague-demon', for the purification of the city (καθήρας τοὺς Ἐφεσίους τῆς νόσου) (Philostratus, *VA* 4.10-11).

121. On the Hellenistic period, cf.: Farnell, *Cults*, 4.277; on the Classical period: Harrison, *Prolegomena*, p. 96; also: W.J. Woodhouse, 'The Scapegoat', *Encyclopaedia of Religion and Ethics*, XI, pp. 218-23, esp. 220.

122. The term Βούλιμος is difficult to translate, sometimes being rendered 'ox-hunger' or 'voracious appetite'. These translations do not fully capture the sense of this term in this ritual. Plutarch does not treat the condition of Bulimy merely as a physical state resulting from the deprivation of food, but rather as a disease which infects the undernourished (cf. Plutarch, *M*. 694c).

123. Though Plutarch calls this ritual a 'sacrifice' (θυσία), he reveals his

to return after the ritual, indicating that the original savage ritual had been replaced by a kind of fictive simulation.

The most obvious example of an apotropaeic ritual in the first century is the expulsion of the scapegoat on the Day of Atonement which continued until the destruction of the temple in 70 CE. Philo testifies that in the first century, the Day of Atonement had special significance for non-observant Jews as well as those who were observant.[124]

A third example involves the expulsion of Februarius (cf. Mamurius Veturius) in the last month of the year, the month of purification (*februare* = purify). Byzantine sources mention how an old man was selected to represent the Old Year. He was wrapped in a mat of rushes, scourged and then expelled from Rome.[125] It is remarkable that similar folk customs were practiced in Greece until very recently. I am referring here again to the expulsion of old Roman Mars, Mamurius Veturius.[126] Again, the Old Year was clothed with skins and then driven out of the city.[127]

The point of these observations is not to suggest that Paul may have consciously borrowed from one of these rituals, though this possibility cannot be ruled out. Rather, of primary importance is simple fact of the universality of the apotropaeic paradigm. This demonstrates that the apotropaeic paradigm was deeply rooted in ancient Mediterranean culture and religion.

---

discomforture with the term 'sacrifice' and his understanding that it is really a purification, when he describes the ritual as 'a sacrifice with an admixture of purification'
(μεμιγμένην τινὰ καθάρμου θυσία). The use of the term 'sacrifice' is a concession to popular usage which referred to all religious ceremonies as 'sacrifices'.

124. 'When the third special season has come in the seventh month...On the
tenth day is the fast [Day of Atonement], which is carefully observed not only by the
zealous for piety and holiness, but also by those who never act religiously in the rest
of their life' (*Spec. Leg.* 1.186).

125. Versnel, *Transition and Reversal*, p. 301, n. 42.

126. F. Schneider, 'Kalendae Januariae und Martiae im Mittelalter, *ARW* 20
(1921), pp. 391-402; J.A. Megas, *Greek Calendar Customs* (Athens: Press and
Information Office, Prime Minister's Office, 2nd edn, 1963), pp. 79-85.

127. Other examples could have been cited in addition to the above, such as
Cyprus and Delphi (Harrison, *Prolegomena*, pp. 106-107; Farnell, *Cults*, pp. 282-
83). There are also more cryptic texts, such as the report by Caesar on the religion of
the Gauls (*Bellum Gallicum* 6.16) (L.A. Constans, *César: Guerre des Gaules* [Paris:
Société d' Edition, 4th cor. edn, 1947); is substantiated by Lactantius Placidi who
says of the scapeman ritual practised in Marseilles, and that this form 'of purifying a
city is a Gallic custom' (*lustrare civitatem humana hostia Gallicus mos est*) (on
Statius, *Theb.* 10.793).

Chapter 3

PAUL'S CONCEPT OF THE CURSED AND SINFUL CHRIST

It has been demonstrated above that apotropaeic rituals were not only widespread throughout the Mediterranean but are also attested in the Hebrew Bible and the New Testament. In addition to these examples, there are notable parallels between the passion of Christ and the apotropaeic paradigm. Like many expulsion victims, Christ was given a special meal in preparation for his death (the Last Supper), was flagellated and invested with special garments (Mk 15.17; Lk. 23.11; Mt. 27.28-29).[1] Finally, Jesus was expelled from society by being condemned as a criminal, by the betrayal and denial of his closest followers, and by being led in procession through the streets of Jerusalem to Golgotha outside the city walls (Mk 15.21-22; Mt. 27.32-33; Lk. 23.26-27). In Mark's gospel, the crucifixion narrative does not emphasise Jesus' death, nor the spilling of his blood, but rather his abandonment by his followers, and his abuse at the hands of the religious and political authorities. As Nils Dahl remarks:

> Jesus is depicted as the rejected one who was betrayed, deserted and denied by his own, slandered, condemned, spat upon and ridiculed, mocked as he hung on the cross, even by those who were crucified with him. Not the physical suffering but the *expulsion from human fellowship* is stressed again and again. Even his cry in deepest need and loneliness, 'My God, my God...' elicits only a crude joke.[2]

According to John Dominic Crossan the original story of Jesus' abuse was influenced by the scapegoat ritual prior to being adopted by the synoptic gospels. He argues that the earliest stratum of the Gospel of Peter was a self-contained narrative of Jesus' passion and resurrection

---

1. Jesus is whipped with a reed (κάλαμος), which is by no means the obvious choice of an instrument for flagellation since it is physically ineffective (Mk 15.19, 15; Mt. 27.30; cf. Isa. 53.5b).

2. N.A. Dahl, 'The Purpose of Mark's Gospel', in C. Tuckett (ed.), *The Messianic Secret* (Philadelphia: Fortress Press, 1983), pp. 29-34, esp. p. 30 (my emphasis).

from which all four canonical versions derive.[3] Whether or not Crossan is correct concerning the influence of the Jewish scapegoat ritual on the canonical passion accounts, the paradigm can be discerned none-the-less.

I have already noted that the *Epistle of Barnabas* (either late first or early second century CE) draws a direct connection between Christ and the scapegoat (*Barn.* 7.7-9). Similarly, Justin Martyr states that Christ was 'sent off as a scapegoat' (*Dial.* 40.4).[4] Tertullian holds that the scapegoat was 'marked with manifest tokens of our Lord's passion' (*Adv. Marc.* 7.7). Origen of Alexandria explicitly compares Jesus to both human apotropaeic victims and to the Levitical scapegoat:

> The apostles not only dared to show to the Jews from the words of the prophets that Jesus was the prophesied one, but also to the other people that Jesus, who had been recently crucified, voluntarily died for humanity, *like those who died for their fatherland, to avert plague epidemics, famines, and shipwreck* (*c. Cels.* 1.31).[5]

> ...the first goat was offered as a victim to the Lord and that the other was chased away 'living'. Listen, in the gospels, Pilate asks the priests and the Jews: 'Which of the two do you want me to release to you, Jesus called Christ or Barabbas?' Then, all the people cried for him to release Barabbas, but deliver Jesus to death. See, the goat was sent 'living into the desert' carrying with him the sins of the people who cried 'crucify! crucify!'. He is therefore the live goat sent into the desert...(Text 25).[6]

3.   He refers to this stratum as the *Cross Gospel* (*The Cross That Spoke: The Origins of the Passion Narrative* [San Francisco: Harper & Row, 1988], Pt. 1). According to Crossan, one of the four stages through which the story of Jesus' abuse passed prior to its appearing in the *Cross Gospel* (*Gos. Pet.* 3.6-9) focused on the typology of the purification goat and scapegoat. These two goats were related to the two comings of Christ through the linkage of Zech. 3.1-5, 12.10. With reference to the scapegoat text in Epistle of Barnabas, Justin and Tertullian, he postulates that the reed of the canonical passion narratives (Mk 15.15-20; Mt. 27.26-31) and the spear (Jn 19.31-37) find their origin in scapegoat typology.

4.   'And the two goats at the [Day of Atonement] fast that are commanded at the fast, which by God's command must be alike, of which one became the scapegoat, and the other an offering, were an announcement of the two advents of Christ; of one advent, in which the elders of your people and the priests, laying their hands on him and putting him to death, sent him off as a scapegoat; and of his second advent, because in the same place of Jerusalem you will recognise him who was dishonoured by you' (Justin Martyr, *Dial.* 40.4 [Text 24]).

5.   M. Borret, *Origène: Contre Celse* (5 vols.; Paris: Cerf, 1967) (my emphasis).

6.   The same may also be true for Gregory of Nazianzus (329–389 CE). In

Each of these authors carefully details the precise manner in which the scapegoat foretells the death of Christ.[7] The explicit and inexplicit parallels between Christian interpretations of Jesus' death and apotropaeic rituals testify to a culturally conditioned habit of mind which was shared by all inhabitants of the Mediterranean basin *including* the evangelists and later Christians.

Does this paradigm also shed light upon Paul's theology of atonement? The fact that the apotropaeic paradigm was widespread throughout the area of Paul's missionary activity and appears in Jewish and Christian writings suggests that this paradigm may also have been part of Paul's world view. Indeed, there is strong evidence that this is so. In 1 Cor. 4.13, Paul explicitly applies '*pharmakos*' terminology to himself: 'We have become like the "refuse" (περικαθάρμα) of the world, the "offscouring" (περίψημα) of all things, to this very day'. Both of these terms, περικάθαρμα and περίψημα (cf. above, nn. 109, 114), are associated with human apotropaeic victims and many scholars have concluded that this is the intended usage here.[8]

In any case, the presence of apotropaeic language in Christian texts generally raises the possibility of its being employed in Paul's writings. This hypothesis will be explored on the basis of three texts: 2 Cor. 5.21, Gal. 3.13 and Rom. 8.3. I shall return to the first two of these texts a second time in Chapter 6 in order to situate them in the overall

Euripides' *Bacchae* (963), Dionysos says to Pentheus, 'Alone you bear the burden for this city' (μόνος σὺ πόλεως τῆσδ' ὑπερκάμνεις) (A.S. Way, 'Bacchanals', in *Euripides* [LCL; 4 vols.; London: Wm. Heinemannn, 1912], II, pp. 1-121). E.R. Dodds thinks that Euripides is here alluding to the *pharmakos* ritual, a motif which later recurs in the stoning of Pentheus (1096–98) (E.R. Dodds, *Euripides: Bacchae* [Oxford: Clarendon Press, 2nd edn, 1960], pp. 196, 215). It is remarkable that Gregory makes virtually the same statement concerning Christ: 'Alone you bear the burden for human nature' (μόνος σὺ φύσεως ὑπερκάμεις βρότων); A. Tuilier (trans.), *Grégoire de Nazianze: La Passion du Christ* (Paris: Cerf, 1969), p. 1525.

7.   For sculptural evidence of apotropaeic Christology see: McLean, 'A Christian Sculpture in Old Corinth', pp. 199-205.

8.   περικάθαρμα is an intensive form of κάθαρμα, one of the two most common terms for human expulsion victims (e.g., Photius φαρμακός, 640; scholiast on Aristophanes *Pl.* 454; scholiast on Aristophanes, *Eq.* 1133; scholiast on Aristophanes, *Ran.* 742, φαρμακοῖσι; Suidas καθάρματα; Tzetzes *H.* 726; *s.v.* περικάθαρμα and περίψημα in: J.H. Moulton and G. Milligan, *The Vocabulary of the Greek Testament Illustrated from the Papyri and Other Non-Literary Sources* (London: Hodder & Stoughton, 1914–1929), I, p. 506, p. 510; F. Hauck, *TDNT*, III, pp. 430-31; Gustav Stählin, *TDNT*, VI, pp. 84-93; BAGD; cf. Rom. 9.3.

development of Paul's thought and to consider the social factors which
may have contributed to their formulation.

The Sinful Christ: 2 Corinthians 5.21

For our sake (ὑπὲρ ἡμῶν) God made Christ to be sin (ἁμαρτία) who
knew no sin (ἁμαρτία), in order that in him we might become the
righteousness of God.

The interpretation of this text largely depends upon the meaning of the
term ἁμαρτία. Does it mean 'sin' or, as some have suggested, a 'sin-
offering'? Relatively few contemporary New Testament scholars hold
the view that ἁμαρτία in 2 Cor. 5.21 means 'sin-offering'. F.F. Bruce
translated it as 'sin offering' by analogy with Isa. 53.6.[9] However, Oscar
Cullmann has persuasively demonstrated that there is no clear reference
to Isa. 53.6 in this verse.[10] The question of the meaning of ἁμαρτία in
v. 21 has been dealt with more exhaustively by Philipp Bachmann than
any other scholar. He has summarized the general scholarly consensus
against the translation of ἁμαρτία as 'sin-offering':[11]

---

9.   F.F. Bruce, *1 and 2 Corinthians* (London: Butler & Tanner, 1971), p. 210;
cf. L. Sabourin, *Rédemption sacrificielle: Une enquête exégétique*, Studia 11 (Bruges:
Desclée de Brouwer, 1961); Daly, *Christian Sacrifice*, p. 239; some Hebrew Bible
scholars also hold this interpretation of 2 Cor. 5.21: de Vaux, *Ancient Israel*, p. 420;
N. Snaith, 'Sacrifices in the Old Testament', *VT* 7 (1957), pp. 308-317, esp. p. 316.
This interpretation was also adopted by Augustine (354–430 CE), Ambrosiaster
(fourth century), Pelagius (c. d. 412), Oecumenius (sixth century), Erasmus (1469–
1536 CE). I am grateful to Daniel P. Bailey for drawing to my attention the following
additional references: U. Wilckens, *Der Brief an die Römer* (Zürich: Berzinger;
Neukirchener–Vluyn: Neukirchener Verlag, 1987), pp. 240-41; M. Hengel, *The
Atonement: The Origins of the Doctrine in the New Testament* (trans. J. Bowden;
Philadelphia: Fortress Press, 1981 [1980]), p. 46; P. Stuhlmacher, 'Sühne oder
Versöhnung?: Randbemerkungen zu Gerhard Friedrichs Studie: "Die Verkündigung
des Todes Jesu im Neuen Testament"', in U. Luz and H. Weder (eds.), *Die Mitte
des Neuen Testaments: Einheit und Vielfalt neutestamentlicher Theologie. Festschrift
für Eduard Schweizer zum siebzigsten Geburtstag* (Göttingen: Vandenhoeck &
Ruprecht, 1983), pp. 291-316, esp. pp. 298-99; Thyen, *Studien*, pp. 188-90.
10.   O. Cullman, *Christology of the New Testament* (trans. S.C. Guthrie and
C.A.M. Hall; Philadelphia: Westminster Press, 1959 [1957]), p. 76.
11.   P. Bachmann, *Der zweite Brief des Paulus an die Korinther* (KNT, 8; ed.
T. Zahn; Leipzig: Deichert, 4th edn, 1922), pp. 272-74; cf. V. Furnish, *2 Corinthians*
(AB, 32A; Garden City, NY: Doubleday, 1984), p. 340; A. Stanley, *The Epistles of St
Paul to the Corinthians* (2 vols.; London: John Murray, 1855), p. 112; H. Alford, *The
Greek New Testament* (4 vols.; London: Rivingtons, 1877), II, p. 666; B. Weiss,

1. The term ἁμαρτία occurs twice in v. 21: 'In our place, God made Christ to be ἁμαρτία, although he knew no ἁμαρτία.' Since Paul gives no indication that a different meaning is intended in these two usages, both instances must be taken to have the same meaning. Since it is indisputable that the second occurrence means 'sin' and not 'sin offering', the first occurrence must mean the same.

2. Though the term ἁμαρτία is occasionally found in the Septuagint to mean 'sin-offering', that is, purification sacrifice (e.g., Lev. 4.21; 6.25; Hos. 4.8; Num. 6.14), there is no example of this usage in the New Testament.

3. The internal logic of 2 Cor. 5.21 has a chiastic structure: Christ, who is sinless, is made to be sin by God; human beings, who are sinful, are made to be righteousness by God. Thus, the *sinful* state of Christ is reciprocally implied by the newly received righteousness of Christians. Each term is the necessary complement of the other. This parallelism is lost if Christ is described as becoming a 'sin-offering', since 'sin-offering' does not constitute a contrast to the 'righteousness of God'.

4. The almost literal affinity of this text to Gal. 3.13 and Rom. 8.3 is widely recognized. In the latter text, the terms 'curse' (κατάρα) and 'sinful flesh' (σάρξ ἁμαρτία) are not open to the same double interpretation as ἁμαρτία.

In view of this evidence, ἁμαρτία must mean 'sin', not 'sin offering'. What then does it mean to say that 'Christ was made to be *sin*'? Any investigation into the significance of this statement must begin by recognising the rhetorical device known as metonymy, the use of an abstract term in place of one which is more concrete.[12] In 2 Cor. 5.21,

---

Commentary on the New Testament (4 vols.; trans. G.H. Schodde and E. Wilson, (New York: Funk & Wagnell, 1906), III, p. 316; J.E. McFadyen, *The Epistles to the Corinthians* (London: Hodder & Stoughton, 1911), p. 322; Plummer, *Second Epistle of St Paul to the Corinthians*, p. 187; H.L. Goudge, *The Second Epistle to the Corinthians* (London: Methuen, 1927), p. 60; Héring, *La Seconde Épître*, p. 54; R.V.G. Tasker *The Second Epistle of Paul to the Corinthians* (Grand Rapids: Eerdmans, 1958), p. 90; Collange *Enigmes*, pp. 277-78; C.K. Barrett, *A Commentary on the Second Epistle to the Corinthians* (HNTC; New York: Harper & Row, 1973), p. 180; E. Best, *Second Corinthians*, Interpretation (Atlanta: John Knox Press, 1987), p. 56.

12. R. Bultmann, *The Second Letter to the Corinthians* (trans. R.A. Harrisville; Minneapolis: Augsburg–Fortress, 1985 [1976]), p. 165. Paul has employed metonymy in other contexts besides this one: for instance the abstract terms 'circumcision' (περιτομή) and 'uncircumcision' (ἀκροβυστία) to specify 'Jews' and 'Gentiles'.

metonymy is used to state emphatically that Christ was made over into 'a carrier of sin'.[13] In the words of J.-F. Collange, 'Christ was made sin in the sense that he personified all the sins of man, he is the curse incarnate'.[14] Thus, Paul describes how Christ who was not guilty of sin was made over into a sin-bearer without ever sinning.

Substitutionary Role

The nature of Christ's role as a sin-bearer is succinctly defined by the prepositional phrase ὑπὲρ ἡμῶν. There are two meanings of ὑπὲρ (+ genitive) which are easily confused: the beneficiary use has the English sense, 'for our benefit'; the substitutionary use means 'in our place'.

Though these two meanings are conceptually distinguishable, they sometimes overlap in actual practice since there are circumstances when one acts for the benefit of another person by taking his place. The beneficiary use of ὑπὲρ ἡμῶν in the New Testament is by no means controversial. Contention has arisen, however, over the translation of ὑπὲρ in a substitutionary sense in 2 Cor. 5.21.

There is widespread evidence in Classical and Hellenistic Greek literature for the substitutionary use of ὑπὲρ (+ gen.). Xenophon uses it to describe a person literally giving his life *instead of* another.[15] Herodotus

---

As we shall see, this device is also at work in Gal. 3.13 where Christ is described as becoming 'a curse' (κατάρα), an abstract term (Cf. H.A.W. Meyer, *Critical and Exegetical Commentary to the Epistle to the Galatians* [CECNT, 7; trans. W.D. Dickson; Edinburgh: T. & T. Clark, 1884], p. 153; J. Bengel, *Gnomen of the New Testament* [trans. C.T. Lewis; 2 vols.; Philadelphia: Perkinpini & Higgins, 1967, [1867]), II, p. 355; C. Ellicott, *A Commentary, Critical and Grammatical on St Paul's Epistle to the Galatians* (Boston: Crosby, Nicholas, Lee, 1860), p. 74; M.-J. Lagrange, *St Paul, Epître aux Galates* (Librairie Lecoffre; Paris: J. Gabalda, 2nd edn, 1925), p. 71; F. Büchsel, κατάρα, *TDNT*, I, pp. 449-51, esp. p. 450; J. Bligh, *Galatians in Greek: A Structural Analysis of St Paul's Epistle to the Galatians* (Detroit: University of Detroit Press, 1966), p. 138.

13. Thyen, *Studien*, p. 188.

14. J.-F. Collange, *Deuxième Epître*, p. 276.

15. 'There was a certain Episthenes of Olynthus who was a lover of boys, and upon seeing a handsome boy, just in the bloom of youth...on the point of being put to death, he ran up to Xenophon and besought him to come to the rescue of the handsome lad. So Xenophon went to Seuthes and begged him not to kill the boy...And Seuthes asked: "Would you even be willing, Episthenes, *to die instead of* (ὑπὲρ τούτου ἀποθανεῖν) this boy?" Then Episthenes stretched out his neck and said "Strike".' (C.L. Brownson [trans.], *Xenophon: Anabasis and Hellenica* [3 vols.; LCL; London: Wm. Heinemann, 1921]), *An.* 7.4.9 (my emphasis).

uses the same expression for lives being lost *instead of* another life.[16] Adolf Deissmann observes the habitual use of substitutionary ὑπέρ in papyri and ostraca in order to explain that the scribe acts in the place of an illiterate person.[17] The substitutionary use of ὑπέρ also occurs in the Septuagint, significantly, in connection with the concept of ransoming:

> For I am the Lord your God, the holy one of Israel, your saviour. I give Egypt as your ransom, Ethiopia and Seba in exchange for you (ὑπὲρ σοῦ). Because you are precious in my eyes, and honoured, and I love you, I give men in exchange for you (ὑπὲρ σοῦ), peoples in exchange for your life (ὑπὲρ τῆς κεφαλῆς) (Isa. 43.3-4).

The substitutionary use of ὑπέρ in connection with the concept of ransoming is also found in Clement of Rome:[18]

> For the love which he had toward us, Jesus Christ our Lord has given...his flesh in place of our flesh (ὑπὲρ τῆς σαρκὸς) and his life instead of our lives (ὑπὲρ τῶν ψυχῶν ἡμῶν) (Clem.R. 5.1).

In the Epistle to Diognetus the preposition ὑπέρ (+ genitive) occurs six successive times, followed by the crowning exclamation, 'Oh what a sweet *exchange* (ἀνταλλαγῆς)!'[19] There is also an instance of the substitutionary use of ὑπέρ in Jn 11.50: 'You do not understand that it is expedient that one man should die *in the place of* (ὑπέρ) the people, and that the whole nation should not perish.'[20]

---

16.   'Now it is a Persian custom to bury persons alive, inasmuch as I learn that Amestris also, the wife of Xerxes, when she grew old, took twice seven children of eminent Persians and made them a present *in her own stead* (ὑπὲρ ἑωυτῆς) to the god that is said to be beneath the earth, by burying them' (Powell [trans.], *Herodotus*, VII. 114, 2).

17.   G. A. Deissmann, *Light from the Ancient East* (trans. L.R.M. Strachan; rev. edn; London: Hodder & Stoughton, 1927), pp. 152, 166, 331, 335. There are similar examples of this in classical literature (e.g., Plato, *R.* 590a; also *Grg.* 515c; Thucydides, 1.141.15; cf. Phlm. 13).

18.   J. Lightfoot, *The Apostolic Fathers* (ed. J.R. Harmer; London: Macmillan, 1893), VII, p. 59.

19.   *Diog.* 9.2, 5: 'He parted with his own son as a ransom for us (λύτρον ὑπὲρ ἡμῶν), the holy instead of (ὑπέρ) the lawless, the guileless instead of (ὑπέρ) the evil, the just instead of (ὑπέρ) the unjust, the incorruptible instead of (ὑπέρ) the corruptible, the mortal instead of (ὑπέρ) the immortal...O the sweet exchange (ἀνταλλαγῆς)!' (Lightfoot, *Apostolic Fathers*, pp. 497, 508-509) (my emphasis).

20.   E.A.C. Abbott, *Johannine Grammar* (London: A. & C. Black, 1906), p. 276; R. Brown, *The Gospel According to John* (AB, 29/30; 2 vols.; New York: Doubleday, 1966–1970), I, p. 440 (my emphasis).

Though other New Testament texts could be considered, it is sufficiently clear at this point that there is widespread evidence for the substitutionary usage outside of the Pauline corpus. Therefore, it is not surprising that Paul also employs ὑπέρ in a substitutionary sense. This is partly explained by the fact that Paul never uses the customarily expected preposition ἀντί in a substitutionary sense.[21] For example, he speaks of 'those who are being baptised *in the place of* the dead' (οἱ βαπτιζόμενοι ὑπὲρ τῶν νεκρῶν [1 Cor. 15.29]). In 2 Cor. 5.14, Paul again uses ὑπέρ in a substitutionary sense: 'For the love of Christ controls us, because we are convinced that one has died *in the place of* all people (ὅτι εἷς ὑπὲρ πάντων ἀπέθανεν); therefore all have died'.[22] In his letter to Philemon, Paul explains, 'I would have been glad to keep Onesimus with me, in order that he might serve me in your place (ὑπὲρ σοῦ) during my imprisonment for the gospel' (Phlm. 13).

The internal logic of 2 Cor. 5.21 also requires a substitutionary meaning.[23] Christ's initial preincarnate status is described as 'not knowing sin' (τὸν μὴ γνόντα ὑμαρτίαν).[24] Christ is sinless only so long as he eschews human form.[25] Once human, he is sinful. Christ does not become human in order to stand in solidarity with humanity but to stand in its place and to participate in a twofold imputation: he receives the burden of humanity's sin while humanity receives God's righteous-

21. The interchangeability of ὑπέρ and ἀντί is demonstrated by Irenaeus: 'Since the Lord thus has redeemed us through his own blood, giving his soul *instead of* (ὑπέρ) our souls, and his flesh *instead of* (ἀντί) our flesh...' (H.W. Wigan, *Sancti Irenaei Episcopi Lugdenensis* [2 vols.; Cambridge, Cambridge University Press, 1857], 5.1.1 [ET; A. Roberts and J. Donaldson (eds.), *The Ante-Nicene Fathers*. I. *The Apostolic Fathers, Justin Martyr, Irenaeus* (Grand Rapids: Eerdmans, 1903)]).

22. Commenting on this text, A.T. Robertson remarks that ὑπέρ should be understood here in a substitutionary sense because Paul uses 'therefore all have died' (ἄρα οἱ πάντες ἀπέθανον) as the conclusion of εἷς ὑπὲρ πάντων ἀπέθανεν (*A Grammar of the Greek New Testament in the Light of Historical Research* [Nashville: Broadman, 1934], p. 631). J.-F. Collage concludes, 'Toutefois, l'antithèse "un-tous" ne permet pas d'en préciser le sens autrement que dans l'optique de la substitution. Le ὑπέρ rapproche ainsi d'un ἀντί' (*Enigmes*, p. 254).

23. M. Zerwick, *Biblical Greek: Illustrated by Examples* (trans. and adapted by J. Smith; Rome: Biblical Institute Press, 1963), p. 30, sect. 91.

24. Hans Windisch has demonstrated this is not a description of Jesus earthly life but of his status as preexistent Christ (Windisch, *Der zweite Korintherbrief*, pp. 197-98).

25. His sinlessness is implied by his sharing in the 'form' (μορφή) of God and divine sonship (Phil. 2.7).

ness. As John McFadyen observes, 'Christ was completely identified with human sin; and with the same completeness as we are identified with divine righteousness...in both cases there is an inner identification, as it were—of Him with sin, and of us with righteousness'.[26]

Within the immediate terms of reference of this passage, Paul does not suggest that Christ was rescued from this circumstance in any way. There is no hint of Christ's subsequent resurrection, nor his triumphant return. As we shall see, these ideas belong to a different paradigm of salvation.

The Cursed Christ: Galatians 3.13

Paul's image of the cursed Christ is cited in the context of arguments against the observance of Jewish law. Therefore, the interpretation of this image is bound up with the larger question of the relationship between transgression, law and faith.

Paul's Rejection of the Law
Why did Paul prohibit the Galatians from observing the Jewish law? The traditional answer to this question is that the law was intrinsically unful-fillable and could only bring condemnation upon those who attempted to keep it (cf. Gal. 3.10; Rom 3.23).[27] Rudolf Bultmann, who agrees with this interpretation, adds a second reason for Paul's prohibition: namely, striving to observe the law often led to the sinful attitudes of self-reliance and boasting, not self-renunciation.[28] Thus, Bultmann thinks that the law

---

26.   J. McFadyen, *Corinthians*, p. 322.

27,   Hans Schoeps interprets πᾶσιν (Gal. 3.10) to refer to the law with its 613 commandments and prohibitions, and interprets ὅλον τὸν νόμον (Gal. 5.3) in this sense (Schoeps, *Paul*, p. 176; also: H. Lietzmann, *An die Galater* [HNT, 10; Tübingen: Mohr (Paul Siebeck), 1910], p. 19; B. Weiss, *Galatians* [CommNT, 3; 4 vols.; trans. G.H. Schodde and E. Wilson; New York: Funk & Wagnal, 1906], III, p. 387; A. Oepke, *Der Brief des Paulus an die Galater* [ThHK, 9; Leipzig: A. Deichertsche Verlag, 1937], p. 105; F. Mussner, *Der Galaterbrief*, in Herder's Theologischer Kommentar zum Neuen Testament, 9 [Freiburg: Herder, 1974], pp. 224-26; U. Luz, *Das Geschichtverständnis des Paulus* [BEvT, 49; Munich: Chr. Kaiser Verlag, 1968], pp. 149-50).

28.   Bultmann, *Theology*, pp. 228-29, 232, 239, cf. p. 263. Bultmann's explanation for Paul's rejection of the law begins with Paul's anthropology. According to Bultmann, Paul portrays human persons fundamentally as creatures, created beings who are dependent upon their Creator for everything they receive. The observance of

is portrayed by Paul as evil because it leads to boasting.

Ulrich Wilckens disagrees with these interpretations, arguing that Paul considers the law to be good in itself: it was given by God in the expectation that Israel would faithfully observe it and realise its promises. To explain why the law cannot save, Wilckens begins with the problem of the universality of transgression: all have sinned, therefore all are under God's wrath (Rom. 1.18–3.20; Gal. 2.15-16; 3.10). The law can save no longer because the sins of humanity have rendered it impotent.[29]

These explanations for Paul's rejection of the law are anthropocentric, each focusing on a particular defect in the human person; either people are unable to keep the law, or they boast when they do keep it, or they have sinned and have thereby rendered the law impotent. None of these explanations can serve as a starting point for the understanding of Galatians because they are all fundamentally flawed. The evidence against these interpretations can be summarised in three arguments.

First, the traditional explanations for Paul's rejection of Jewish law imply that the law *could* have been a means of salvation, if only Galatians were able to observe all its ordinances, and do so without boasting. However, according to Paul, God never intended that the law should serve as a path to salvation (Gal. 2.21; 3.21). He describes the purpose of the law in the plainest possible terms in Gal. 3.19: 'Therefore why the law? It was added in order to bring about transgressions.'[30] In the light of Christ, Paul depicts the law as that which provokes transgression by inciting humanity's rebellious nature; it serves to 'enclose

---

the law encourages a self-reliant attitude in the creatures. As a result, the created beings begin to trust in the created order rather than acknowledging their absolute dependency upon the Creator (*Theology*, pp. 240-43).

29. U. Wilckens, 'Was heisst bei Paulus: "Aus Werken des Gesetzes wird kein Mensch gerecht"?', in *Rechtfertigung als Freiheit: Paulusstudien* (Neukirchen-Vluyn: Neukirchener Verlag, 1974), pp. 77-109, esp. pp. 79-94; U. Wilckens, *Der Brief an die Römer. 1–3* (2 vols.; EKKNT; Cologne: Benziger; Neukirchen-Vluyn: Neukirchener, 1978–82), I, pp. 84, 122, 152-53; 122, 240-41; II, pp. 99-100; U. Wilckens, 'Christologie und Anthropologie im Zusammenhang des paulinischen Gesetzesverständnisses', *ZNW* 67 (1976), pp. 64-82, esp. pp. 71, 74.

30. Τί οὖν ὁ νόμος; τῶν παραβάσεων χάριν προσετέθη. The word χάριν indicates purpose or goal (cf. BAGD, 877, no. 1). Brice Martion comments that the question of the purpose of the law should be analyzed by distinguishing between the *ostensible* and the *real* reason. Ostensibly, God gave the law to prevent sin; but the real purpose was to increase sin (B. Martion, *Christ and the Law in Paul*, NovTSup 62 [Leiden: Brill, 1989], ch. 1).

everything under sin' (Gal. 3.22) in order to prepare the world to receive Christ's eschatological kingdom.[31]

Secondly, explanations which begin with the notion of people's inability to keep the law are contradicted by Paul's own description of himself as 'blameless' with regard to 'righteousness under the law' (Phil. 3.6). The cornerstone passage for the 'unfulfillability theory' is Romans 7, a passage which many scholars from Luther onwards have interpreted as Paul's autobiographical confession of his own despair over his inability to keep the law.

Werner Kümmel has refuted this interpretation of Romans 7, demonstrating that this chapter cannot be read as Paul's pre-conversion turmoil over keeping the law.[32] Krister Stendahl has further argued that Paul's conscience was robust and untroubled both before and after his conversion. It is not Paul's plagued conscience which he left behind at his conversion but his 'glorious achievements as a righteous Jew' (2 Cor. 1.12; 5.11; 1 Cor. 4.4; Gal. 1.13-14); it is Paul's *accomplishments* which seemed worthless in comparison with the value of knowing Christ.[33]

Thirdly, all anthropocentric explanations share a common flaw in their approach to Paul in that they begin with the plight of Christians under the law and then move to the solution—Jesus Christ. E.P. Sanders convincingly argues that Paul does not reason from plight to solution, but from solution to plight: 'for Paul, the conviction of a universal solution preceded the conviction of a universal plight.'[34] Once Paul is convinced

31. In Romans Paul explains that the law served to 'multiply sin' in order that grace may abound (Rom. 5.20; 4.15). It led people to spiritual death in order that the offer of new life might be irresistible.

32. The most difficult problem of Rom. 7.7-25 is the identity of the 'I' who speaks. Is Paul speaking about his own personal experience, or is the first person pronoun used rhetorically. Kümmel has convincingly demonstrated the rhetorical understanding of the 'I' showing that it designates all non-Christians (W.G. Kümmel, *Römer 7 und das Bild des Menschen im Neuen Testament* [Munich: Chr. Kaiser Verlag, 1974], pp. 74-138).

33. K. Stendahl, *Paul Among Jews and Gentiles, and Other Essays* (Philadelphia: Fortress Press, 1976), p. 80. Paul acknowledges his physical handicaps and sufferings, not his sin (2 Cor. 12.7, 10; Gal. 4.13). Stendahl blames Augustine and Luther for imposing their own introspective consciences onto Paul (*Paul*, p. 83, cf. pp. 85-87).

34. E.P. Sanders, *Paul and Palestinian Judaism: A Comparison of Patterns of Religion* (Philadelphia: Fortress Press, 1977), p. 474. Sanders has severely criticized Bultmann's approach to Paul in particular on the grounds that it proceeds from plight to solution (pp. 474-76, cf. 442-43). Frank Thielman has attempted to reassert the

that Christ is *the* Way, all *other* ways are wrong because they are not
Christ: 'If salvation comes only in Christ, no one may follow any other
way whatsoever', including the law.[35] This train of reasoning is apparent
in Paul's statement, 'if justification were through the law, then Christ
died to no purpose' (Gal. 2.21). The obvious inference here is that since
Paul believes that Christ did not die in vain, the law must necessarily be
void.

Sanders has distinguished between Paul's *real* reason for rejecting the
law and his arguments intended to defend this position. The real reason
behind Paul's conviction that righteousness must be by faith is not his
despair over humanity's plight under the law, nor because the law leads
to boasting, nor because it cannot be kept, nor even because of the
universality of transgression. These are mere arguments mustered to
defend Paul's *real* reason for rejecting the law. These arguments are all
dependent upon his prior Christ-centred perspective.

What then is Paul's real reason for rejecting the law? Albert
Schweitzer was the first to argue that Paul's real reason for rejecting the
law was his belief that in Christ, God had inaugurated this new creation
in which the law was no longer valid.[36] The law being designed for sinful
humanity, was incompatible with the new age created for a redeemed

traditional 'plight to solution pattern' (F. Thielman, *From Plight to Solution: A
Jewish Framework for Understanding Paul's View of Law in Galatians and
Romans*, NovTSup 61 [Leiden: Brill, 1989], p. 35). He interprets the role of the Torah
in Judaism juristically instead of in terms of the covenant (p. 35) and argues that Paul
is in continuity with Judaism in this respect. The problem, according to Thielman, is
not the law, but the human inability to keep the law and the sin which results; 'it is the
individual and sin, not the law, which are responsible for the human plight of disobedience to God' (p. 111). In following this line of argument he attempts to explain
away the force of Phil. 3.6 (pp. 109-111). As a whole he seems to misinterpret
Sanders since Sanders is concerned with how Paul *arrived* at his religious convictions not, as in Thielman's case, how Paul *argued* his convictions.

35. Sanders, *Paul*, p. 474. Similarly, Terence Donaldson, building on the insights
of Thomas Kuhn, concludes that 'Paul can be seen as one who underwent a paradigm
shift, a transfer of allegiance from one set of world-structuring convictions to another'
('Zealot and Convert: the Origin of Paul's Christ Torah Antithesis', *CBQ* 51 [1989],
pp. 655-82, esp. p. 682; cf. T. Donaldson, in B.H. McLean [ed.], *Origins and
Method: Towards a New Understanding of Judaism and Christianity. Studies in
Honour of John C. Hurd* [JSNTSup, 86; Sheffield: JSOT Press, 1993], pp. 190-98).

36. Schweitzer says that Paul had in effect 'sacrificed the Law to eschatology'
(A. Schweitzer, *The Mysticism of Paul the Apostle* [New York: Seabury, 1931],
p. 192).

humanity.[37] In fact, everything belonging to the old order lost its validity when this new creation began.[38] The whole of Galatians presupposes this overarching antithesis between Christ's *new* creation and the *old* unredeemed creation of the flesh, sin and death. The new creation is the domain of God's Spirit, blessing, faith and freedom. The old creation is the domain of both law and lawlessness (Gal. 2.16; 3.1-5; 5.1-6), circumcision and uncircumcision (5.6; 6.14).

There is substantial evidence that Paul's understanding of the Jewish law is distorted. For example, Hans Schoeps has demonstrated how Paul's portrayal of the law has been strongly influenced by the theology of the Septuagint. The Septuagint displays a marked tendency to ethicise Judaism by understanding it as *moral* law, disconnected and isolated from the controlling reality of the Sinai covenant. In contrast, Palestinian Jews understood the *Torah* as a gift from God and the observance of Torah as a means of grace. The septuagintal translation of 'Torah' as 'law' (νόμος) underlines this general shift towards legalism. Another example of the legalism in the Septuagint is its translation of *tsedeq* (צדק) which from a Jewish perspective includes the ideas of grace and mercy, as well as righteousness. But the Septuagint, often preferring the juristic sense, usually translates *tzedeq* as δικαιοσύνη ('righteousness').[39]

Heikki Räisänen concludes that 'for Paul, Judaism was legalism'.[40] Taking a more nuanced position, Stephen Westerholm argues that Paul has distorted Judaism by reweighting the relative importance of grace and works in his presentation of Judaism, giving more emphasis to the latter than was commonly given in Judaism itself. According to Westerholm, this is not a complete distortion but only a difference in weighting.[41] In some ways, Schoeps, Räisänen and Westerholm do not

---

37. Schweitzer, *Mysticism*, pp. 64, 69, 189-91.

38. Many scholars have followed Schweitzer's conclusion. Hans Schoeps for example remarks that the point of departure of Paul's theology is that 'the times are now post-Messianic' as a consequence of Christ's death and resurrection (Schoeps, *Paul*, p. 173; cf. B.R. Gaventa, 'The Singularity of the Gospel: A Reading of Galatians', in D.J. Lull [ed.] [SBLSP, 27; Missoula: Scholars Press, 1988], pp. 17-26, esp. 18-19, 22-26; J.L. Martyn, 'Paul and His Jewish-Christian Interpreters', *USQR* 42 [1988], pp. 1-15, esp. p. 4).

39. Schoeps, *Paul*, pp. 175-77, esp. p. 176.

40. H. Räisänen, 'Legalism and Salvation by the Law', in S. Pedersen (ed.), *Die paulinische Literatur und Theologie* (Aarthus: Aros, 1980), pp. 63-83, esp. p. 64; cf. H. Räisänen, *Paul and the Law* (Philadelphia: Fortress Press, 1983), pp. 162-64.

41. Therefore the two ways of works and faith cannot be taken to represent the

go far enough in identifying the divergence between Paul's understanding of the law and that of the Hebrew Bible. In Galatians, Paul employs the term 'law' to designate a reality much broader than simply 'Jewish law' (*torah*). 'Law' has become a comprehensive symbol for the way of the old world, whether Jewish or non-Jewish.

Paul's all-encompassing use of the term 'law' is apparent in his statement that the Jews are *under* the 'elemental cosmic powers' (τὰ στοιχεῖα τοῦ κόσμου) along with the Gentiles (cf. Gal. 3.19-25; 4.1-3, 8-10).[42] In Paul's terminology, being *'under* the law' is merely another way of being *under* the 'elemental cosmic powers'. The law is merely an instrument of the powers of the old age, the powers of the flesh, sin and death.

The whole of Galatians is preoccupied with the ramifications of the breaking in of this new age into the old age. With the resurrection of

distinct self-understandings of the Jewish and Christian communities respectively since Jews did not think that they earned God's favour. However, Westerholm does think that works had a soteriological function in Judaism (S. Westerholm, *Israel's Law and the Church's Faith: Paul and His Recent Interpreters* [Grand Rapids: Eerdmans, 1988], pp. 147-50). Sanders characterizes first-century Judaism by the term 'covenantal nomism' meaning that Israel's place in God's overall plan is determined by God's prevenient grace in choosing Israel to be a separate and privileged people by giving them the covenant (Deut. 4.31; 2 Macc. 8.15; *Pss. Sol.* 9.10; CD 6.2; 8.18). God gave the law as an integral part of the covenant to show Israel how to live within the covenant (e.g. Deut. 4.1, 10, 40; 5.29-33; 6.1-2, 18, 24). Israel's obedience to the law does not represent Israel's legalistic attempt to earn salvation but its faithful and loving response to God's initial act of grace in giving the covenant (*Paul*, pp. 75, 420, 544; so also L. Gaston, *Paul and the Torah* [Vancouver: University of British Columbia Press, 1987], pp. 25-26). Thielman has challenged this portrayal of Judaism and attempted to reaffirm the traditional portrayal of Judaism as consistently sinning and 'inescapably tainted with sin' (Thielman, *From Plight to Solution*, p. 29).

42. For the translation of the difficult term τὰ στοιχεῖα I follow Eduard Schweizer in his recent article, meaning the four basic elements of the world (earth, water, air, fire) which had the power to prevent one from entering the after-life, as well as cause earthquakes, storms and eruptions of volcanoes (E. Schweizer, 'Slaves of the Elements and Worshippers of Angels: Gal. 4.3 and Col. 2.8, 18, 20', *JBL*, 107/3 [1988], pp. 455-68). In a similar fashion, W. Kern considers this term to refer to the aspects of the created world that surround and condition humankind, and whom humanity idolatrously invests with power over it (W. Kern, 'Die antizipierte Entideologisierung oder die 'Weltelemente' des Galater—und Kolosserbriefes heute', *ZKT* 96 [1974], pp. 185-216). Therefore in this thesis I shall translate the term τὰ στοιχεῖα as 'elemental cosmic powers'. In the context of Paul's thought, these 'powers' should perhaps be understood as the flesh, sin and death.

Christ, God has inaugurated a new creation in juxtaposition to the old creation. Membership in Christ's new creation (Gal. 2.19-21; 3.26-29) can only be achieved by renouncing all previous associations with the old including the renunciation of the Jewish law (Gal. 5.1; cf. 1.3-4, 11-17; 4.8-11; 6.14-15). Therefore, Paul does not argue that Christians *are not obliged* to follow the law, but rather that they *must not* follow the law. They must be freed from the old order in order to live exclusively in the new.[43]

Life under the Law (Gal. 3.13-14)
In Paul's mind, Christians who continue to observe the law (and thereby retain loyalty to the old creation) are 'under a curse' (ὑπὸ κατάραν, Gal. 3.10). This statement serves as a preamble to Paul's scriptural quotations in 3.10 (Deut. 27.26) and 3.13 (Deut. 21.23). It is a generalising statement or thesis concerning the predicament of the Galatian compromisers and those who listen to them (see Chapter 6).

> For all who rely on works of the law are under a curse; for it is written, 'Cursed is everyone who does not observe and obey all the things written in the book of the law'. (Gal. 3.10)

In contrast, those who have *renounced* the law (and therefore allegiance to the old creation) are free to be partakers in God's blessing (Gal. 3.7-9). It is logical that the corresponding fate to 'carrying a blessing' is 'bearing a curse' since the act of blessing is the diametric opposite of cursing.[44] Here Paul does not envision any middle ground—one is either blessed or cursed depending on one's decision about Torah.

Paul takes pains to support his argument by quoting Deut. 27.26. This citation is taken from the closing statement of the curses pronounced on Mount Ebal, and it serves as a summary of the preceding narrative. In order to comprehend the implied meaning of this text in Paul's argument, it is helpful to compare his citation of Deut. 27.26 with that of the Masoretic text and the Septuagint:

43. Gaventa, 'Singularity of the Gospel', pp. 20, 23, 26.
44. For this reason, the forms given to curses and blessing are frequently parallel (e.g., Deut. 11.29; Jer. 17.5-8). Six tribes stood on Mount Ebal to curse those who disobeyed the law while at the same time the six remaining tribes stood on Mount Gerazim to pronounce the corresponding blessing (Deut. 27.11–28.6). The close identity between cursing and blessing is evident in Jas 3.9-10: 'With the tongue we bless the Lord and Father, and with it we curse men...From the same mouth comes blessing and cursing.'

Masoretic Text

אָרוּר אֲשֶׁר לֹא־יָקִים אֶת־דִּבְרֵי הַתּוֹרָה־

הַזֹּאת לַעֲשׂוֹת אוֹתָם וְאָמַר כָּל־הָעָם אָמֵן:

LXX

'Επικατάρατος πᾶς ἄνθρωπος, ὃς οὐκ ἐμμενεῖ ἐν πᾶσιν τοῖς λόγοις τοῦ νόμου τούτου τοῦ ποιῆσαι αὐτούς.

Galatians 3.10

'Επικατάρατος πᾶς [...] ὃς οὐκ ἐμμένει [...] πᾶσιν τοῖς γεγραμμένοις ἐν τῷ βιβλίῳ τοῦ νόμου [...] τοῦ ποιῆσαι αὐτά.

The Hebrew text reads: 'Cursed is he who does not keep the words of this law, in order to do them.' The Septuagint has intensified the gravity and comprehensiveness of the statement with the addition of the words πᾶς and πᾶσιν, stressing that *everyone* who does not fulfill *all* the injunctions of this law is cursed.

The 'laws' to which the Hebrew Bible and Septuagint refer are narrowly defined and limited in number. Deut. 27.26 specifies 'the sayings of *this* law' which is to say, the twelve statutes previously cited in Deut. 27.15-26. In contrast, Paul's version of Deut. 27.26 includes the *entire* Jewish law (πᾶσιν τοῖς γεγραμμένοις ἐν τῷ βιβλίῳ τοῦ νόμου). Dietrich-Alex Koch argues that the newly added phrase γεγραμμένοις ἐν τῷ βιβλίῳ τοῦ νόμου has been imported from Deut 29.19 where it is also employed in connection with a curse formula:[45]

Deuteronomy 27.26

...ἐν πᾶσιν τοῖς λόγοις τοῦ νόμου τούτου τοῦ ποιῆσαι αὐτούς.

Galatians 3.10

...πᾶσιν τοῖς γεγραμμένοις ἐν τῷ βιβλίῳ τοῦ νόμου τοῦ ποιῆσαι αὐτά.

45. D.-A. Koch, *Die Schrift als Zeuge des Evangeliums: Untersuchungen zur Verwendung und zum Verständnis der Schrift bei Paulus* (BHT, 69; Tübingen: Mohr [Paul Siebeck], 1986), p. 164. Though a similar phrase is found in Deut. 28.58 (πάντα τὰ ῥήματα τοῦ νόμου τούτου τὰ γεγραμμένα ἐν τῷ βιβλίῳ), the word sequence is altered and γεγραμμένα κτλ is not part of the announcement of a curse. The announcement of the curse begins in Deut. 28.59. The use of τὰ ῥήματα suggests derivation from Deut. 28.58 (see Deut. 27.26 τοῖς λόγοις). However, in Gal. 3.10 both οἱ λόγοι and τὰ ῥήματα are missing (Koch, *Die Schrift*, p. 164, n. 22).

Deuteronomy 29.19
...πᾶσαι αἱ ἀραὶ τῆς διαθήκης ταύτης αἱ γεγραμμέναι ἐν τῷ
βιβλίῳ τοῦ νόμου τούτου...

Koch refers to the 'formula-like character' of Paul's modified wording
of Deut. 27.26 and states that the possibility of a pre-Pauline tradition
cannot be ruled out.[46] However, he thinks that the modified character of
Deut. 27.26 is so well-suited to Paul's hermeneutic purpose that it is
more probable that Paul adapted the text himself:

> In Gal. 3.10, Paul wants to show more clearly the harmful character of the
> law, and the connection between law and curse. He wants to do this in
> contrast to the connection between δικαιοσύνη and πίστις (3.8; 3.11b,
> 12), and πίστις and εὐλογία τοῦ 'Αβραάμ (3.9; 3.14) respectively. The
> inclusion of additional terms firmly rooted in the added curse-formulae of
> Deut. 28–30 suit this purpose. The inclusion of τὰ γεγραμμένα, the
> direct reference to the βίβλιον τοῦ νόμου, and the simultaneous
> omission of λόγοι, all do their part to emphasise the scriptural character of
> the law in a one-sided manner. Thus, the law is interpreted as γράμμα,
> and especially as γράμμα, in Paul's opinion, it will lead people to death
> (2 Cor. 3.6). Therefore, a Pauline origin of this modified quotation can be
> viewed possible.[47]

According to Paul, the whole law must be observed *in toto* or else a
curse is invoked. For Paul, it is not that the law itself is a curse, but the
law pronounces a curse on all who transgress it.[48] Paul could have used
the original text of the Septuagint to combat the compromisers without

---

46.   'Besides, πᾶσιν τοῖς λόγοις is not only expanded by γεγραμμένοις κτλ.
but τοῖς λόγοις is also omitted. Moreover, this simultaneous text abbreviation cannot
be based on parallel influence' (Koch, *Die Schrift*, p. 165, also n. 23). Koch notes that
in all parallel passages, γεγραμμέν κτλ. is related to the noun that directly precedes
it. In Deut. 28.58, the omission of λόγοις cannot be explained (τὰ ῥήματα τὰ
γαγραμμένα κτλ.) (p. 165, no. 24).

47.   Koch, *Die Schrift*, 165. In his discussion of Paul's rendering of LXX citations, Koch demonstrates that Paul may either quote the text literally or change the
wording according to the requirements of his argument. He argues that Paul's
freedom with texts is not typical of Jewish exegetical practice in the first century CE.
Variations from written texts are the result of conscious interpretive activity, not mere
lapses of memory. This suggests that his exegesis is non-scholastic and non-
professional in nature.

48.   F.F. Bruce, *Commentary on Galatians* (NIGTC; Grand Rapids: Eerdmans,
1982), pp. 162-64; cf. R. Hays, *Echoes of Scripture in the Letters of Paul* (New
Haven: Yale University Press, 1989), p. 203, n. 24.

adaptation since their selective observance of the law probably did not include all the ordinances contained in Deut. 27.15-26. However, Paul was able to sharpen his attack by generalizing the application of Deut. 27.26. In the words of Koch,

> In 3.10 Paul aims at the general statement that everyone who is ὑπὸ νόμου (see Gal. 4.21) or ἐξ ἔργων νόμου, is also at the mercy of the curse of the law. Because only when κατάρα has hit everyone who is 'under the law', is the declaration, also a general one, of a ransom from the κατάρα τοῦ νόμου in 3.13 a meaningful one.[49]

In its adapted form, Deut. 27.26 serves as an uncompromising indictment of the compromisers and their gospel for they do not keep the *whole* law (Gal. 6.13, cf. 5.3). Paul warns that the selective observance of the law as taught by the compromisers can have no future; the transgression of but a single ordinance leads to bearing a curse.[50]

This curse which is associated with sin must not be psychologised or spiritualised by modern interpreters.[51] In the ancient world, curses were real, so real in fact that they were used as weapons (e.g., Judg. 9.57; Prov. 11.26; 30.10).[52] When Jesus cursed the fig tree it 'withered at once' (Mt. 21.19-20). On account of their inherent power, curses often accompanied the declaration of punishments (Gen 3.14, 16; 4.11), the utterance of threats (Jer. 11.3; 17.5; Mal. 1.4), and the proclamation of laws (Deut. 11.26-28; 27.15-26) in order to provide the necessary deterrent. Curses could also cause plagues, famines and the defeat of armies (cf. Chapter 2). In fact, throughout the ancient Near East, curses

49. Koch, *Die Schrift*, p. 265.

50. On the surface, Deut. 27.26 seems to contradict Paul's assertion that all who follow the law are under a curse. The positive inference of Deut. 27.16 is that as many as observe the law faithfully are *not* cursed. I have already stated that Paul's theology proceeds from solution to plight; Christ's provision of a new creation has invalidated the old creation including the law. The law has been nullified. Since loyalty to the law is the same as loyalty to the old unredeemed order, it offers not a blessing but a curse.

51. Cf. W. Wrede, *Paul* (Lexington: American Library Association Committee on Reprinting, repr. edn, 1962), pp. 92-93.

52. The custom of cursing presumes a close association between a spoken wish and its fulfilment. Edward Westermarck explains this as follows:

> The wish is looked upon in the light of energy which may be transferred—by material contact, or by the eye, or by means of speech—to the person concerned, and then becomes a fact. This process, however, is not taken quite as a matter of course; there is always some mystery about it' (E. Westermark, *The Origin and Development of Moral Ideas* [2 vols.; London: Macmillan, 1906–1908], I, p. 563).

were used as threats and punishments upon those who transgressed the will of the deity.[53] This context applies equally to Paul's writings. Paul's concept of being *'under* a curse' should be understood in *physical* terms; he means to say that the transgressors truly incur a deadly curse and are subject to its power.[54]

From this perspective, it is apparent that Paul's portrayal of this curse is very similar to his understanding of sin. Paul describes sin, not merely as the sum of wrong doings, but as a physical power which is both infectious and dangerous. Sin is an active, menacing, independent power which physically clings to the human flesh as a hostile power (Rom. 7.17, 20) and enslaves people (Rom. 5.12-14; 6.6-23; 7.14). Hence the phrase *'under* a curse' (ὑπὸ κατάραν) in Gal. 3.10 is synonymous with the analagous phrase *'under* sin' (ὑπὸ ἁμαρτίαν, Gal. 3.22; Rom. 3.9).[55]

Therefore, even if Christians were able to observe *all* the ordinances of the law, they would remain doomed because, in Paul's view, the law does not lead to blessing but cursedness (Gal. 3.10; cf. 2.21; 3.21). It is an inferior entity belonging to the old creation. It was not ordained by God but by intermediaries (Gal. 3.19-20). In brief, the law is limited both in terms of validity and function: it was in effect only until Christ came (Gal. 3.19), and it functioned merely as a custodian (Gal. 3.23).

The Cursed Christ

> Christ freed [literally 'purchased'] us from the curse of the law by becoming a curse in our place, for it is written 'cursed is everyone who hangs on a tree' (Gal. 3.13).

53. E.g., B.H. McLean, 'Attic Christian Epitaph: the Curse of Judas Iscariot', *OCP* 58 (1993), pp. 241-44.

54. Johann Bengel interprets the phrase to mean, 'the curse under which they lie' (Bengel, *Gnomon of the New Testament*, II, p. 355). A.T. Robertson speaks of Christ taking us 'out from under the curse' (Robertson, *Grammar*, p. 631). In the New Testament ὑπό (+ acc.) frequently means under the power, rule, command of someone or something (G.B. Winer, *A Grammar of New Testament Diction* [trans. E. Masson; Edinburgh: T. & T. Clark, 1861], p. 507, sect. 49; cf. BAGD 843, 2b).

55. The phrase 'under a curse' (ὑπὸ κατάραν) is a *hapax legomenon* in the New Testament. It is clearly related to the expression *'under* the law' (ὑπὸ νόμον, Gal. 4.4, 5; 5.18; Rom. 6.14), since observing the law according to Paul implies bearing its curse; cf. similar expressions such as *'under* guardians and trustees' (ὑπὸ ἐπιτρόπους ἐστὶν καὶ οἰκονόμους) which is equivalent to 'being slaves to the elemental powers' (ὑπὸ τὰ στοιχεῖα τοῦ κόσμου...δεδουλωμένοι, Gal. 4.2, 3; cf. 4.8, 9).

I have demonstrated how Paul portrays all who observe the law as being burdened by a curse which prohibits their entrance into Christ's new creation. They remain prisoners of the old creation and ruled by its powers of sin and death. In the immediate context of Galatians, this predicament is limited to the Galatian compromisers and their followers (see Chapter 6). In a broader context, it describes the pre-conversion situation of all Christians.

As a remedy, God transferred this curse from humanity to a substitutionary victim, Christ. The consequence of this action for Christ is set forth in Paul's startling statement 'Christ *became a curse* (γενόμενος κατάρα) in our place.' This statement represents Paul's own formulation as a preface to Deut. 21.23.[56] As in the case of 2 Cor. 5.21, this is another example of Paul's use of metonymy, the use of an abstract term for one which is more concrete.[57] Paul signals to the reader that he is using this rhetorical device in Gal. 3.13 by complementing the abstract term 'curse' (κατάρα) with the adjective 'cursed' (ἐπικατάρατος). Moreover, the absence of an accompanying article with the term 'curse' suggests that a category of quality is intended.[58] These grammatical features indicate that the statement, 'Christ became a curse' is an emphatic way of saying 'Christ became the object of a curse'. In the words of Marie-Joseph Lagrange, Christ is 'the one upon whom the curse is discharged'.[59] Joseph Lightfoot's explanation is more detailed:

> The expression is to be explained...by the religious conception which it involves. The victim is regarded as bearing the sins of those for whom atonement is made. The curse is transferred from them to it. It becomes in a certain sense the impersonation of the sin and of the curse. This idea is very prominent in the scapegoat.[60]

---

56.   Koch, *Die Schrift*, p. 124, n. 17; Luz, *Geschichtsverständnis*, p. 152 A 66; contra G. Jeremias, *Der Lehrer der Gerechtigkeit* (Göttingen: Vandenhoeck & Ruprecht, 1963), p. 134.

57.   Meyer, *Galatians*, p. 153; Bengel, *Gnomen*, 2.355; Ellicott, *Galatians*, p. 74; Lagrange, *Galates*, p. 71; F. Büchsel, κατάρα, *TDNT*, I, esp. p. 450; Bligh, *Galatians in Greek*, p. 138. This same expression (γίνομαι + κατάρα) occurs in the Protoevangelium of James where Anna laments her barrenness in an impassioned prayer to God: 'I have become a curse in the opinion of the Israelites' (κατάρα ἐγενήθην ἐγω ἐνώπιον τῶν υἱῶν Ἰσράηλ (C. Tischendorf, 'Protoevangelium of James', in *Evangelia Apocrypha* [Hildesheim: Georg Olms, 1876], p. 3).

58.   Meyer, *Galatians*, p. 153.

59.   Lagrange, *Galates*, p. 72.

60.   Lightfoot, *Galatians*, p. 139.

The use of the abstract for the concrete describes Christ's resultant state in the strongest possible terms. The discharge of the curse is absolute and irrevocable with the result that Christ physically embodies the curse, or as Lagrange concludes, 'Christ became a curse personified'.[61] The Didache seems either to allude to Gal 3.13 or express this same notion: 'But they that endure in their faith shall be saved by him [Christ], the Curse [σωθήσονται ὑπ' αὐτοῦ τοῦ καταθέματος]' (Did. 16.5).

The curse borne by Christ (3.13) is the same curse previously borne by Christians before their baptism, and even now by the Galatian compromisers and their followers. A review of biblical texts makes it clear that being cursed is often accompanied by social rejection and divine excommunication.[62] Likewise, the state of cursedness resulting from observance of the law implies expulsion from the Christian community (cf. Gal. 1.8; 1 Cor. 16.22; 2 Cor. 5.4-5) and expulsion from Christ's new creation characterized by the reception of God's blessing and Spirit (Gal. 3.14; cf. Rom. 9.3). It is this same expulsion which is suffered by Christ upon bearing the curse. The imposition of a curse established an unbreachable separation between Christ and the now redeemed Christians. No choice remained but to remove the danger by executing him thereby making the transfer irrevocable.

As in the case of 2 Cor. 5.21, Paul gives no hint of Christ's resurrection or glorious return in this passage. Paul's use of the resurrection paradigm and apotropaeic paradigm are localized in his theology. Just as the notion of Christ the 'first Adam' does not cohere with the image of Christ 'the paschal lamb', so also the theology of Christ the Cursed Victim is independent of his concept of Christ the 'resurrection one'.

---

61. Lagrange, *Galates*, p. 72.

62. After Adam and Eve were cursed they were driven out of the garden and armed cherubim were stationed at the entrance to prevent their return (Gen. 3.16-19, 23-24). After the cursing of Cain, God banished him as a fugitive. Cain laments: 'Behold you have driven me this day away from the ground; and from your face I shall be hidden; and I shall be a fugitive and a wanderer on the earth' (Gen. 4.14). Simeon and Levi are cursed and then scattered in Israel (Gen. 49.7). According to Deut. 29.18 the Lord brought curses upon those who forsook the law and he 'uprooted them from their land…and cast them into another land' (Deut. 29.25, 27-28). The prophet Jeremiah warns: 'Cursed is the man who trusts in man…whose heart turns away from the Lord…He shall dwell in the parched places of the wilderness, in an uninhabited salt land' (Jer. 17.5-6).

Christ's Substitutionary Role

As was the case in 2 Cor. 5.21, Christ's role in this process is succinctly defined by the prepositional phrase ὑπὲρ ἡμῶν Here again, the phrase is used in a substitutionary sense: 'Christ became a curse *in our place* (ὑπὲρ ἡμῶν).'[63] In the words of Dietrich-Alex Koch,

> the curse of the law does not apply 'to us' anymore, since it fell on Christ in its full force; and Paul feels compelled to assume that Christ himself became the 'curse' (ὑπὲρ ἡμῶν)—namely by his curse-laden death.[64]

Criticism of this substitutionary interpretation, though more widely argued in the nineteenth century,[65] has been virtually abandoned.[66] In the controversy of the nineteenth century, it was not so much the semantic features of the text as the ongoing theological (Protestant/Catholic) debate which generated the controversy.[67] A.T. Robertson's

---

63. In the second century CE, Justin Martyr interpreted Gal. 3.13 precisely as a substitutionary transference saying that 'the Father of the universe purposed that His own Christ should receive on himself the curses of all, *in the place of men of every race'* (*Dial.* 95.2) (my emphasis).

64. Koch, *Die Schrift*, p. 124.

65. Substitutionary meaning was denied by Johann F. von Flatt (1828), Leopold I. Rückert (1833), Johann C.K. von Hoffmann (1863), Franz X. Reithmayr (1865) and H.A.W. Meyer (1884).

66. However, I have found only one twentieth-century scholar, Ernest de Witt Burton, who has adopted this position. He offers no arguments against a substitutionary interpretation. He only argues in favour of a beneficiary usage, meaning 'to accomplish something for someone', by analogy with Gal. 1.4 (E. de Witt Burton, *A Critical and Exegetical Commentary on the Epistle to the Galatians* [Edinburgh: T. & T. Clark, 1921], pp. 12, 172). Modern proponents of the substitutionary interpretation include: P. Bonnard, *L'Epître de Saint Paul aux Galates* (CNT, 9; Neuchatel: Neuchatel & Niestlé, nd), p. 69; C.K. Barrett, *Freedom and Obligation: A Study of the Epistle to the Corinthians* (HNTC; New York: Harper & Row, 1973), p. 30; J. Bligh, *Galatians in Greek: A Structural Analysis of St Paul's Epistle to the Galatians* (Detroit: University of Detroit Press, 1966), p. 138; Lagrange, *Galates*, p. 72; Mussner, *Galaterbrief*, p. 232; C.B. Cousar, *Galatians* (Atlanta: John Knox Press, 1982), p. 72; J.A. Fitzmyer, 'The Letter to the Galatians', in *JBC*, pp. 236-46, esp. p. 242; D. Guthrie, *Galatians* (NCB; London: Nelson, 1969), p. 103; W. Neil *The Letter of Paul to the Galatians* (Cambridge: Cambridge University Press, 1967), p. 54; H. Riesenfeld, ὑπέρ, *TDNT*, VIII, pp. 507-16, esp. p. 509; Joachim Jeremias says that it was clear to Paul that 'Jesus...died on the Cross as a substitute for the sins of the many' (J. Jeremias, 'The Key to Pauline Theology', *ExpTim* 76 [1964], pp. 27-30, esp. p. 29).

67. Many other scholars from John Calvin onwards have adopted the *substitu-*

explanation of this substitutionary usage is most instructive and worthy of being quoted *in extenso*:[68]

> There are a few other passages where ὑπέρ has the resultant notion of 'instead' and only violence to the context can get rid of it. One of these is Gal. 3.13. In v. 10, Paul has said that those under the law were under a curse (ὑπὸ κατάραν). In v. 13 he carries on the same image. Christ brought us 'out from under' the curse (ἐκ τῆς κατάρας τοῦ νόμου) of the law by becoming a curse 'over us' (γενόμενος ὑπὲρ ἡμῶν κατάρα). In a word, we were *under* the curse; Christ took the curse on himself and thus *over* us (between the suspended curse and us) and thus rescued us *out from under* the curse. We went free while he was considered accursed (v. 13).

The substitutionary interpretation is confirmed by the verb ἐξαγοράζω which, in the context of Gal. 3.13 means the handing over of Christ's life as a payment *in exchange for* the lives of others. This exceedingly rare verb occurs only twice in connection with Christ in the New Testament (Gal. 3.13; 4.5). It is attested only once in the Septuagint (Dan. 2.8), and only rarely attested in other Greek literature.

Excursus on the Meaning of ἐξαγοράζω
The translation of this verb must be carefully argued since the question has been the subject of some debate. Before assigning a meaning to this rare compound verb, it is useful to observe that the unprefixed form ἀγοράζειν (derived from ἀγορά) means literally 'to buy' in a commercial sense (e.g., Rev. 3.18; Isa. 55.1). This is a common verb used for all types of purchases including the purchase of slaves.[69] Generally speaking, it describes a commercial transaction whereby ownership is transferred from one person to another. Paul uses this same verb when

---

tionary interpretation. Joseph Lightfoot takes pains to underline *both* the substitutionary and the beneficiary meaning: 'Christ has ransomed us from this curse pronounced by the law, Himself *taking our place* and becoming a curse *for our sakes* (Lightfoot, *Galatians*, p. 139).' B. F. Westcott remarks: 'I cannot see how we can extrude from the passage before us, the thought of vicarious suffering. "Christ redeems" us by "becoming a curse"—that is by taking on Himself the penalty involved in the failure to achieve the claims of God's Holiness (Westcott, *St Paul and Justification*, p. 54); also: Ellicott, *Galatians*, p. 74).

68. Robertson, *Grammar*, p. 631; also: Zerwick, *Biblical Greek*, p. 30, sect. 91.

69. Purchase of slaves: *OGIS* 338.23 (133 BCE); *P.Oxy.* VIII, 1149.5 (second century CE); cf. W. Elert, 'Redemptio ab hostibus', *TLZ* 72/5 (1947), pp. 265-70, esp. p. 267.

he asserts that Christians are slaves of the world who have been 'bought' (ἠγοράσθητε) at a 'price' (τιμή) and therefore belong to Christ (1 Cor. 7.23; 6.20).

However, Paul does not employ this verb with the same semantic rigor which some scholars might presume since he does not make a distinction between 'buying *to own*' and 'buying *to set free*'. In other words, he does not distinguish between purchasing and manumitting/redeeming. This fact is partially to be explained by Paul's intentional paradox that the slave of Christ is also free (1 Cor. 7.22). Moreover, it should also be added that even in the daily life of the Hellenistic people, the distinction between purchasing and redeeming slaves was equally vague. When owners permitted their slaves to purchase their own freedom, they usually did so on the condition that they remained bound to their owner by a special contract (παραμονή) whereby they would remain under obligation to work for the same master, although now for pay.[70]

It is the compound form, ἐξαγοράζειν which occurs in Gal. 3.13 (cf. 4.5). The first general entry in the Greek lexica for this verb is always 'to buy'.[71] Most lexica also include the second meaning 'to redeem', referring the manumission of slaves.[72] All Greek lexica cite the same four texts in support of the translation 'to redeem': Gal. 3.13; 4.5; Diodorus 15.7.1; 36.2.2. Putting aside the two Galatian passages for a moment, a close examination of the text of Diodorus reveals this translation to be

---

70. S. Treggiari, *Roman Freedmen during the Late Republic* (Oxford: Clarendon Press, 1969), p. 16.

71. The two texts always cited are Polybius 3.42.2 ('to buy from') and Plutarch, *Crassus* 2.5 ('to buy up'); LSJ also cites the geographer Dicaearchus 1.22.

72. Including F.L.C.F. Passow, *Wörterbuch der griechischen Sprache* (Göttingen: Vandenhoeck & Ruprecht, 1874); W. Pape, *Wörterbuch der griechischen Eigennamen* (2 vols.; Braunschweig: F. Vieweg, 1884); H. Cremer, *Biblico-Theological Lexicon of New Testament Greek* (trans. W. Urwick; Edinburgh: T. & T. Clark, 1880); W. Bauer, *Griechisch–Deutsches Wörterbuch zu den Schriften des Neuen Testaments* (Giessen: Töpelmann, 1928); BAGD; F. Zorell, *Lexicon Graecum Novi Testamenti* (Rome: Pontificium Institutum Biblicum, 1931); LSJ; Friedrich Büchsel is so convinced by this apparent distinction between ἀγοράζειν ('to buy') and ἐξαγοράζειν ('to redeem') that he makes no mention of the fact that ἐξαγοράζειν can also mean 'to buy', nor does he mention the hapax occurrence of ἐξαγοράζειν in the Septuagint (Dan. 2.8) which also concerns 'buying' (F. Büchsel, ἀγοράζειν, ἐξαγοράζειν, *TDNT*, I, pp. 124-27, esp. p. 126).

false.[73] The verb simply means 'to purchase'.

Taking a different approach, Adolf Deissmann has argued in favour of the translation of ἐξαγοράζειν as 'to redeem' on the basis of the custom of sacral manumission practised by the priests of Apollo in Delphi. He thinks that this practice has strongly influenced Paul's use of ἐξαγοράζειν. He proposes that in Gal. 3.13 Paul is alluding to the Delphic practice in which a deity would redeem a slave in order to describe 'a single summary act performed [by Christ] once and for all in the past [for Christians]'.[74] Deissmann's views go far beyond the

---

73. In the first text (Diod. 15.7.1), a nobleman named Dionysios becomes so offended by the statements of Plato that he sells him in the slave market for twenty minas. The sale of Plato may be explained by analogy with Roman law, where a Roman citizen could be reduced to slavery if convicted of certain crimes (J. Crook, *Law and Life of Rome* [New York: Cornell University Press, 1967], pp. 272-73). Plato's friends purchased (ἐξηγόρασαν) him and he then returned to Greece as a freeman. Stanislaus Lyonnet argues against translating ἐξαγοράζειν as 'to redeem', objecting that this passage does not refer to a 'redemption' because it is not a slave who is being redeemed, but a freeman who regains his freedom (S. Lyonnet, 'L'emploi paulinien de ἐξαγοράζω au sens de 'redimere' est-il attesté dans la littérature gréque?', *Bib* 42 [1961], pp. 85-89, esp. p. 87). In the second instance, a Roman knight falls in love with a beautiful servant girl who belonged to another master (Diod. 36.2.2). The text reads 'He purchased her (ἐξηγόρασεν αὐτήν) for seven Attic talents.' Lyonnet again argues that the verb simply means 'to buy' in the common commercial sense (Lyonnet, 'L'emploi paulinien de ἐξαγοράζω', p. 87). Similarly Henri Estienne concludes 'ἐξαγοράζειν pro simplici ἀγοράζειν' (H. Estienne, *Thesauros tes hellenikes glosses: Thesaurus graecae lingae* [3 vols.; Paris: A.F. Didot, 1865], ἐξαγοράζειν).

74. Deissmann, *Light*, pp. 321-30, esp. p. 330. Owners of slaves followed a regular policy of manumitting them as a reward for hard work; all domestic slaves could reasonably expect to be manumitted after ten to twenty years (S.S. Bartchy, ΜΑΛΛΟΝ ΧΡΗΣΑΙ: *First-Century Slavery and the Interpretation of 1 Corinthians 7.21* [SBLDS, 11; Missoula, MT: Scholars Press, 1973], p. 83, n. 308). Manumission served the owner's self-interest because the slaves would work more efficiently in anticipation of this reward (A.M. Duff, *Freedmen in the Early Roman Empire* [Cambridge: W. Heffer, 2nd edn, 1958], p. 14). More than one thousand manumission records have survived from Delphi dating from 200 BCE to 74 CE. In Delphi, the typical legal manumission document records the name of the owner (nominative) (as vendor), the name of Apollo (dative) (the purchaser) and the formula, πρᾶσις ἐπ' ἐλευθερία ('sale for freedom') with the name of the slave. In Deissmann's most famous inscription (dating 200–199 BCE), it is not the vendor who is mentioned in the nominative case but the purchaser, the god Apollo, who 'buys' a slave for freedom: 'The Pythian Apollo bought (ἐπίατο) from Sosibios of Amphissa, freedom (ἐπ' ἐλευθερίαι), a woman by the name of Nicaia, of Roman nationality, for the price of

available evidence. Though there are common features between the Delphic practice of manumission and Paul's presentation of redemption, the contrasts are more striking than the similarities. First, the verb used in the Delphic inscriptions for 'buying' is πρίασθαι ('to buy'). This term is never used in the New Testament. By contrast, neither ἐξαγοράζω nor ἀγοράζω are ever used in connection with sacral manumission in the New Testament or in any Greek inscription or writing.[75] Secondly, the phrase ἐπ' ἐλευθερίᾳ ('[purchased] for freedom') is never used by Paul in connection with either ἐξαγοράζω or ἀγοράζω.[76] Thirdly, whereas the noun σῶμα is always used at Delphi to mean 'a person in slavery', Paul never uses this term in this way. Lastly, examples of manumission formulae at Delphi which describe the god as the buyer (in nominative case) are rare. This form is not found in any non-Delphic first-century inscriptions. The usual formula is an '*owner* sells "so-and-so" *to* Apollo'.[77]

To sum up. The verb ἐξαγοράζειν does not specifically allude to the sacral manumission practiced at Delphi, nor is it a technical term for manumission in general. It simply means 'to buy', without specifying the intent of the author, whether it be 'buying to own', or 'buying to set free'. In the context of Gal. 3.13, it is used in the latter sense. Paul's description of unredeemed humanity presupposes a state of being enslaved under the elemental principles of the old creation: 'We [Christians] were slaves to the elemental cosmic spirits of the universe' (Gal. 4.3, cf. 4.7-9, 24-25; 5.1; 2.4-5). Indeed, in Paul's mind, living under the law (Gal. 4.5)

three and a half silver minas' (*Light*, p. 323; *SIG³* no. 845). Though Apollo mediated the ransom, it was the slave Nicaia who actually bought her own freedom by depositing the money with the temple priests. The money was provided by the slave out of her own savings (W.L. Westermann, *The Slave Systems of Greek and Roman Antiquity* [Philadelphia: American Philosophical Society, 1955], p. 122; R. Taubenschlag, *The Law of Greco-Roman Egypt in the Light of the Papyri [332 BC–AD 640]* [rev. enlarged; Warsaw: Panstwowe Wydawnictwo Naukowe, 2nd edn, 1955], pp. 87-89).

75. In his exhaustive study on the subject, Elpidius Pax says that he has never found either of these two verbs used in the context of sacral manumission (in Lyonnet, 'L'emploi paulinien de ἐξαγοράζω', p. 89, n. 1; Bartchy, ΜΑΛΛΟΝ ΧΡΗΣΑΙ, p. 124; cf. Elert, 'Redemptio ab hostibus', p. 267).

76. Bartchy, ΜΑΛΛΟΝ ΧΡΗΣΑΙ, p. 124.

77. Cf. F. Bömer, *Untersuchungen über die Religion der Sklaven in Griechenland und Rom* (AAWLMG; Wiesbaden: Steiner, 1957-1963), II, pp. 101-106, 134-137, 140; R. Dareste, B. Hausoullier and T. Reinach (eds.), *Recueil des inscriptions juridiques greques* (2 vols.; Rome: L'Erma di Bretscheider, 1892–1965), II, p. 253.

was also a form of slavery since it was simply another way of being a slave to the elemental cosmic principles. By being *purchased* from this slavery to the law, Christians are likewise freed from the curse which the law entails.

This interpretation accords with the substitutionary use of ὑπὲρ ἡμῶν. Commercial exchanges are substitutionary in nature since the value of the payment is commensurate with the value of the goods purchased. In other words, money is rendered as a substitute for the goods. Thus, Gal. 3.13 states that Christ offered his own life as payment for (in exchange for) the lives of Christians who were slaves to the law. This commercial metaphor explains how Christians are freed from the curse at the cost of Christ's life which was given in exchange.

Paul's Application of Deuteronomy 21.22-23 to the Crucifixion of Jesus

> [22]And if a man has committed a crime punishable by death and he is put to death, and you *hang him on a tree*, [23]his body shall not remain all night upon the tree, but you shall bury him the same day; for a hanged man is accursed by Elohim (Deut. 21.22-23).

In Deut. 21.22, the meaning of the verb 'to hang' (*tâwuy*) is ambiguous. On the one hand, it could refer to execution by 'hanging' on the gallows. According to this interpretation the phrase 'he is put to death, and you hang him on a tree' refers to a single event: the criminal is put to death by hanging him on the gallows ('tree'). On the other hand, the verb 'to hang' may refer to the public exhibition of a corpse by hanging it on a wooden pole *after* execution. In other words, the verse implies a sequence: first, the criminal is executed; secondly, his corpse is exposed publicly 'on a tree'. An examination of the use of the verb 'to hang' (*tâwuy*) elsewhere in the Hebrew Bible suggests that the latter interpretation is the correct one.[78]

---

78. The reference to 'hanging' in the story of the execution of the Pharaoh's chief baker seems ambiguous until one recognizes the pun 'lifted up the head' which is repeated three times (Gen. 40.13, 19, 20). This refers to their execution by decapitation: 'within three days Pharaoh will lift up your head from you [decapitate the baker], and [after beheading you he will] hang you [gibbet your corpse] on a tree; and the birds will eat your flesh'. Though the example in 2 Sam. 21.12 is ambiguous, the passage does seems to separate the events of execution (v. 9) and act of hanging (v. 12), and emphasize the prolonged public exposure (cf. 2 Sam. 21.9-10). Similarly, the evidence in Josh. 10.26, 8.29 and 2 Sam. 4.12 seems to indicate the exposure of corpses by hanging on an '*êts* ('pole').

Deuteronomy 21.22-23 concerns the rules governing the disposal of a corpse after its public exhibition.[79] According to the Jewish law, all corpses were impure. A corpse which was left hanging for decomposition was thought to pollute the land.[80] It is for this reason that the gibbeted corpses of the king of Ai (Josh. 8.29) and the five Canaanite kings (Josh. 10.27) were taken down the same day. Thus, Deut. 21.23 is an explanation for why a gibbeted body should be taken down before nightfall. Rabbinic sources in general agree with this interpretation of Deut. 21.22-23.[81]

However, other Jewish sources interpret the passage differently. For example, the Temple Scroll interprets Deut. 21.23 to mean execution by gallows. This is evident by the change in the word order of the Masoretic text from 'and he is put to death and you hang him on a tree' to 'and you shall hang him on the tree, and he shall die'. Yigael Yadin thinks that the author of the Temple Scroll purposely altered the Masoretic text in order to 'establish the plain meaning of the text [Deut. 21.23], namely that *tâwuy* certainly indicates the 'means of execution' in order to oppose the prevalent misinterpretation of Deut. 21.23 by the tannaitic schools.[82] Similarly, the Targum to Ruth describes four methods of carrying out juridical execution (1.17), including 'strangulation' which in rabbinic terminology is 'hanging on a tree'. J. Heinemann argues that this tradition preserves an ancient pre-Tannaitic tradition whose traces have all but disappeared from halakic literature. He thinks that this tradition proves that the Jews had a difference of opinion over the plain

---

79. Lightfoot, *Galatians*, p. 154; Lagrange, *Galates*, p. 73; Bruce, *Galatians*, pp. 164-65; Bligh *Galatians: A Discussion*, p. 268.

80. The land on which the Israelites lived had to be maintained in a ritually holy state for it was the abiding place of the temple of YHWH (cf. Hos. 5.3; Deut. 23.14).

81. E.g. *m. Sanh.* 6.4. The Sifre on Deuteronomy denounces the practice of hanging a man while still alive, basing its position on the word order of the Hebrew text of Deut. 21.23: 'Might it be interpreted that he is to be hanged alive, as is done by the state? Therefore Scripture says: "and he is put to death, and you hang him on a tree"' (R. Hammer [trans.], *Sifre: A Tannaitic Commentary on the Book of Deutermonomy* [New Haven: Yale University Press, 1986], *s.* 232). The argument is spelled out in greater detail in the *b. Sanh.* 46b (I. Epstein, *Babylonian Talmud* [London: Soncino Press, 1935–1952], LI, 305).

82. Y. Yadin, *The Temple Scroll* (2 vols.; Jerusalem: Ben Zvi, 1983), I, pp. 374-75. Similarly, the Syriac midrash on Deut. 21.23 reads: 'He is hanged on a tree and put to death' (*Temple Scroll*, I, p. 375).

meaning of Deut. 21.23.[83] Similarly, S. Lieberman observes that the plain meaning of Deut. 21.23 as understood by ha-Neziv was that the phrase 'you shall hang him on a tree' was a conditional statement, not an additional injunction.[84] Thus, even though Deut. 21.22-23 did not originally concern a form a execution, many post-biblical Jewish writers did interpret the text in this way, though never in terms of crucifixion as Paul did.[85]

The following verse, Deut. 21.23, also poses exegetical problems. The Masoretic text of Deut. 21.23 contains the shortest and most difficult version to interpret: כי־קללת אלהים תלוי. On the one hand, 'Elohim' can be taken as the subject of the action (subjective genitive) meaning 'he that

83. J. Heinemann, *Tarbits* 38 (1969), p. 296 (Hebrew) (ET = Y. Yadin, *Temple Scroll*, I, p. 376).

84. S. Lieberman, private correspondance to Y. Yadin (published in *Temple Scroll*, I, p. 377). In addition to the above evidence there are also a number of Jewish examples of execution by hanging which were never thought to contradict the plain meaning of Deut. 21.23. *4QpNah* recounts Alexander Janneus' order to 'hang alive' those Pharisees who encouraged Demetrius 3 to invade Israel. The text justifies the means of the execution, claiming that Janneus acted in accordance with the law of Moses. The passage speaks of the Lion 'who hangs men alive [on the tree as this is the law] in Israel as of old since the hanged one is called "alive" on the tree' (*4QpNah*. 1.7-8; Y. Yadin, 'Pesher Nahum [4QpNah] Reconsidered', *IEJ* 21 [1971], pp. 1-12, esp. pp. 7-8; J.M. Baumgarten, 'Does *tlh* in the Temple Scroll Refer to Crucifixion?', *JBL* 91 [1972], pp. 472-81; M. Hengel, 'Mors Turpissima Crucis' [*Rechtfertigung: Festschrift für Ernst Käsemann zum 70*; Göttingen: Vandenhoeck & Ruprecht, 1976], pp. 125-84). There is also a historical account of the hanging on the gallows of eighty witches in one day in Ashkelon by Simeon ben Shetah (a contemporary of Alexander Jannaeus). The testimony shows that some people did not consider that execution by hanging contradicted the intent of Deut. 21.23 (*b. Sanh.* 45b [51, 300]; *j. Hag.* 2.2; *Sanh.* 6.3). When the Sages describe the methods of punishment in hell, they described a great variety of strange (e.g., hanging by tongues) and sundry methods of hanging alive (L. Ginzberg, 'Sin and Its Punishment: A Study in Jewish and Christian Visions of Hell' [*Louis Ginzberg Jubilee Volume*, Hebrew Section; New York: Jewish Publication Society, 1946], pp. 249-70 [ET = Yadin, *Temple Scroll*, I, p. 377]).

85. It is unlikely that *tlh* in *11QTemple* 64.12 refers to death by crucifixion. The execution by *tlyyh* described in *11QTemple* 64.12 does not refer to crucifixion because if it did, the biblical rule of burial before sundown would necessitate some extraneous means of hastening death. When the sectarians refer to crucifixion as in *4QpNah* 1.6-8, they use the explicit phrase, *ytlh 'nsym hyym* and describe the condemned as *tlwy hy 'l h's* (Baumgarten, '*tlh* in the Temple Scroll', pp. 472-81; cf. Yadin, 'Pesher Nahum', pp. 1-12); cf. Koch, *Die Schrift*, p. 124, n. 18.

is hanged is cursed by Elohim'. Alternatively, 'Elohim' can be taken as the object of the action (objective genitive), meaning 'he that is hanged is an insult/reproach to Elohim'.[86] However, my task is simplified by the fact that the Septuagint, and those who used it including Christians, interpreted the text as a subjective genitive, meaning, 'a corpse hanged on a tree is cursed by God'.[87]

In his citation of Deut. 21.23, Paul introduced two major changes to the text of the Septuagint. First, Paul replaces the participle (κεκατηραμένος) with the adjective 'accursed' (ἐπικατάρατος). Secondly, he omits the phrase 'by God' (ὑπὸ θεοῦ). Both deviations have exegetical significances which aid in the reconstruction of Paul's overall argument:

Deuteronomy 21.23 (LXX)
κεκατηραμένος ὑπὸ θεοῦ πᾶς κρεμάμενος ἐπὶ ξύλου.

Galatians 3.13
ἐπικατάρατος [...] πᾶς ὁ κρεμάμενος ἐπὶ ξύλου.

The Addition of the Adjective 'Accursed'
The term 'accursed' (ἐπικατάρατος) occurs naturally in Paul's citation of Deut. 27.26 (Gal. 3.10), but unexpectedly in his citation of Deut. 21.23 (Gal. 3.13) since the term does not occur in the Septuagintal version. While it is possible that Paul may have used a different Greek recension, this hypothesis is unlikely. Koch states that there is insufficient evidence to support the assumption of a pre-Pauline text development. Only in citations of Deut. 21.23 by the Church Fathers is the term ἐπικατάρατος attested. The earliest witness being Justin (*Dial.* 96.1) who was no doubt influenced by Paul's text. Nor can one argue that Paul relied on the Hebrew text as did Alexandrinus (A) and Tbilisi (θ)

---

86. There is also a third possibility: 'Elohim' may be being used as an intensive genitive to mean 'he that is hanged is a shocking disgrace (to the land)'. For the intensive interpretation see: Zorell, *Lexicon Hebraicum*, p. 54, col. 2, II, 1; Bligh, *Galatians: A Discussion*, p. 268).

87. The LXX emphasizes the gravity and universality of the ordinances with the addition of πᾶς· *'every'* man' who is hanged on a tree is cursed. Philo reproduces the text of the LXX almost exactly (κεκατηραμένον ὑπὸ θεοῦ τὸν κρεμάμενον ἐπὶ ξύλον, *Poster.* 26); Justin reproduces Paul's text (*Dial.* 96.1-2). The Temple Scroll (11QTemple 64.12) reads, 'Those who are hanged upon the tree are accursed by God and men' (Yadin, *Temple Scroll*, I, p. 375).

which read κατάρα θεοῦ κρεμάμενος[88] since in these versions, πᾶς and ἐπὶ ξύλου (which are vital to Paul's quotation) are missing.[89]

It can hardly be coincidental that the only other occurrence of ἐπικατάρατος in the whole of the New Testament is in Gal. 3.10, three verses prior to its unexpected appearance in Gal. 3.13.[90] Clearly, Paul has inserted ἐπικατάρατος into his quotation of Deut. 21.23 from Deut. 27.26.

Why did Paul alter the text of the Septuagint by inserting 'accursed' (ἐπικατάρατος)?[91] The answer appears to be that the repetition of this term in v. 13 serves to create a verbal parallelism between the curse mentioned in v. 10 and the second curse in v. 13. In this way, Paul is able to make a clear connection between the curse of the transgressors (v. 10) and the curse borne by Christ (v. 13).[92] This parallelism reinforces Paul's assertion that the two curses are in fact one, as explained by Koch:

> Paul wants to prove that the κατάρα, which applied to all according to Paul, ὅσοι ἐξ ἔργων νόμου εἰσίν (3.10a), is abolished by Christ for 'us'. Paul proves the cursing character of the law with Deut. 27.26 (3.10b), and

---

88. Cf. H. Vollmer, *Die alttestamentlichen Citate bei Paulus* (Leipzig: Metzger & Wittig, 1869), p. 29).

89. Koch, *Die Schrift*, p. 166.

90. Moreover, Philo's text includes this term (*Poster. C.* p. 26).

91. In classical Greek, the more primitive and simpler forms ἀρατός, ἐπάρατος and κατάρατος are used instead of ἐπικατάρατος. However, this is no basis to conclude that ἐπικατάρατος has a distinctive technical sense over and against its classical cognates. The double suffix on this term is merely a sign of later *koine* Greek, not an indication of a technical term. The genesis of this doubly-compounded form (ἐπί + κατά + ἀρατός) is not significant since an almost endless number of double and even triple compounds evolved throughout the Hellenistic period. Though we have insufficient data to determine when the transition from the classical cognates to ἐπικατάρατος may have occurred, there are no philological grounds for distinguishing it from its parent cognates (Deissmann, *Light*, p. 96). The term occurs in the LXX (42 times), in Jewish and Christian writings (Philo, *Leg. All.*, 3.111, 113; *1 En.* 102.3; Gal. 3.10, 13) and in inscriptions. Adolf Deissmann published two inscriptions which employ the term ἐπικατάρατος. An inscription from Euboea (second century CE) is found on a tomb monument (*SIG*³ 891). This inscription cannot be Jewish or Christian for it begins by naming the goddesses Erinyes, Charis and Hygeia. The second inscription (GIBM 918.6) comes from Halicarnassus (second-third century CE).

92. Vollmer, *Die alttestamentlichen Citate*, p. 29; Lagrange, *Galates*, p. 72; Bruce, *Galatians*, p. 165; G. Bertram, 'κρεμάννυμι', *TDNT*, II, pp. 917-19; Str.-B. III.544-45.

the removal of the content of the curse by Christ with Deut. 21.23 (3.13b).
Paul emphasises the correlation of the content of the two quotations by
employing a linguistic adjustment of Deut. 21.23 and Deut. 27.26. The
identity of the curse that exists in the law as such, the curse that afflicted
itself on Jesus Christ, is well expressed in the language used.[93]

There may have been a second motivation for Paul's insertion of this
term. The Epistle of Barnabas quotes an unidentified source in which the
scapegoat is called ἐπικατάρατος three times (*Barn.* 7.7, 9). Paul's
inclusion of this term in Gal. 3.13 may also be an allusion to the scapegoat image, though this point should not be pressed.

Omission of the Prepositional Phrase 'by God' (ὑπὸ θεοῦ)
The Septuagintal version of Deut. 21.23 reads: 'Cursed *by God* is
everyone who hangs on a tree'. In Gal. 3.13, the text has been changed
by the omission of the words 'by God' such that it now reads 'Cursed is
everyone who hangs on a tree'. Paul may have omitted these words
deliberately or inadvertently due to a lapse of memory. The resolution of
this matter revolves around a theological question: did Paul intend to
dissociate God from Christ's cursed condition?

It is interesting to note that Tertullian believed Gal. 3.13 to preserve
the original text of Deut. 21.23. He accused the Jews of intentionally
falsifying the Greek text, alleging an anti-Christian interest was responsible for the insertion of the name of God into the Septuagint ('cursed
by God').[94] This fact underlines the importance which early Christians
laid upon each individual word.

Koch demonstrates that the omission of ὑπὸ θεοῦ cannot be traced
back to Jewish interpretations of the text. In the Temple Scroll (Deut.
21.23), the curse belongs to God and his people who curse those who
are executed. *m. Sanh* 6.6 does not interpret Deut. 21.23 as a statement
about God's curse on someone, but as a curse *on God* by an executed
person: the criminal is hung up after his execution because he has cursed
Elohim.[95]

Some scholars argue that Paul purposely omitted 'by God' (ὑπὸ θεοῦ)
in order to suggest that Christ became accursed only in appearance, but
not in reality (i.e. not really 'by God'). According to this argument,
Christ's death by 'hanging on a tree' only has the *appearance* of being

93.   Koch, *Die Schrift*, p. 166.
94.   Tertullian, *Adv. Jud.*, ch. 10.
95.   Koch, *Die Schrift*, p. 125.

accursed though in reality he was not cursed at all.[96]

Taking the opposing position, H.A.W. Meyer argues that Paul intends to say that Christ truly became accursed by taking upon himself the curse of humanity. He explains the omission as an inadvertent error, a result of Paul's quoting from free recollection. From this point of view, the omission is incidental since for Paul, the point of the passage was the *fact* of Christ's cursedness, not the *agency* of transfer.[97]

A resolution to this question is to be found in 2 Cor. 5.21 and Rom. 8.3 which present a paradigm which is very similar to that of Gal. 3.13. The former clearly states that '*God made* Christ to be sin', or in other words, Christ was made to be sin *by God*. Romans 8.3 states that *God sent* his Son 'in the visible appearance of sinful flesh'. It is improbable that Paul should make such explicit statements in 2 Cor. 5.21 and Rom. 8.3 and then imply the opposite in Gal. 3.13. Moreover, since the passive voice in Gal. 3.13 implied for Paul and his readers divine agency, there is within this verse the idea that God was active in transferring the curse from Christians to Christ.

This does not, however, imply that it was *God's* curse. Indeed, the sense of the passage is that the curse originated from the law, not from God. Thus, Paul deliberately omitted 'by God' in order to stress that the curse was initiated by the law. In the words of Koch:

> Without any interpreting clarification it would have been an impossible statement for Paul to say that Christ's crucifixion represents a curse on Christ by God. Only by the omission of ὑπὸ θεοῦ could Deut. 21.23 become applicable in a Christian way for Paul. This new interpretation of the quote as a statement about the curse of the law (not: the curse of God)

---

96. John Bligh, for example, says that Paul only intends to say that Christ 'became accursed in the opinion of men' (Bligh, *Galatians: A Discussion*, p. 270). Similarly, Joseph Lightfoot argues that Christ 'was in no literal sense κατάρατος ὑπὸ θεοῦ and that Paul instinctively omits those words which do not strictly apply, and which, if added, would have required some qualification' (Lightfoot, *Galatians*, p. 141). This position is also held by: T. Zahn, *Der Brief an die Galater* (KNT, 9; Leipzig: Deichert, 3rd edn, 1922), pp. 156-57; F. Sieffert, *Der Brief an die Galater* (Göttingen: Vandenhoeck & Ruprecht, 9th edn, 1899), pp. 186-87; H. Schlier, *Der Brief an die Galater* (Göttingen: Vandenhoeck & Ruprecht, 14th edn, 1971), p. 138; J.C.K. von Hoffmann, *Der Brief Pauli an die Galater* (Nördlingen, 2nd edn, 1872). This position is summarized by one of its opponents, H.A.W. Meyer: 'the whole proof adduced would amount only to a semblance, and not to a reality' (*Galatians*, p. 155, n. 1).

97. Meyer, *Galatians*, pp. 153-54.

corresponds to the tendency of Gal. 3.19-20 to separate the law from God
and to assign to it a lower origin and therefore a lower rank of content,
since it was ordered by ἄγγελοι and delivered by a μεσίτης.[98]

Paul uses Deut. 21.23 to demonstrate how Christ could become subject
to the curse imposed by the law upon Christians.[99] According to H.D.
Betz, the quotation proves that 'a curse [on Christ] became effective
through the act of hanging on the cross'.[100] It was the crucifixion which
transferred the curse from Jews and Gentiles to Christ.[101] The main
difference between 2 Cor. 5.21 and Gal. 3.13 is that the former describes
the divine agency of the transfer (God), whereas the latter describes the
concrete means by which the transfer was achieved ('by hanging on a
tree').

Resultant State of Christians

Is it possible to state more precisely, from the point of view of Galatians,
who were the beneficiaries of Christ's action? When Paul tells the
Galatians that 'Christ redeemed *us* from the curse of the law' (3.13), to
whom does he refer? Does Paul intend to specify Jews alone, or Jews
and Gentiles?

The opinion of many scholars is that v. 13 is addressed to Jews alone.

98.   Koch, *Die Schrift*, p. 125; also Mussner, *Galaterbrief*, p. 233; cf. Burton,
Galatians, p. 174; Oepke, *Galater*, p. 107.

99.   Guthrie, *Galatians*, p. 103.

100. Betz, *Galatians*, 152; similarly, F. F. Bruce remarks:

> The curse which Christ "became" was his people's curse [borne in their pre-Christian
> life], as the death which he died was their death...Christ endured the curse on his
> people's behalf (by being "hanged on a tree") in order to redeem them from the curse
> pronounced on those who failed to keep the law [in their pre-conversion life]' (F.F.
> Bruce, *The Epistle of Paul to the Galatians: A Commentary on the Greek Text* [Exeter:
> Paternoster Press, 1982], p. 166, cf. p. 164)

101. Terence Donaldson adds that Christ's cursedness may also be a consequence
of his condemnation by the religious authorities:

> For Paul the case of Jesus of Nazareth corresponded precisely to the situation addressed
> by Deut. 21.22-23, except that in Jesus' case "hanging" was the form of execution
> rather than [a means] of publicizing the fact that the execution had been carried out by
> another means. As in Deuteronomy, the man in question had been judged by a Jewish
> court and found guilty of a crime punishable by death (cf. *b. Sanh.* 43)—perhaps even
> blasphemy (Mk 14.64). Paul could have believed that Jesus was under the curse pro-
> nounced by the Torah not because of the mere fact of crucifixion, but because the
> crucifixion was the result of the Sanhedrin's judgment against him' ('Zealot and
> Convert', p. 677).

The main argument in favour of this position is that Gentiles were not 'under the law,' and therefore cannot be redeemed from the curse of the law (v. 13).[102] In answer to this objection, I have already demonstrated that Paul's concept of 'law' in Galatians is much broader than the ordinances of the Torah. According to Paul, 'the law' is part of the 'elemental cosmic principles' (Gal. 3.19-25; 4.1-3, 8-10) which govern the old creation as a whole. In fact, he uses the phrase 'under the law' as a kind of convenient short-form to mean being enslaved by the old order. Walter Hansen demonstrates that Paul argues for the inclusion of the Gentiles among the faithful children of Abraham by dissociating the Abrahamic promise from the Mosaic law (Gal. 3.15-22).[103] According to Richard Hays 'Paul can treat Scripture as a word about Gentile Christians only because these Gentiles have become—in a remarkable metonymic transfer—Abraham's seed, heirs of God's word to Israel, as a result of God's act in Jesus Christ'.[104] Therefore, there is no reason to exclude the Gentiles in the application of this verse since, for Paul, there is no difference between being 'under the law' and being 'under the elemental cosmic principles'.

Galatians 3.14 describes the benefits which the Gentile and Jewish Galatian Christians will receive as a result of Christ becoming a curse, if they remain faithful to his gospel:

> …in order that (ἵνα) the blessing of Abraham might come to the Gentiles in Christ,
> in order that (ἵνα) we might receive the promise of the Spirit through faith.

Both clauses of this verse are introduced by ἵνα in order to signal to the reader that these benefits are contained within the purpose of v. 13. In other words, both of these benefits are contingent upon Christians being

102. Lietzmann, *Galater*, p. 19; Oepke, *Galater*, p. 57; G. Klein, *Rekonstruktion und Interpretation*, BEvT 50 (1969), pp. 207-208; K. Kertelge, 'Zur Deutung des Rechtfertigungsbegriffs im Galaterbrief', *BZ* 12 (1968), pp. 211-22, esp. p. 210; Luz, *Geschichtsverständnis*, pp. 152-53; Mussner, *Galaterbrief*, p. 233; Büchsel, ἐξαγοράζω, *TDNT*, I, p. 127; Büchsel, κατάρα, *TDNT*, I, p. 450; H. Riesenfeld, ὑπέρ, *TDNT*, VIII, p. 509; Bruce, *Galatians*, pp. 166-67).

103. G.W. Hansen, *Abraham in Galatians: Epistolary and Rhetorical Contexts* (JSNTSup, 29; Sheffield: JSOT Press, 1989), pp. 95-154.

104. Hays, *Echoes of Scripture*, p. 121; further, Hays remarks, 'Paul now construes that truth [of Deut. 21.23] in an ironic mode: by hanging upon the tree, Jesus became cursed in order that blessing might accrue to others. The eschatological *apokalypsis* of the cross has wrought an inversion in Paul's reading of the text' (Hays, *Echoes of Scripture*, p. 169).

freed from the curse of the law. People must be freed from the old order before receiving the benefits of the new.

Taken together, these two ἵνα ('in order that') clauses describe the final state of the Christians resulting from the transfer of their curse to Christ: first, they will be partakers of Abraham's blessing (cf. Gal. 3.8-9). Secondly, they will receive God's Spirit. The second ἵνα clause expresses 'coincidence of time' with the first clause.[105] God bestows his blessing and Spirit upon the Galatians in one gracious act.

The Sinful Christ: Romans 8.3

[25]So then, with my mind I am a slave to the law of God, but with my flesh I am a slave to the law of sin. [1]There is therefore now no condemnation for those who are in Christ Jesus. [2]For the law of the Spirit of life in Christ Jesus has set you free from the law of sin and death. [3]For God has done what the law, weakened by the flesh, could not do: by sending his own Son in the visible appearance of sinful flesh (ἐν ὁμοιώματι σαρκὸς ἁμαρτίας) and to deal with sin (περὶ ἁμαρτίας), he condemned sin in the flesh...(Rom. 7.25–8.3).

Having considered Gal. 3.10-14 in considerable detail, the reader will find many of the ideas in this text very familiar. Paul opposes two ways of life: life as 'a slave to the law of sin' and life lived under the 'law of the Spirit' (Rom. 7.25–8.2). In order to provide a way for Christians to exchange one way of life for another, God sent Christ 'in the visible appearance of human flesh (ἐν ὁμοιώματι σαρκὸς ἁμαρτίας)' (Rom. 8.3). A more precise understanding of Christ's role depends upon the clarification of two key terms: ὁμοίωμα and σάρξ ἁμαρτίας.

'Visible Appearance' (ὁμοίωμα)

Some translators render ὁμοίωμα as 'likeness' in contrast to the concept of 'identity'. So states C.H. Dodd, according to whom Christ 'was sent in the guise of sinful flesh...in the guise of that flesh which in Adam is sinful'.[106] The obvious motive for this interpretation is to harmonise

---

105. Ellicott, *Galatians*, p. 75.

106. C.H. Dodd, *The Epistle of Paul to the Romans* (MNTC; New York: Harper & Row, 1959), pp. 119-20. Similarly, J. Schneider:

> The ὁμοίωμα [in Rom. 8.3] thus indicates two things, first the likeness in appearance, and secondly the distinction in essence...Paul is showing that for all the similarity between Christ's physical body and that of men there is an essential difference between Christ and men...He became man without entering the nexus of human sin' (ὁμοίμα, *TDNT* 5 [1968], p. 196).

this passage with other texts in the New Testament which insist upon Christ's sinlessness.[107] However, this interpretation of ὁμοίωμα contradicts its consistent use, both in the Septuagint[108] and Paul's writings,[109] where it signifies 'the perceptible expression of a reality'.[110] Whether it be Ezekiel's 'vision of the expression of the glory of the Lord (ὁμοίωμα δόξης κυρίου)' (Ezek. 1.28), or the Gentiles consulting τὰ ὁμοιώματα of their idols (1 Macc. 3.48), the term is used to express the visible and actual appearance of a reality, not a mere likeness.

This same usage occurs in Phil. 2.7 where Paul states that Christ was born 'in the visible appearance of a human' (ἐν ὁμοιώματι ἀνθρώπων). One does not find commentators of Phil. 2.7 arguing that Christ was born in the guise or mere semblance of human flesh, because such notions conflict with the Chalcedonian definition of Christ as fully human. Yet commentators readily misconstrue the same term in Rom. 8.3 in order to protect another dogma, namely the sinlessness of Christ. But, as C.K. Barrett remarks:

> The word 'form' or 'likeness' (ὁμοίωμα) has already been used several times in the epistle [to the Romans] (1.23; 5.14; 6.5), and in none of these places does it mean simply 'imitation'. Compare also Phil. 2.7, where Paul certainly does not mean to say that Christ only appeared to be a man. We are probably justified therefore in our translation,[111] and in deducing that

Also: Schlier, *Der Römerbrief*, p. 241; E. de Witt Burton, *Spirit, Soul and Flesh* (Chicago: University of Chicago, 1918), p. 195, n. 2; S. Lyonnet, *Exegesis epistulae ad Romanos, Cap. V ad VIII* (Rome: Biblical Institute Press, 1966), p. 161; M.H. Scharlemann, 'In the Likeness of Sinful Flesh', *CTM* 32 (1961), p. 136; P. von der Osten-Sacken, *Römer 8 al Beispiel paulinischer Soteriologie* (FRLANT, 112; Göttingen: Vandenhoeck & Ruprecht, 1975), p. 230 n. 10; E. Käsemann, *Commentary on Romans* (Grand Rapids: Eerdmans, 1980), p. 207; C.E.B. Cranfield, *A Critical and Exegetical Commentary on the Epistle to the Romans* (ICC; 2 vols.; Edinburgh: T. & T. Clark, 1925), p. 193; T. Zahn, *Der Brief des Paulus an die Römer* (Leipzig: Deichert, 3rd edn, 1925), p. 382; J. Murray, *The Epistle to the Romans* (NICNT; Grand Rapids: Eerdmans, 1963), p. 280.

107. E.g., 1 Pet. 2.22; Heb. 4.15; 7.26; 1 Jn 3.5; cf. Mt. 4.1-14; Jn 8.46; Acts 3.14.

108. Ezek. 1.28; 1 Macc. 3.48; 4 Kgdms 16.10; Josh. 22.28; Sir. 38.28.

109. Rom. 1.23; 5.14; 6.5; 8.3; Phil. 2.7.

110. U. Vanni, 'Ὁμοίωμα in Paolo (Rom. 1, 23; 5, 14; 6, 15; 8, 2; Fil. 2, 7). Un'interpretazione esegetico-teologica alla luce dell'uso dei LXX', *Greg* 58 (1977), pp. 431-70, esp. pp. 339, 468.

111. Namely, 'by sending his own Son in the form of flesh which had passed under sin's rule'.

Christ took precisely the same fallen nature that we ourselves have...[112]

Thus, in Rom. 8.3, Paul clearly identifies Christ with human sin. The nature of this identification is explained by Vincent Branick:

> The sense of the word [ὁμοίωμα] in Rom. 8.3, therefore, by no means makes a distinction or a difference between Christ and sinful flesh. If Christ comes ἐν ὁμοιώματι of sinful flesh, he comes as the full expression of that sinful flesh. He manifests it for what it is. Sinful flesh is fully visible in the flesh of Christ.[113]

This concept of Christ being incarnated in sinful flesh finds its logical corollary in Paul's earlier statements: whether Christ was 'made to be sin' (2 Cor. 5.21), or cursed (Gal. 3.13), the concept is essentially the same.

'Sinful Flesh' (σάρξ ἀμαρτίας)

Paul's use of the term 'flesh' (σάρξ) is noted for it tremendous diversity, ranging from a designation of physical existence, to a cosmic power responsible for human perversity.[114] According to E. Brandenburger, Paul never uses 'flesh' (σάρξ) in a neutral sense; it always has a theo-logical significance.[115] When Paul states that Christ was sent 'in the visible appearance of sinful flesh' (Rom. 8.3) he is combining two theo-logical ideas: (1) flesh as power; and (2) flesh as way of substitution.

When Paul states that Christ took on 'the visible appearance of sinful flesh', he not only means that Christ became fleshy, visible and corpo-real, but also that he was born into the grips of the deadly power of sin. Paul portrays the flesh as a power which makes demands upon people and puts them under the obligation of debt (Rom. 8.12). As a power, it opposes the Spirit (Rom. 8.5-6; Gal. 5.17), has its own 'desires' (πρόνοια/ἐπιθυμίαι) and 'passions' (παθήματα) (Rom. 13.14; Gal. 5.16, 24), and can direct human thoughts and deeds (Rom. 8.4, 5, 13; 2 Cor. 1.17; 5.16; 10.2, 3; Gal. 5.19).

This interpretation of flesh as a power in Rom. 8.3 is confirmed by its accompanying adjective, '*sinful* flesh' (cf. 2 Cor. 5.21). For Paul, sin is

112. Barrett, *Romans*, p. 147.

113. V.P. Branick, 'The Sinful Flesh of the Son of God (Rom. 8.3): A Key Image of Pauline Theology', *CBQ* 47 (1985), pp. 246-61, esp. p. 250.

114. J.D.G. Dunn, 'Jesus—Flesh and Spirit: An Exposition of Romans 1.3-4', *JTS* 24 (1973), pp. 40-63; cf. R. Jewett, *Paul's Anthropological Terms: A Study of Their Use in Conflict Settings* (Leiden: Brill, 1971), pp. 49-166.

115. E. Brandenburger, *Fleisch und Geist. Paulus und die dualistische Weisheit* (WMANT, 29; Neukirchen–Vluyn: Neukirchener Verlag, 1968), p. 48.

not merely a juridical state of guilt, but an active power.[116] When sin
came into the world through human failing (Rom. 5.12), it was in effect
the unleashing of a deadly power which would enslave humanity (Rom.
5.12-14). Thus, Paul describes sin using active verbs such as 'being
master of' (κυριεύω, Rom. 6.14) and 'ruling' (βασιλεύω, 5.21, 6.12),
even denying people command of their own actions (Rom. 7.17, 20).
Conversely, humans become 'enslaved' to this power (Rom. 6.6, 16-17,
20) and 'obey' it (Rom. 6.16). Consequently, Christians are 'under [the
burden] of sin (ὑφ' ἁμαρτίαν)' (Rom. 3.9; 7.14; Gal. 3.22; cf. 2 Cor.
5.21).[117] Hence there is no significant difference between Christ becoming
'in the visible appearance of sinful flesh' (Rom. 8.3), becoming sin
(2 Cor. 5.21) or becoming a curse (Gal. 3.13). They all represent Christ's
subjection to the deadly cosmic powers of the old order.

'Flesh' in Rom. 8.3 also specifies a way of substitution. God puts
Christ in subjection to the power of the flesh in order that humanity
might be released from this power. Christ was not sent in sinful flesh to
stand *in solidarity* with sinful humanity, but *in substitution for* it. Thus,
the paradigm in Romans is conceptually identical to the paradigms in
2 Cor. 5.21 and Gal. 3.13. The principle idea is that of interchange: the
pre-existent sinless Christ becomes identified with human sin in order
that humans might be made sinless, where God is the active agent in this
double imputation.

Paul's Apotropaeic Christology

The imprint of the apotropaeic paradigm on Paul's theology of atonement can be summarised as follows. All apotropaeic rituals reflect the
desire to eradicate the deadly forces or curses beyond society's control

116. One of the classic theological problems of Romans is how to deal with the
combination of forensic language (esp. Rom. 1–4) with cosmological language (esp.
pp. 6-8). As a solution, Martinus C. de Boer proposes a 'two track' theory of Jewish
apocalyptic eschatology. He believes that Paul's conversation partners in Rome are
steeped in the traditions of Jewish forensic eschatology and that Paul uses their
language in order to reinterpret it in terms of cosmological apocalyptic eschatology.
Based on Romans 5 he concludes that Paul's theology falls on the side of cosmological categories, with death and sin being cosmic powers defeated in Christ (M.C. de
Boer, *The Defeat of Death: Apocalyptic Eschatology in 1 Corinthians and Romans 5*
[JSNTSup, 22; Sheffield: JSOT Press, 1988]).

117. Gaston, *Paul*, p. 114; H. Ridderbos, *Paul: An Outline of His Theology* (Grand
Rapids: Eerdmans, 1975), pp. 91-93; Brandenburger, *Fleisch und Geist*, pp. 55-57.

which threaten communal order and well-being. Many of these curses result from the transgression of sacred laws. In the case of the Levitical scapegoat ritual, transgression against the Torah, the sacred law of the Jews, resulted in a corporate sin and curse upon the people. Similarly, Paul thinks that the Jewish law imposes a curse upon all who attempt to live under the law, including Christians. Only by the removal of this burden can they experience the blessing of Abraham and God's Spirit.

The apotropaeic victim functions in a substitutionary role by taking the place of the threatened community and assuming this burden. For example, the Athenian *pharmakoi* would take upon themselves the curse causing the plague or drought which threatened the citizens. Likewise, Christ is said to have died in substitution for all who are oppressed by the powers of the old order—sin and its curse—in order that those who relinquish all ties with this old order may be rescued from them.

As a direct consequence of the ritual, the victim physically embodies the curse or threat of the group. When threatening curses were transferred to the head of an Egyptian steer, it became a lethal receptacle of the power of this curse. In similar fashion, Paul teaches that Christ became the receptacle of the power of sin and its curse. He accomplished this at the personal cost of forfeiting his sinless nature (2 Cor. 5.21). Though innocent and sinless, Christ becomes a transgressor through an act of substitution. Paul is not satisfied with noetic processes: it is not enough for God to reckon humanity to be righteous, nor is a new self-understanding among Christians sufficient. A real transfer of sin and curse to Christ was essential. Christ must truly become polluted.

Following the completion of the ritual, the continued presence of the victim in the society posed a very real threat to the group's newly found safety. In order to prevent contamination, the victim had to be removed from society by expelling him, sometimes followed by execution. In the case of the Levitical scapegoat, we can see the equality with which these two alternatives were viewed. In earlier days, the scapegoat was banished to the symbolic nothingness of the wilderness. By the first century, the goat was taken into the desert and killed by pushing it over a cliff. Similarly, the Christian freedom from sin and the curse of the law could only be completed by Christ's execution. A real death was necessary to put real distance between saved Christians and the power of sin.

The result of the victim's expulsion from society or death was the restoration of social well-being and order. When Jonah is tossed into the raging sea and swallowed by a great fish the sailors immediately experienced salvation from the perilous storm. Christians, freed from their sin and curse by the execution of Christ enter a new order characterised by God's blessing and the reception of his Spirit.

Part II

A DEVELOPMENTAL STUDY OF PAUL'S SOTERIOLOGY

Chapter 4

THE CHRONOLOGY OF PAUL'S LETTERS AND THE DEVELOPMENT OF HIS THOUGHT

The method which one adopts for any research always precedes, pre-conditions and may even interfere with one's analysis. This observation is no less true for the field of Pauline studies. Conversely, the development of new methods often results in important advances in understanding. A case in point is the revival of Pauline studies associated most closely with John Knox, the twentieth-century New Testament scholar.[1] Though I shall not undertake to rehearse a detailed history of this scholarship,[2] it will suffice to discuss three of its most important methodological insights which are relevant to this study, namely: (1) the use of Acts in Pauline studies; (2) the determination of the chronological sequence of Paul's letters; (3) the distinction between epistles and letters.

1.   J. Knox, *Chapters in a Life of Paul* (Nashville: Abingdon Press, 1950); J. Knox, '"Fourteen Years Later": A Note on Pauline Chronology', *JR* 16 (1936), pp. 341-49; J. Knox, 'The Pauline Chronology', *JBL* 58 (1939), pp. 15-29; J. Knox, 'On the Pauline Chronology: Buck-Taylor-Hurd Revisited', in R.T. Fortna and B.R. Gaventa (eds.), *The Conversation Continues: Studies in Paul and John in Honor of J. Louis Martyn* (Nashville: Abingdon Press, 1991), pp. 258-74.

2.   Some of the key figures in this work are: D. Riddle, *Paul: Man of Conflict: A Modern Biographical Sketch* (Nashville: Abingdon Press, 1940); R. Jewett, *A Chronology of Paul's Life* (Philadelphia: Fortress Press, 1979); J. Hurd, *The Origin of 1 Corinthians* (London: SPCK, 1965), pp. 3-41 (reprinted with retrospective pre-face; Macon GA: Mercer University Press, 1984); J. Hurd, 'Pauline Chronology and Pauline Theology', in W.R. Farmer *et al.* (ed.), *Christian History and Interpretation: Studies Presented to John Knox* (Cambridge: Cambridge University Press, 1967), pp. 225-48; J. Hurd, 'The Sequence of Paul's Letters', *CJT* 14/3 (1968), pp. 189-200; G. Lüdemann, *Paul, Apostle to the Gentiles: Studies in Chronology* (ET; trans. F.S. Jones; Philadelphia: Fortress Press, 1984 [1980]), pp. 1-5; G. Lüdemann, *Opposition to Paul in Jewish Christianity* (trans. M.E. Boring; Minneapolis: Fortress Press, 1983–1989); cf. most recently N. Hyldahl, *Die paulinische Chronologie* (Acta Theologica Danica, 19; Leiden: Brill, 1986).

The Use of Acts in Pauline Studies

The traditional approach of scholars in reconstructing a chronology of Paul's life has been to relate the book of Acts to world history, and to relate Paul's letters to Acts. Thus, while Paul's letters were used to understand his theology, Acts was used to reconstruct his biography, making use of Paul's letters only secondarily. Since this study is principally concerned with Paul's *thought*—not biography—one might reasonably ask what bearing such an observation has on this study. There is a simple answer to the question. When Acts is used to reconstruct a 'life' of Paul, it also determines the occasion when Paul founded each of his churches and, what is more important, *when* Paul wrote each of his letters and their relative chronological sequence. Among the numerous implications of this approach are the consequences for understanding Paul's theology.

If Paul's letters are dated according to the information gleaned from Acts, the picture that emerges is that they were all written within a very short period of time towards the very end of his missionary career. If this were indeed the case, then one could hardly expect to find any theological development in Paul's thought. Moreover, the apparent chronological letter sequence produced by using Acts is such that no theological development is evident. If, on the other hand, Paul's letters are dated with respect to the *internal* evidence in Paul's own letters, a decidedly different picture emerges.[3] First, the letters appear to have been written over a lengthy period of time throughout his whole career. Secondly, the letters seem to have been written in an altogether different sequence than the one suggested by Acts. Thirdly, a development of Paul's thought becomes evident.[4]

This raises an important question: to what extent can Acts be relied upon to convey accurate chronological and historical information? In fact, Acts is an extremely unreliable source of information on such matters. The following five points will illustrate this fact:

1. Acts provides very incomplete coverage of Paul's life in that it

3. Cf. Hurd, 'Sequence', pp. 189-200.
4. C.H. Buck and G. Taylor, *Saint Paul: A Study in the Development of his Thought* (New York: Charles Scribner's Sons, 1969); C.H. Dodd, *New Testament Studies* (Manchester: Manchester University Press, 1953), pp. 83-228; J. Hurd, 'Pauline Chronology'; G. Lüdemann, 'Paul, Christ and the Problem of Death', in B.H. McLean (ed.), *Origins and Method*.

omits most of the biographical information found in Paul's letters.[5]

2. At points where Acts and Paul's letters overlap, the disagreements are more notable than the agreements.[6] For example, modern reconstructions of Paul's life usually begin with the two best attested historical events in his life, namely, his trips to Jerusalem and his collection of money for the 'saints' in Jerusalem. Luke betrays a lack of personal acquaintance with these incidents. With respect to the former, it is patently clear from Paul's letters that he visited Jerusalem only three times after his conversion.[7] Acts on the other hand records at least five post-conversion visits.[8] The reason for this disparity is that the author of Acts has failed to consolidate his sources, leaving the narrative with too many visits to Jerusalem.

A second example concerns the movements of Timothy to and from Thessalonica.[9] According to 1 Thess. 3.1-2, Paul and Timothy were staying in Athens together when Paul sent Timothy to Thessalonica. Timothy subsequently returned to Paul in Athens from Thessalonica (1 Thess. 3.6). According to Acts, Timothy did *not* accompany Paul to Athens, but remained in Beroea with Silas (Acts 17.14-15), in other words, Timothy was *never* in Athens. Only later did he join Paul in Corinth (Acts 18.1, 5). In a desperate attempt to reconcile the contradictions created by the witness of Acts, scholars have often conflated the two accounts, assuming that each account reports what the other has omitted.[10] In the fanciful reconstruction that results, the only information

5.   See extensive list in Hurd, *Origin*, pp. 24-25.

6.   Hurd, *Origin*, p. 25; Hurd, 'Pauline Chronology', p. 230.

7.   First visit: after 'three years [in Damascus]', Paul visits Peter and also James (Gal. 1.18-20). By Paul's own admission, this was his only visit prior to the Jerusalem conference (Gal. 3.15-16). Second visit: after 14 years of sojourn, he went to the Jerusalem Conference (Gal. 2.1-10). Third visit: after fulfilling his original plan to winter in Corinth (1 Cor. 16.6, though delayed), he travels to Jerusalem in the Spring to deliver the Collection (Rom. 16.25, 31).

8.   (1) Acts 9.26-29; (2) 11.27-30; (3) 12.25 (Variant reading: UBSGNT [4th edn.] assigns a {C} rating: 'to Jerusalem'; text in NA[26], UBSGNT, and NRSV); (4) 15.4; (5) Acts 18.22 (though the name Jerusalem does not appear; Knox, *Chapters*, 61–62, 68); (6) 21.17-23.30; cf. K. Lake, 'The Chronology of Acts', in F.J.F. Jackson and K. Lake (ed.), *The Beginnings of Christianity* (5 vols.; London: Macmillan, 1920–1933), V, 445-74; Hurd, *Origin*, pp. 19-41; cf. see Paul Achtemeier's attempt to solve this problem (P. Achtemeier, *The Quest for Unity in the New Testament Church: A Study in Paul and Acts* [Philadelphia: Fortress Press, 1987]).

9 .   Hurd, *Origin*, pp. 25-26.

10.   W. Neil, *The Epistle of Paul to the Thessalonians* (MNTC; London: Hodder

which Paul's testimony and Acts share in common are three proper names, Paul, Timothy and Athens! In every other detail, they differ.[11]

3. Acts is inaccurate or vague in chronological matters.[12] Examples of erroneous dating abound.[13] For example, in Acts 4.6, Luke incorrectly thinks that Annas—not Caiaphas—was ruling high priest.[14] In Acts 5.36-37, the chronological order of Theudas and Judas are reversed.[15] The author's dating of the famine to the days of Claudius (Acts 11.28) contradicts secular sources and the context of Acts 11.28[16] indicating either that he has adopted famine-sources uncritically, or transformed a local famine-tradition into something universal.[17] At many other points in the composition the author seems to be uncertain of the length of the intervals between events (e.g., Acts 6.1; 12.1; 11.27; 19.23). For example, he ignores the gap of several years between Acts 12.19 and 12.20. Furthermore, the years in Acts do not add up to the 17 year interval recounted in Gal. 1.15–2.1—no matter how they are added.[18]

4. Acts is built up of diverse sources beyond recovery.[19] In the Acts account of Paul's visits to various cities, Paul's adventures usually occur

---

& Stoughton, 1950), p. 62; E. Haenchen, *Die Apostelgeschichte* (Göttingen: Vandenhoeck & Ruprecht, 13th edn, 1961), p. 471, n. 1; C. Masson, *Les Deux Epître de Saint Paul aux Thessaloniciens* (Neuchâtel: Delachaux & Niestlé, 1957), p. 39; J. Bicknell, *The First and Second Epistles to the Thessalonians* (London: Methuen, 1932), pp. xv-xvi; G.G. Findlay, *The Epistles to the Thessalonians* (Cambridge: Cambridge University Press, 1898), p. 81.

11. (1) Paul arrives in Athens *alone* (Acts; contrary to simple explanation of 1 Thess. 3.1); (2) Timothy later joins Paul in Athens (omitted by both); (3) Paul sends Timothy to Thessalonica (omitted by Acts); (4) Paul goes to Corinth alone (omitted by Paul); (5) Paul later joined by Silvanus and Timothy (Acts).

12. Hurd, *Origin*, pp. 22-23; Lüdemann, *Paul*, pp. 10-11.

13. Lüdemann, *Paul*, pp. 8-11.

14. Annas: 6–15 CE; Caiaphas: 17/19–37 CE.

15. Theudas entered public life at the time of the procurator of Fadus (ca. 44 CE; cf. Josephus, *Ant*. 20.97-99). According to Acts, he lived before Gamaliel and before the census (6 BCE). Contrary to Acts, Judas preceded Theudas. Luke is also wrong in connecting Judas' revolt with census (Josephus, *Ant*. 18.3-5).

16. Since the Antiochene congregation was able to assist the brothers in Judaea, it must not have been affected by the famine and therefore the famine was not 'worldwide'. Sources witness to regional famines in this period (H. Conzelmann, *Apostelgeschichte* [HNT, 7; Tübingen: Mohr, 2nd edn, 1972], p. 76.

17. Dio Cassius 60.6.6 (cf. Lüdemann, *Paul*, pp. 164-65).

18. Hurd, *Origin*, p. 23.

19. Hurd, *Origin*, p. 28.

on the first visit, though he may visit the same city several times afterward. This suggests that Acts has concentrated all traditions concerning
Paul's visit to a given city to one visit.[20] Evidence of this compression
can be found in the account of Paul's visit to Corinth. In Acts 18.1-4
Paul is said to be staying with Aquilla and Priscilla; a few verses later,
Paul is living with Titius Justus (vv. 5-11). Similarly, in 18.8, Crispus is
said to be the ruler of the synagogue, while in v. 17, it is Sosthenes who
is the ruler.[21]

One can deduce from this that the connection of a given episode in
Paul's life with a *particular* visit to a city has very low historical value.[22]
Thus, even though Acts 18.12 indicates that Paul was attacked by the
Jews in Corinth during the proconsulship of Gallio (which can be dated
by the well-known inscription), Acts is not a reliable witness as to *which*
of Paul's visits to Corinth was the occasion for Paul being brought
before Gallio.[23] Therefore, the incident cannot be used to establish an
absolute date for Pauline chronology.[24]

5. Perhaps, most important is the fact that the author of Acts has
deliberate theological and literary motivations which have strongly
influenced the presentation of his material.[25] Acts was written as an epic

20. Hurd, *Origin*, pp. 27-32. The entrenched resistance of scholars to give up
using Acts as a historically reliable source is evident in Jürgen Wehnert's recent
study of the 'we-passages' in the second half of Acts. Wehnert argues that this
stylistic device was inspired by the Jewish tradition and that it functions to mark the
tradition concerning Paul's journeys which Luke obtained from Silas. Despite the
fact that he concludes that the 'we-passages' are clearly redactional and have been
inserted by the author to create a historiographical quality, he argues that the content
of these passages was probably communicated orally to Luke by a reliable informer,
Silas (J. Wehnert, *Die Wir-Passagen Apostelgeschichte: Ein lukanisches Stilmittel
aus jüdischer Tradition* [Göttingen: Vandenhoeck & Ruprecht, 1989], pp. 47-124,
188-90). This assures that Paul in effect is allowed to speak through his reliable
witness. The thesis is peculiar since Wehnert argues that the actual eyewitness, Silas,
was given no personality by Luke in order to guarantee the reliability of the tradition
relayed through him.

21. Hurd, *Origin*, p. 31.

22. Cf., Hurd *Origin*, pp. 28-29, cf. 30-31.

23. G.A. Deissmann supplies a full bibliography through 1925 in his *Paul: A
Study in Social and Religious History* (trans. W.E. Wilson; New York: Doran, 2nd
rev. edn, 1926), p. 270, n. 1; cf. *Origin*, p. 31, n. 2.

24. D. Slingerland, 'Acts 18.1-17 and Lüdemann's Pauline Chronology', *JBL*
109/4 (1990), pp. 686-90.

25. Hurd, *Origin*, pp. 32-33, 42. Richard Pervo argues that argues that Acts is

for the emerging institutional Church. It presents a heroic tale of the rapid spread of Christianity under the aegis of the twelve apostles and Paul from Jerusalem to Asia Minor, Achaia and ultimately to Rome. By a convergence of related themes, such as the work of the Spirit, the proclamation of the gospel, the 'Jewishness' of Paul, and Paul's subordination to the Twelve, this theological saga achieves its objective. From a historical perspective, it is equally clear that this epic is largely a product of the imagination of its author. Historical sources, such as they can be identified, have been deliberately subordinated, altered and suppressed in order to achieve the author's overarching purpose.[26] The subordination of history to authorial intent is most evident in the striking parallelisms between different parts of Acts, and between Acts and Luke as a whole.[27]

To sum up: Given the marked unreliability of Acts in historical and chronological matters, it is not possible to use chronological evidence in Acts for Pauline studies with any confidence whatsoever unless confirmation is found in Paul's letters. It is now clear that Paul's letters and Acts represent two different kinds of sources for Pauline study: primary versus secondary. A primary source is one which is in direct contact with the mind of the author. Only Paul's letters are primary sources for Paul's life and thought. Though Acts is a primary source for the thought of the author of Luke–Acts, it is a secondary source for Pauline study

best understood not in relation to ancient histories and biographies, but in relation to the ancient novel (R. Pervo, *Profit with Delight: The Literary Genre of the Acts of the Apostles* (Philadelphia: Fortress Press, 1987).

26. Colin Hemer, in attempting to ascertain the value of Acts as 'an historical source for primitive Christianity', ignores the whole question of theological motifs by arguing that 'all sophisticated history is in its degree interpretative, and history and theology may not necessarily conflict, but run on parallel lines' (C. Hemer, *The Book of Acts in the Setting of Hellenistic History* [WUNT, 49; Tübingen: Mohr (Siebeck), 1989], p. 49).

27. C.C. Talbert, *Literary Patterns, Theological Themes, and the Genre of Luke–Acts* (Missoula, MT: Scholars Press, 1974), pp. 15-65. Robert Tannehill is representative of many modern scholars who recognize that Acts was not written to convey history, as moderns understand the term. Consequently, he interprets the text as it stands, without discussing the historicity of particular events or reconstructing a 'more plausible' version of events. Rather, he identifies the carefully constructed literary structure of Acts, the balance and movement of the narrative, both as a whole, and in its separate parts (R.C. Tannehill, *The Narrative Unity of Luke–Acts: A Literary Interpretation*. II. *The Acts of the Apostles* [Minneapolis: Fortress Press, 1990]).

and should be treated with the utmost of caution.[28] It may only be used for clarification, and then only after each tradition has been rigorously interrogated with reference to the plan and purpose of Luke–Acts as a whole.[29] John Knox has said this forcefully:

> So important is the distinction between primary and secondary sources in this case [of Acts] that we can justly say that a fact only suggested in the letters [of Paul] has the status which even the most unequivocal statement of Acts, if not otherwise supported, cannot confer.[30]

It should be clear that Acts should not be used to determine the relative chronology of Paul's letters. The method of reconstructing the life of Paul on the basis of purely historical criteria in Paul's own letters is described by John Knox:

> This method has been to give exclusive attention to Paul's own letters until they have been 'wrung dry' of biographical data; next, to construct on the basis of these data alone an outline of Paul's career as an apostle…and only then to consider what the book of Acts, critically examined, can yield by way of filling the gaps—having always in mind that materials from Acts can never have the certainty and authority that materials in the letters possess.[31]

The Chronological Sequence of Paul's Letters

The first problem posed by Paul's letters, after that of genuineness and integrity, is the matter of their original chronological sequence. Though it is difficult to establish an absolute chronology (i.e., a calendar dating), a relative chronology which arranges letters and events in relationship to one another is more easily attained since internal evidence can be used by itself.

The most accurate method of arranging Paul's letters into a chronological sequence is to rely upon internal evidence in Paul's letters which is of a historical nature (esp. Gal. 1.13–2.14; Rom. 15.9-33; 2 Corinthians 8–9; cf. 2 Cor. 11.23–12.9; Phil. 3.3-16). Whereas numerous studies have attempted to arrange the letters on the basis of Paul's apparent eschatological development, the validity of a chronological sequence

28. Knox, *Chapters*, p. 32.
29. Cf. G. Lüdemann, *Early Christianity According to the Traditions in Acts* (Minneapolis: Fortress Press, 1989).
30. Knox, *Chapters*, p. 33.
31. Knox, 'On the Pauline Chronology', p. 258; Lüdemann, *Paul*, pp. 21-22.

produced by this approach clearly rests upon the presupposition that Paul's theology did indeed develop.[32] Scholars who hold that Paul's thought was fully mature when he wrote his letters and that apparent changes in his theology are to be accounted for by the changing needs and situations to which they were addressed, would reject any chronological reconstruction based upon the concept of theological development.[33] Since I intend to argue for the development of Paul's soteriology, I discard at the outset all attempts to arrange his letters into a chronological sequence on the basis of theological development, in order to avoid a circular argument.

Though a precise ordering of all the documented events in Paul's life continues to elude scholars, as does an absolute chronology of these events, a relative chronology can be constructed if one accepts the primacy of Paul's letters over Acts. John Knox began his reconstruction with the 'three-Jerusalem-visit' pattern (termed here 'J1', 'J2', 'J3'), the historical reliability of which is of the highest order.[34] The first visit took place three years after his conversion (Gal. 1.18-20). Paul did not go up to Jerusalem for a second visit until fourteen years after his return from his sojourn in the districts of Syria and Cilicia (Gal. 1.21; 2.1).[35] The occasion for this second visit was the so-called 'Jerusalem conference' which, among other things, initiated Paul's collection 'for the poor' in Jerusalem' (Gal. 2.10).[36] Paul intended to visit Jerusalem a third time in order to deliver the collection (Rom. 15.25-32; cf. 1 Cor. 16.4).

A second and equally reliable criterion for establishing a chronology of Paul's letters are references to the collection itself. When Paul wrote 1

---

32. E.g., C.H. Dodd, *New Testament Studies*, pp. 108-118; Buck, *Saint Paul*; R.H. Charles, *A Critical History of the Doctrine of a Future Life in Israel, in Judaism, and in Christianity* (London: A. & C. Black, 2nd rev. edn, 1913); A.M. Hunter, *Paul and his Predecessors* (London: SCM Press, rev. edn, 1961), pp. 98-102, 148.

33. E.g., J. Weiss, *The History of Primitive Christianity* (2 vols.; trans. and ed. F.C. Grant *et al.*; New York: Wilson–Erickson, 1936), p. 206; G.S. Duncan, *The Epistle of Paul to the Galatians: A Reconstruction* (London: Hodder & Stoughton, 1929), p. xxi; Neil, *Thessalonians*, pp. 25-26.

34. Knox, *Chapters*, pp. 32-42; Knox, '"Fourteen Years Later"', pp. 341-49; Knox, 'The Pauline Chronology', pp. 15-29; cf. n. 7 above.

35. Lüdemann, *Paul*, pp. 61-64.

36. Cf. B.H. McLean, 'Galatians 2.7-9 and the Recognition of Paul's Apostolic Status at the Jerusalem Conference: A Critique of G. Lüdemann's Solution', *NTS* 37 (1991), pp. 67-76.

Corinthians the collection was still in the organizing phase (1 Cor. 16.1-4).[37] By the time he writes 2 Corinthians 1–9,[38] the collection is well underway and the Corinthian Christians are in need of further encouragement (cf. 2 Cor. 8–9).[39] When Paul writes Romans, the Collection is near completion and Paul is planning his third trip to Jerusalem in order to deliver the funds. A merging of information concerning Paul's visits to Jerusalem and the Collection produce the following sequence:

$$J1 \rightarrow J2 \rightarrow 1\ Corinthians \rightarrow 2\ Corinthians\ 1–9 \rightarrow Romans \rightarrow J3$$

It is clear from Galatians 1–2 that *Galatians* was written following Paul's second visit to Jerusalem (and the Jerusalem conference), and prior to his third visit. Paul's reference to instructing the Galatians about the collection in 1 Cor. 16.1 suggests that he was unaware of any difficulty with the Galatian churches when he wrote 1 Corinthians. However, by the time Paul writes Galatians, his attention is focused on the Galatian controversy to such an extent that he makes no mention of the Galatian contribution to the collection which was anticipated in 1 Cor. 16.1. These two observations suggest that Galatians was written sometime after 1 Corinthians. Though Galatians is customarily grouped with Romans on the basis of their overlapping subject matter, it is not possible to determine the relative sequence of Galatians and Romans with any degree of certainty.[40] These observations can be integrated into the above sequence as follows:

$$J1 \rightarrow J2 \rightarrow 1\ Corinthians \rightarrow 2\ Corinthians\ 1–9 \rightarrow Romans \rightarrow J3$$
$$<----------Galatians---------->$$

---

37. Lüdemann, *Paul*, pp. 83-87.

38. Excluding 2 Cor. 6.14–7.1 which most scholars take to be an interpolation because: (1) drastic change in subject matter; (2) its excision produces a smoother reading; (3) it is a self-contained unit which reads like a short homily; (4) the evidence that 2 Cor. is effected by other editorial compilation (e.g., 2 Cor. 10–13). N. Dahl thinks that this is a non-Pauline fragment which Paul may have inserted into its present context as a warning against associating with the superapostles (N. Dahl, *Studies in Paul: Theology for the Early Christian Mission* [Minneapolis: Augsburg, 1977], 62-69; see also David Rensberger, '2 Corinthians 6.14–7.1—A Fresh Examination', *Studies Biblica et Theologica* 8 [1978], pp. 25-49).

39. Lüdemann, *Paul*, pp. 87-88.

40. Building upon the work of Knox, C.H. Buck expanded the sequence to include Galatians immediately prior to Romans (C.H. Buck, 'The Collection for the Saints', *HTR* 43/1 [1950], pp. 1-29).

Several letters remain to be fitted into this sequence. A number of historical factors converge in support of the conclusion that 1 Thessalonians was written in the period between Paul's first and second visits to Jerusalem, and prior to 1 Corinthians:[41]

J1→*1 Thessalonians*→J2→*1 Corinthians*

These can be summarized as follows:

Paul's mission to Macedonia probably followed immediately after his travels in Syria and Cilicia (Gal. 1.21) and prior to his second visit to Jerusalem (Gal. 2.1).[42] 1 Thess. 4.13-18 clearly reflects the period in the church's history when few Christians had died, a problem which the first Christian preaching had not addressed since many early Christians believed that the parousia would precede the death of all or most believers.[43] The increase in the number of Christian dead presupposed by 1 Cor. 15.51-52 in comparison with 1 Thess. 4.13-18 suggests that 1 Thessalonians was written prior to 1 Corinthians.[44] Moreover, the absence of any reference to the collection in 1 Thessalonians suggests that it was written prior to the Jerusalem Conference (J2).

This leaves a number of letters out of the sequence. Since 2 Corinthians 10–13 and Philemon are not relevant to this thesis, no decision regarding their placement is necessary. Colossians and Ephesians can also be omitted on the grounds of inauthenticity. The remaining letters, 2 Thessalonians and Philippians require further discussion.

2 Thessalonians: Authenticity

For many scholars, the question of the authenticity of 2 Thessalonians revolves upon the dating of 1 Thessalonians according to Acts (Acts 18.5 = 1 Thess. 3.6).[45] As John Hurd observes, when 1 Thessalonians is dated on the on the basis of Acts, it is either considered to be a baffling addendum to 1 Thessalonians or inauthentic.[46] The remarkable similarly

---

41. Lüdemann, *Paul*, pp. 201-238, 262; cf. M.J. Suggs, 'Concerning the Date of Paul's Macedonian Ministry', *NovT* 4 (1960), pp. 60-68.

42. Lüdemann builds a compelling argument that the Paul's mission to Macedonia, Thessalonica and Corinth antedate the Jerusalem conference (*Paul*, pp. 60-61, 103-109, 195-200; cf. 164-70).

43. Lüdemann, *Paul*, pp. 213-20, 238.

44. Lüdemann, *Paul*, pp. 239-41.

45. Hurd, *Origins*, pp. 26-27.

46. Hurd, 'Sequence'; Hurd, *Origins*, p. 27, n. 2 lists scholars who reject the authenticity of 2 Thessalonians. Following Buck and Hurd, Knox agrees that

between 2 Thessalonians and 1 Thessalonians has led many to conclude
that 2 Thessalonians was written by a pseudonymous author who relied
heavily upon 1 Thessalonians as an exemplar. John Hurd has called into
question the logic of this kind of argument. Since this article is unpublished I shall quote at length:

> The proposal that similarity shows inauthenticity involves the notion that
> text can be *too* similar as the result of copying, and it depends on the
> assumption that the author in question would not repeat himself to any
> considerable extent. But this last assumption requires defense. Which of
> us in writing Christmas 'thank you' notes has not repeated himself, at
> times even word by word. Thus the term 'wooden imitation' or even
> 'plagiarism' would aptly apply to our genuine output. Of course, the
> author of 2 Thessalonians is not writing Christmas notes, but then neither
> is he being accused of major plagiarism...In fact, a number of the com-
> monly listed similarities between the Thessalonian letters relate to letter
> style. Therefore the argument from similarity should be viewed with con-
> siderable caution...If two types of argument [i.e., argument from differ-
> ence, argument from similarity] are not carefully distinguished, then a
> 'heads I win; tails you lose' situation is inevitable. Features which are
> similar in the two documents are taken as evidence of borrowing; features
> which are different, as evidence of non-genuineness. Everything about the
> text can be explained with this type of hybrid method, and a method which
> explains everything is not subject to falsification.[47]

Robert Jewett concludes his recent examination on the history of the
academic debate on the subject of the authenticity of 2 Thessalonians by
saying

> the evidence concerning the authenticity of 2 Thessalonians is equivocal,
> with the likelihood remaining fairly strongly on the side of Pauline author-
> ship. While 1 Thessalonians remains on the list of indisputable Pauline
> letters, 2 Thessalonians must be placed in a category of 'probably
> Pauline'.[48]

2 Thessalonians precedes 1 Thessalonians, if genuine, though Knox personally rejects
the letter as inauthentic (Knox, 'Buck–Taylor–Hurd', p. 261).

47. J.C. Hurd, 'Concerning the Authenticity of 2 Thessalonians' (Unpublished
paper for the Thessalonians Seminar of the SBL annual meeting; Dallas, Texas, 19–
22 December, 1983); cf. Ken Neumann's computer-assisted stylostatistical analysis
of the question which concludes in favour of authenticity of 2 Thessalonians
(K. Neumann, *The Authenticity of The Pauline Epistles in the Light of Stylostatistical
Analysis* [SBLDS, 120; Atlanta, GA: Scholars Press, 1990]).

48. R. Jewett, *The Thessalonian Correspondence: Pauline Rhetoric and
Millenarian Piety* (FFNT; Philadelphia: Fortress Press, 1986), pp. 3-18, esp. 16-17.

A decision on the authenticity of 2 Thessalonians is in no way crucial to the question of the apotropaeic paradigm in Paul's thought. However, if authentic, it does provide valuable information concerning the starting point of Paul's theology.

1 and 2 Thessalonians: Relative Chronology
If 2 Thessalonians is authentic, then the question of its chronological sequence with respect to 1 Thessalonians and the remainder of the Pauline corpus is inescapable. It need hardly be said that the canonical ordering of 1 and 2 Thessalonians is meaningless in this regard since the canonical sequence of Paul's letters to his churches is determined on the basis of letter length alone: 2 Thessalonians follows 1 Thessalonians simply because it is shorter. Many scholars have concluded that there is convincing evidence that 2 Thessalonians was written prior to 1 Thessalonians.[49] This evidence can be summarized as follows:[50]

1. In 2 Thess. 3.6-12, the problem of Christians refraining from work because of the nearness of the Parousia seems to be a new problem, whereas in 1 Thess. 4.11 the problem is old.
2. In 2 Thess 1.6-7, persecution is an present reality, whereas in 1 Thessalonians (1.6, 2.14, 3.3-5), persecution is referred to both as an event of the past and as a present reality.
3. In 2 Thess. 2.1, only living Christians gather to meet to the Lord. In 1 Thess. 4.13-18, dead Christians as well as the living meet the Lord. Moreover, in 1 Thessalonians the problem posed by the death of some fellow Christians is new.
4. In response to some Thessalonian Christians who fear that they have missed the coming of the Lord, Paul describes an apocalyptic sequence which is in progress in the immediate present (2 Thess. 2.2). However, the description of the Parousia in 1 Thess. 5.1-11 is more timeless and less apocalyptic.

49. Weiss, *Primitive Christianity*, p. 289; J.C. West, 'The Order of 1 and 2 Thessalonians', *JTS* 15 (1914), pp. 66-74; W. Hadorn, *Die Abfassung der Thessalonicherbriefe in der Zeit der dritten Missionsreise des Paulus* (BFCT, 24; Gütersloh: C. Bertelsmann Verlap, 1919), pp. 116-26; F.J. Badcock, *The Pauline Epistles and the Epistle to the Hebrews in Their Historical Setting* (London: SPCK, 1937), pp. 43-52; L.O. Bristol, 'Paul's Thessalonian Correspondance', *ExpT* 55 (1944), p. 223; T.W. Manson, *Studies in the Gospels and Epistles* (Manchester: Manchester University Press, 1962), pp. 267-77.

50. J.C. Hurd, '2 Thessalonians', in *IDBSup*, pp. 900-901, esp. p. 901.

Therefore, on the basis of internal evidence alone, there are a number of reasons in favour of dating 2 Thessalonians as the earlier of the two letters:

J1→2 Thessalonians→1 Thessalonians→J2→1 *Corinthians*

Philippians

Of all Paul's letters, Philippians is perhaps the most difficult to insert into this sequence. In his resume of the scholarly discussion of the dating of Philippians and its place of composition, Ralph Martin concludes that recent discussion has 'run into an impasse' on the subject.[51] On the basis of literary parallels, Joseph Lightfoot argued that Philippians bears a resemblance to Romans.[52] Buck, Taylor and Hurd conclude that Philippians was written immediately before 2 Corinthians 1–9 and after 1 Corinthians and the 'Severe Letter'.[53] Donald Riddle sorted Paul's letters into three groups according to whether there is no mention of the Judaizing crisis (1 Thess., 2 Thess., 1 Cor., Phil. [excepting 3.2-16 as belonging to a separate letter]), or Paul is directly involved with the Judaizers (2 Cor. 10–13, Gal., Phil. 3.2-16), or the Judaizing crisis is viewed in retrospect (2 Cor. 1–9, Rom.).[54] According to this scheme, Philippians belongs to the period prior to the composition of Galatians, Romans and 2 Corinthians (group 1).

John Knox notes that Philippians does not mention of the collection. It

---

51. R.P. Martin, *Carmen Christi: Philippians 2.5-11 in Recent Interpretation and in the Setting of Early Christian Worship* (Grand Rapids: Eerdmans, 1976), pp 36-57, esp. 56.

52. J.B. Lightfoot, *Saint Paul's Epistle to the Philippians* (London: Macmillan, new edn, 1879), pp. 41-46. Many scholars have argued in favour of the non-integrity of Philippians. It has been proposed that Phil. 3.1 marks the end of the letter, with 3.2 beginning the text of a second letter, or that 3.2-16 is a fragment of another letter (cf. R.P. Martin, *Philippians* [NCB Commentary; Grand Rapids: Eerdmans, 1976], pp. 10-21; E.J. Goodspeed, *An Introduction to the New Testament* [Chicago, 1937], pp. 90-96). Since this study deals exclusively with the 'Christ hymn' (2.5-11) which all would agree is found in the *first* letter (Phil. 1-2) (if indeed Philippians is composed of more than one letter), the question of the integrity of the letter is not relevant to this thesis.

53. Buck, *St. Paul*, pp. 145-46; Hurd, 'Pauline Chronology', pp. 166-67; Hurd, 'Sequence', pp. 198-99.

54. Riddle, *Paul, Man of Conflict*, pp. 205-211; for a comparison of the solutions worked out by Riddle and Knox see: Hurd, 'Pauline Chronology and Pauline Theology', pp. 225-48.

is clear that Macedonia was greatly involved in the collection (cf. 2 Cor. 9.1-5). If Philippians was written is the middle of the period of the collection (i.e., according to the dating of Buck, Taylor and Hurd), it is difficult to explain how could Paul fail to mention the collection. On the basis of this significant omission, Knox concludes that Philippians was written either before 1 Corinthians or after Romans, though he considers the later dating more likely.[55]

The question of a precise placement of Philippians continues to elude scholarship. In my opinion, the letter was written sometime after 1 Corinthians since there is no hint that he expects to be alive at the coming of the Lord: 'For to me, living is Christ and dying is gain...my desire is to depart and be with Christ...' (Phil. 1.21-25; cf. 2.17). Moreover, Paul's reflection of the meaning of his sufferings in relation to those of Christ's has much closer affinity with Paul's later letters.[56]

Fortunately, a precise decision of this issue is not crucial for the elaboration of my thesis since the key christological text, namely the Christ hymn in Phil. 2.5-11, is a pre-Pauline tradition. Paul's recitation of this hymn is part of his rhetorical strategy begun in Phil. 2.1-4 to encourage unity and mutual consideration. To this end, he attempts to persuade the Philippians to subordinate themselves to one another after the example of Christ who subordinated himself as a servant to God. Though Paul obviously affirms the general content of this hymn, it is not his own composition (cf. Appendix 2). Therefore, one should not expect a developmental relationship between this non-Pauline passage and passages composed by Paul immediately before or after it. In any case, the fact that the chronological placement of the letter cannot be determined with precision would make any such attempt highly dubious.

All of the above conclusion can now be integrated to produce a working chronology for this study:

J1→2 *Thessalonians*→1 *Thessalonians*→J2→1 *Corinthians*→
2 *Corinthians* 1–9→*Romans*→J3
<-------*Galatians*------->

The analysis of the development of Paul's theology in chs. 5–6 will discuss each of these letters according to this chronological sequence. As

55. Knox, 'Buck-Taylor-Hurd', p. 263.
56. According to Paul, his own sufferings would have redemptive value because they matched the sufferings of Christ: 'I want to know Christ and the power of his resurrection and the sharing of his sufferings, by becoming like him in his death, if somehow I may attain the resurrection from the dead' (Phil. 3.10; cf. ch. 6).

a matter of convenience, Galatians will be dealt with after 2 Corinthians 1–9, though my conclusions would remain unaltered if it were treated before 2 Corinthians 1–9 or after Romans.

Letters versus Epistles

Following the first publications of non-literary papyri collections from Egypt, there was a watershed in the scholarly understanding of what constitutes a letter.[57] Adolf Deissmann was the first to make a distinction between a letter and an epistle.[58] According to him, a letter represents a stream of consciousness written not for posterity or to a general readership but to a specific addressee. An epistle, on the other hand, is more structured and addresses a general audience.

The work of scholars such as William Doty, Stanley Stowers, Calvin Roetzel and John Lee White has both enlarged and corrected the insights of Deissman.[59] It is now clear that the common letter was far more structured than once supposed and was no mere stream of consciousness.[60] Moreover, they also demonstrated that the structure of ancient letters varied in accordance with their function and the relationship between the writer and recipient(s).

Letters share a number of characteristics which distinguish them from epistles. First, a letter addressed a particular recipient in a particular situation at a particular time. An epistle, on the other hand, addresses a general audience and general situation. Secondly, letters avoid the repetition of

57. One series beginning in 1895 and another publication, *The Oxyrhynchus Papyri*, in 1898.

58. Deissmann, *Light*, p. 192.

59. W.G. Doty, *Letters in Primitive Christianity* (Guides to Biblical Scholarship; Philadelphia: Fortress Press, 1973); J.L. White, 'The Ancient Epistolography Group in Retrostect', in *Semeia* 22 (Chica, CA: Scholars Press, 1982), pp. 1-14; J.L. White, *The Form and Function of the Body of the Greek Letter: A Study of the Letter-Body in the Non-Literary Papyri and in Paul the Apostle* (SBLDS, 2; Missoula: University of Montana Printing Department for SBL, 1972); J.L. White, 'The Greek Documentary Letter Tradition Third Century BCE to Third Century CE', *Semeia* 22 (Chica, CA: Scholars Press, 1982), pp. 89-106; J.L. White, 'Apostolic Mission and Apostolic Message: Congruence in Paul's Epistolary Rhetoric, Structure and Imagery', in B.H. McLean (ed.), *Origins and Method*, pp. 145-61; S.K. Stowers, *Letter Writing in Greco-Roman Antiquity* (Library of Early Christianity, 5; Philadelphia: Westminster Press, 1986).

60. Cf. L.G. Bloomquist's discussion of letter writing in antiquity (*The Function of Suffering in Philippians* [JSNTSup, 78; Sheffield: JSOT Press, 1993], pp. 72-96).

information which is already known to the recipient(s) whereas epistles presuppose little previous knowledge and supply all information necessary for the argument.

It is now widely recognized that, with the possible exception of Romans, Paul wrote letters not epistles.[61] He wrote in response to particular questions, needs, interests and conflicts arising in his churches. Hence, his letters frequently refer to messages and letters previously received; and at other points Paul appears to be quoting questions or statements made in such communications. Therefore, a letter written by Paul represents only one half of a conversation, not a self-contained systematic discourse on a subject. Paul's writings also reflect his own personal situation at the time of writing. Thus, Paul's letters cannot be understood properly apart from the context of both the recipients and Paul himself. This observation has implications for the way in which a scholar should approach Paul's writings.

Since a letter represents only one half of a conversation, the interpretation of any letter must include a reconstruction of the other half of this conversation. What are the immediate congregational issues? What is the present status of Paul's relationship to the congregation? In the words of T.W. Manson: 'We must try...to discover what purpose lay behind the enquiry, what answer they hoped to receive, how the question and Paul's answer square with Jewish, Jewish-Christian, and Gentile (Graeco-Roman) sentiments and convictions.'[62]

One vital exegetical principle follows from the above observation: the hermeneutic unit for understanding Paul's thought is the individual letter. This principle is distinctly at odds with the habitual method of interpreting Paul, characterised by comparing and conflating text in all of his letters on the basis of subject matter. As John Hurd observes:

> ...much of Pauline study could be improved if scholars were more precise in their recognition of the hermeneutical unit. Texts are extremely complex entities, built up of words, sentences, paragraphs, and other larger structures...Frequently sentences or paragraphs are compared from one Pauline letter to another with little regard to the historical circumstances

61. Hurd, *Origin*, 1–6; C. Roetzel, *The Letters of Paul: Conversations in Context* (Atlanta: John Knox Press, rev. edn, 1982–1983); B. Rigaux, *The Letters of St Paul* (Chicago: Franciscan Herald, 1968), pp. 40-67; W. Meeks, *The Writings of St. Paul* (Norton Critical Editions; New York: W.W. Norton, 1972); G.J. Bahr, 'Paul and Letter Writing in the First Century', *CBQ* 28 (1966), pp. 465-77.

62. Manson, *Studies*, p. 192.

which gave rise to each letter or to the particular structure of argument in which the passage is embedded. Quite simply, the hermeneutical unit is the letter. Most Pauline scholars will agree to this statement in principle, but its significance in practice does not seem to be widely understood.[63]

The abandonment of this exegetical principle leads to the hazardous practice of comparing texts which may have been written a decade or more apart and which address different situations and audiences, before understanding each text in the context of the letter in which it occurs.[64]

The above observations make the task of tracing the development of Paul's thought more complex. The notion of development presupposes a discernable theological continuity from letter to letter. This is theoretically possible because the author remains the same, and therefore one expects a degree of continuity and organic development in Paul's articulation of his theological beliefs from one letter to the next.

On the other hand, the occasional nature of Paul's letters wherein he reacts to unexpected questions, crises and conflicts in the churches, tends to obscure the detail of this development. These varied circumstances forced Paul to address issues and problems which were not of his own choosing. Such occasions pushed Paul to be imaginative, inventive and experimental. In such instances, the continuity and development of Paul's more fundamental ideas may be less apparent.

It would be quite artificial to attempt to make absolute distinctions between those texts which respond to congregational need, and those which arise from Paul's detached theological reflection. Clearly, both factors are operative in any given text, though their relative significance will vary from passage to passage. In the following two chapters, I will attempt to describe both of these factors. First, I will endeavour to observe the principle that the hermeneutical unit of interpretation is the letter by identifying the pressing congregational factors which motivated the composition and argument of each letter and interpreting the key

63. J.C. Hurd, 'Paul Ahead of His Time: 1 Thess. 2.13-16', in P. Richardson and D. Granskou (eds.), *Anti-Judaism in Early Christianity* (ESCJ; 2 vols.; Waterloo, ON: Wilfrid Laurier University Press, 1986), pp. 21-36, esp. p. 30.

64. W.L. Knox, *St Paul and the Church of the Gentiles* (Cambridge: Cambridge University Press, 1939), pp, 125-26; Lake, *Earlier Epistles*, pp. 215-16. For an example of how not to proceed, I mention the recent work by Judith Gundry Volf who, rather than dealing with each letter as a distinct hermeneutic unit, assumes 'a certain coherence and consistency in [Paul's] thought until the texts...prove otherwise' (*Paul and Perseverance In and Falling Away* [WUNT, 2.37; Tübingen: Mohr–Siebeck, 1990], p. 3).

soteriological text in the context of these congregational factors.

This raises the problem posed by Romans. Romans is Paul's only letter written to a congregation which he neither founded nor visited (at least prior to writing the letter). This unusual situation, coupled with the lengthy and convoluted nature of its discourse, has given rise to a protracted debate on the purpose or reason of Romans.[65] For example, is Paul responding to a particular situation which has arisen in the congregation at Rome? Or is he simply attempting to demonstrate that he is not an antinomian in order to encourage their material assistance in his planned mission to Spain? Since Romans cannot be related to congregational factors with any degree of certainty, this letter will not be considered here. However, given the fact that the expulsion language in Romans has already been discussed, and that Galatians and 2 Corinthians 1–9 are representative of Paul's adoption of the apotropaeic paradigm, little is lost in this omission.

Immediately following a consideration of congregational factors in each letter and the relevance of Paul's own experiences (especially his affliction in Asia), I will attempt to describe the general trend in the development of Paul's thought.

---

65. Note for example the recent appearance of three new books on the subject: K.P. Donfried (ed.), *The Romans Debate* (Peabody, MA: Hendrickson, rev. edn, 1991); A.J.M. Wedderburn, *The Reasons for Romans* (Edinburgh: T. & T. Clark, 1988); L.A. Jervis, *The Purpose of Romans: A Comparative Letter Structure Investigation* (JSNTSup, 55; Sheffield: JSOT Press, 1991).

Chapter 5

THE DEVELOPMENT OF PAUL'S SOTERIOLOGY IN HIS EARLY CAREER:
2 THESSALONIANS, 1 THESSALONIANS, 1 CORINTHIANS

The study of Paul has been traditionally divided into two areas: his life and his thought. The former has to do with the social context in which lived; the latter, with the symbolic system of his thought. It follows from this that Pauline Christianity is at once a product of social and symbolic realities, especially as they concern meaning. Both must be integrated if interpretative reductionism is to be avoided.

Bearing this in mind, I shall turn to the question of the development of Paul's soteriology from his early letters through to his later letters. This study does not aim to be exhaustive in its study of Paul's soteriological texts. In other words, I do not intend to comment upon all texts which have soteriological significance, much less, to relate all soteriological texts to some overarching thesis concerning the development of Paul's thought. My purpose here is less ambitious, namely: to relate the apotropaeic paradigm found in Paul's later letters to some of the most important paradigms of his earlier letters. I will illustrate that there is a general shift in Paul's soteriology from an emphasis on Christ's parousia and resurrection (Chapter 5) to an emphasis on Christ's resurrection and his death as an apotropaeic victim (Chapter 6). Before this broader purpose can be achieved it is necessary to locate some of Paul's key soteriological texts within the specific situations arising in his churches and within his own life experiences.

Jesus the Warrior: 2 Thessalonians

The unifying message of Jewish apocalyptic writings is a pastoral one whose essence is encouragement.[1] Jewish apocalyptic literature was

1.   When inquiring into the understanding of the afterlife in Jewish apocalyptic writings, it is perplexing to find a great diversity of ideas even in a single work. For

written to exhort the faithful to courage, steadfastness and hope in the face of overwhelming persecution. It accomplished this by assuring them that God will soon vindicate his people. The following passage from *1 Enoch* illustrates this theme:

> Be hopeful, because formerly you have pined away through evil and toil. But now you shall shine like the lights of heaven, and you shall be seen; and the windows of heaven shall be opened for you. Your cry shall be heard. Cry for judgment, and it shall appear for you; for all your tribulations shall be (demanded) for investigation from the (responsible) authorities—from everyone who assisted those who plundered you. Be hopeful, and do not abandon your hope, because there shall be a fire for you; you are about to be making a great rejoicing like the angels of heaven. You shall not have to hide on the day of the great judgment, and you shall not be found as the sinners; but the eternal judgment shall be for all the generations of the world. Now fear not, righteous ones, when you see the sinners waxing strong and flourishing.[2]

Thus, at the heart of Jewish apocalyptic belief was a theology of hope; hope in a final judgment for the wicked and a glorious new life for the righteous. There is an assurance that what God did not do for the Jews in this life, he would surely do in the next. Thus, Jewish apocalyptic literature was primarily not speculative in nature but pragmatic and pastoral. It can be summed up in the exhortation: 'Be of good courage now because you have grown old in troubles and tribulations...your cry shall be heard' (*1 En.* 104.2).

At the outset of his new life as a Christian, Paul's mind was steeped in the language and images of Jewish apocalypticism. He assures the Thessalonian Christians that Jesus, the heavenly warrior, will soon come

---

example, in *4 Ezra*; one reads of the immortality of the soul similar to Greek conceptions (*4 Ezra* 7.78, 88), the revivication of human life at judgment (7.32), and the glorious transformation of the righteous (7.96-98). Likewise, in *1 En.* both the righteous and the unpunished wicked are resurrected in book 1 (22.9-11), while in book 5, one finds a doctrine of immortality (100.4; 103.4); the pious are said to enjoy a peaceful sleep in death from which they will be 'awakened' at a time appointed by God (91.10; 92.3; 100.5; cf. 1 Thess. 4.13-17; 1 Cor. 15.52). Examples could easily be multiplied but the point is clear; this genre of literature manifests no singular position on resurrection versus immortality, on general resurrection versus resurrection of the righteous alone, on the Messianic kingdom on earth versus life in the heavenly abode.

2.   E. Isaac (trans.), '1 (Ethiopic Apocalypse of) Enoch', in J.H. Charlesworth (ed.), *The Old Testament Pseudepigrapha*. I. *Apocalyptic Literature and Testaments* (Garden City, NY: Doubleday, 1983), pp. 5-89.

down from heaven with his army of mighty angels to punish the wicked and vindicate persecuted Christians. Paul writes:

> God deems it just to repay with affliction those who afflict you, and to grant rest with us to you who are afflicted, when the Lord Jesus is revealed from heaven with his mighty angels in flaming fire, inflicting vengeance upon those who do not know God and upon those who do not obey the gospel of our Lord Jesus Christ. They shall suffer the punishment of eternal destruction and exclusion from the presence of the Lord and from the glory of his might, when he comes on that day to be glorified among his saints, and to be marvelled at in all who have believed...(2 Thess. 1.6-10).

The persecuted Christians living in Thessalonica undoubtedly found comfort in these words. It goes without saying that Paul's apocalyptic images, including his portrayal of a heavenly redeemer, were not his own invention.[3] C.H. Dodd describes the theology of this letter as being 'painted in colours from the crudest palette of Jewish eschatology'.[4] Paul shared in the language of the Jewish apocalypticism of his own day, but modified it so as to make it recognizably Christian.

One searches this letter in vain for references to later Pauline themes such as the cross, atonement, resurrection. All these are yet to come in the development of Paul's thought. In his first days as a Christian, the parousia was the pivotal salvation event.[5] The resurrection, such as it can be inferred from the context, served only to install Jesus in readiness for his triumphant return. Furthermore, at this point, it has not occurred to Paul that some Christians may die before the parousia. He is convinced that all Christians are living in the very last days of the aeon and will witness Christ's triumphant return.

---

3. The Jewish apocalypticism of Paul's day can be briefly summarised as follows. First, it was characterized by the expectation of the imminent end of the world and God's vindication and salvation of his covenantal people. Secondly, the heavenly world was thought to include angelic beings and a pre-existent saviour. It was separated from the realm of human existence by a series of intermediate worlds which were occupied by good and evil spirits. Thirdly, God himself was cosmologically removed from this world, but made use of intermediaries such as the Son of Man, the heavenly Logos, and angels, to intervene in human affairs (K. Koch, *The Rediscovery of Apocalyptic: A Polemical Work on a Neglected Area of Biblical Studies and Its Damaging Effects on Theology and Philosophy*, SBT 2/22 [1972], pp. 18-35).

4. Dodd, *New Testament Studies*, p. 121.

5. The 'coming' (ἡ παρουσία) of Jesus at the end of the age is traditionally referred to as the parousia.

Jesus the Rapturer: 1 Thessalonians

What Paul could not have known is that there were more 'last days' than he had expected, so many in fact, that a number of Christians would die waiting for the parousia. This surprising turn of events raised doubts about the well-being of Christians who had died before Christ's triumphant return. This is the background against which Paul tells the Thessalonians 'not to grieve' over fellow Christians who have died 'as others do who have no hope' (1 Thess. 4.13). Paul assures them that the dead in Christ have *not* missed out on their deliverance; they will not be at a disadvantage at the parousia.

> But we do not want you to be uninformed, brothers, about those who have died, so that you may not grieve as others do who have no hope. For since we believe that Jesus died and rose again, even so, through Jesus, God will bring with him those who have died. For this we declare to you by the word of the Lord, that we who are alive, who are left until the coming of the Lord, will by no means precede those who have died. For the Lord himself, with a cry of command, with the archangel's call and with the sound of God's trumpet, will descend from heaven, and the dead in Christ will rise first. Then we who are alive, who are left, will be caught up in the clouds together with them to meet the Lord in the air; and so we will be with the Lord forever. Therefore, encourage one another with these words (1 Thess. 4.14-18).

Paul's introductory phrase, 'we do not want you to be uninformed, brothers' (Οὐ θέλομεν δὲ ὑμᾶς ἀγοεῖν, ἀδελφοί [4.13]) consists of a disclosure formula followed by a noun in the vocative case. This formula is a strong epistolary signal that Paul is about to tell the Thessalonians something he has never told them before. In other words, this teaching was not part of Paul's original preaching when he founded a church in Thessalonica.

Paul assures the Thessalonians that, not only will the dead not be at a disadvantage, they will be raised *first* when Christ returns; only then will the living be taken up quickly 'in the clouds to meet the Lord in the air' (v. 17). Paul finds no difficulty in stating that the living and the dead are put on an equal basis despite the fact that they begin with different types of bodies.[6] Paul does not turn his attention to the problem of bodily transformation until 1 Corinthians 15.

---

6. W. Wiefel, 'Die Hauptrichtung des Wandels im eschatologischen Denkens des Paulus', *TZ* 30 (1974), pp. 65-81, esp. 81; J. Gillman, 'Signals of Transformation in 1 Thess. 4.13-18', *CBQ* 47 (1985), pp. 263-81, esp. p. 281.

For the modern reader, this disclosure formula (4.13) serves as a sign-post to a development in Paul's thought. In this, Paul's second extant letter, the subject of the rapture of the dead in Christ is mentioned for the first time. Christ will return, not only to punish the wicked and reward faithful Christians, but also to raise the dead. Clearly the issue at stake is pastoral: Paul ends this section by instructing the Thessalonians to 'encourage one another with these words' (v. 18).

Though much of the apocalyptic battle imagery of 2 Thessalonians persists (e.g., the coming of a heavenly redeemer, the 'cry of command', 'the archangel's cry', the sound of the 'trumpet'), the emphasis is on salvation rather than retribution: Jesus the warrior has become Jesus the rapturer. The issue in the forefront is no longer persecution but the untimely death of Christians.

The resurrection of Jesus is still of subordinate significance at this stage in Paul's thought. Paul does *not* assure the Christians that their life beyond the grave is related to Christ's resurrection; he does *not* argue, 'because Christ was raised, so also Christians will be raised', as he will in 1 Corinthians. The logic is different here: rather it is because Christ will return that Christians will be raised.

If Jesus' resurrection is of secondary significance in this letter, what does Paul say of Jesus' crucifixion? Jesus' death is mentioned in the same breath as the death of the prophets (1 Thess. 2.15). In Paul's early years as Christian, he believed that Jesus' death demonstrated the con-tinued hard-heartedness of the Jews, but he attached no theological significance to it. The death of Jesus was a regrettable but understand-able set-back in a world where violence and conflict ruled the day. As I shall demonstrate below, the unimportance of Christ's death and resur-rection in Paul's early theology is reminiscent of the Palestinian and Syrian Christologies of two other early Christian writings, the Sayings Gospel, Q, and the Gospel of Thomas (see Appendix 1).

The Resurrected Christ: 1 Corinthians

1 Corinthians is the 'resurrection letter' par excellence. For this reason, it has done more to secure the theological centrality of resurrection in the Christian tradition than any other Pauline letter. Seen from the vantage point of historical hindsight, this observation is unremarkable. However, when viewed in relation to Paul's own preaching up to this point, not to mention from the vantage point of contemporary Palestinian Christianity, the development is noteworthy indeed.

The canonical First Letter to the Corinthians is actually Paul's second correspondence with the Corinthian Christians.[7] In this letter, Paul pointedly addresses the concerns and questions raised by a number of representatives of the church in Corinth: Chloe's people had brought oral news (1.11); Stephanus, Fortunatus and Achaicus had also arrived bearing both an oral report and a letter (1 Cor. 16.17). Paul responded to these oral and written communications by writing 1 Corinthians.

This letter breaks into a number of separate and self-contained sections, each dealing with one of the matters raised by the Corinthians. These matters are frequently introduced by the formula περὶ δὲ ἐγράψατε ('now concerning the matters about which you wrote').[8] In each case, the exegete must attempt to reconstruct the question raised by the Corinthians from Paul's own answer. 1 Corinthians 15 introduces one of these 'matters' about which they had written, namely the problem of the resurrection of believers. The chapter begins with Paul's recitation of the so-called 'witness tradition'.

The Witness Tradition Delivered to Paul
The analysis of 1 Corinthians 15 is complicated at the outset by the fact that Paul begins with a witness tradition which was passed on to him: 'For I have handed on to you as of first importance *what I in turn had received*' (1 Cor. 15.3). In this brief prefatory remark Paul signals the reader that the 'witness tradition' which follows (vv. 3-7) is not his own theological formulation but a tradition which he had received from others. This tradition can be broken down into five consecutive statements:

1. 'that Christ died for our sins in accordance with the [Jewish] scriptures and that he was buried', (vv. 3b-4a)
2. 'he was raised (ἐγήγερται) on the third day in accordance with the scriptures', (v. 4b)
3. 'he appeared (ὤφθη) to Cephas and *then* (εἶτα) to the twelve'; (v. 5)
4. '*afterward* (ἔπειτα) he appeared to more than five hundred brothers at one time, most of whom are still alive, though some have died'. (v. 6)
5. '*afterward* (ἔπειτα) he appeared to James, *then* (εἶτα) to all the apostles'. (v. 7)

7. Paul wrote the so-called 'previous letter' while in Ephesus (1 Cor. 5.9).
8. This 'now concerning' (περὶ δὲ) formulae occurs 6 times (1 Cor. 7.1, 25; 8.1; 12.1; 16.1; 16.12; cf. Hurd, *Origins*, p. 63).

This tradition is the earliest of all extant resurrection accounts in the New Testament. That it originated in the Gentile—not Jewish—churches can be deduced from the following observations. First, Paul not only states that he 'received' this witness tradition (1 Cor. 15.3), but also that the Jerusalem church 'added nothing' to his gospel (Gal. 2.6). This suggests that he did not receive the witness tradition from the Jerusalem church. Secondly, the ambiguous phrase, 'in accordance with the [Jewish] scriptures' lacks the precision which one would expect of a Jewish author. It suggests a Hellenistic author who did not know the Jewish scriptures well but was convinced that Christ's death and resurrection somehow fulfilled these scriptures. Thirdly, the term 'Christ' (Χριστός) is used as a proper name (v. 3). In the first century, the term 'christ' (*messiah*) was not a title or office, but a designation of someone chosen by God to perform a function on behalf of the covenant people.[9] A Jew would have used it in its proper sense with a definite article, *'the* christ' (ὁ χριστός).

The emergence of this witness tradition in the Gentile churches is very significant since there is no evidence of a parallel witness tradition in the earliest Jewish churches (Appendix 1), nor in Paul's earliest theology (2 Thess., 1 Thess.). This suggests that the witness traditions of the canonical gospels were a product of Gentile Christianity.

Why did the Gentile Church articulate its faith in Jesus Christ in terms of post-death appearance stories? What situation in the life of the Gentile churches contributed towards the formulation of this witness tradition? An analysis of the content of 1 Cor. 15.3-7 suggests that the two principal factors were: (1) the validation of leadership claims; (2) the need to explain how Jesus, having been crucified, could continue to bestow benefits on his followers.

Validation of Leadership Claims

Adolf von Harnack has observed the parallelism in 1 Cor. 15.3-7 between 'Cephas' and 'the twelve' on the one hand, and 'James' and 'all the apostles' on the other.[10] He has also drawn attention to the careful use of the particles 'then' (εἶτα) and 'afterward' (ἔπειτα).

---

9. A. Segal, *Rebecca's Children: Judaism and Christianity in the Roman World* (Cambridge, MA: Harvard University Press, 1986), p. 65.

10. A. von Harnack, 'Die Verklärungsgeschichte Jesu, der Bericht des Paulus (1 Kor 15.3f.) und die beiden Christus-Visionen des Petrus' (SPAW; Berlin: Akademie der Wissenshaften, 1922), pp. 62-80.

Christ appeared to Cephas and *then* (εἶτα) to the twelve[11]...

afterward (ἔπειτα) he appeared to James, *then* (εἶτα) to all the apostles.

According to Harnack, these structural features indicate that the witness tradition was originally structured upon two lists, one headed by Cephas (Peter), the second by James. Harnack and E. Bammel conclude that these two lists represent the rival leadership claims of Cephas and James.[12]

Those who came forward as leaders in the emerging churches validated their authority by claiming a christophany, a personal vision of the resurrected Lord. By crediting Cephas with the first witness of the risen Lord, then 'the twelve', and then only secondarily, James and the other apostles, the witness tradition accords preeminence to the Cephas-party and subordinates the authority of the James-party.[13]

This conclusion is consistent with Paul's own testimony. In the first years of Paul's life as a Christian, Cephas was the chief leader in Judaea. When Paul describes his visit with Cephas in Jerusalem, James is mentioned only secondarily and treated as belonging with 'the other apostles' (Gal. 1.18). However, by the time Paul returns to Jerusalem over fourteen years later for the so-called 'Jerusalem conference' the political situation has changed: Cephas, once the principal authority, has been replaced by a triumvirate of three 'pillars', James, Cephas and John, with James at the head.[14] The obvious tension between Cephas and James is dramatised by Cephas' fear of the followers of James over the issue of table-fellowship with Gentiles (Gal. 2.11-14). Thus, the emergence of the pre-Pauline witness tradition is bound up with the recognition of individual authority and leadership in the early churches.

11. This cannot be Paul's expression since Paul never refers to 'the twelve' (R.H. Fuller, *The Formation of the Resurrection Narratives* [New York: Macmillan, 1971], p. 28). The idea of twelve disciples is a Lukan creation. On the basis of this parallelism, Reginald Fuller considers the reference to Christ's appearance to the five hundred to be a later addition to the tradition.

12. von Harnack, 'Die Verklärungsgeschichte Jesu', pp. 62-80; E. Bammel, 'Herkunft und Funktion der Traditionselemente in 1 Kor 15.1-11', *TZ* 11 (1955), pp. 401-419. Though Bammel disagrees with Harnack as to how the list should be divided.

13. This explains why the fourth gospel stresses that Peter entered the empty tomb first, despite the fact that John arrived at the site ahead of him (Jn 20.3-6).

14. B.H. McLean, 'Galatians 2.7-9 and the Question of the Recognition of Paul's Apostolic Status at the Jerusalem Conference: A Critique of Gerd Lüdemann's Reconstruction', *NTS* 37.1 (1991), pp. 67-76; Lüdemann, *Paul*, pp. 64-65; Manson, *Studies*, p. 196.

Immediately following his recitation of the witness tradition, Paul records his own christophany, thereby inserting himself into this witness tradition: 'Last of all, as to one untimely born, he appeared also to me' (1 Cor. 15.8). In so doing Paul hoped to validate his own authority as a genuine apostle.

Although Paul felt no immediate need for official authorisation of his apostleship by the apostles in Jerusalem at the time of his conversion,[15] his apostolic status was later challenged. This challenge pushed Paul to seek official recognition from the 'pillar' apostles in order to assure that he 'was not running, or had not run, in vain' (Gal. 2.2; cf. 1.21; 2.1).[16] Paul's insertion of himself in the witness tradition was undoubtedly part of Paul's defence of his apostleship when he visited the pillar apostles in Jerusalem. His subsequent reiterations of his christophany are part of his ongoing need to defend his own apostolic authority in the face of his detractors.[17] Therefore, far from being detached theological discourse, Paul's recitation of the witness tradition is closely bound up with his self-validation and authority as an apostle.

Rationale for Christ Bestowing Benefits

While Paul's account of Christ the warrior and rapturer is immersed in the language and ideas of Jewish apocalypticism, his depiction of Christ's resurrection appearances is rooted in the tradition of the Graeco-Roman witness stories which tell of the after-death sightings of certain 'divine men'.

15. There can be no doubt that Paul considered himself an apostle at the point of his conversion. In the words of Ferdinand Hahn, Paul's 'concept of apostleship is characterized by the fact of his being simultaneously converted, entrusted with the gospel, and sent out to the Gentiles' (F. Hahn, *Mission in the New Testament* [London: SCM Press, 1965], pp. 95-110, esp. p. 98). As John Knox observes, Paul's customary use of the term 'apostle' means 'one who saw the Lord and was commissioned directly by him. Certainly when Paul saw himself as an 'apostle', he invariably has this higher meaning in mind' (Knox, *Chapters*, p. 117).

16. McLean, 'Galatians 2.7-9', pp. 67-76.

17. R. Bultmann, 'New Testament and Mythology', in H.W. Bartsch (ed.), *Kerygma and Myth: A Theological Debate* (trans. R.H. Fuller; London: SPCK, 1953), pp. 1-44, esp. pp. 39-40. Similarly, James Tabor argues that Paul recounts his extraordinary journey to Paradise (2 Cor. 12.2-4), like the epiphany at his conversion, in order to support his own claims to apostolic authority (J. Tabor, *Things Unutterable: Paul's Ascent to Paradise in its Greco-Roman, Judaic, and Early Christian Contexts* [Studies in Judaism; Lanham, MD: University Press of America, 1986], ch. 3).

In antiquity, certain men were singled out for their exceptional virtue, wisdom or power, and venerated as 'divine men' (θεῖοι ἄνδρες).[18] The stories about such men share many common characteristics: these men were all conceived through the union of an eternal god with a virgin; each was taken up into heaven after his death (if he died at all), after which there are accounts of mysterious post-death appearances and deifications (ἀποθεώσεις).

One of the best known examples is that of the neopythagorean mystic and wandering teacher, Apollonius of Tyana.[19] He was born from the union of Apollo and a mortal virgin named Karinus. The records imply that he was miraculously translated to heaven. He then appeared to one of his disciples who had not accepted his teacher's instruction on the immortality of the soul. Those who were present with this disciple could not see or hear Apollonius. The disciple explained: 'it would seem that

18. The figure of the 'divine man' (θεῖος ἀνήρ) is one of the classic insights of the *religionsgeschichtliche Schule*. Based on the research of Richard Reitzenstein (*Hellenistische Wundererzählungen* [Leipzig: B.G. Teubner, 1906]) and Ludwig Bieler (*ΘΕΙΟΣ ΑΝΗΡ: Das bild des 'gottlichen Menschen' in Spatantike und Fruhchristentum* [2 vols.; Darmstadt Wissenschaftliche Buchgesellschaft, 1930–1935]), this concept was used to explain the background to the miracle stories of the gospels. More recently, David Aune concludes that the canonical gospels fit comfortably as a sub-type within the parameters of ancient biographical conventions (D. Aune, *The New Testament in Its Literary Environment* [ed. W.A. Meeks; Library of Early Christianity, 8; Philadelphia: Westminster Press, 1987], ch. 2). For a complete bibliography cf. J.E. Alsup, *The Post-Resurrection Stories on the Gospel Tradition* (Calwer Theologische Monographien; Stuttgart: Calwer Verlag, 1975); C. Talbert, *What is a Gospel?* (Philadelphia: Fortress Press, 1982). Most recently, cf. Barry Blackburn who accepts the method but argues that the locus for parallels with Mark's Gospel is the Jewish, not Hellenistic world. His work focuses on healing stories (B. Blackburn, *Theos Aner and the Markan Miracle Traditions: A Critique of the Theios Aner Concept as an Interpretive Background of the Miracle Traditions Used by Mark* [WUNT, 2.40; Tübingen: Mohr (Paul Siebeck), 1991], pp. 10-11, 229-30, 265). Though Blackburn concedes the fusion of Jewish and Hellenistic worlds, his thesis artificially divides the two and, in my view, accords too much weight to the Jewish.

19. On affinities between the *Vita Apollonii* and the gospels cf. G. Petzke's essay in H.D. Betz, G. Delling and W.C. van Unnik, (eds.), *Die Traditionen über Apollonius von Tyana und das Neue Testament*, (SCHNT, 1; Leiden: Brill, 1970), pp. 61-62. Though the only extant account of his life was preserved in Philostratus (c. 249 CE), it is almost certain that he was working with traditions which were contemporaneous with those of the New Testament (J.E. Alsup, *Post-Resurrection Appearance Stories*, p. 222).

he is come to converse with myself alone concerning the tenets which I would not believe.'[20]

There are many other examples of the divine man phenomenon. For example, Romulus was the son of Mars and the virgin Ilia Sylvia.[21] He was taken up during a sudden darkness,[22] and later appeared to a friend on a road demanding to be worshipped as the god Quirinius.[23] Empedocles, a renowned poet, philosopher and statesman, after offering sacrifice and sharing a meal with some friends, remained at the table until the others had retired and then vanished. One of his friends claimed to have seen a brilliant light and heard a mysterious voice summoning Empedocles to heaven.[24]

Aristeas of Proconnesus was resurrected while sealed in the locked room of a textile shop where he died. When the word of his death spread throughout the region, one man protested saying that he had just met Aristeas on the road to Cyzicus and conversed with him. The miraculous disappearance of Aristeas' body was testified by his relatives who went to the textile shop in order to prepare the body for burial. Aristeas' resurrection was proven by the fact that the chamber which contained his body was empty.[25]

Events such as these served to prove the passage of these men from

20. F.C. Conybeare (trans.), *The Life of Apollonius of Tyanna* (2 vols.; New York: Macmillan, 1912), 8.31.

21. 'She [Illia] had been united in marriage to the divinity [Mars] in the place and as a result of her violation should bear two sons [Romulus and Remus] who would far excel all men in valour and warlike achievements' (E. Cary [trans.], *The Roman Antiquities of Dionysius of Halicarnassus* [7 vols.; Cambridge, MA: Harvard University Press, 1937], 1.77.2).

22. 'Romulus disappeared suddenly, and no portion of his body or fragment of his clothing remained to be seen...The light of the sun failed, and night came down upon them...with...thunder and furious blasts (cf. Acts 2.2)...and when the storm had ceased, and the sun shone out...the nobles...exhorted them all [the multitude] to honour and revere Romulus, since he had been caught up into heaven, and was to be a benevolent god for them instead of a good king' (B. Perrin [trans.], 'Romulus', in *Plutarch's Lives* [LCL; 11 vols.; Cambridge, MA: Harvard University Press, 1967], 27.5.7).

23. Dionysius Halicarnassus, *Rom. Ant.* 2.63, 3-4.

24. R.D. Hicks (trans.), *Dionysius of Halicarnassus: The Lives of Eminent Philosphers* (LCL; 2 vols.; Cambridge, MA: Harvard University Press, 1958), 8.57.

25. Herodotus, *Hist.* 4.14-15. Other examples of 'divine men' include Cleomedes of Astypaleia, Alcmene, Peregrinus Proteus and Demainete (Alsup, *Post-Resurrection Appearance Stories*, pp. 226-29).

the human to the divine realm. What is more, they also provided a rational explanation of how such men could bestow blessings upon their followers who were left behind. When the delay of Christ's parousia called into question his power beyond the grave, the stories of Christ's post-death appearances communicated the Christian conviction that Christ had indeed passed into the divine realm. It also explained how Christ could be a source of divine blessing in the present, and finally, how he could come and vindicate steadfast Christians in the future.

In the light of the divine man tradition, it would appear that it was not the uniqueness of Christ's appearance stories which made them significant for early Christians, but their similarity to the appearance stories of other divine men. Though Christ was pre-eminent for Christians and their devotion was reserved for him alone, this does not imply that the stories of his post-death appearance were unparalleled. Rather, Christ's resurrection numbered him among that elite group of divine men who had special powers with which to bless their followers. The significance of the resurrection and appearance stories lay in the fact that they proclaimed the Christian conviction that Jesus is a divine man whose relationship with his followers continues.

Paul's Resurrected Christ

Having established the context of Paul's witness tradition in terms of both claims to apostleship and the divine man tradition, there remains the primary question: why is Paul 'reminding' (γνωρίζω [1 Cor. 15.1]) the Corinthians of this tradition at this time? Or, put another way, why does Paul state that *this* teaching is imperative for one's salvation (15.2)? What exactly was Paul's controversy with the Corinthians?

Paul is not attempting to prove the facticity of Jesus' resurrection as Rudolf Bultmann and Wolfhart Pannenberg have suggested.[26] Bultmann thinks that Paul had misunderstood the Corinthians' objection, interpreting it to mean a rejection of the whole notion of life after death. Bultmann argues that the Corinthians had actually adopted a Gnostic[27]

---

26. W. Pannenberg, *Jesus: God and Man* (Philadelphia: Westminster Press, 2nd edn, 1977), p. 89; Bultmann, *Theology of the New Testament*, p. 295.

27. The task of describing Gnosticism is complicated at the outset by a modern confusion of terminology. English speaking scholars generally speak of 'Gnosticism' by which they mean the numerous amorphous schools of thought resulting from the fusion of Christianity with Greek philosophy in the second century CE. German scholars, on the other hand, tend to think in terms of 'Gnosis' which is a more inclusive

interpretation of the resurrection saying 'the resurrection has already occurred'.[28] The real problem, says Bultmann, was rooted in a pneumatic-Gnostic movement in the Corinthian church which denied the future reality of the resurrection of the dead and the final judgment.

According to Walther Schmithals, the principal demonstration of their Gnostic beliefs is to be found in their pride in γνῶσις (1 Cor. 8.1-13). Schmithals argues that Paul's proclamation of the resurrection of the dead in 1 Corinthians 15 was the climax of his anti-gnostic polemic which he sustained throughout the Corinthian letters. Since the denial of the resurrection is a fundamental dogma of Gnosticism, Paul chose to sum up his anti-gnostic polemic by teaching on the resurrection in ch. 15.[29] Similarly, Robert Jewett has argued that Paul's ψυχικός language in particular (1 Cor. 15.21, 44-49; cf. 2.14-16) is evidence of the Corinthians' adhesion to the basic duality of Gnosticism, ψυχή and πνεῦμα. According to Jewett, this proves that Paul was arguing with Gnostics in Corinth and that Paul himself had Gnostic tendencies.[30]

The difficulty posed by the Gnostic interpretation of 1 Corinthians is its questionable assumption that Gnosticism did indeed exist during the first century CE.[31] Although the word γνῶσις occurs twenty-nine times in the New Testament, ten times in 1 Corinthians, and six in 2 Corinthians, there is no indication that this is γνῶσις in the Gnostic sense. The concept of 'knowing' God is also attested in Qumran writings,[32] in the

term meaning the belief that salvation is by knowledge. The situation is further complicated by the adjective 'gnostic' which is used in the literature to describe both Gnosticism and Gnosis. French scholars have maintained a useful distinction between *la gnose* and *le gnosticisme*. There is a growing tendency in English scholarship to either adopt the French distinction or recognise the validity of the German term 'Gnosis' as a comprehensive word which expresses its diffuse and complex character with diverse expressions in Christian, Jewish and so-called 'pagan' culture.

28. Bultmann, *Theology of the New Testament*, p. 169. This 'Gnostic hypothesis' was first put forward by W. Lütgert (*Freiheitspredigt und Scharmgeister in Korinth* [Gütersloh: C. Bertelsmann, 1908]) and subsequently taken up by A. Schlatter, R. Reitzenstein and R. Bultmann (who found the Gnostic redeemer myth lurking behind 1 Cor. 2.8 [*Theology of the New Testament*, p. 175]).

29. Schmithals, *Gnosticism*, pp. 156-285.

30. Jewett, *Paul's Anthropological Terms*, pp. 340-54.

31. Cf. Heinz O. Guenther detailed discussion of the gnostic hypothesis in the Corinthian church (H.O. Guenther, 'Gnosticism in Corinth?' in McLean [ed.], *Origins and Method*, pp. 44-81).

32. W.D. Davies, 'Knowledge in the Dead Sea Scrolls and Matthew 11.25-30', *HTR* 46 (1953), pp. 379-80.

Odes of Solomon[33] and in the *Mandaic* writings.[34]

Moreover, one must avoid the trap of reading Gnostic ideas which may reflect subsequent developments within the terminology itself into Paul's terminology. One cannot assume that the significances of these particular terms in the fully developed Gnostic system can be attached to the same terms in 1 Corinthians. Though there are elements in 1 Corinthians 15 which could be perceived as Gnostic, the letter contains no Gnostic myth and no Gnostic system, nor can any Gnostic document be dated as early as 1 Corinthians.[35] All that can be said is that these similarities represent partial analogies with Gnosis or Gnosticism.[36] One finds in the Corinthian correspondence the first tentative beginnings of what would later develop into Gnosticism. In other words, 1 Corinthians demonstrates how conditions were ripe for the development of Gnostic theology in the second century.

Bultmann's contention that Paul misunderstood the Corinthians to mean that they denied the whole possibility of an afterlife is untenable. For example, Paul knew that they were vicariously baptising the living on behalf of the dead. Clearly, Paul did not think the Corinthians had denied the reality of life beyond the grave, nor the resurrection of Christ. As Hans Conzelmann points out, 1 Cor. 15.12-18 indicates that the Corinthians had already accepted Jesus' resurrection.[37]

The Corinthians did not contest *Christ's* resurrection. They were familiar with the appearance stories and Christ's resurrection was probably part of Paul's preaching to them. The Corinthians accepted Jesus' resurrection as an isolated fact but they did not accept its relationship to those among them who had died.[38] Hence, Paul's quotation of the slogan of the Corinthians: 'Now if Christ is proclaimed as raised from the dead, *how can some of you say there is no resurrection of the dead?*' (1 Cor. 15.12).

Why, and on what basis, did some Corinthians claim that there was no

33. K. Rudolph, 'War der Verfasser der *Oden Salomos* ein 'Qumran Christ'—Ein Beitrag zur Diskussion um die Anfänge der Gnosis', *RevQ* 4 (1963), p. 525.

34. Rudolph, 'War der Verfasser', p. 525.

35. C.H. Dodd, *The Interpretation of the Fourth Gospel* (Cambridge: Cambridge University Press, 1968), p. 98.

36. R. Haardt, 'Gnosis', in K. Rahner *et al.* (eds.), *Sacramentum Mundi* (6 vols.; Montreal: Palm Publishers, 1968), II, pp. 372-79, esp. 378.

37. Conzelmann, *1 Corinthians*, pp. 299-320.

38. K. Barth, *The Resurrection of the Dead* (New York: Fleming H. Revell, 1933), pp. 102, 152.

resurrection of the dead? The solution to the question is afforded by an analysis of the development of Paul's thought up to this point. In Paul's early preaching, the theological centrepiece was Christ's parousia, not his resurrection. The resurrection simply served to install Christ in a position of readiness for his triumphant return. More to the point, it was the parousia—not the resurrection—which was the principal salvation event. The living and dead in Christ were both taken up into heaven at the parousia. No mention was made of participation in Christ's resurrection.

For the Corinthian Christians, Christ's resurrection constituted his victory over death, his exaltation to heaven and his enthronement as the Lord who would one day return and gather Christians. However, they continued to believe that Christ's parousia was the fundamental salvation event. Indeed, Paul continues to teach that the dead and living will be taken up at the parousia. In other words, the dead are not resurrected individually at the time of their deaths. Salvation for the living and the dead is still an event which takes place in the future when the 'last trumpet' will sound (15.52; cf. 1 Thess. 4.16). This event is still instantaneous, taking place 'in the twinkling of an eye' (1 Cor. 15.52).

In this light, it is hardly surprising that the Corinthians perceived no direct connection between Christ's resurrection and their own future beyond the grave. It seems that some Corinthians had put forward the teaching that their spiritual union with Christ through baptism and their present endowment with the Spirit, meant that each of them had a new spiritual self which would actually survive death. In other words, they denied the necessity of the bodily resurrection of the dead in favour of a doctrine of immortality.[39] According to John Hurd, they found the notion of bodily resurrection 'gross and unspiritual'.[40]

Paul, on the other hand, believed that the fate of deceased Christians was tied to the resurrection of Christ. They could not simply pass through death as spiritual beings. Like Christ, Christians must truly die and then be raised again with spiritual bodies. Paul's defence in 1 Corinthians 15 represents his first extant attempt to describe *how* the dead in Christ are resurrected bodily.

In order to establish this proposition Paul had to address two issues. First, he needed to explain why this belief is necessary. To this end,

---

39. A.J.M. Wedderburn, 'The Problem of the Denial of the Resurrection in 1 Corinthians 15', *NovT* 23 (1981), pp. 229-41, esp. 236-39; Hurd, *Origins*, p. 229.
40. Hurd, *Origins*, p. 229.

Paul's enlarges upon the significance of the Christ's resurrection such that it no longer serves simply as an explanation of how Christ was made ready for his return at the parousia. Rather, Paul conceives of the resurrection more broadly in relation to believers. Secondly, Paul attempts to answer the questions '*How* are the dead raised? With what kind of body do they come?' (1 Cor. 15.35).

Why Belief in the Resurrection is Necessary
Paul argues that to dispute one's own resurrection is to abrogate the possibility of future life beyond the grave. In vv. 12-34 Paul attempts to prove the absurdity of the Corinthian's denial of the resurrection of the dead. He argues by *reductio ad absurdum* in order to prove that the Corinthian denial of their own resurrection implies a denial of Christ's resurrection. The resurrection of Christ from the dead (ἐκ νεκρῶν) necessarily implies the final resurrection of the dead (ἀνάστασις νεκρῶν) (15.12). In other words, Christ's resurrection does not have an isolated meaning for Christ alone but is set fundamentally on the same level as the resurrection of all Christians.[41]

Paul's assertion that there is a causal connection between Christ and the dead Christians is based on his mystical theology of participation in Christ which he explains using Adam typology (1 Cor. 15.20-22, 45-50). Both Adam and Christ are described by the term 'human' (ἄνθρωπος); as death came into the world through the primal human (Adam), so also resurrection was made possible by the redeemer human (Christ). Human beings are naturally 'in Adam' and thereby participate in death. But by virtue of their baptism, Christians are also 'in Christ', the second Adam. Therefore, Christ is only 'the first fruits of those who sleep' (1 Cor. 15.20).[42] His resurrection was the first in a series of subsequent raisings. It is not complete in its fullest sense unless the dead in Christ are also resurrected in a bodily form. Conversely, no resurrection of the dead would mean that Christ had not been resurrected (15.13).

How Are the Dead Raised?
Paul also attempts to answer the questions '*How* are the dead raised? With what kind of body do they come?' (1 Cor. 15.35). As we have

41. H. Braun, *Gesammelt Studient zum Neuen Testament* (Tübingen: Mohr [Paul Siebeck], 1966), pp. 198-201.
42. H. Riesenfeld, 'Paul's '"Grain of Wheat" Analogy and the Argument of 1 Corinthians 15', in *Studies zum Neuen Testament und Patristik: Erich Klostermann zum 90. Geburstag dargebracht* (Berlin: Akademie-Verlag, 1961), pp. 43-55.

seen, Paul did not deal with the problem of bodily transformation when he wrote the Thessalonians. He simply stated that 'the dead in Christ will rise first' and be caught up into the air (1 Thess. 4.16-17). The Corinthian 'immortality theory' has pushed Paul to formulate a coherent defence of his resurrection teaching, and hence his discourse on the nature of the resurrected body (1 Cor. 15.35-49).

Paul describes the earthly body as a ψυχικός σῶμα ('soul-dominated body') which belongs to the realm of transient corruptible life. The term ψυχικός (soul-dominated) is not easily translated. In Greek thought, the ψυχή (soul) was under the control of the conflicting passions, while the mind was under divine control. Some persons were thought to be so dominated by their passions that they were bereft of mind altogether.[43] Thus, a 'soul-dominated' body (ψυχικός σῶμα) is a body which is controlled by the passions. Owing to the negative connotations of the term ψυχή (soul), Paul chose to identify the πνεῦμα (spirit) with the σῶμα (body) in his description of the resurrected body. This 'spirit'/'soul' (or 'spirit-dominated'/'soul-dominated') distinction can be detected throughout Paul's argument.[44]

According to Paul, Christians die with a 'soul-dominated body', but are resurrected with a 'spirit-dominated body' (πνευματικός σῶμα) or 'spiritual body' (1 Cor. 15.44). This was Paul's term for the resurrected state of the believer.[45] Implied here is a dualism between what is subject to the destructive forces of the passions and what is subject to divine

43. It is this kind of person which is described in 1 Cor 2.14 (P. Perkins, *Resurrection: New Testament Witness and Contemporary Reflection* [Garden City, NY: Doubleday, 1984], p. 301).

44. The πνευματικός/ψυχικός language in this section is quite unique within Paul's letters. In his study of this language in 1 Cor. 15, B.A. Pearson observes that the kind of distinctions which are presupposed in 1 Cor. 15 are found in this letter only: e.g. ψυχικός (soul-dominated) is limited to 1 Cor. 2.14; 15.44, 46; χοϊκός (earthly) occurs only in 1 Cor. 15.47-49 in the New Testament; σαρκικός (fleshly) occurs as an anthropological category only in 1 Cor. 3.1, with its cognate appearing in Rom. 7.14; πνευματικοί (spiritual persons) only occurs in co-ordination with other anthropological categories in 1 Corinthians (B.A. Pearson, *The Pneumatikos-Psychikos Terminology in 1 Corinthians: A Study in the Theology of the Corinthian Opponents of Paul and its Relation to Gnosticism* [Missoula: Scholars Press, 1973], pp. 1-6).

45. N.A. Dahl, *The Resurrection of the Body* (London: SCM Press, 1962), p. 75; A.T. Lincoln, *Paradise Now and Not Yet: Studies in the Role of the Heavenly Dimension in Paul's Thought with Special Reference to His Eschatology* (Cambridge: Cambridge University Press, 1981), p. 39.

control, and between the natural person and the spiritual person.[46] Thus, Paul is not contrasting the spirit with the body, or the soul with the body, but two different types of bodies, namely the 'soul-dominated body' and the 'spirit-dominated body'—the body which is destined for corruption and the body destined for glory.

Paul also contrasts the terms 'body' (σῶμα) and 'flesh' (σάρξ), a distinction which is easily missed by the modern reader. In Paul's terminology, the 'body' (σῶμα) is the factor which supplies continuity after death.[47] It is the outward form of a person, not his physical substance. The substance or matter of the 'body' in its natural state is described as 'flesh' (σάρξ). The 'body' is like a container which is filled with 'flesh'. At the final resurrection, this 'flesh' is replaced with 'glory' (δόξα), while the body-container remains intact. Thus, Paul's 'soul-dominated body' is composed of 'flesh', and his 'spirit-dominated body' is composed of glory.

In addition to Paul's explanation of why and how Christians are resurrected, Paul also developed a theology for the (now greatly expanded) intervening period between Christ's resurrection and parousia. Christ's resurrection becomes the beginning of his conflict with God's enemies. The parousia is no longer the commencement of Christ's war with God's enemies but the 'mopping up' of the last battle (15.23-28). Moreover, the enemies which Christ subdues are no longer limited to the earthly persecutors of Christians but include spiritual enemies, 'every rule and every authority and power' including the power of death, conceived of as a quasi-personal power (1 Cor. 15.24, 26).[48] The final consummation of history will come only when Christ hands this conquered kingdom over to the Father (15.24). Thus, Paul has compensated for the delay of the parousia by expanding the significance of Christ's resurrection, both with reference to the individual Christian and the world at large.

In his recitation of the witness tradition Paul also affirms that Christ died 'for our sins' (15.3). This idea of atonement is fundamental to this

46. Perkins, *Resurrection*, pp. 301-302. Paul previously made this distinction in 1 Cor. 2.14 where he disputes the Corinthians' claim to divine wisdom because they were ψυχικός (soul-dominated), not πνευματικός (spirit-dominated), for only this explains why they do not understand his theology of the cross.

47. E. Schweizer, Πνεῦμα, πνευματικός, *TDNT*, VI, pp. 332-455, esp. 420-21.

48. Conzelmann, *1 Corinthians*, p. 270; Dodd, *New Testament Studies*, pp. 121-22.

study and central to Paul's apotropaeic paradigm and thus merits some comment. Paul does not develop the concept of atonement in any detail in 1 Corinthians except to say that if Christ was not raised then Christians would still be in their sins (1 Cor. 15.17). The implied inference from this statement is that Christians are in fact no longer in their sins.

How did Christ's resurrection accomplish this for Christians? Though Paul does not make explicit in this letter the connection between Christ's resurrection and the atonement of sin, the notion may be bound up with his Adam typology. Adam and Christ are represented as human 'images' or prototypes, with the primordial Adam being principally a sinner. As Joachim Jeremias remarks, these two Adams portray 'a type of the destiny of believers who, when they have first borne the image of the earthly, will then be transformed into the image of the heavenly'.[49] The first Adam was ψυχικός ('soul-dominated') and χοϊκός (earthly), while the second Adam (Christ) is 'spirit-dominated' (πνευματικός) (15.46-47). Death came into the world through the first Adam, a death which was the result of disobedience. Human death proceeded from Adam because the whole of humanity is contained in him.[50] Likewise, participation in the celestial Adam means that Christians will not only bear Christ's image (εἰκῶν) but also be delivered from the sin of the first Adam.

---

49. J. Jeremias, 'The Origin of the Typology Adam/Christ', *TDNT*, I, pp. 142-43, esp. 142.

50. Cf. Sir. 25.24; U. Bianchi, 'La rédemption dans les livre d'Adam', in *Selected Essays on Gnosticism, Dualism and Mysteriosophy* (NovTSup, 38; Leiden: Brill, 1978), pp. 1-8, esp. p. 2.

Chapter 6

THE DEVELOPMENT OF PAUL'S SOTERIOLOGY IN HIS LATER CAREER:
2 CORINTHIANS AND GALATIANS

The principal interest of this study is Paul's theology of the cursed and
sinful Christ. This concept appears only in letters written after Paul's
'affliction is Asia'. This observation raises several questions which are
worthy of exploration. How does the soteriology of Paul's later missionary career differ from his earlier thought? Why is his apotropaeic
soteriology localised in one period of his life? Is there a causal connection
between the development of this concept and Paul's crisis in Asia?

Paul's 'Affliction in Asia'

Following Paul's dispatch of the 'Severe Letter' to Corinth (cf. 2 Cor.
2.2-4, 7.8-12), Paul became quite anxious about its reception (2 Cor. 7.8)
and decided to send Titus to Corinth to ascertain how the Corinthians
had received it, and also to persuade them to recommit themselves to
the collection (2 Cor. 7.6-7, 14-15; cf. 2.13). Being anxious to know
more about the situation in Corinth, Paul decided to change his travel
plans and travel with Timothy to Corinth via Troas and Macedonia
(2 Cor. 2.12; cf. 1 Cor. 16.3-9). He hoped thereby to meet up somewhere along the way with Titus who was making his way back from
Corinth. Sometime prior to their departure from Asia to Macedonia,
Paul and Timothy experienced the so-called 'affliction (θλῖψις) in Asia':

> We do not want you to be unaware, brothers, of the affliction we experi-
> enced in Asia; for we were so utterly, unbearably crushed that we despaired
> of life itself. Indeed, we felt that we had received the sentence of death;
> but that was to make us rely not on ourselves but on God who raises the
> dead. He who rescued us from so deadly a peril will continue to rescue us
> (2 Cor. 1.7-10).

The opening disclosure formula in the passage, 'We do not want you to be unaware' (οὐ γὰρ θέλομεν ὑμᾶς ἀγνοεῖν), followed by the vocative (ἀδελφοί), is a strong epistolary signal[1] which indicates to the reader that this is new information for the Corinthians.[2] It follows from this that the affliction took place within the last few months of Paul's stay in Asia, sometime after his dispatch of Titus to Corinth. It must have occurred either at the end of his Ephesian sojourn, or during his travels in Asia Minor prior to his departure from the port of Troas.

Though the precise nature of this affliction is a matter of speculation, it is clear that Paul did not expect to survive the crisis. He speaks of it as a 'deadly peril' and as a 'death sentence'. It weighed him down 'utterly beyond his power of endurance' (καθ' ὑπερβολήν ὑπέρ δύναμιν) such that he envisaged no possibility of survival (ὥστε ἐξαπορηθῆναι ἡμᾶς καὶ τοῦ ζῆν).

Several conflicting suggestions have been made concerning the precise nature of this affliction. Many scholars consider it to be some sort of external threat to Paul's life. In favour of an Ephesian provenance of such persecutions, Alfred Plummer observes how Paul has previously made reference to his 'many adversaries' in Ephesos (1 Cor. 16.9; cf. 15.16-17).[3] Is Paul here referring to the riot in Ephesos (Acts 19.23-40),[4] or perhaps to persecutions elsewhere in Asia following upon this riot?[5]

On the other hand, some scholars argue that Paul's affliction is not an external danger, but an internal threat such as a deadly illness.[6] For

---

1.   Cf. 1 Thess. 4.13; 1 Cor. 10.1; 12.1; Rom. 1.13; 11.25; cf. 2 Cor. 8.1.

2 .   Furnish, *2 Corinthians*, p. 122; cf. Barrett, *Second Epistle to the Corinthians*, pp. 43-64; therefore, it cannot refer to the incident of 'the wild beasts' in Ephesos in 1 Cor. 15.32, an interpretation first made by Tertullian (1 Cor. 15.32) (*De Resurrectione Carnis*, XLVIII, in J.-P. Migne [ed.], *Patrologia Latina*, II, col. 865).

3.   Plummer, *Second Epistle of Saint Paul to the Corinthians*, pp. 16-17; also: Windisch, *Der zweite Korintherbrief*.

4.   Bruce, *1 and 2 Corinthians*, p. 179.

5.   Duncan thinks that Paul was imprisoned three times during the period covered by Acts 19.1–20.1, twice in Ephesos, and once somewhere else in Asia, probably in Laodicea, the setting of Paul's 'affliction in Asia' (G.S. Duncan, *St Paul's Ephesian Ministry: A Reconstruction* [London: Hodder & Stoughton, 1929], pp. 136, 198-99; cf. Hans Lietzmann, *An die Korinther I, II* [HNT, 9; Tübingen: J.C.B. Mohr, 5th edn, 1969], pp. 100-101).

6.   E.g., H. Clavier, 'La Sante de l'apôtre Paul', in J.N. Sevenster and W.C. van Unnik (eds.), *Studia Paulina in honorem Johannis de Zwaan Septuagenari* (Haarlem: Bohn, 1953), pp. 66-82, esp. p. 77: 'Mais il semble qu'aux fatiques, privations, accidents, ou mauvais traitments, il faille ajouter une autre cause d'affaiblissement: un "vie pneumatique" intense, dont les répercussions physiques

example, E.B. Allo thinks the affliction was a lasting and recurrent fever. Allo's interpretation relies heavily upon the interpretation of the perfect tense of ἐσχήκαμεν, this tense being 'taken in the full force of the perfect, of a past act which has not been cancelled, and the consequences still continue' and not merely as a weakened aorist.[7] Allo's interpretation is almost certainly incorrect. First, most scholars disagree with Allo's interpretation of the perfect tense in this verse and consider it to be an aoristic use of the perfect to express in the present a vivid recollection of a past experience (as it is in 2 Cor. 2.13).[8] Secondly, the fact that Paul counts this affliction as being under the category of 'sufferings of Christ' (παθήματα τοῦ Χριστοῦ) indicates that this affliction was proper to the Christian in particular, whereas the non-Christian as well as the Christian is vulnerable to illness.[9] Thirdly, one would expect an illness to be described by symptoms, not by a place reference.[10] Fourthly, Allo's theory does not fit well with Paul's exclusive use of the plural pronoun.[11] A life endangering threat shared by two or more persons is more likely

sont d'autant plus violentes que l'organisme est plus délabreé'; cf. also Alford, *Greek Testament*, IV, p. 630; C.H. Dodd, 'The Mind of Paul: I', *(NTS*; Manchester: Manchester University Press, 1953), pp. 67-82, esp. p. 68.

7. E.B. Allo, *Saint Paul: Seconde épître aux Corinthiens* (Paris: Cerf, 1937), pp. 11-12, 15-19; cf. M. Goguel, *Introduction au Nouveau Testament* (Paris: E. Leroux, 1925), 4.132.

8. R.P. Martin, *2 Corinthians* (WBC, 40; Waco: Word Books, 1986), p. 14; Furnish, *II Corinthians*, p. 113; J.H. Moulton classifies ἐσχήκαμεν here with ἔσχηκα (2 Cor. 2.13) and ἔσχηκεν (2 Cor. 7.5) as 'genuinely aoristic perfects' (*Grammar of New Testament Greek. I. Prolegomena of A Grammer of the New Testament* (Edinburgh: T. & T. Clark, 3rd edn, 1908), pp. 144-45; BDB 343; so also Bultmann, *Second Letter to the Corinthians*; Plummer, *2 Corinthians*, p. 18; Windisch, *Der Zweite Korintherbrief*, p. 46; cf. analysis in P.E. Hughes, *Paul's Second Epistle to the Corinthians* (Grand Rapids: Eerdmans, 1962), p. 19, n. 16).

9. H.A.W. Meyer, *Critical and Exegetical Handbook to the Epistles to the Corinthians* (ed. and trans. W.P. Dickson; Edinburgh, 1870), p. 141; P.W. Schmiedel, *Die Briefe an die Thessaloniker und an die Korinther* (HKNT, 2.1; Freiburg, 2nd edn, 1891), p. 211.

10. M.E. Thrall, *The Second Epistle to the Corinthians* (ICC; 2 vols.; Edinburgh: T. & T. Clark, 1994), p. 116.

11. Paul states 'we' experienced the affliction; 'we' were utterly crushed; 'we' felt we had experienced the sentance of death; and that God's purpose in all of this was to make 'us' rely on God; God delivered 'us' from the peril and 'we' have set our hope on him (vv. 8-9). The use of the plural pronoun strongly suggests that Paul is referring to an experience which he shared with at least one other person, probably his travelling companion Timothy (2 Cor. 1.1).

to be an external danger than some form of disease. Finally, this affliction should not be identified with Paul's 'thorn in the flesh' (2 Cor. 12.7) since, as Margaret Thrall observes, this latter passage is obscure and there are considerable differences between the two passages.[12]

Thus, Paul's affliction is probably an external threat of some kind. It may be numbered among Paul's list of perils in 2 Cor. 11.23-28. The plausibility of this proposal depends in part of upon the relative dating of 2 Corinthians 10–13 with respect to 2 Corinthians 9. If 2 Corinthians 10–13 is a portion of the so-called 'Severe Letter',[13] then it predates 2 Corinthians 1–9,[14] and the affliction mentioned in 2 Corinthians 1–9 would not have been new information to the Corinthians since they would have already learned of it in a previous letter (namely 2 Cor. 10–13) including 11.23-28. However, Buck argues that 2 Corinthians 10–13 is not a fragment of the 'Severe Letter'.[15] If correct, then 2 Corinthians 10–13 likely dates from a period subsequent to 2 Corinthians 1–9. This being so, then Paul's 'affliction in Asia' is probably included in this list since one would hardly expect Paul to omit so profound an affliction from his catalogue of hardships (2 Cor. 11.25-28).[16]

---

12. Thrall, *Corinthians*, p. 116, n. 248.

13. Friedrich Bleek was the first scholar to argue that 2 Cor. 2.3-4 and 7.8-9 refer to a letter, now lost, written after 1 Corinthians. This letter is known as the 'Severe Letter' or the 'Tearful Letter'. Its tone was so severe that Paul subsequently regretted having sent it (7.8) (F. Bleek, 'Erörterungen in Beziehung auf die Briefe Pauli an die Korinther', *Theologische Studien und Kritiken*, 3 [1830], pp. 614-32).

14. This identification was first made by Adolf Hausrath (*Der Vier-Capitelbrief des Paulus an die Korinther* [Heidelberg: Bassermann, 1870]) and was followed by most scholars after him; Riddle identifies the letter with the crisis over the relationship between Jewish and Gentile Christians which arose after the Jerusalem conference (Riddle, *Paul, Man of Conflict*, pp. 205-211); Dodds, *New Testament Studies*, pp. 80-81; Knox at first reluctantly placed 2 Cor. 10–13 after 2 Cor. 1–9, though his chronology allowed little time between 2 Cor. 1–9 and Paul's arrest in Jerusalem (Knox, *Chapters*, pp. 51, 85-88). In his later life, he reversed his opinion, placing it before 1 Cor. 1–9 (Knox, 'Buck-Taylor-Hurd', pp. 264-65); for a summary of other proposed solutions see Hurd, *Origins*, pp. 55-57.

15. According to Buck, the opponents mentioned in 2 Cor. 10–13 came from outside the Corinthian congregation, and therefore should be identified with the single Corinthian offender whose punishment is alluded to in 2 Cor. 1–9 (2.5-11). On this basis, he places it later in Paul's career (Buck, 'Collection', pp. 7-8).

16. E.g., Robert Strachan thinks that this affliction was some form of serious physical violence which is 'hidden among those many hazards and perils to which Paul refers in 2 Cor. 11.23ff' (R. Strachan, *The Second Epistle of Paul to the*

Johann von Hoffmann thinks that Paul's affliction is the shipwreck followed by a night and day in the sea mentioned in 2 Cor. 11.25.[17] However, it is difficult is explain how this hardship at sea qualifies as taking place 'in Asia'. Arthur P. Stanley suggests that the words θλίψεως (v. 8), ἐβαρήθημεν (v. 8), αὐτοὶ ἐν ἑαυτοῖς (v. 9), and the general context of 1 Cor. 1.7-10 'point to...inward care occasioned probably by his anxiety for the Corinthian church' (2 Cor. 11.28).[18] This suggestion seems ill-suited to the context since, as Margaret Thrall observes, 'however acute his anxiety, it would not have threatened his life, nor would it have been relevant to mention the location. Moreover, the aorist participle γενομένης indicates an event rather than a state of mind'.[19]

On the other hand, Paul's statement that he had received the 'sentence of death' (ἀπόκριμα τοῦ θανάτου) may shed some light on the problem. 'Απόκριμα is a technical term denoting some kind of official report or decision.[20] If taken literally, it suggests a legal sentence delivered upon Paul and his companion Timothy which Paul thought would end their lives. Perhaps this death sentence was subsequently mitigated to a severe beating, either with a lash (11.24) or rods (11.25), or Paul was released to the mob for stoning (11.25), as enumerated in Paul's hardship list.

The frustration experienced by all exegetes who would endeavour to identify the precise historical incident to which Paul refers is due to the fact that Paul's allusion to his affliction is no mere historical reminiscence, but rather is part of his rhetorical strategy in 2 Corinthians 1–9 relating to the 'superlative apostles'. As Karl Plank observes

Corinthians [London: Hodder & Stoughton, 1935], p. 51, cf. p. 52).

17. J.C.K. von Hoffmann, *Der zweite Brief Pauli an die Korinther* (HSNT, 2; Nördlingen, 1866).

18. A.P. Stanley, *The Epistles of St Paul to the Corinthians* (2 vols.; London: John Murray, 4th edn, 1855), p. 19; so also G.H. Rendall who suggests extreme depression and spiritual anguish (G.H. Rendall, *The Epistles of St. Paul to the Corinthians* [London: Macmillan, 1909], p. 49).

19. Thrall, *Second Epistle to the Corinthians*, p. 115; cf. Allo, *Saint Paul*, p. 16, H.L. Goudge, *The Second Epistle to the Corinthians* (London: Methuen, 2nd edn, 1928), p. 3.

20. According to Colin Hemer, ἀπόκριμα may be used 'for an official decision in answer to the petition of an embassy' ('A Note on 2 Corinthians 1.9', *TynBul* 23 [1972], pp. 103-107, esp. p. 118; cf. BAGD; Windisch, *Der Zweite Korintherbrief*, p. 46).

the writings of Paul have a density that deflects historical reconstruction
and allows the apostle to remain elusive at least until the critic comes to
terms with the literary character of the text which imply his portrait...
[Paul's letters] provide historical evidence only in an indirect and oblique
manner.[21]

With this in mind, I shall consider the rhetorical strategy of Paul's
affliction text in relation to 2 Corinthians 1–9 as a whole, and then
return to the matter of Paul's affliction below.

The Sinful Christ: 2 Corinthians 1-9

I have demonstrated above how the formulation of Paul's soteriology is
closely related to identifiable crises in his churches. Such was the
urgency of each situation that it was often necessary for Paul to articulate new ideas rather than reinforce previous preaching. Similarly, the
soteriology in 2 Corinthians 1–9 is not a rarefied spiritual treatise
divorced from the world of power and politics, but rather is closely
bound up with Paul's fear that his authority in the Corinthian church
was under siege.

The events which led up to this situation are as follows. When Titus
failed to show up in Troas, Paul and Timothy travelled on to Macedonia
where they finally met up with their friend Titus and were consoled by
his news that the Corinthian church had responded well to Paul's
'Severe Letter' (2 Cor. 2.12-17; 7.5-8, 13-15; 9.4). However, Titus also
reported that Paul was no longer the only apostle with authority in
Corinth: other apostles had arrived in Corinth who claimed to be
'preeminent' or 'superlative apostles' (ὑπερλίαν ἀποστόλων [2 Cor.
11.5]).[22] Paul wrote 2 Corinthians in response to this news while he was
wintering in Macedonia.

These superlative apostles identified themselves as apostles of Christ
and servants of righteousness. Paul refers to them as 'false apostles'

21. K. Plank, *Paul and the Irony of Affliction* (Atlanta,: Scholars Press, 1987),
p. 3.
22. According to Peter Marshall's reconstruction, Paul had been offered a gift by
the Corinthians and refused it so as not to put himself under an 'unwanted
obligation'. This act of refusal offended the Corinthians who then planned traditional
forms of invective which included seeking out rival apostles. These rival apostles took
control of Corinth and humiliated Paul on his second visit (P. Marshall, *Enmity in
Corinth: Social Conventions in Paul's Relations with the Corinthians* [WUNT, 2.23;
Tübingen: Mohr (Paul Siebeck), 1987]).

(2 Cor. 11.13) and servants of Satan (11.14-15).[23] The key issue which underlies the whole of 2 Corinthians 1–9 is the correct criteria for identifying who are the legitimate apostles, especially with reference to the competing apostolic claims of Paul and the superlative apostles.[24] This conflict was fought on four fronts: pay for apostles (e.g., 2.17), proof of apostleship (e.g., 3.1, 5-6; 4.5; 6.3), the proper evaluation of ministries (e.g., 4.5; 5.6; 6.3), and the practice of comparing ministries (e.g., 5.12).[25]

Thus a sort of struggle for power ensued in the Corinthian congregation. 'Power' in this sense should not be conceived of 'in realist terms as a simple datum' for, as Simon Price has demonstrated, 'power' is not a 'thing' but a construct which can only be analysed in terms of relationships.[26] This same point is argued by Michel Foucault who states that 'power is not an institution, a structure, or a certain force with which certain people are endowed; it is the name given to a *complex strategic situation* in a given society'.[27] Price distinguishes between 'power' and 'force' stating that only power is a relational term. The ability of 'A' to have power over 'B' is dependent upon there being a relationship between 'A' and 'B', and 'B' being compliant with 'A'. As soon as one of these two criteria is broken, 'A' has no 'power' over 'B' since a strategic situation no longer exists. The exercise of 'force', on the other hand, requires neither a relationship between 'A' and 'B' nor the

---

23. Though 2 Cor. 10–13 is a separate letter, the issue of the legitimacy of apostleship is the same, and the opponents are probably the same. Therefore, 2 Cor. 10–13 can be used to reconstruct the teaching of Paul's opponents in 2 Cor. 1–9.

24. J. Sumney, *Identifying Paul's Opponents: The Question of Method in 2 Corinthians* (JSNTSup, 40; Sheffield: JSOT Press, 1990), p. 182.

25. Jerry Sumney has produced this summary from the sophisticated method which he has developed for identifying opponents in Paul's writings. This methodology considers: (1) what sources may be used to reconstruct Paul's opposition; (2) how this reconstruction is to function when identifying the opponents; (3) the question of the 'single front' behind Paul's letters'; (4) the issue of whether or not Paul misunderstood his opposition (Sumney, *Identifying Paul's Opponents*, Part 1). Cilliers Breytenbach argues that Paul puts forward his teaching about reconciliation in the context of his apostleship, though he accepts the partition theory wherein 2.14–7.48 (without 6.14–7.1) is the next letter following 1 Corinthians (Breytenbach, *Versöhnung: Eine Studie zur paulinischen Soteriologie* [WMANT, 60; Neukirchen–Vluyn: Neukirchener Verlag, 1989], pp. 107-108).

26. S.R.F. Price, *Rituals and Power: The Roman Imperial Cult in Asia Minor* (Cambridge: Cambridge University Press, 1984), p. 241; cf. P. Bachrach and M.S. Baratz, *Power and Poverty* (New York: Oxford University Press, 1970).

27. M. Foucault, *La volonté de savoir* (Paris: Gallimard, 1976), p. 123.

compliance of 'B'. Force is the opposite of power in that it is non-relational and non-rational.

It follows from this that Paul's exercise of power over the Corinthians required that he be in an ongoing relationship with them, and equally important, that the congregations respond with compliancy. 2 Corinthians 1–9 fulfilled the requirement of an ongoing relationship in that it served as a substitute for Paul's presence. Similarly, Paul's defence of his apostolic status and gospel served to foster compliance. He defended his apostolic status on the basis of: (1) his superior personal credentials; (2) his definitive gospel.

Paul's Superior Personal Credentials

After stating that he will not compare his credentials with those of the superlative apostles (10.12), Paul goes on to do precisely this (11.5-29). He justifies this defence on the grounds that 'since many boast according to the flesh, I will boast also' (11.18). In the course of the letter Paul boasts of superior apostleship, preaching, pneumatic experiences and gospel, and he urges the Corinthians to take pride in his superiority: 'We are not commending ourselves to you again but *giving you cause to be proud of us*, so that you may be able to answer those who pride themselves on a man's position and not on his heart' (5.12).[28] Paul's description of his affliction in Asia (2 Cor. 1.3-11) is part of his self-commendation or 'boast' to the Corinthians.[29] John Fitzgerald summarizes this strategy as follows:

> He [Paul] wants the Corinthians to see that there is something in him for which *they* can be grateful. He is confident that once they realise the full truth about him, they will see him as their true benefactor. The basic problem at Corinth, as Paul sees it, is a *lack of gratitude* on their part. He is grateful for them; they are his pride; he wants them to be grateful for him and proud of him.[30]

Paul used the account of his affliction to demonstrate his superior apostolic credentials. He tells of his great faith, hope and trust in God (v. 9-10). He interprets his deliverance from death as God's blessing ($\chi\acute{\alpha}\rho\iota\sigma\mu\alpha$) whereby the continuation of his ministry among the Corinthians was

---

28. Lüdemann, *Opposition to Paul*, p. 87.

29. J.T. Fitzgerald, *Cracks in an Earthen Vessel: An Examination of the Catalogues of Hardships in the Corinthian Correspondence* (Atlanta: Scholars Press, 1988), pp. 153-57.

30. Fitzgerald, *Cracks*, p. 156.

made possible. In other words, Paul is telling the Corinthians that his life and continued ministry to the Corinthians is God's gift to them (2 Cor. 1.4-7). Paul exhorts the Corinthians to give thanks for this gift, of which they should be proud (1.11, 14).[31]

Paul's Definitive Gospel

Paul not only claims to have superior apostolic credentials, he also claims to have a superior gospel. Paul tells the reader that the superlative apostles had proclaimed 'another Jesus' which is made available by a 'different Spirit' and a 'different gospel,' and many Corinthians have accepted it.[32] Here, Paul is citing an event of the recent past:[33]

> For if someone proclaims another Jesus [ἄλλον 'Ιησοῦν] than the one we proclaimed, or if you receive a different spirit from the one you received [through Paul's preaching], or if you receive a different gospel from the one you accepted, you submit to it readily enough (2 Cor. 11.4).

This is the context in which Paul makes his statement about atonement (2 Cor. 5.21). Though the subject of human sin has been mentioned in his previous letters, Paul has never explained to the reader exactly *how* sins are removed. Why does Paul develop this teaching at this point in his ministry?

An examination of the context reveals that this text defines an essential point of Paul's gospel which the Corinthians must accept if they are to be reconciled to God.[34] Paul describes those who remained loyal to

31. S.J. Hafemann, *Suffering and the Spirit: An Exegetical Study of 2 Corinthians 2.14–3.3 within the Context of the Corinthian Correspondence* (WUNT, 2; Tübingen, Mohr [Paul Siebeck]: 1986), p. 75.

32. Scholars have related Paul's reference to 'another Jesus' to 5.16 ('even though we once knew Christ according to the flesh, we know him no longer in that way'), arguing that opponents appealed to their contacts with the historical Jesus. Lüdemann is uncertain about the connection (*Opponents*, p. 266, n. 110). On this problem: D. Georgi, *The Opponents of Paul in Second Corinthians: A Study of Religious Propaganda in Late Antiquity* (Philadelphia: Fortress Press, 1985), pp. 252-53, 272; J. Blank, *Paulus und Jesus* (SANT, 18; Munich: Chr. Kaiser Verlag, 1968), pp. 304-326 (bib.); D.W. Oostendorp, *Another Jesus: A Gospel of Jewish-Christian Superiority in II Corinthians* (Kampen: Kok, 1967), pp. 52-58 (bib).

33. Lüdemann, *Opponents*, p. 88.

34. Breytenbach critiques Käsemann's identification of 2 Cor. 5.19-21 as pre-Pauline (Käsemann, in E. Dinkler [ed.], *Zeit und Geschichte: Dankesgabe an Rudolf Bultmann* [Tübingen: Mohr [Paul Siebeck], 1964], pp. 47-59), arguing that only 5.19 should be so identified (Breytenbach, *Versöhnung*, pp. 118-19).

this gospel as being 'in Christ' (ἐν Χριστῷ). In other words, they continued to accept Paul's gospel which is summarised in 2 Cor. 5.21. In the politicised context of the Corinthian congregation, acceptance of this teaching was as much a test of loyalty as a point of catechism. In this situation, allegiance with either side required compliance with their respective gospels.

Since it was impossible to comply with both sides, those who embraced the Jesus and gospel of superlative apostles could not support Paul. In response, Paul broke off his relationship with them. From Paul's point of view, they had accepted 'the grace of God in vain' (6.1) and were no longer part of the new creation (cf. 2 Cor. 5.17-18). From a strategic point of view, Paul had lost his 'power' over these Christians because they were no longer compliant, nor were they in a relationship with him. This is the background for Paul's appeal them to 'be reconciled to God'. He bids them to once again submit to his authority and gospel. He entreats them saying 'we are ambassadors for Christ, since God is making his appeal through us; we entreat you on behalf of Christ, be reconciled to God' (5.20). In this light, 2 Cor. 5.21 explains the means by which Christians, especially the *lapsed* Corinthians who supported the superlative apostles, could be reconciled to God.

What can be said about the theology of 2 Cor. 5.21 in reference to Paul's earlier soteriology? First, as already noted, this passage does not mention Christ's resurrection or parousia. This is not to suggest that Paul had abandoned his belief in the resurrected Christ. Paul was able to develop multiple discrete paradigms which stand independently of each other. Whereas the resurrection paradigm related the after-death existence of Christians to Christ's life beyond the grave, this paradigm related the atonement of Christians to Christ who was made over into a carrier of 'sin' (ἁμαρτία).

2 Corinthians 5.21 and Paul's Affliction in Asia

Though the occasion for Paul's account of his affliction in Asia was part of his self-commendation to the Corinthians, its significance for Paul should not be limited to its use in this rhetorical strategy.[35] The experi-

---

35. Similarly, Gregory Bloomquist concludes that Paul's discussion of suffering in Philippians serves a rhetorical function in Paul's rhetorical address: 'the theological role of suffering must be understood to be dependent on the epistolary and rhetorical functions of the component parts of the letter and on the role of suffering plays in those component parts' (Bloomquist, *Function of Suffering*, p. 190).

ence had a broader significance for Paul. He likens his deliverence to God's resurrection of the dead (2 Cor. 1.9-10). In 2 Cor. 4.7-12 he uses the categories of the 'death of Jesus' (τὴν νέκρωσιν τοῦ 'Ιησοῦ) and the 'life of Jesus' (ἡ ζωὴ τοῦ 'Ιησοῦ) to interpret his own experience of suffering and deliverance. As John Schütz observes:

> Paul understands his tribulation and suffering as Christ's suffering (i.e., Christ's death), and his comfort as the equivalent of the new life in Christ. The death and resurrection of Christ inform the life of the apostle with perfect analogies in his own life.[36]

Paul classed his affliction as being one of many 'sufferings of Christ' which abound to him (2 Cor. 1.5).[37] This analogy between Paul's sufferings and Christ's 'suffering' (death) had revelatory character for him in that he thought that his affliction actually manifested Christ's own suffering. Correspondingly, Paul's deliverance from this affliction and continued mission manifested Christ's resurrected life. This point is made explicit in 2 Cor. 4.10 where he states that he carries around 'the death of Jesus in the body' in order than the 'life' of Jesus might be revealed (φανερωθῇ) in his body. In the words of Scott Hafemann:

> …it is precisely this tension between the present and the future in Paul's eschatology which enables him to interpret his *own* suffering and deliverance in terms of the decisive eschatological events of the death and resurrection of Christ. Thus, in Paul's view, because the kingdom is not yet present in its fullness it becomes necessary for him to continue to carry in his body the 'death of Jesus'. Nevertheless, because the new age has already decisively broken into the present aeon in the resurrection of Christ, it is also possible for Paul's *present* suffering to be at the *same* time a *present* revelation of God's resurrection power, i.e. ἡ ζωὴ τοῦ 'Ιησοῦ. For as 2 Cor. 1.8-11 illustrates, God's deliverance of Paul from his suffering is intended to be interpreted as an expression of God's ability to raise the dead.[38]

Paul's interpretation of his own suffering and his deliverance from suffering is deeply rooted in his theology of individual transformation, or

---

Through his words on suffering, Paul 'endears himself to the Philippians' (Bloomquist, *Function of Suffering*, p. 192).

36. J. Schütz, *Paul and the Anatomy of Apostolic Authority* (SNTSMS, 26; Cambridge: Cambridge University Press, 1975), pp. 242-43.

37. P.E. Hughes, *Paul's Second Epistle to the Corinthians* (Grand Rapids: Eerdmans, 1962), p. 17.

38. Hafemann, *Suffering and the Spirit*, p. 72.

sanctification. In contrast to the eschatology of Paul's previous letters, 2 Corinthians 1–9 no longer confines individual transformation to the parousia at which time Christians were transformed in an instant. Rather the experience of transformation is a gradual ongoing process and part of the *present* life and suffering of the Christian (2 Cor. 5.17-18; 6.2). Paul states that the inner natures of Christians are 'being renewed *every day*' (2 Cor. 4.16) and they 'are being changed' even now into the likeness of Christ (3.18). Thus, 2 Corinthians marks a significant new development in Paul's theology. No longer is Christ's second coming the pivotal salvation event but instead, Christ's first coming. Christ's greatest accomplishment is no longer defined in terms of what he will do at the end of history as a heavenly deliverer, but rather defined in terms of what he has already made possible for Christians in human history.

This radical transformation of Paul's theology from one which is future oriented and apocalytic, to a theology which is oriented to the present and related to Christian suffering, trials and persecution, coincides with Paul's brush with death in Asia. This suggests that Paul's affliction in Asia may have been instrumental in this transformation. It may have served as a catalyst for the development of Paul's theology, moving him to develop theologies of the Cross which were rooted in his own suffering and near death experience. F.F. Bruce sees the lasting effect of Paul's affliction in 2 Cor. 4.7–5.10.[39] Similarly, C.H. Dodd treats Paul's affliction in Asia as 'a sort of second conversion', a watershed by reference to which his letters can be dated, either to the preceding period, or the period following:

> But when he [Paul] accepted his limitations he was liberated afresh... When he wrote again (2 Cor. 1–9), it was in a strangely chastened mood. It is not only that he apologises for the tone of his previous letter [the Severe Letter], and pleads for a restoration of his Corinthian friends' alienated affection. He also makes it plain that he has gone to the depths and made terms with the last realities. There is nothing in earlier letters like the quiet self-abandonment of 2 Cor. 4–5. Whether or not I am right in isolating this particular spiritual crisis as a sort of second conversion, it is at any rate plain that in the later epistles there is a change of temper. The traces of fanaticism and intolerance disappear, almost if not quite completely, along with all that anxious insistence on his own dignity.[40]

39. Bruce, *1 and 2 Corinthians*, pp. 179-80.
40. Dodd, *New Testament Studies*, p. 81.

Though it is not possible to prove a causal relationship between Paul's affliction and the development of his theology, it is remarkable how Paul's first theological articulation of the Christ's suffering coincides with his profound experience of his own suffering and mortality. Once again, human experience seems to be driving his theology. Only a suffering and persecuted Christ could be meaningful to the suffering and persecuted apostle. The once powerful thought of Christ's victorious return, now inordinately postponed, seemed empty to Paul in the midst of his personal anguish.

The Cursed Christ: Galatians

Paul's letter to the Galatians was written in response to the teaching of certain persons who had, intentionally or unintentionally, contradicted Paul's gospel and thereby 'stirred up' the Galatian congregations (Gal. 1.6-9; 5.7-12). Paul's concept of the 'cursed Christ' in Gal. 3.13 is cited as part of his rhetorical debate with the Galatians. Two questions must be raised at the outset. First, who are these agitators? Secondly, what did they teach, and why did Paul find their teaching so provocative?

The Galatian 'Compromisers'
The situation in the Galatian churches bears many resemblances to the occasion of 2 Corinthians 1–9. Paul contrasts two groups: those who remain committed to his gospel, identified as 'the adherents to the faith' (οἱ ἐκ πίστεως) and certain trouble-makers and their followers whom he calls 'the doers of the law' (ὅσοι ἐξ ἔργων νόμου εἰσίν [Gal. 3.10]).[41] Scholars frequently refer to these trouble-makers as Paul's 'opponents' or as 'Judaizers'. Louis Martyn has noted how the term 'opponents' prejudices the inquiry from the outset: it suggests that these persons had gained their identity by their opposition to Paul, and that their preaching was a reaction to his. In Martyn's judgment, it is not a matter of these people deliberately opposing Paul's gospel, but *Paul* reacting to their

---

41. Gal. 3.7, 9; cf. Gal. 2.16; 3.2, 5; Rom. 3.26; 4.16. The construction ἐκ (+ gen.) is frequently employed by Paul. In Hellenistic literature generally, the genitive construction is used to denote a member of a certain class, party, sect or school, by indicating what is characteristic of the group in question (Zerwick, *Biblical Greek*, p. 45, sect. 134); cf. analagous designations: e.g., οἱ ἐκ περιτομῆς (Gal. 2.11); οἱ ἐκ νόμου (Rom. 4.14).

independent preaching.[42] They may have been conducting an independent mission which happened to include some of the Galatian churches.

The most popular label for these Galatians preachers after that of 'opponents' is the term 'Judaizers'. This term also invites misunderstanding for it suggests that the Galatian preachers were either law-observant Jews or law-observant Jewish Christians who sought to persuade Paul's converts to follow the *whole* Jewish law. They cannot have been *Jewish* missionaries because Paul's first reference to them indicates that they were preaching 'another *gospel*' (Gal. 1.6-9). Despite the fact that he denies that there is any other gospel, his concession that their teaching is *called* a 'gospel' indicates that they were preaching about Christ, not Torah.[43] Therefore, they must have been *Christian* evangelists, not *Jewish* missionaries. If the term 'Judaizers' were adopted by scholars to designate these Christian missionaries, it would imply that they advocated the observance of the *whole* Jewish law. Yet, with the exception of circumcision (Gal. 6.12) and the observance of certain Jewish feasts (Gal. 4.10), Paul says that they 'do not themselves keep the [whole] law' (Gal. 6.13; cf. 5.3).

Both terms, 'Judaizers' and 'opponents', distort the identity of these Galatian preachers. In place of such misleading terminology, Beverly Gaventa suggests 'compromisers', meaning Christian preachers (originally of Jewish or Gentile descent) who have advocated a compromise between the complete abandonment of the law and the rigorous observance of the whole law.[44]

A perplexing array of answers has been given regarding the identity of these 'compromisers', including *Jewish* Christians, *Gentile* Christians, Jewish Gnostics (either Christians or unconverted Jews), the 'James party' in Jerusalem, or Judaean zealots.[45] Any assessment of these divergent

42. Martyn, 'A Law-Observant Mission', p. 320.

43. Gaventa, 'The Singularity of the Gospel', p. 17; Martyn, 'A Law-Observant Mission', p. 314.

44. Gaventa, 'Singularity of the Gospel', p. 20. Martyn prefers the more neutral term 'teachers' ('A Law-Observant Mission', p. 313).

45. F.R. Crownfield concludes that they were Jewish–Christian syncretists who favoured circumcision for symbolic reasons (F.R. Crownfield, 'The Singular Problem of the Dual Galatians', *JBL* 44 [1945], pp. 491-500). Günther Bornkamm, K. Wegenast and H. Koester all argued that they were Jewish–Christian missionaries who were rooted in a syncretistic brand of Judaism in Asia Minor (G. Bornkamm, *Paul* [ET; trans. D.M.G. Stalker; New York: Harper & Row, 1975 (1969)], pp. 18-19; K. Wegenast, *Das Verständnis der Tradition bei Paulus und in den Deuteropaulinen*

descriptions of the identity of the compromisers must begin with a reconstruction of their teaching.

The Teaching of the Compromisers

What can be said about the content of the compromisers' teaching? I have already observed that they claimed to be preaching the 'gospel' of Christ (Gal. 1.6-9). Moreover, it is evident that they encouraged circumcision (Gal. 6.12; cf. 5.12). In light of these two observations, one can deduce that they preached that Jesus Christ made it possible for Gentiles to become full partners with the Jews in the Covenant through the rite of circumcision. This much information can be inferred more or less directly from Paul's text.

A more detailed reconstruction of the teaching of the compromisers involves one important assumption, that each element in the argument of Galatians is a response to, and contingent upon, the specific arguments of the compromisers. J.C. Beker for instance argues that Paul's insistence upon the disjuncture between law and Christ, and between law and faith, presupposes the compromisers' teaching which emphasised the continuity of these antitheses. Likewise, H.D. Betz's thesis that the central concept in Galatians is *freedom* hinges upon the assumption that the central point of the compromisers' gospel was *submission* to the law.[46]

[WMANT; Neukirchen-Vluyn: Neukirchener Verlag, 1962], pp. 36-40; Koester, *GNOMAI DIAPHOROI*, pp. 143-47). Johannes Munck argues that they were Gentiles who had recently become circumcised members of a Judaizing Christian movement and had no connection to Jerusalem (J. Munck, 'The Judaizing Gentile Christians: Studies in Galatians', in *idem*, *Paul and the Salvation of Mankind* [trans. F. Clarke; London: SCM Press, 1954–1959], pp. 87-134). Walter Schmithals thinks that they were Jewish Gnostics who promoted circumcision, but did not demand observance of the moral demands of the Jewish law (W. Schmithals, 'The Heretics in Galatia', in *idem*, *Paul and the Gnostics* [trans. J. Steely; Nashville: Abingdon, 1965–1972], pp. 13-64; W. Schmithals, *Paul and James* [trans. D. Barton; London: SCM Press, 1963–1965], pp. 103-117). David Bronson tries to connect the opponents with political pressure from Jerusalem, and specifically with the 'James party' (D. Bronson, 'Paul, Galatians, and Jerusalem', JAAR 35 [1967], pp. 119-28). Robert Jewett speculates that zealots in Judaea might be responsible (R. Jewett, 'The Agitators and the Galatian Congregation', *NTS* 17 [1971], pp. 198-212).

46. J.C. Beker, *Paul the Apostle: The Triumph of God in Life and Thought* (Philadelphia: Fortress Press, 1980), pp. 56-58; Betz, *Galatians*, pp. 28-33. Gaventa observes that the result of both these readings is that they begin with chs. 3 and 4 of Galatians as the hermeneutic starting point for the interpretation of the letter, while the remaining chapters are bracketed off as secondary. Galatians 5–6 is isolated as

In response to this line of argument, Beverly Gaventa argues that in Galatians there is a balance between contingency and coherence. On the one hand, Paul is indeed reacting to particular individuals whose ideas are hostile to his gospel. On the other hand, it must also be recognised that in his attack upon the compromisers' teaching, Paul's has his own understanding of the gospel which he is trying to express. Therefore, while the overall thrust of Galatians is against the compromisers, each of Paul's individual arguments is not necessarily contingent upon a prior argument of the compromisers but rather represents a subcomponent of his own defence. As Gaventa comments:

> Although the [Galatian] letter arises out of the issue of the law, the under-lying theological convictions that shape Paul's response to the problem derive not from his interpretation of the law but from his christology...
> My argument is not that Paul takes from his theological store house the appropriate response for this setting [the Galatian controversy], but that the theology expressed in the letter is not determined by merely adding up responses to a particular problem. Just because the present problem concerns the law does not mean that, in Paul's perspective, the central theological issue at stake is the law.[47]

It was Paul's prior commitment to Christ as understood in Gal. 3.13 that excluded the option of observing the law. Paul can be said to be responding to the teaching of the compromisers only in the overall thrust of his argument, namely, in his rejection of their demand for the observance of Jewish law and circumcision. However, the detail of Paul's argument does not represent a point by point attack of the specific arguments of the compromisers, but his coherent defense of his gospel. Therefore, it is not of primary importance to the exegesis whether the compromisers were Jewish, Gentile or Gnostic Christians, or even whether or not they had any connection with the Jerusalem church. It is Paul's gospel which is at stake, not the ethnic identity of the compromisers.

I have demonstrated above how Paul's gospel, with its promise of the blessing and God's Spirit, it bound up with issues of the Jewish law and Christ's apotropaeic death (cf. ch. 3). Thus, Paul's atonement paradigm, far from being detached theological theory, was employed in the service of the congregational crises in Galatia provoked by the teaching of the

traditional paraenesis. Chapter 1, being a defence of Paul's apostleship, is treated as if it sheds no light on his theology (Gaventa, 'Singularity of the Gospel', p. 18).

47. Gaventa, 'Singularity of the Gospel', pp. 18-19.

compromisers. Paul had to demonstrate why life under the law was incompatible with his gospel.

To this end, Paul reinterprets Christ's death with reference to the Jewish law. He argues that life under the law is a dead end. The Galatian Christians who follow it bear a deadly curse. Entry into Christ's new creation is contingent upon relinquishing both the law and its curse. Otherwise, they will remain slaves of the old creation and the prey to the powers of sin and death.

The Galatian Christians could choose to abandon their allegiance to the Jewish law by an act of volition. However, Paul believes that it is beyond human ability to throw off the curse imposed by the law. Only Christ's death as an apotropaeic victim could accomplish this. The curse could only be thrown off by Christ offering himself as a substitutionary victim. Paul believed that those who continue to follow the law remain under this curse and render Christ's substitutionary death ineffective. In other words, Christ died in vain if the Galatian Christians accept the teaching of the compromisers.

The Function of Paul's Participatory Language

Paul frequently describes the believer as being mystically incorporated into Christ: the Christian is 'baptised into Christ' (Gal. 3.27; Rom. 6.3), is 'dying with Christ', is 'in Christ', is 'with Christ', and belongs to Christ (5.24). Paul even states Christ lives in him (Gal. 2.20). According to Albert Schweitzer, this concept of 'being-in-Christ' is the prime enigma of Paul's teaching and 'once grasped it gives the clue to the whole'.[48]

Many scholars have attempted to identify the background ideas to Paul's participatory language.[49] For example, it is commonly noted how participation in the ritual *seder* supper made the Exodus story meaningful to Jews in the present (Exod. 13.8; *m. Pes.* 10.5). Is Paul's mysticism an adaptation of the Jewish Passover experience? In his detailed analysis

---

48. Schweitzer, *Mysticism*, p. 3; cf. Bloomquist, *Function of Suffering*, p. 191, cf. pp. 35-49.

49. G. Wagner, *Pauline Baptism and the Pagan Mysteries* (Edinburgh: Oliver & Boyd, 1967); R. Shedd, *Man in Community* (London: Epworth, 1958); A.D.M. Wedderburn, *Baptism and Resurrection* [WUNT, 55; Tübingen: Mohr [Paul Siebeck], 1987), pp. 342-56; R. Tannehill, *Dying and Rising with Christ* (BZNW, 32; Berlin: Töpelmann, 1967); K. Grayston, 'Paul's Use of Objective and Participatory Language in Speaking of the Death of Christ', *Epworth Review* 8.3 (1981), pp. 65-71.

of this question, A.D.M. Wedderburn has stated that Paul's notions of participation with Christ are not 'peculiarly connected with the Exodus; rather they are basic ideas, ways of looking at things, to which the Jews had given classic expression in their Passover liturgy'.[50] He concludes, 'Paul's language of our dying with Christ then is probably his own; at least I have found no convincing enough parallel to it which might explain whence he derived it'.[51] So prevalent is this concept of mystical participation in antiquity that Paul could easily have employed this concept without borrowing it directly from any identifiable source. Thus, as in the case of all participatory languages, Paul's mysticism is taxonomically unique.

However, to recognise that Paul's participation language has no exact parallel is not to suggest that it is *sui generis*. Paul's participatory language is sometimes portrayed as deeply 'mystical' and that union with Christ is at once more profound than the *seder* experience and incomparable in Graeco-Roman antiquity. For example, Schweitzer argues that Paul's mysticism was not merely metaphorical language, but rather it expressed a real 'co-experiencing of His dying and rising again'.[52] Consequently the believer can truly experience the 'dawning of the supernatural world' by participating in Christ's resurrection.[53] However, it should be borne in mind that the belief systems of many religious groups share the general concept that ritual enactment of the founding story of a community can give this story contemporary relevance for the community.

Some clarity on this matter is afforded by a comparison of Pauline mysticism with the participatory language of the Passover *seder*. That we know of no Jew who employed the *same* participatory language as Paul, confessing 'I am in the Passover lamb', or 'I have died with the Passover lamb' or 'I was circumcised into the Passover lamb', does not change the fact that both Paul and the *seder* ritual employ participatory language. In the context of a *seder*, the language is functional and sermonic in that it helps to define who belongs to the community and define the relationship of the community to its communal foundation story, the Exodus. Paul's participation language is also functional and sermonic. As Alan Segal observes, Paul's description of Christians being

50. Wedderburn, *Baptism and Resurrection*, p. 344, n. 9.
51. Wedderburn, *Baptism and Resurrection*, p. 356.
52. Schweitzer, *Mysticism*, p. 13.
53. Schweitzer, *Mysticism*, p. 23.

'in Christ' serves to define the Christian covenant community entered into through baptism.[54] It likewise explains the relationship between the Christian community and the story of its founding figure, Christ.

Paul's participatory language functioned in the same way as other participatory language in that it explained how events connected with the story of a group's founding figure in the remote past could have present consequences for a particular community. In Paul's case, participation language explains how the life and death of Jesus in the past can have significance for Christians living in the present, even for Christians separated from Christ by culture and language. In other words, without such participatory language, Paul could not keep the past and present together.

This point can be illustrated as follows. If a group of people was sentenced to death, or sold into slavery, and someone intervened as a substitute, by being killed or becoming a slave in their place, the relevance of this person's actions would be immediately apparent to the surviving group. This logic breaks down when applied to the substitutionary intervention of a saviour figure in the past. Two difficulties arise: time span and individual relevance. First, since the saviour's act of substitution took place in the *past*, it is necessary to demonstrate *how* this past event can tangibly effect people living in the present. Secondly, it is necessary to explain why this past substitutionary act has relevance specifically for this group and not another. Thus, participatory language addressed the problems posed by time span and individual relevance.

Similarly, Paul made use of participatory language in order to overcome these two difficulties. By assuring Christians that through baptism (Rom. 6.3-6) and eucharist (1 Cor. 10.14-16) they are in Christ, and Christ is in them, events in Christ's life—even if in the remote past—can have relevance for Christians in particular, because their lives are intertwined. Paul's participatory language was ideally suited for his resurrection paradigm because of the obvious parallelism which it provides between Christ and believers. Christ as 'the first fruits' (1 Cor. 15.20) establishes the way in which others will follow, by virtue of the mystical

---

54. Segal, *Rebecca's Children*, 108. He states that Paul was a 'pragmatic man' preeminently concerned with building and maintaining a unified community of Christians 'in Christ'. Paul's goal is the unity of the community, not the articulation of doctrine (A. Segal, *Paul the Convert: The Apostolate and Apostasy of Saul the Pharisee* [New Haven: Yale University Press, 1990], pp. 210-41).

union. Like Christ, all believers will die, and like Christ, all will be resurrected.

What is the relationship between participatory language in general and the apotropaeic paradigm? It should be noted that the non-biblical texts quoted in this study do not employ participatory language. The reason is clear: these texts are predominantly *ritual* texts, and participatory language is much less necessary for ritual than myth because the obstacles of time and relevance are not present. For example, the observance of an apotropaeic ritual is not an event in the remote past, but a present experience which coincides with a particular crisis. Moreover, the victim is not a founding figure of a former time, but someone known and chosen by the threatened community. Thus, the connection between the victim and the threatened community is direct and self-evident. On the other hand, when the apotropaeic paradigm is expressed in *myth* (i.e., a communal foundation story), participatory language can mitigate the attendant impediments of time span and individual relevance.

This observation concerning the relative importance of participatory language in myth versus ritual can be illustrated with an example from Greek mythology, namely Euripides' *Bacchae*. This story relates the *myth* of Dionysos to the *ritual* of Dionysiac sacrifice by means of participatory language. According to the story, Pentheus refused to acknowledge that Dionysos was a god. In punishment, Dionysos turns Pentheus into a sacrificial victim in place of the usual animal victim. He does this, ostensibly, in order to prove his existence to the skeptical Pentheus.

Pentheus is immediately dismembered as a victim (*sparagmos*) and consumed raw by the maenads. As E.R. Dodds points out, the eating of such a victim in Dionysiac religion was a commemorative rite like the Lord's supper 'in memory of the day when the infant Dionysos was himself torn to pieces and devoured'.[55] Dodds goes on to explain:

> The practice seems to rest on a very simple piece of savage logic. The homeopathic effects of a flesh diet are known all over the world. If you want to be lion-hearted, you must eat a lion; if you want to be subtle, you must eat a snake...By parity of reasoning, if you want to be like god you must eat god (or at any rate something which is *theion*). And you must eat him quick and raw, before the blood has oozed from him.[56]

55. E.R. Dodds, *The Greeks and the Irrational* (Berkeley: University of California Press, 1964), p. 277; citing the scholiast on Clement of Alexandria.
56. Dodds, *Greeks and the Irrational*, p. 277.

Thus, when Pentheus is made into a ritual victim he is in fact transformed into a surrogate Dionysos; the act of his followers eating this raw flesh was in fact the ingesting of Dionysos himself. The myth serves to awaken the reader to the continuing reality of Dionysos. The substance of this reality is not merely that Dionysos lives, but that Dionysos lives *within* the believer.[57] This is a mystical teaching about 'being-in-Dionysos'. It is analogous to Paul's teaching about 'being-in-Christ'. Both express the notion of participation in the life of the deity. This demonstrates that the Greeks, like Paul, employed participatory language when the primary event was a communal foundation story or myth, rather than a ritual.

Paul's apotropaeic soteriology, which was based upon the Christian communal story of Christ's death, likewise implies mystical participation in Christ. The transfer of sin and its curse from Christians to Christ necessitated a mystical contact between them. However, the logic is different from that of the resurrection paradigm: after this transfer of sin and its curse is complete, the mystical union must be severed, for to remain united with Christ would be to remain cursed and sinful.

Here is the difference between the resurrection paradigm and the apotropaeic paradigm. There is an implied tension between these two notions of mystical participation, one of which is permanent, and the other transitory. Paul's resurrection paradigm was useful as a way of explaining how believers could be resurrected. However, it could not explain how the sin of believers was atoned for because the parallelism breaks down. In this case, the logic 'as with Christ, so also with the believer' is untenable, for the Christian has no wish to be permanently united with a bearer of sin and its curse.

Paul addressed the problem of atonement by developing the apotropaeic paradigm which focuses, not on Christ's resurrection, but on his expulsion and death. The apotropaeic paradigm is also based upon mystical participation with Christ, but not the permanent mystical bonding of the resurrection paradigm. Rather than setting up a parallelism between the fate of Christ and believers, Paul constructed a divergence. Once the burden of sin has been transferred from the believer to Christ, the mystical union must be severed, and Christ expelled and killed. Paul refrained from drawing attention to the inherent tension between the resurrection paradigm and the apotropaeic paradigm because his

---

57. W.D. O'Flaherty, *Other Peoples' Myths* (London: Macmillan, 1988), pp. 104-11.

purposes were pastoral, not theoretical and systematic. They represent two distinctive ways of understanding the benefits of being in Christ.

Conclusion

In Paul's first years as a Christian, Christ's parousia formed the centre of his soteriology. This parousia-centred theology addressed the problems of persecution in Thessalonica (2 Thess.) and of the premature death of Thessalonian Christians (1 Thess.). At this early juncture in Paul's missionary preaching, the notion that Christ's death and resurrection had salvific significance was foreign to Paul, a feature which he shared with some of the earliest Palestinian and western Syrian Christians (see Appendix 1).

By the time Paul wrote 1 Corinthians, the concept of Christ's resurrection had come to the forefront of his thought and was of equal, if not greater, importance to the parousia. This new emphasis on Christ's resurrection was related to Paul's response to some Corinthian Christians who continued to understand Christ's saving work in accordance with Paul's original preaching, which stressed Christ's parousia as the ultimate salvation event. In Paul's early preaching, the significance of Christ's resurrection had been limited to Christ himself. Thus the Corinthians contended that they would live beyond the grave at the parousia, not because of Christ's resurrection, but because of their present endowment with the Spirit through baptism.

Following his affliction in Asia, Paul's soteriology underwent a radical transformation. It became more focused on the relevance of Christ for Christian life on *this* side of the grave than on life beyond the grave or at the parousia. Paul's articulation of this subject is deeply embedded in his notion of mystical participation in Christ. On the one hand, Paul employed participatory language to deal with the issues of personal transformation, suffering and persecution. By virtue of baptism, the Christian participates in Christ's life in the present. Through suffering, Christians share in Christ's 'suffering' (death); and in experiences of rescue from danger, they even now partake of Christ's resurrected life. This mystical theology of Christ's cross and resurrection became the foundation of Paul's teaching that the inner nature of Christians was transformed gradually over time, not instantaneously at the parousia.

Paul also adopted participatory language to address the problem posed by the observance of the Jewish law and related issues of the sin and curse brought on by the law. Through baptism, sinful and curse-bearing Christians are mystically united with the sinless Christ who subsumes this burden of sin and curse. In this way, Christ atones for sin and frees Christians to receive God's righteousness and blessing. Thus, it was Christ's death as a curse-bearer which put a permanent distance between Christians and their sin and curse.

Paul's resurrection and apotropaeic paradigms stand side by side in a complementary relationship. Whereas the resurrection paradigm addressed issues such as suffering, persecution and death, it was unable to come to terms with the problem of the law, and the sin and curse which it laid upon Christians. Similarly, while the apotropaeic paradigm addressed the problem of the law, it shed no light these other pressing existential matters.

Though complementary in the context of Paul's pastoral praxis, these paradigms are mutually exclusive from a conceptual standpoint. Christ 'the resurrected one' and Christ 'the curse-laden victim' are two distinct images which stand independently and in tension with each another. Such tensions are typical of Paul's theology. For example, his portrayal of Christ as 'Paschal Lamb' does not cohere with Christ 'the Second Adam'; nor for that matter can Paul's distinctive concepts of redemption and justification, which presuppose the metaphors of slave manumission and the law courts respectively, be collapsed into a single paradigm. The terrain of Paul's soteriology is rich in such provocative juxtapositions, included within which are the resurrection and apotropaeic paradigms.

Paul's use of the apotropaeic paradigm illustrates but one soteriological model which can be conceptually isolated from his rich repertoire of soteriological paradigms. Through a creative synthesis, Paul has deeply imprinted this paradigm with his profound faith in Jesus Christ. Though the image of Christ as a curse-laden victim is foreign to modern sensibilities, this should not distract the reader from recognizing in it the deeper reality of Paul's conviction that Christ died for all.

GREEK AND LATIN EXPULSION TEXTS

Text 1: Philo, On Special Laws 1.188

προστάττει γὰρ δύο χιμάρους ἀνάγειν καὶ κριόν, εἶτά φησι δεῖν τὸν μὲν ὁλοκαυτοῦν, διακληροῦν δὲ τοὺς χιμάρους, καὶ τὸν μὲν λαχόντα τῷ θεῷ θύειν, τὸν δ' ἑτέρω εἰς ἀτριβῆ καὶ ἄβατον ἐρημίαν ἐκπέμπειν ἐφ' ἑαυτῷ κομίζοντα τὰς ὑπὲρ τῶν πλημμελησάντων ἀράς.

F.H. Colson and G.H. Whitaker (trans.), *Philo in Ten Volumes* (LCL; Cambridge: Cambridge University Press, 1930), VII.

Text 2: Epistle of Barnabas 7.6-10

[6]Πῶς οὖν ἐνετείλατο; προσέχετε· 'Λάβετε δύο τράγους καλοὺς καὶ ὁμοίους καὶ προσενέγκατε, καὶ λαλβέτω ὁ ἱερεὺς τὸν ἕνα εἰς ὁλοκαύτωμα ὑπὲρ ἁμαρτιῶν.' [7]Τὸν δὲ ἕνα τί ποιήσουσιν; ''Επικατάρατος', φησίν, 'ὁ εἷς.' Προσέχετε, πῶς ὁ τύπος τοῦ Ἰησοῦ φανεροῦται. [8]'Καὶ ἐμπτύσατε πάντες καὶ κατακεντήσατε καὶ περίθετε τὸ ἔριον τὸ κόκκινον περὶ τὴν κεφαλὴν αὐτοῦ, καὶ οὕτως εἰς ἔρημον βληθήτω.' Καὶ ὅταν γένηται οὕτως, ἄγει ὁ βαστάζων τὸν τράγον εἰς τὴν ἔρημον καὶ ἀφαιρεῖ τὸ ἔριον καὶ ἐπιτίθησιν αὐτὸ ἐπὶ φρύγανον τὸ λεγόμενον ῥαχῆ, οὗ καὶ τοὺς βλαστοὺς εἰώθαμεν τρώγειν ἐν τῇ χώρᾳ εὑρίσκοντες. Οὕτως μόνης τῆς ῥαχῆς οἱ καρποὶ γλυκεῖς εἰσιν. [9]Τί οὖν καὶ τοῦτο; προσέχετε· 'Τὸν μὲν ἕνα ἐπὶ τὸ θυσιαστήριον, τὸν δὲ ἕνα ἐπικατάρατον', καὶ ὅτι τὸν ἐπικατάρατον ἐστεφανωμένον. 'Επειδὴ ὄψονται αὐτὸν τότε τῇ ἡμέρᾳ τὸν ποδήρη ἔχοντα τὸν κόκκινον περὶ τὴν σάρκα καὶ ἐροῦσι· 'Οὐχ οὗτός ἐστιν, ὅν ποτε ἡμεῖς ἐσταυρώσαμεν ἐξουθενήσαντες καὶ κατακεντήσαντες καὶ ἐμπτύσαντες; ἀληθῶς οὗτος ἦν, ὁ τότε λέγων ἑαυτὸν υἱὸν θεοῦ εἶναι.' [10]Πῶς γὰρ ὅμοιος ἐκείνῳ; εἰς τοῦτο 'ὁμοίους' τοὺς τράγους καὶ 'καλούς', ἴσους, ἵνα ὅταν ἴδωσιν αὐτὸν τότε ἐρχόμενον, ἐκπλαγῶσιν ἐπὶ τῇ ὁμοιότητι τοῦ τράγου. Οὐκοῦν ἴδε τὸν τύπον τοῦ μέλλοντος πάσχειν Ἰησοῦ.

P. Prigent and R.A. Kraft, *Epître de Barnabé* (Paris: Les Éditions du Cerf, 1971).

Text 3: Tertullian, Adversus Marcionem 3.7.7
[7]Si enim et duorum hircorum qui ieiunio offerebantur faciam interpretationem, nonne et illi utrumque ordinem Christi figurant? Pares quidem atque consimiles propter eundem dominum conspectum, quia non in alia venturus est forma, ut qui agnosci habeat a quibus laesus est. Alter autem eorum circumdatus coccino, maledictur et consputus et convulsus et compunctus, a populo extra civitatem adiciebatur in perditionem, manifestis notatus insignibus dominicae passionis.

E. Evans (ed. and trans.) *Tertullian: Adversus Marcionem* (2 vols.; Oxford: Clarendon Press, 1972), p. 190.

Text 4: Herodotus, History 2.39.1-4
[1]ἀγαγόντες τὸ σεσημασμένον κτῆνος πρὸς τὸν βωμὸν ὅκου ἂν θύωσι, πῦρ ἀνακαίουσι, ἔπειτα δὲ ἐπ' αὐτοῦ οἶνον κατὰ τοῦ ἱρηΐου ἐπισπείσαντες καὶ ἐπικαλέσαντες τὸν θεὸν σφάζουσι, σφάξαντες δὲ ἀποτάμνουσι τὴν κεφαλήν. [2]σῶμα μὲν δὴ κτήνεος δείρουσι, κεφαλῇ δὲ κείνῃ πολλὰ καταρησάμενοι φέρουσι, τοῖσι μὲν ἂν ᾖ ἀγορὴ καὶ Ἕλληνές σφι ἔωσι ἐπιδήμιοι ἔμποροι, οἱ δὲ φέροντες ἐς τὴν ἀγορὴν ἀπ' ὦν ἔδοντο, τοῖσι δὲ ἂν μὴ παρέωσι Ἕλληνες, οἳ δ' ἐκβάλλουσι ἐς τὸν ποταμόν. [3]καταρῶνται δὲ τάδε λέγοντες τῇσι κεφαλῇσι, εἴ τι μέλλοι ἢ σφίσι τοῖσι θύουσι ἢ Αἰγύπτῳ τῇ συναπάσῃ κακὸν γενέσθαι, ἐς κεφαλὴν ταύτην τραπέσθαι. [4]κατὰ μέν νυν τὰς κεφαλὰς τῶν θυομένων κτηνέων καὶ τὴν ἐπίσπεισιν τοῦ οἴνου πάντες Αἰγύπτιοι νόμοισι τοῖσι αὐτοῖσι χρέωνται ὁμοίως ἐς πάντα τὰ ἱρά, καὶ ἀπὸ τούτου τοῦ νόμου οὐδὲ ἄλλου οὐδενὸς ἐμψύχου κεφαλῆς γεύσεται Αἰγυπτίων οὐδείς.

W.G. Waddell, *Herodotus: Book II* (London: Methuen, 1939).

Text 5: Helladios in Photius, Bibliotheca, 534a
ὅτι ἔθος ἦν ἐν Ἀθήναις φαρμάκους ἄγειν δύο, τὸν μὲν ὑπὲρ ἀνδρῶν, τὸν δὲ ὑπὲρ γυναικῶν, πρὸς τὸν καθαρμὸν ἀγομένους. καὶ ὁ μὲν τῶν ἀνδρῶν μελαίνας ἰσχάδας περὶ τὸν τράχηλον εἶχε, λευκὰς δ' ἄτερος. συβάκχοι δέ φησιν ὠνομάζοντο. τὸ δὲ καθάρσιον τοῦτο λοιμικῶν νόσων ἀποτροπιασμὸς ἦν, λαβὸν τὴν

ἀρχὴν ἀπὸ ᾽Ανδρόγεω τοῦ Κρητός, οὗ τεθνηκότος ἐν ταῖς ᾽Αθήναις παρανόμως τὴν λοιμικὴν ἐνόσησαν οἱ ᾽Αθηναῖοι νόσον, καὶ ἐκράτει τὸ ἔθος ἀεὶ καθαίρειν τὴν πόλιν τοῖς φαρμάκοις.

R. Henry, *Photius: Bibliotheca* (8 vols.; Paris: Société d'éditon, 1959–1977).

Text 6: Scholiast on Aristophanes, Equites 1136
δημοσίους δὲ τοὺς λεγομένους φαρμακούς, οἵπερ καθαίρουσι τὰς πόλεις τῷ ἑαυτῶν φόνῳ, ἢ τοὺς δημοσίᾳ καὶ ὑπὸ τῆς πόλεως τρεφομένους. ἔτρεφον γάρ τινας ᾽Αθηναῖοι λίαν ἀγενεῖς καὶ ἀχρήσιους καὶ ἐν καιρῷ συμφορᾶς τινος ἐπελθούσης τῇ πόλει, λοιμοῦ λέγω ἢ τοιούτου τινός, ἔθυον τούτους ἕνεκα τοῦ καθαρθῆναι τοῦ μιάσματος, οὓς καὶ ἐπωνόμαζον καθάρματα.

W.G. Rutherford (ed.), *Scholia Aristophanies* (3 vols.; London: Macmillan, 1896).

Text 7: Lysias, Contra Andokikes 53
νῦν οὖν χρὴ νομίζειν τιμωρουμένους καὶ ἀπαλλαττομένους ᾽Ανδοκίδου τὴν πόλιν καθαίρειν καὶ ἀποδιοπομπεῖσθαι καὶ φαρμακὸν ἀποπέμπειν καὶ ἀλιτηρίου ἀπαλλάττεσθαι, ὡς ἐν τούτων οὗτός ἐστι.

W.R.M. Lamb (trans.), *Lysias* (LCL; London: Heinemann, 1930).

Text 8: Diogenes Laertius, Lives of Eminent Philosophers, 2.44
ἐγεννήθη δὲ Σωκράτης...Θαργηλιῶνος ἕκτῃ, ὅτε καθαίρουσι τὴν πόλιν ᾽Αθηναῖοι καὶ τὴν ῎Αρτεμιν γενέσθαι Δήλιοί φασιν.

R.D. Hicks, *Diogenes Laertius: Lives of Eminent Philosophers* (LCL; 2 vols.; London: Heinemann, 1925).

Text 9: Hipponax
Frg. 4 (Tzet. 47), 5 (48), 6 (49), 7 (50), 8 (51), 9 (52), 11:

[4]πόλιν καθαίρειν καὶ κράδῃσι βάλλεσθαι.
[5]βάλλοντες ἐν λειμῶνι καὶ ῥαπίζοντες κράδῃσι καὶ σκίλλῃσιν ὥσπερ φαρμακόν.
[6]δεῖ δ᾽ αὐτὸν εἰς φαρμακὸν ἐκποιήσασθαι,

⁷κάφῇ παρέξειν ἰσχάδας τε καὶ μᾶζαν, καὶ τυρόν, οἷον ἐσθίουσι φαρμακοί·
⁸πάλαι γὰρ αὐτοὺς προσδέχονται χάσκοντες κράδας ἔχοντας, ὡς ἔχουσι φάρμακοις.
⁹λιμῷ γένηται ξηρός, ἐν δὲ τῷ θυμῷ φαρμακὸς ἀχθεὶς ἑπτάκις ῥαπισθείη.
¹¹ὡς οἱ μέω ἀγεῖ Βουπάλῳ κατηρῶντο.

T. Bergk, *Poetae Lyrici Graeci* (Leipzig: Teubner, 4th edn, 1882), frg. 4–9, 11; A.D. Knox (ed. and trans.), 'Fragments of Hipponax', in *Herodes, Cercidas and the Greek Choliamibic Poets* (LCL; London: Heinemann, 1929), pp. 15-65.

Text 10: J. Tzetzes, The Thousand Histories, 726–735

726. ὁ φαρμακός, τὸ κάθαρμα, τοιοῦτον ἦν τὸ πάλαι.
727. ἂν συμφορὰ κατέλαβε πόλιν θεομηνίᾳ,
728. εἴτ᾽ οὖν λιμὸς εἴτε λοιμὸς εἴτε καὶ βλάβος ἄλλο,
729. τὸν πάντων ἀμορφότερον ἦγον ὡς πρὸς θυσίαν,
730. εἰς καθαρμὸν καὶ φαρμακὸν πόλεως τῆς νοσούσης.
731. εἰς τόπον δὲ τὸν πρόσφορον στήσαντες τὴν θυσίαν
732. τυρόν τε δόντες τῇ χειρὶ καὶ μάζαν καὶ ἰσχάδας,
733. ἑπτάκις γὰρ ῥαπίσαντες ἐκεῖνον εἰς τὸ πέος
734. σκίλλαις, συκαῖς ἀγρίαις τε καὶ ἄλλοις τῶν ἀγρίων
735. τέλος πυρὶ κατέκαιον ἐν ξύλοις τοῖς ἀγρίοις.

P.A.M. Leone (ed.), *Tzetzae: Historiae* (Naples: Libreria Scientifica Editrice, 1968).

Text 11: Harpocration

s.v. Φαρμακός· δύο ἄνδρας ᾽Αθήνησιν ἐξῆγον καθάρσια ἐσομένους τῆς πόλεως ἐν τοῖς θαργηλίοις, ἕνα μὲν ὑπὲρ τῶν ἀνδρῶν, ἕνα δὲ ὑπὲρ τῶν γυναικῶν. ὅτι δὲ ὄνομα κύριόν ἐστιν ὁ φαρμακός, ἱερὰς δὲ φιάλας τοῦ ᾽Απόλλωνος κλέψας ἁλοὺς ὑπὸ τῶν περὶ τὸν ᾽Αχιλλέα κατελεύσθη, καὶ τὰ τοῖς Θαργηλίοις ἀγόμενα τούτων ἀπομιμήματά ἐστιν, ῞Ιστρος ἐν α᾽ τῶν ᾽Απόλλωνος ἐπιφανειῶν εἴρηκεν.

W. Dindorf, *Valerius Harpocration* (2 vols.; Oxford: Oxford University Press, 1853), I, p. 298.

Text 12: Hesychius, Lexicon 915
κραδίης νόμος· νόμον τινὰ ἐπαυλοῦσι τοῖς ἐκπεμπομένοις
φαρμακοῖς, κράδαις καὶ θρίοις ἐπιρραβδιζομένοις.

M. Schmidt (ed.), *Hesychii Alexandrini: Lexicon* (Ienae: Frederici, 1863).

Text 13: Petronius in Servius on Virgil's Aeneid 3.57
'Auri sacra fames': sacra, id est execrabilis. Tractus est autem sermo ex
more Gallorum. Nam Massilienses, quotiens pestilentia laborabant, unus
se ex pauperibus offerebat alendus anno integro publicis sumptibus et
purioribus cibis. Hic postea ornatus verbenis et vestibus sacris circum-
ducebatur per totam civitatem cum exsecrationibus, ut in ipsum recider-
ent mala totius civitatis, et sic proiciebatur. Hoc autem in Petronio
lectum est.

M. Heseltine (trans.), 'Fragments', in *Petronius* (LCL; London:
Heinemann, 1961), fr. 1 pp. 322-35; A.F. Stocker and A.H. Travis,
Servianorum in Vergilii Carmina Commentariorum (3 vols.; Oxford:
Oxford University Press, 1965), fr. 1.

*Text 14: Lactantius Placidi on 'Lustralemne' in Statius, Thebais, X,
793*
Lustrare civitatem humana hostia Gallicus mos est. Nam aliquis de
egentissimis prolicicbatur praemiis, ut se ad hoc venderet. Qui anno toto
publicis sumptibus alebatur purioribus cibis, denique certo et sollemni die
per totam civitatem ductus ex urbe extra pomeria saxis occidebatur a
populo.

R. Jahnke (ed.), *P. Papinius Stati. III. Lactantii Placidi Qui Dicitur
Commentarios in Statii Thebaida Commentarium in Achilleida*
(Leipzig: Teubner, 1898).

Text 15: Diegesis, 2.29-40 on Callimachus, fr. 90
[30]ἀγινεῖ 'Αβδήροις ὠνητὸς ἄνθρω-
[31]πος καθάρσιον τῆς πόλεως, ἐπὶ πλίν-
[32]θου ἑστώς φαιᾶς, θοίνης ἀπολαύων
[33]δαψιλοῦς, ἐπειδὰν διάπλεως γένηται,
[34]προάγεται ἐπὶ τὰς Προυρίδας καλου-
[35]μένας πύλας· εἶτ' ἔξω τοῦ τείχους

³⁶περίεισι κύκλῳ περικαθαίρων (?)
³⁷αὐτῷ τὴν πόλιν, καὶ τότε ὑπὸ
³⁸τοῦ βασιλέως καὶ τῶν ἄλλῶν λι-
³⁹θοβολεῖται, ἕως ἐξελασθῇ τῶν
⁴⁰ὁρίων.

R. Pfeiffer (ed.), *Callimachus* (2 vols.; Oxford: Clarendon, 1949), I, p. 97.

Text 16: Scholiast on Ovid, 'Aut te devoveat' (Ibis, 467)
Mos erat in Abdera civitate singulis annis hominem immolari pro peccatis civium, sed prius VII diebus excommunicari ut sic omnium peccata solus haberet.

R. Ellis, 'Scholia' in *P. Ovid Ovidii Nasonis Ibis* (Oxford: Clarendon Press, 1881), pp. 43-104, esp. p. 81.

Text 17: Hesychius, Lexicon, 1514 on Hipponax, fr. 7
Φαρμακοί· καθαρτήριοι, περικαθαίρουντες τὰς πόλεις, ἀνὴρ καὶ γυνή.

M. Schmidt (ed.), *Hesychii Alexandrini: Lexicon* (Ienae: Frederici, 1863).

Text 18: Strabo, Geography, 10.2.9
ἦν δὲ καὶ πάτριον τοῖς Λευκαδίοις κατ' ἐνιαυτὸν ἐν τῇ θυσίᾳ τοῦ 'Απόλλλωνος ἀπὸ τῆς σκοπῆς ῥιπτεῖσθαί τινα τῶν ἐν αἰτίαις ὄντων ἀποτροπῆς χάριν, ἐξαπτομένων ἐξ αὐτοῦ παντοδαπῶν πτερῶν καὶ ὀρνέων ἀνακουφίζειν δυναμέωνω τῇ πτήσει τὸ ἅλμα, ὑποδέχεσθαι δὲ κάτω μικραῖς ἁλιάσι κύκλῳ περιεστῶτας πολλοὺς καὶ περισῴζειν εἰς δύναμιν τῶν ὅρων ἔξω τὸν ἀναληφθέντα.

H.L. Jones (ed. and trans.), *The Geography of Strabo* (LCL; 8 vols.; London: Heinemann, 1917).

Text 19: Photius, Lexicon, s.v. περίψημα
s.v. περίψημα· κατά(μα)γμα ἢ ὑπὸ τὰ ἴχνη ἢ ἀπολύτρωσις· καὶ οὕτως ἐπέλεγον τῷ κατ' ἐνιαυτὸν ἐμβαλλομένωι τῇ θαλάσσηι νεανίαι ἐπὶ ἀπαλλαγῇ τῶν συνεχόντων κακων· περίψημα ἡμῶν γενοῦ, ἤτοι σωτηρία καὶ ἀπολύτρωσις· καὶ οὕτως ἐνέβαλον τῇ θαλάσσῃ, ὡσανεὶ τῷ Ποσειδῶνι θυσίαν ἀποτιννύντες.

214   The Cursed Christ

S.A. Naber, *Photii Patriarchae Lexicon* (Amsterdam: Adolf M. Hakkert, 1864).

Text 20: Photius, Lexicon, s.v. Λευκάτης
s.v. Λευκάτης· σκόπελος τῆς 'Ηπείρου ἀφ' οὗ ῥίπτουσιν αὐτοὺς εἰς τὸ πελαγος οἱ ἱερεῖς.

S.A. Naber, *Photii Patriarchae Lexicon* (Amsterdam: Adolf M. Hakkert, 1864).

Text 21: Ampelius 8.4
In summo monte fanum est Apollinis, ubi sacra fiunt; et cum homo inde desiluit, statim excipitur lintribus.

Erwin Assmann, *Lucii Ampelii* (Stuttgart: Teubner, 1966), p. 14.

Text 22: Livy, 10.28.14–29.1
[14]Haec locutus M. Livium pontificem, quem descendens in aciem digredi vetuerat ab se, praeire iussit verba quibus se legionesque hostium pro exercitu populi Romani Quiritium devoveret. [15]Devotus inde eadem precatione eodemque habitu quo pater P. Decius ad Veserim bello Latino se iusserat devoveri, [16]cum secundum sollemnes precationes adiecisset prae se agere sese formidinem ac fugam caedemque ac cruorem, [17]caelestium inferorum iras, contacturum funebribus diris signa tela arma hostium, locumque eundem suae pestis ac Gallorum ac Samnitium fore,—[18]haec exsecratus in se hostesque, qua confertissimam cernebat Gallorum aciem concitat equum inferensque se ipse infestis telis est interfectus. [1]Vix humanae inde opis videri pugna potuit.

B.O. Foster (trans.), *Livy* (LCL; 13 vols.; London: Heinemann, 1926).

Text 23: Suidas, Lexicon
s.v. κάθαρμα· ὑπὲρ δὲ καθαρμοῦ πόλεως ἀνῆρουν ἐστολισμένον τινά, ὅν ἐκάλουν κάθαρμα.

A. Adler (ed.), *Suidas: Lexicon* (5 vols.; Leipzig: Teubner, 1928).

Text 24: Justin Martyr, Dialogue with Trypho, 40.4
καὶ οἱ ἐν τῇ νηστείᾳ δὲ τράγοι δύο ὅμοιοι κελευσθέντες γίνεσθαι, ὧν ὁ εἷς ἀποπομπαῖος ἐγίνετο, ὁ δε ἕτερος εἰς προσ-

φοράν, τῶν δύο παρουιῶν τοῦ Χριστοῦ καταγγελία ἦσαν· μιᾶς μέν, ἐν ᾗ ὡς ἀποπομπαῖον αὐτὸν παρεπέμψαντο οἱ πρεσβύτεροι τοῦ λαοῦ ὑμῶν καὶ οἱ ἱερεῖς, ἐπιβαλόντες αὐτῷ τοῦ παρουσίας· ὅτι ἐν τῷ αὐτῷ τόπῳ τῶν 'Ιεροσολύμων ἐπιγνώσεσθε αὐτόν, τὸν ἀτιμωθέντα ὑφ' ὑμῖν, καὶ προσφορὰ ἦν ὑπὲρ πάντων τῶν μετανοεῖν βουλομένων ἁμαρτωλῶν καὶ ναστευόντων ἦν καταλέγει.

J.C.T. Otto (ed.), *Corpus Apologetorum Christianorum*, III (Jena: Libraria H. Dufft, 1879).

Text 25: Origin, Homily 10.2.20-30
Tamen quoniam dives est sermo Dei et secundum sententiam Salomonis non simpliciter, sed et dupliciter et tripliciter describendus in corde est, temptemus etiam nunc addere aliqua ad ea, quae dudum pro viribus dicta sunt, ut ostendamus, quomodo in typo futurorum etiam hic unus hircus Domino oblatus est hostia et alius vivus dimissus est. Audi in Evangeliis Pilatum dicentem ad sacerdotes et populum Iudaeorum: Quem vultis ex duobus dimittam vobis, Iesum, qui dicitur Christus, aut Barabban? Tunc clamavit omnis populus, ut Barabban dimitteret, Iesum vero morti traderet. Ecce habes hircum, qui dimissus est vivus in eremum peccata secum populi ferens clamantis et dicentis: Crucifige, crucifige. Iste est ergo hircus vivus dimissus in eremum et ille est hircus, qui Domino oblatus est hostia ad repropitianda peccata et veram propitiationem in se credentibus populis fecit.

M. Borret (trans.), *Origène: Homélies sur le Lévitique* (2 vols.; Paris: Cerf, 1981), pp. 134-35.

Appendix 1

MAPPING PAUL'S EARLY THOUGHT ON THE TERRITORY OF EARLY CHRISTIANITY

It is difficult for the non-specialist to imagine the life of Jesus without viewing him through the lens of the synoptic gospels, or to reflect upon the significance of his death without seeing it through the eyes of Paul. Such is the authority of the writings selected for the New Testament canon that the contemporary reader could easily presume that the canonical gospels are entirely representative of first-generation Christianity, and that Paul's letters are the definitive theological commentary on the gospels.

The last two hundred years of biblical criticism have made it clear that the gospels and Pauline writings hold up to the reader a highly selective and interpreted portrait of Jesus. To such an observation, the reader might counter that the New Testament preserves the most historically reliable records of Jesus life—whether selective and interpreted or not. However, the impact of scholarship and archaeology over the past century has rendered such an assertion highly dubious.

Perhaps the most important archaeological discovery for the re-appraisal of Christian origins was that of the Gospel of Thomas, discovered in the Nag Hammadi library in 1945.[1] Scholars subsequently identified this as the same gospel partially preserved in three previously unidentified Greek papyri discovered in 1897, 1903 and 1904.[2]

With hindsight, it is now clear that the discovery of the Greek Gospel of Thomas coincided with what might be termed the 'discovery' of a second gospel, which is to say, the scholarly recognition of the Sayings Gospel Q.[3] Adolf von Harnack's

---

1.   For critical edition of Coptic, and Greek with ET see. B. Layton (ed.), 'The Gospel According to Thomas', in *Nag Hammadi Codex II,2-7 Together with XIII,2*, Brit. Lib. Or. 4926(1) and P. Oxy. 1, 654, 655* NHS 20–21 (Leiden: Brill, 1989), pp. 38-109.

2.   P.Oxy. 1 = *Gos. Thom.* (Coptic) 28-33, 77a; P.Oxy. 654 = *Gos. Thom.* (Coptic) 1-7; P. Oxy. 655 = *Gos. Thom.* (Coptic) 24, 36-39 (B.P. Grenfell and A.S. Hunt, *Logia Iesou: Sayings of Our Lord* [London: Egypt Exploration Fund, 1897]; B.P. Grenfell and A.S. Hunt, *New Sayings of Jesus and Fragment of a Lost Gospel from Oxyrhynchus* [London: Egypt Exploration Fund, 1903]; B.P. Grenfell and A.S. Hunt, *The Oxyrhynchus Papyri, Part IV* [London: Egypt Exploration Fund, 1904], pp. 1-28)

3.   The Sayings Gospel 'Q' from the German word *Quelle* ('Source') is used (minimally) to refer to all material held in common between Matthew and Luke but not found in Mark. The view that this source tradition was a written document is based on two main arguments: (1) the degree of

reconstruction of the Sayings Gospel Q in 1907 precipitated a heightened scholarly awareness of Q as a distinct document.[4] The ensuing study of both these gospels have dramatically altered our understanding of Christian origins.

The Two Oldest Gospels: Thomas and the Sayings Gospel Q

The Gospel of Thomas (*Gos. Thom.*) consists of 114 sayings of Jesus, 68 of which have parallels in the New Testament, mostly in the canonical gospels. Given the striking overlap between the sayings of *Gos. Thom.* and the synoptic gospels, controversy has arisen over the relationship between these textual traditions. Was *Gos. Thom.* written before the gospels and independently of them, or was it written later than them and dependent upon them?

The search for an answer to this question was led astray from the start by two misconceptions: the first involved the confinement of *Gos. Thom.* to second-century Gnosticism; the second comprised the notion that the text of *Gos. Thom.* is a fixed (stable) text. I have argued elsewhere that both of these propositions are false.[5] Both *Gos. Thom.* and the Sayings Gospel Q were written in the mid-50's and pre-date the composition of the canonical gospels.[6]

In view of the antiquity and priority of *Gos. Thom.* and the Sayings Gospel Q, what can be said about the nature of the Christianity which they express? The Gospel of Thomas has rightly been called a 'sayings gospel' because it consists of 114 sayings of Jesus without any narrative context. Likewise, the Sayings Gospel Q, as its name would suggest, consists of Jesus-sayings fixed in a minimum of narrative.

verbal agreement between Lukan and Matthaean non-Markan material is so high that it can be explained only by the use of a common written source; (2) the order of this non-Markan material is so often the same in Luke and Matthew that only a written common source can account for it.

4. A. von Harnack, *The Sayings of Jesus: The Second Source of St. Matthew and St. Luke* (trans. J.R. Wilkinson; London: Williams & Norgate; New York: G.P. Putnam's Son's, 1907–1908); also: G.H. Müller, *Zur Synopse: Untersuchung über die Arbeitsweise des Luke und Matt. und ihre Quellen* (FRLANT, 11; Göttingen: Vandenhoeck & Ruprecht, 1908). As John Kloppenborg has pointed out:

> Prior to Harnack's reconstruction of Q, various discussions of the synoptic problem had used the notion of 'Q' virtually as an algebraic variable for solving the relationship among the extant Synoptics...With Harnack's reconstruction, the mathematical, almost whimsical, use of the *idea* of Q vanished and Q as a *document* of early Christianity appeared (Review of Helmut Koester's 'Ancient Christian Gospels', [unpublished; delivered to SBL, Nov. 1991], p. 2).

The subsequent attempts to reconstruct the Q text by Wolfgang Schenk, Athanasius Polag and most recently by the ongoing International Q Project parallel the efforts to reconstruct the text of *Gos. Thom.* (W. Schenk, *Synopse zur Redenquelle der Evangelien: Q Synopse und Rekonstruktion in deutscher Übersetzung mit kurzen Erläuterungen* [Düsseldorf: Patmos, 1981]; A. Polag, *Fragmenta Q: Textheft zur Logienquelle* [Neukirchen–Vluyn: Neukirchener Verlag, 1979]; J.M. Robinson *et al.*, 'The IQP Project: Work Sessions 12–14', *JBL* 111/3 (1992), pp. 500-508.

5. B.H. McLean, 'On the Gospel of Thomas and Q', in R.A. Piper (ed), *The Gospel Behind the Gospels* (Leiden: Brill, 1995), pp. 321-46, esp. pp. 322-33.

6. J.M. Robinson, 'On Bridging the Gulf from Q to the Gospel of Thomas (or Visa Versa)', in C.W. Hedrick and R. Hodgson Jr. (ed.), *Nag Hammadi, Gnosticism, and Early Christianity*, (Peabody, MA: Hendrickson, 1986), pp. 127-75, esp. 142-64.

Neither gospel makes any reference to Jesus' infancy, boyhood, ministry, miracles, death, resurrection, ascension or parousia. Hence, the beliefs of Christians living in the Christian communities represented by the Gospel of Thomas and the Sayings Gospel Q were substantially different from those of the communities represented by the canonical gospels.

John Kloppenborg has demonstrated that, far from being a random collection of sayings, the Sayings Gospel Q exhibits a definite structure as a product of distinct moments of compositional activity.[7] He has delineated three compositional strata in Q: the most primitive stratum, known as Q^1, consists of sapiential sayings; a secondary redactional stage (Q^2) incorporates apocalyptic material and references to John the Baptist;[8] finally, in a third stage of compositional activity the temptation story was appended (Q^3).[9]

A careful analysis of the 68 parallels between *Gos. Thom.* and the New Testament reveals that 40 of them belong to the Sayings Gospel Q. In other words, there is a greater overlap between *Gos. Thom.* and Q than between any other writing in the New Testament.[10] Of the 40 *Gos. Thom.* sayings parallelled in Q, twenty-eight belong to Q^1, its most primitive stratum.[11] Thus, the earliest collection of Q material—the

---

7. Delineation of strata is accomplished by a compositional approach which analyses Q texts according to two criteria, continuity (of theme, implied audience and forms of speech), and discontinuity, or redactional breaks, between and within defined blocks of text. This compositional approach begins with the final form of Q, as best as it can be deduced, and then works backwards to distinguish its constituitive layers. Thus, the delineation of strata does not begin with individual sayings but with Q's unifying structures which subsume compositional clusters of sayings and single sayings into a cohesive literary composition. Kloppenborg remarks:

> The detection of the presence of redaction in a sayings collection such as Q cannot proceed simply by cataloguing and sorting the individual Q sayings into two or three 'piles' either on the basis of common form, or shared motifs, or the extent of external attestation. Rather than beginning with the individual saying, it must start with the larger composed units, i.e., with the form in which the sayings are now framed. This, of course, implies, that the issue of the original order of Q is a necessarily preliminary (J.S. Kloppenborg, 'The Formation of Q Revisited: A Response to R. Horsley', in D.J. Lull [ed.], *SBL 1989 Seminar Papers* [Atlanta: Scholars Press, 1989], pp. 204-25, esp. p. 205).

Such a compositional approach disengages the analysis from *a priori* sociological judgments about the nature of primitive Christianity, whether it be characterised as being sapiential, prophetic or apocalyptic. Instead, the criteria are internal and literary (J.S. Kloppenborg, *The Formation of Q: Trajectories in Ancient Wisdom Collections* [Studies in Antiquity and Christianity; Philadelphia: Fortress Press, 1987]; J.S. Kloppenborg, 'Tradition and Redaction in the Synoptic Sayings Source', *CBQ* 46 [1984], pp. 34-62; cf. also D. Lührmann, *Der Redaktion der Logienquelle* [WMANT, 33; Neukirchen–Vluyn: Neukirchener Verlag, 1969]).

8. Cf. J.S. Kloppenborg, 'Symbolic Eschatology and the Apocalypticism of Q', *HTR* 80/3 (1987), pp. 287-306.

9. Q 4.1-13; 11.42c; 16.17; by convention Q texts are cited according to Lukan chapter and verse.

10. Cf. list in H. Koester, *Ancient Christian Gospels: Their History and Development* (Philadelphia: Trinity Press; London: SCM Press, 1990), pp. 87-89.

11. The overlaps are especially numerous between Q1's 'Sermon' (Q 6.20b-49, 16.13, 13.26-27) with nine parallels. In several of the 'Sermon' parallels, *Gos. Thom.* frequently preserves a more

sapiential sayings of Q^1—incorporates the highest number of *Gos. Thom.* parallels.

Equally significant is the fact that the apocalyptic sayings which are proper to Q^2 are not parallelled in *Gos. Thom.* Thus, the core of the Sayings Gospel Q, like that of *Gos. Thom.*, consists of sapiential sayings. James Robinson has named this genre 'sayings of the wise' (*logoi sophîn*).[12] The Sayings Gospel Q is not a paraenetic supplement to the synoptic gospels, much less a 'heretical' or 'pseudo-' gospel, but like *Gos. Thom.*, is a gospel of a different genre; namely, a gospel written in the wisdom sayings genre.[13]

In the course of time, this wisdom genre underwent two significant modifications. First, it bifurcated: while *Gos. Thom.* remained a pure sayings collection, the redactor of Q's second stratum (i.e., Q^2) subordinated the original Q^1 collection of wisdom sayings to apocalyptic themes.[14] This forking widened further when Matthew and Luke integrated Mark's narrative kerygma with the Sayings Gospel Q.[15]

Given the antiquity of the wisdom sayings in the *Gos. Thom.* and the Sayings Gospel Q, these sources have much to contribute towards the reappraisal of the origins of Christianity.[16] The fundamental principle of the sayings genre is that the

original form of the saying than Q (e.g., *Gos. Thom.* 68/Q 6.22; *Gos. Thom.* 95/Q 6.34; *Gos. Thom.* 47ab/Q 16.13; Koester, *Ancient Christian Gospels*, pp. 89-90).

12. J.M. Robinson, 'LOGOI SOPHON: On the Gattung of Q', in Robinson and Koester (eds.), *Trajectories through Early Christianity* (Philadelphia: Fortress Press, 1971), pp. 74-85; J.M. Robinson, 'On Bridging the Gulf from Q to the Gospel of Thomas (or Visa Versa)', in C.W. Hedrick and R. Hodgson, Jr (eds.), *Nag Hammadi, Gnosticism, and Early Christianity* (Peabody, MA: Hendrickson, 1986), pp. 164-75; H. Koester, 'GNOMAI DIAPHOROI: The Origin and Nature of Diversification in the History of Early Christianity', in Robinson and Koester (eds.), *Trajectories*, pp. 114-57, esp. pp. 135-36). Robinson has demonstrated that the incipit *logoi* is more primitive than the subscription *gospel* ('LOGOI SOPHON', pp. 78-80).

13. Robinson, 'On Bridging the Gulf', p. 164.

14. H. Koester, 'One Jesus and Four Primitive Gospels', in Robinson and Koester (eds.), *Trajectories*, pp. 158-204, esp. pp. 186-87; Koester, 'GNOMAI DIAPHOROI', p. 138.

15. J.M. Robinson, 'Jesus—From Easter to Valentius (or to the Apostles' Creed)', *JBL* 101 (1982), pp. 5-37, esp. pp. 22, 36. According to Dominic Crossan, the burial and tomb stories were first developed in *Gospel of Peter* as a reflection on Deut. 21.22-23 and Josh. 10.18, 26-27, and only subsequently historicised in the canonical gospels. He thinks that the earliest stratum of the Gospel of Peter was a self-contained non-historical narrative of Jesus' passion and resurrection which he refers to as the *Cross Gospel*. According to Crossan's reconstruction, Mark used the *Gospel of Peter* as his whole source. Matthew and Luke used it along with Mark, and John used it in conjunction with the synoptic narratives (Crossan, *Cross That Spoke*, Pt. 1). The first three stages of the passion tradition were: (1) the historical passion about which Jesus' disciples knew nothing; (2) an application of prophetic and psalmic passages to a passion narrative which was virtually devoid of memory; (3) the *Cross Gospel*, a coherent sequential narrative of Jesus' passion (cf. D. Crossan, *Four Other Gospels: Shadows on the Contour of Canon* [Minneapolis: Winston, 1985]).

16. Having identified the genre of Q and *Gos. Thom.* as *logoi sophôn*, other texts come to the fore that embody this same genre. For example, 1 Cor. 1–4 reports of Christians who claimed that secret wisdom was revealed to them by Jesus (S.L. Davies, *The Gospel of Thomas and Christian Wisdom* [New York: Seabury Press, 1983], p. 145). In his attack on this wisdom theology, Paul employs a saying which also appears in *Gospel of Thomas* 17 (1 Cor. 2.9). Similarly, Mark's *parables* approach what *Gos. Thom.* calls *secret sayings*. They are really allegorical riddles intended to obscure the mystery of the Kingdom to outsiders (e.g., Mk 4.10-12, 21-22, 33-34; 7.17), but to be

'teacher is present in the word which he has spoken'.[17] Both *Gos. Thom.* and the Sayings Gospel Q presuppose that Jesus' importance lay in his words alone: he is portrayed as a teacher of wisdom. His death and resurrection have no theological import.[18]

Taken together, Helmut Koester says, *Gos. Thom.* and Q 'challenge the assumption that the early church was unanimous in making Jesus' death and resurrection the fulcrum of Christian faith'.[19] The execution of Jesus was not the point of departure for some of Jesus' first followers. The Christians associated with *Gos. Thom.* and the Sayings Gospel Q may have viewed Jesus' death as a regrettable set-back in their mission, but there was no 'scandal' in his cross, nor was the meaning of Jesus' life thought to be summed up by this event.

The discussion thus far has been based on textual and literary evidence. Working independently on another front, Graydon Snyder has examined the extant archaeological evidence of the first four centuries in an attempt to describe the beliefs of early Christians. He interprets these exemplars of early Christian iconography as representative of *popular* Christian religion as opposed to *official* Christianity. He observes that 'artistic analogies of self-giving, suffering, sacrifice, or incarnation [of Jesus] are totally missing [in the archaeological evidence]. The suffering Christ on a cross first appeared in the fifth century, and then not very convincingly'.[20] Snyder concludes that in the popular Christian religion of the first three centuries 'there is no place... for a crucified Christ, or a symbol of divine death. Only when Christ was all powerful, as in the iconography of the Emperor, could that strength be used for redemption and salvation as well as deliverance'.[21]

Snyder may overstate the distinction between popular and official Christianity. He has also overlooked some relevant data such as the special writing of the Greek term σταυρός in Christian manuscripts as an explicit reference to Jesus' kerygmatic death.[22] However, iconography provides a better index of popular Christian culture,

---

revealed to the inner circle of Jesus' followers (Robinson, 'LOGOI SOPHON', pp. 91-94; E. Boring, *Sayings of the Risen Jesus*, [Cambridge: Cambridge University Press], pp. 80-81 [cf. 1 Cor. 2.6-7; Lk. 12.2-3]).

17.   Koester, 'GNOMAI DIAPHOROI', p. 138; Robinson, 'Bridging the Gulf', p. 168. According to Robinson, the sayings genre was absorbed by the narrative genre of the synoptic tradition because it was unacceptable to orthodox Christianity without a radical alternation of its form and theological intention ('LOGOI SOPHON', pp. 112-13; J.M. Robinson, 'The Problem of History in Mark, Reconsidered', *USQR* 20 [1965], p. 135).

18.   *Gos. Thom.*'s incipit which refers to *the living Jesus* does not seem to imply a *resurrected* Jesus but rather, as Koester points out, Jesus is simply referred to, 'without any concern for the problem of his death, and without any recognition of the fact that his life has become past history' (Koester, 'One Jesus', pp. 167-68; contra B.E. Gärtner, *The Theology of the Gospel According to Thomas* [New York: Harper & Row, 1960/1961], pp. 112-13).

19.   Koester, *Ancient Christian Gospels*, p. 86.

20.   G. Snyder, *Ante Pacem: Archaeological Evidence of Church Life Before Constantine* (Mercer, GA: Mercer University Press, 1985), p. 165.

21.   Snyder, *Ante Pacem*, p. 29.

22.   Matthew Black, 'The Chi-Rho Sign: Christogram and/or Staurogram?' in W.W. Gasque and R.P. Martin (ed.), *Apostolic History and the Gospel: Biblical and Historical Essays Presented to*

albeit of the wealthy, than do ancient New Testament manuscripts. Thus, despite these reservations, the essence of Snyder's argument remains intact. Taken together, the archaeological and textual evidence lead us to a reassessment of traditional portrayals of the nature of early Christianity.

Paul's gospel of the Cross and Resurrection which became dominant by the time of the Constantinian Church was not the only interpretation of Jesus' life in the first century, nor was it *Paul's* only interpretation. I have noted above how, in Paul's early years as a Christian, he interpreted Jesus' death as a sign of the continued hard-heartedness of the Jews, but nothing more: Jesus' death is mentioned in the same breath as the death of the prophets (1 Thess. 2.14-15): 'You [Thessalonians] suffered the same things from your own compatriots as they did from the Jews, who killed the Lord Jesus and the prophets, and drove us out.'

Paul's treatment of Christ's death in his first years as a Christian is remarkably similar to that of the Sayings Gospel Q. In the Sayings Gospel Q, Jesus' ministry is placed against the narrative background of the suffering, persecution and death of God's other prophets:

> Therefore also the Wisdom of God said, 'I will send them prophets and apostles some of whom they will kill and persecute', so that this generation may be charged with the blood of all the prophets shed since the foundation of the world, from the blood of Abel to the blood of Zechariah (Lk. 11.49-51).

In this passage and others, the Sayings Gospel Q had the opportunity to reflect upon the meaning of Jesus' death, but instead chose to go in a different direction, employing the deuteronomistic motif of persecution of God's envoys.[23] Thus, neither Q nor Paul in his early ministry particularise the meaning of Jesus' death, but rather generalise it by grouping it along with the persecution and murder of Israel's prophets over the entire sweep of history.

The similarities between Paul's early thought and the teaching of the Sayings Gospel Q and *Gos. Thom.* should not overshadow the fact that they flourished in different geographical regions and were divergent in their orientations. Burton Mack considers the Christianity of Q and *Gos. Thom.* to be representative of Jesus' movements in and around Palestine and western Syria.[24] In contrast to this is the Christianity which prospered in Asia Minor, Macedonia and Achaia, which he terms the 'Christ cult' or 'congregations of the Christ', best exemplified in Pauline Christianity.[25] Unlike the Jesus movements of Palestine, Paul evinced little or no interest in the sayings tradition of Jesus. Instead, Paul's soteriology began with the language rooted in Jewish apocalypticism.[26]

F.F. Bruce on his Sixtieth Birthday (Grand Rapids: Eerdmans, 1970), pp. 319-27; cf. Jack Finegan on the Christian adaptation of cross marks (*The Archaeology of the New Testament* [Princeton: Princeton University Press, rev. edn, 1992]).

23. Cf. J.S. Kloppenborg, ' 'Easter Faith' and the Sayings Gospel Q', in R. Cameron (ed.), *The Apocryphal Jesus and Christian Origins*, Semeia 49 (1990), pp. 71-99; cf. D. Seeley, 'Jesus' Death in Q', *NTS* 38 (1992), pp. 222-34.

24. Mack, *Myth of Innocence*, pp. 79-95; cf. Koester, 'GNOMOI DIAPHOROI', pp. 119-42.

25. Mack, *Myth of Innocence*, pp. 98-123; cf. Koester, 'GNOMOI DIAPHOROI', pp. 143-57.

26. Though Mack's schema does tend to oversimplify the complex emergence of Christianity,

However, Paul's conception of Christ was not static, but dynamic and constantly evolving into something new. From the vantage point of first-generation Christianity, the development of Paul's theology of the crucified and resurrected Christ in 1 Corinthians was not the 'centre' of his entire theology, much less the centre of early Christian belief. Rather it is but one of many models, albeit a very significant model for Paul, which he developed to explain the saving work of Christ. As I have demonstrated, numbered among these other models is the apotropaeic paradigm.

nevertheless it remains a useful interpretative tool for the identification of two important streams in the diverse Jesus movements; cf. for example Robert Funk's division of the genre of 'gospel' into five categories: narrative gospels, sayings gospels (e.g, *Gos. Thom.*, *Dial. Sav.*, *Ap. Jas*, Q), infancy gospels, passion gospels (e.g., *Gos. Pet.*, *Acts Pil.*), and gospel fragments (e.g., Egerton, *Gos. Eb.*, *Gos. Eg.*, etc.) (New Gospel Parallels. I. The Synoptic Gospels [2 vols.; Philadelphia: Fortess Press, 2nd edn, 1985], pp. x-xi; Koester, *Ancient Christian Gospels*, pp. 49-348).

Appendix 2

PHILIPPIANS 2.5-11

Most scholars agree that Phil 2.5-11 should be understood as a self-contained poetic unit. This can be justified on both stylistic[1] and linguistic grounds.[2] It may have been composed for liturgical use and have been set to music.[3] There is general concurrence that this hymn is an anonymous pre-Pauline tradition which was composed independently of, and prior to, Paul's letter to the Philippians, and that it was inserted into this letter by Paul himself.[4] The hymn begins by describing Christ as pre-existent, being 'in the form of God' (ἐν μορφῇ θεοῦ ὑπάρχων, v. 6). The meaning of the term μορφή has been the occasion of much debate.[5] Christ voluntarily relinquishes 'the form of God' when he 'becomes in the ὁμοιώματι of humans' (v. 7c), in exchange for 'the form of a servant' (μορφὴν δούλου λαβών. v. 7b). The term 'form' (μορφή) should be understood in the same sense in both v. 6 and v. 7b. There is now general concensus that the term does not simply refer to the mere semblance of external appearance but, as Moulton and Milligan state, the 'form which truly and fully expresses the being which underlies it'.[6]

---

1.   R.P. Martin, *Carmen Christi*, pp. 12-13.

2.   J.T. Sanders, *The New Testament Christological Hymns: Their Historical and Religious Background* (SNTSMS; Cambridge: Cambridge University Press. 1971), pp. 1-5; R. Deichgräber, *Gotteshymnus und Christushymnus in der fruhen Christenheit: Untersuchungen zur Form, Sprache und Stil der fruhchristlichen Hymnen* (Göttingen: Vandenhoeck & Ruprecht, 1967), pp. 11-21.

3.   For examples of other passages which may also be hymns cf. Col. 1.15-20; Jn 1.1-14; 1 Tim. 2.5-6; 3.16; 6.15-16; Heb. 1.3.

4.   For a summary of arguments against Pauline authorship see: P.T. O'Brien, *The Epistle to the Philippians: A Commentary on the Greek Text* (Grand Rapids: Eerdmans 1991), pp. 198-202; Martin, *Carmen Christi*, pp. 45-54; arguments in favour of Pauline authorship: Martin, *Carmen Christi*, pp. 55-57. One of the key points of debate concerning this hymn focuses on the problem of reproducing the structure of the hymn on the basis of its literary and rhetorical devices. Most recently, Morna Hooker has argued: first, that the hymn falls into two (not three) parts (vv. 6-8, 9-11) with one finite verb in each section; secondly, that all the words and phrases should be accepted as part of the original hymn (M. Hooker, 'Philippians 2.6-11', in E.E. Ellis and E. Gräßer [ed.], *Jesus und Paulus: Festschrift für Werner Georg Kümmel zum 70 Geburtstag*; Göttingen: Vandenhoeck & Ruprecht, 1975], pp. 151-64, esp. pp. 157-59).

5.   Summarized by P. O'Brien, *Philippians*, pp. 207-211.

6.   J.H. Moulton and G. Milligan, *The Vocabulary of the Greek New Testament Illustrated from the Papyri and Other Non-Literary Sources* (London: Hodder & Stoughton, 1914-1929), p. 417.

Similarly, ὁμοιώματι signifies 'the perceptible expression of a reality' not the mere semblance thereof.[7] Hence, the passage describes Christ becoming fully and truly human and, what is more, becoming the lowest form of human life, 'the form of a slave' (μορφὴ δούλου). Christ, now a humiliated slave, is obedient, even at the personal cost of being killed. This act of self-humbling and death, is followed by his exultation by God to a place of highest honour. In recognition of this supreme act of condescension, God then exalted him as 'Lord'. The internal logic of the hymn is different from all the paradigms considered thus far. Instead of Paul's ascending and descending Christ (resurrection/parousia), the hymn recounts three phases of Christ's existence, Christ pre-existent, Christ according to the flesh, and finally Christ according to the Spirit by the resurrection.[8]

Clearly, this hymn does not manifest the expulsion paradigm. First, though Christ humbles himself, becoming human, and dies on a cross, there is no transfer to him of sin or a curse. In other words, Christ does not abase himself to become a substitutionary victim. Secondly, in contrast to the apotropaeic victim, Christ in this hymn is ultimately exalted by God after his temporary abasement.

Many attempts have been made to identify the linguistic and conceptual background of this hymn.[9] However, there is as yet no consensus. Collange concludes that the hymn is 'not primarily a Christianised copy of prior speculations'.[10] Whether this hymn stimulated Paul's thought in the direction of the notion of Christ becoming a substitutionary victim, it is impossible to say. However, it does illustrate Paul's general tendency of drawing upon numerous mutually exclusive conceptual models as the occasion requires.

---

7.   Vanni, ''Ομοίωμα in Paolo', p. 339; cf. discussion of this term ch. 3 in discussion of Rom. 8.3.

8.   Branick, 'Sinful Flesh', p. 253.

9.   See summary in O'Brien, *Philippians*, pp. 263-71.

10.   J.-F. Collange, *The Epistle of Saint Paul to the Philippians* (trans. A.W. Heathcote; London: Macmillan, 1979), p. 88.

BIBLIOGRAPHY

Abbott, E.A., *Johannine Grammar* (London: A. & C. Black, 1906).

Achtemeirer, P.J., *The Quest for Unity in the New Testament Church: A Study in Paul and Acts* (Philadelphia: Fortress Press, 1987).

Ackerman, R., *J.G. Frazer: His Life and Work* (Cambridge: Cambridge University Press, 1987).

Alford, H., *The Greek New Testament* (4 vols.; London: Rivingtons, 1877).

Alliot, M., *Le Culte d'Horus à Edfou au temps des Ptolemees* (Cairo: Impr. de l'Institut français d'Archeologie orientale, 1946).

Allo, E.B., *Seconde Epître aux Corinthiens* (Paris: Cerf, 1937).

Alsup, J.E., *The Post-Resurrection Stories of the Gospel Tradition* (Calwer Theologische Monographien; Stuttgart: Calwer Verlag, 1975).

Assmann, E., *Lucii Ampelii* (Stuttgart: Teubner, 1966).

Aune, D., *The New Testament in Its Literary Environment* (W.A. Meeks [ed.]; Library of Early Christianity, 8; Philadelphia: Westminster Press, 1987).

Babbitt, F.C., *Plutarch's Moralia* (LCL; 16 vols.; London: Heinemann, 1969).

Bachmann, P., *Der zweite Brief des Paulus an die Korinther* (T. Zahn [ed.], KNT, 8; Leipzig: Deichert, 4th edn, 1922 [1918]).

Bachrach, P. and M.S. Baratz, *Power and Poverty* (New York: Oxford University Press, 1970).

Badcock, F.J. *The Pauline Epistles and the Epistle to the Hebrews in Their Historical Setting* (London: SPCK, 1937).

Bahr, G.J., 'Paul and Letter Writing in the First Century', *CBQ* 28 (1966), pp. 465-77.

Bammel, E., 'Herkunft und Funktion der Traditionselemente in 1 Kor 15.1-11,' *TZ* 11 (1955), pp. 401-419.

Barr, J.,*The Semantics of Biblical Language* (London: Oxford University Press, 1961).

Barrett, C.K., *A Commentary on the Epistle to the Romans* (BNTC; London: A. & C. Black, 1957).

—*A Commentary on the Second Epistle to the Corinthians* (HNTC; New York: Harper & Row, 1973).

—*Freedom and Obligation: A Study of the Epistle to the Galatians* (London: SPCK, 1985).

Bartchy, S.S., ΜΑΛΛΟΝ ΧΡΗΣΑΙ: *First Century Slavery and the Interpretation of 1 Corinthians 7.21* (SBLDS, 11; Missoula, MT: Scholars Press, 1973).

Barth, K., *The Resurrection of the Dead* (New York: Revell, 1933).

Bauer, W., *Griechisch-Deutsches Wörterbuch zu den Schriften des Neuen Testaments* (Giessen: Töpelmann, 1928).

Baumgarten, J.M., 'Does *tlh* in the Temple Scroll Refer to Crucifixion?', *JBL* 91 (1972), pp. 472-81.

Baus, K., *Der Kranz in Antike und Christentum, eine religionsgeschichtliche Untersuchung mit besonderer Berucksichtigung Tertullians* (Bonn: Peter Hanstein, 1940).

Beker, J.C., *Paul the Apostle: The Triumph of God in Life and Thought* (Philadelphia: Fortress Press, 1980).

Belkin, S., *Philo and the Oral Law: The Philonic Interpretation of Biblical Law in Relation to the Palestinian Halakah* (Cambridge, MA: Harvard University Press, 1940).

Bengel, J.A., *Gnomon of the New Testament* (C.T. Lewis [trans.]; Philadelphia: Perkinpini & Higgins, 1860/1867).

Bergk, T., *Poetae Lyrici Graeci* (Leipzig: Teubner, 4th edn, 1882).

Bernard, J.H., *The Second Epistle to the Corinthians* (W.R. Nicoll [ed.]; EGT, 3; New York: George H. Doran & Co., 1903).

Berthiaume, G., *Les rôles du Mágeiros: étude sur la boucherie, la cuisine et le sacrifice dans la Grèce ancienne* (Leiden: Brill; Montréal: Les Presses de l'Université de Montréal, 1982).

Bertram, G., 'κρεμάννυμι', *TDNT*, III, pp. 917-19.

Best, E., *Second Corinthians* (Atlanta: John Knox, 1987).

Betz, H.-D., *Galatians* (Hermeneia; Philadelphia: Fortress Press, 1980).

Bianchi, U., 'La rédemption dans les livre d'Adam', in *Selected Essays on Gnosticism, Dualism and Mysteriosophy* (NovTSup, 38; Leiden: Brill, 1978), pp. 1-8.

Bicknell, J., *The First and Second Epistles to the Thessalonians* (London: Methuen, 1932).

Black, M., 'The Chi-Rho Sign: Christogram and/or Staurogram?' in W.W. Gasque and R.P. Martin (eds.), *Apostolic History and the Gospel: Biblical and Historical Essays Presented to F.F. Bruce on his Sixtieth Birthday* (Grand Rapids: Eerdmans, 1970), 319-27.

Blackburn, B., *Theios Aner and the Markan Miracle Traditions: A Critique of the Theios Aner Concept as an Interpretive Background of the Miracle Traditions Used by Mark* (WUNT, 2.40; Tübingen: Mohr [Paul Siebeck], 1991).

Blank, J., *Paulus und Jesus* (SANT, 18; Munich: Chr. Kaiser Verlag, 1968).

Blau, J., 'The Red Heifer: A Biblical Purification Rite in Rabbinic Literature', *Numen* 14 (1967), pp. 70-78.

Bleek, F., 'Erörterungen in Beziehung auf die Briefe Pauli an die Korinther', *TSK* 3 (1830), pp. 614-32.

Bligh, J., *Galatians: A Discussion of St Paul's Epistle* (London: St Paul Publishing, 1969).

—*Galatians in Greek: A Structural Analysis of St Paul's Epistle to the Galatians* (Detroit: University of Detroit Press, 1966).

Bloomquist, L.G., *The Function of Suffering in Philippians* (JSNTSup, 78; Sheffield: JSOT Press, 1993).

Blunt, A.W.F., *The Epistle of Paul to the Galatians* (Oxford: Clarendon Press, 1925).

Boer, M.C. de, *The Defeat of Death: Apocalyptic Eschatology in 1 Corinthians and Romans 5* (JSNTSup, 22; Sheffield: JSOT Press, 1988).

Bömer, F., *Untersuchungen über die Religion der Sklaven in Griechenland und Rom* (4 vols.; AAWM; Wiesbaden: Steiner, 1957–1963).

Bonnard, P., *L'Epître de Saint Paul aux Galates* (CNT, 9; Neuchatel: Delachaux & Niestlé, 1953).

Bonnet, H., *Reallexikon der ägyptischen Religionsgeschichte* (Berlin: De Gruyter, 1952).

Boring, E., *Sayings of the Risen Jesus* (Cambridge: Cambridge University Press, 1982).

Bornkamm, G., *Paul* (D.M.G. Stalker [trans.]; New York: Harper & Row, 1969–1975).

Borret, M., *Origène: Contre Celse* (5 vols.; Paris: Cerf, 1967).

Borret, M. (trans.), *Origène: Homélies sur le Lévitique* (2 vols.; Paris: Cerf, 1981).

Brandenburger, E., *Fleisch und Geist: Paulus und die dualistische Weisheit* (WMANT, 29; Neukirchen–Vluyn: Neukirchener Verlag, 1968).

Branick, V.P., 'The Sinful Flesh of the Son of God (Rom. 8.3): A Key Image of Pauline Theology', *CBQ* 47 (1985), pp. 246-61.

Braun, H., *Gesammelt Studient zum Neuen Testament* (Tübingen: Mohr, 1966).

Brelich, A., 'Symbol of a Symbol', in J.M. Kitigawa and C.H. Long (eds.), *Myths and Symbols: Studies in Honor of Mircea Eliade* (Chicago: University of Chicago Press, 1969), pp. 195-207.

Bremmer, J., 'Scapegoat Rituals in Ancient Greece', HSCP 87 (1983), pp. 299-320.

Breytenbach, C., *Versöhnung: Eine Studie zur paulinischen Soteriologie* (WMANT, 60; Neukirchen–Vluyn: Neukirchener Verlag, 1989).

Brichto, H.C. 'On Slaughter and Sacrifice, Blood and Atonement', *HUCA* 47 (1976), pp. 19-55.

Bright, J., *A History of Israel* (Philadelphia: Westminster Press, 3rd edn, 1959).

Bristol, L.O. 'Paul's Thessalonian Correspondence', *ExpTim* 55 (1944), p. 223.

Bronson, D.B., 'Paul, Galatians, and Jerusalem', *JAAR* 35 (1967), pp. 119-28.

Brown, R., *The Gospel According to John* (AB 29/30; Garden City, NY: Doubleday, 1966–1970).

Brownson, C.L. (trans.), *Xenophon: Anabasis and Hellenica* (LCL; 3 vols.; London: Heinemann, 1921).

Bruce, F.F., *1 and 2 Corinthians* (London: Butler & Tanner Ltd, 1971).

—*The Epistle of Paul to the Galatians: A Commentary on the Greek Text* (Exeter: Paternoster Press, 1982).

Büchsel, F., 'ἀγοράζειν, ἐξαγοράζω', *TDNT*, I, pp. 124-27.

—'ἱλαστήριον', *TDNT*, III, pp. 318-23.

—'κατάρα', *TDNT*, I, pp. 449-51.

Buck, C.H., 'The Collection for the Saints', *HTR* 43.1 (1950), pp. 1-29.

Buck, C.H., and G. Taylor, *Saint Paul: A Study in the Development of his Thought* (New York: Charles Scribner's Sons, 1969).

Budge, E.A.W., *From Fetish to God in Ancient Egypt* (Oxford: Oxford University Press, 1949).

Bultmann, R., 'New Testament and Mythology', in H.W. Bartsch (ed.), *Kerygma and Myth: A Theological Debate* (R.H. Fuller [trans.]; London: SPCK, 1953), pp. 1-44.

—*The Second Letter to the Corinthians* (R.A. Harrisville [trans.]; Minneapolis: Augsburg, 1976–1985).

—*Theology of the New Testament* (K. Grobel [trans.]; New York: Charles Scribner's Sons, 1951–1955).

Burkert, W., *Greek Religion* (J. Raffa [trans.]; Cambridge, MA: Harvard University Press, 1985).

—'Greek Tragedy and Sacrificial Ritual', *GRBS* 7 (1966), pp. 87-121.

—*Homo Necans: The Anthropology of Ancient Greek Sacrificial Ritual and Myth* (P. Bing [trans.]; Berkeley: University of California Press, 1972–1983).

—'The Problem of Ritual Killing', in *Violent Origins: Walter Burkert, René Girard,* and Jonathan Z. *Smith on Ritual Killing and Cultural Formation* (Stanford, CA: Stanford University Press, 1987), pp. 149-76.

—*Structure and History in Greek Mythology and Ritual* (Sather Classical Lectures, 47; Berkeley: University of California Press, 1979).

Burton, E. de Witt, *A Critical and Exegetical Commentary on the Epistle to the Galatians* (Edinburgh: T. & T. Clark, 1921).

—*Spirit, Soul and Flesh* (Chicago: University of Chicago Press, 1918).

Busnell, H., *The Vicarious Sacrifice* (London: Richard D. Dickinson, 1880).

Cary, E. (trans.). *The Roman Antiquities of Dionysius of Halicarnassus* (7 vols.; Cambridge, MA: Harvard University Press, 1937).

Casabona, J., *Recherches sur le vocabulaire des sacrifices en Grec, des origines à la fin de l'époque classique* (Publication des Annales de la Faculté des lettres, NS 59; Aix-en-Provence: Editions Ophrys, 1966).

Charles, R.H., *A Critical and Exegetical Commentary on the Book of Daniel* (Oxford: Clarendon Press, 1929).

Chilton, B., *Targumic Approaches to the Gospels* (Lanham, MD: University Press of America, 1986).

Clavier, H. 'La Sante de l'apôtre Paul', in J.N. Sevenster and W.C. van Unnik (eds.), *Studia Paulina in honorem Johannis de Zwaan Septuagenarii* (Haarlem: Bohn, 1953), pp. 66-82.

Cohoon, J.W., *Dio Chrysostom* (LCL; 5 vols.; Cambridge, MA: Harvard University Press, 1961–1971).

Collange, J.-F., *Enigmes de la Deuxième Epître de Paul aux Corinthiens: Etude Exegetique de 2 Cor. 2.14–7.14* (Cambridge: Cambridge University Press, 1972).

—*The Epistle of Saint Paul to the Philippians* (A.W. Heathcote [trans.]; London: 1979).

Colson, F.H. and G.H. Whitaker (trans.), *Philo in Ten Volumes* (LCL; Cambridge: Cambridge University Press, 1930).

Constans, L.A., *César: Guerre des Gaules* (Paris: Société d'Edition, 5th edn, 1947).

Conybeare, F.C. (trans), *Flavius Philostratus: The Life of Apollonius of Tyanna* (2 vols.; New York: Macmillan, 1912).

Conzelmann, H., *1 Corinthians* (G.W. Macrae [trans.], J.W. Leitch [ed.]; Philadelphia: Fortress Press, 1975–1969).

Cosgrove, C.H. *The Cross and the Spirit: A Study in the Argument and Theology of Galatians* (Macon, GA: Mercer University Press, 1988).

Cousar, C.B., *Galatians* (Atlanta: John Knox, 1982).

Cranfield, C.E.B. *A Critical and Exegetical Commentary on the Epistle to the Romans* (ICC; 2 vols.; Edinburgh: T. & T. Clark, 1925).

Crawey, A.E. 'Cursing and Blessing', in James Hastings (ed.), *Encylopaedia of Religion and Ethics* (Edinburgh: T. & T. Clark, 1920), 4.367-374.

Cremer, H., *Biblico-Theological Lexicon of New Testament Greek* (W. Urwick; Edinburgh: T. & T. Clark, 1880).

Crook, J., *Law and Life of Rome* (New York: Cornell University Press, 1967).

Crossan, J.D. *The Cross That Spoke: The Origins of the Passion Narrative* (San Francisco: Harper & Row, 1988).

—*Four Other Gospels: Shadows on the Contour of Canon* (Minneapolis: Winston, 1985).

Crownfield, F.R. 'The Singular Problem of the Dual Galatians', *JBL* 44 (1945), pp. 491-500.

Cullman, O., *Christology of the New Testament* (S.C. Guthrie and C.A.M. Hall [trans.]; Philadelphia: Westminster Press, 1957–1959).

Dahl, N.A., *Studies in Paul: Theology for the Early Christian Mission* (Minneapolis: Augsburg, 1977), pp. 62-69.

—'The Purpose of Mark's Gospel', in C. Tuckett (ed.), *The Messianic Secret* (Philadelphia: Fortress Press, 1983), pp. 29-34.

—*The Resurrection of the Body* (London: SCM Press, 1962).

Daly, R.J., *Christian Sacrifice* (Washington: Catholic University of America Press, 1978).

—'The Soteriological Significance of the Sacrifice of Isaac', *CBQ* 39 (1977), pp. 45-75.

Dan, J., 'Sacrifice', *EncJud* (C. Roth [ed.]; New York: Macmillan 1971), XIV, 599-616.

Danby, H., *The Mishnah* (London: Oxford University Press, 1933).

Dareste, R., B. Hausoullier, and T. Reinach (eds.). *Recueil des inscriptions juridiques greques* (Rome: L'Ermna di Bretscheider, 1892–1965).

Davies, D., 'An Interpretation of Sacrifice in Leviticus', *ZAW* 89 (1977), pp. 387-99.

Davies, N. de Garis, *Archaeological Survey of Egypt. XXI. Five Theban Tombs* (F.L. Griffith [ed.]; London: Egyptian Exploration Fund, 1913).

Davies, P.R., and B.D. Chilton, 'The *Aquedah*: A Revised Tradition of History', *CBQ* 40 (1978), pp. 514-46.

Davies, S.L., *The Gospel of Thomas and Christian Wisdom* (New York: Seabury, 1983).

Davies, W.D. 'Knowledge in the Dead Sea Scrolls and Matthew 11.25-30', *HTR* 46 (1953), pp. 379-80.

Degani, H., *Hipponactis testimonia et fragmenta* (Bibliotheca scriptorum Graecorum et Romanorum Teubneriana; Leipzig: Teubner, 1983).

Deichgräber, R., *Gotteshymnus und Christushymnus in der fruhen Christenheit: Untersuchungen zur Form, Sprache und Stil der fruhchristlichen Hymnen* (Göttingen: Vandenhoeck & Ruprecht, 1967).

Deissmann, G.A., *Bibelstudient: Beiträge, zumeist aus den Papyri und Inschriften, zur Geschichte der Sprache, des Schriftums und der Religion des hellenistischen Judentums und des Urchristentums* (New York: Georg Olms, 1977).

—*Light from the Ancient East* (L.R.M. Strachan [trans.]; London: Hodder & Stoughton, rev. edn, 1927).

—*Paul: A Study in Social and Religious History* (W.E. Wilson [trans.]; New York: Doran, 2nd rev. edn, 1926).

Delcor, M., 'Le mythe de la chute des anges', *RHR* 190 (1976), pp. 3-53.

Detienne, M., 'Culinary Practices and the Spirit of Sacrifice', in M. Detienne and J.-P. Vernant (eds.), *The Cuisine of Sacrifice among the Greeks* (ET; P. Wissing [trans.]; Chicago: University of Chicago Press, 1989 [1979]), pp. 1-20.

—*Dionysus mis à mort* (Paris: Gallimard, 1977).

—'The Violence of Wellborn Ladies: Women in the Thesmophoria', in G. Duby and M. Perrot (eds.), *A History of Women. I. From Ancient Goddesses to Christian Saints* (Cambridge, MA: Belknap Press of Harvard University Press, 1992), pp. 338-76.

Deubner, L., *Attische Feste* (Berlin: Akademie Verlag, 1932).

Dietauer, U., *Tier und Mensch im Denken der Antike* (Amsterdam: Gruner, 1977).

Dindorf, W. (ed.)., *Aristophanes* (4 vols.; Oxford: Oxford University Press, 1838).

—*Valerius Harpocration: Lexicon in decem oratores atticos* (2 vols.; Oxford: Oxford University Press, 1853).

Dittenberger, W. (ed.), *Orientis Graeci Inscriptiones selectae* (2 vols.; Leipzig: H. Hirzel, 1903–1905).

—*Sylloge Inscriptionum Graecarum* (4 vols.; Leipzig: S. Hirzelium, 3rd edn, 1915–1924).

Dodd, C.H., *The Epistle of Paul to the Romans* (MNTC; New York: Harper & Row, 1959).

—*The Interpretation of the Fourth Gospel* (Cambridge: Cambridge University Press, 1968).

—*New Testament Studies* (Manchester: Manchester University Press, 1953).

Dodds, E.R., *Euripides: Bacchae* (Oxford: Clarendon Press, 2nd edn, 1960).

—*The Greeks and the Irrational* (Berkeley: University of California Press, 1964).

Donaldson, T., 'Thomas Kuhn, Convictional Worlds, and Paul', in B. Hudson McLean (ed.), *Origins and Method: Towards a New Understanding of Judaism and Christianity. Studies in Honour of John C. Hurd* (JSNTSup, 86; Sheffield: JSOT Press, 1993, pp. 190-98.

—'Zealot and Convert: the Origin of Paul's Christ Torah Antithesis', *CBQ* 51 (1989), pp. 655-82.

Donfried, K.P. (ed.)., *The Romans Debate* (Peabody, MA: Hendrickson, rev. edn, 1991).

Doty, W.G., *Letters in Primitive Christianity* (Guides to Biblical Scholarship; Philadelphia: Fortress Press, 1973).

Douglas, M., *Implicit Meanings: Essays in Anthropology* (London: Routledge & Kegan Paul, 1975).

—*Natural Symbols: Explorations in Cosmology* (New York: Pantheon, 2nd edn, 1982).

—*Purity and Danger: An Analysis of Concepts of Pollution and Taboo* (New York: Praeger, 1966).

Driver, G.R., 'Three Technical Terms in the Pentateuch', *JSS* 1 (1956), pp. 97-105.

Duff, A.M., *Freedmen in the Early Roman Empire* (Cambridge: W. Heffer, 2nd edn, 1958).

Duncan, G.S., *The Epistle of Paul to the Galatians: A Reconstruction* (London: Hodder and Stoughton, 1929).

—*St Paul's Ephesian Ministry: A Reconstruction* (London: Hodder & Stoughton, 1929).

Dunn, J.D.G., 'Jesus—Flesh and Spirit: An Exposition of Romans 1.3-4', *JTS* 24 (1973), pp. 40-63.

—*Romans 1–8* (Dallas: Word Books, 1988).

Durand, J.-L., 'Greek Animals: Toward a Topology of Edible Bodies', in M. Detienne and J.-P. Vernant (eds.), *The Cuisine of Sacrifice among the Greeks* (ET; P. Wissing [trans.]; Chicago: University of Chicago Press, 1989 [1979]), pp. 87-118.

Edmonds, J.M. (trans.), 'The Poems (Idylls) of Theocritus', in *The Greek Bucolic Poets* (LCL; London: Heinemann, 1912), pp. 8-207.

Eichrodt, W., *Theology of the Old Testament* (J.A. Baker [trans.]; Philadelphia: Westminster Press, 1961).

Eitrem, S., *Opferritus und Voropfer der Griechen und Römer* (Oslo: Jacob Dybwad, 1915).

Elert, W., 'Redemptio ab hostibus', *TLZ* 72/5 (1947), pp. 265-70.

Ellicott, C.J., *A Critical and Grammatical Commentary on St Paul's Epistle to the Galatians* (Boston: Crosby, Nicholas, Lee & Co., 1860).

Ellis, R., 'Scholia', in *P. Ovid Ovidii Nasonis Ibis* (Oxford: Clarendon Press, 1881), pp. 43-104.

Epstein, I. (trans.), *Babylonian Talmud* (London: Soncino Press,1935–1948).

Erman, A., *A Handbook of Egyptian Religion* (A.S. Griffith [trans.]; London: A. Constable, 1907).

Estienne, H., *Thesauros tes hellenikes glosses. Thesaurus graecae lingae* (3 vols.; Paris: A.F. Didot, 1865).

Etheridge, J.W. (trans.), *The Targums of Onkelos and Jonathan ben Uzziel on the Pentateuch with Fragments of the Jerusalem Targum* (New York: Ktav, 1968).

Evans, E. (trans.), *Tertullian: Adversus Marcionem* (2 vols.; Oxford: Clarendon Press, 1972).

Evans-Pritchard, E., *A History of Anthropological Thought* (New York: Basic Books, 1981).

—*Theories of Primitive Religion* (Oxford: Oxford University Press), 1965.

Farnell, L.R., *The Cults of the Greek States* (5 vols.; Oxford: Clarendon Press, 1907).

Fauth, W., 'Römische Religion im Spiegel der "Fasti" des Ovid', in *ANRW* II, 16.1 (1978), pp. 104-182.

Fee, G.D., *The First Epistle to the Corinthians* (NICNT; Grand Rapids: Eerdmans, 1987).

Findlay, G.G., *The Epistles to the Thessalonians* (Cambridge: Cambridge University Press, 1898).

Finegan, J., *The Archaeology of the New Testament* (Princeton: Princeton University Press, rev. edn, 1992).

Finkelstein, L., *The Pharisees: The Sociological Background of Their Faith* (2 vols.; Philadelphia: Jewish Publication Society, 3rd edn, 1962).

Fitzer, G., 'Der Ort der Versöhnung nach Paulus. Zu Frage des Sühnopfers Jesus', *TZ* 22 (1966), pp. 161-83.

Fitzgerald, J.T., *Cracks in an Earthen Vessel: An Examination of the Catalogues of Hardships in the Corinthian Corresondence* (Atlanta, GA: Scholars Press, 1988).

Fitzmyer, J.A., 'The Letter to the Galatians', in R.E. Brown *et al.* (eds.), *The Jerome Biblical Commentary* (Englewood Cliffs, NJ: Prentice–Hall, 1968), pp. 236-46.

Foster, B.O. (trans.)., *Livy* (LCL; 13 vols.; London: Heinemann, 1926).

Foucault, M., *La volonté de savoir* (Paris: Gallimard, 1976).

Frazer, J.G., *The Golden Bough*. VI. *The Scapegoat.* (London: Macmillan, 1st edn, 1890; 2nd edn, 1900; 3rd edn, 1911–1915).

Friedrich, J., *Aus dem hethitischen Schrifttum* (2 vols.; Der Alte Orient, 24; Leipzig: Hinrichs, 1925).

Fuller, R.H., *The Formation of the Resurrection Narratives* (New York: Macmillan 1971).

Funk, R., *New Gospel Parallels*. I. *The Synoptic Gospels* (2 vols.; Philadelphia: Fortress Press, 2nd edn, 1985).

Furnish, V., *2 Corinthians* (AB, 32A; Garden City, NY: Doubleday, 1984).

Gärtner, B.E., *The Theology of the Gospel According to Thomas* (New York: Harper & Row, 1961).

Gaster, T.H., 'Azaze'l', *IDB*, I, pp. 325-26.

—'Demon, Demonology', *IDB* (G.A. Buttrick *et al.* [eds.]; New York: Abingdon Press, 1962), 1.817-24.

Gaston, L., *Paul and the Torah* (Vancouver: University of British Columbia Press, 1987).

Gaventa, B.R., 'The Singularity of the Gospel: A Reading of Galatians', in D.J. Lull (ed.) (SBLSP 27; Missoula, MT: Scholars Press, 1988), pp. 17-26.

Gebhard, V., *Die Pharmakoi in Ionien und die Sybakchoi in Athen*, (dissertation; Amberg: H. Böes Söhne, 1926).

Gelzer, T. and C. Whitman (trans.), *Callimachus* (LCL; Cambridge, MA: Heinemann, 1965).

Georgi, D., *The Opponents of Paul in Second Corinthians: A Study of Religious Propaganda in Late Antiquity* (Philadelphia: Fortress Press, 1985).

Gese, H., *Essays on Biblical Theology* (K. Crim [trans.]; Minneapolis: Ausburg, 1977–1981).

Gillman, J., 'Signals of Transformation in 1 Thess. 4.13-18', *CBQ* 47 (1985), pp. 263-81.

Ginouvés, R., *Balaneutikè: Recherches sur le bain dans l'antiquité* (Paris: E. de Boccard, 1962).

Ginzberg, L., 'Sin and Its Punishment. A Study in Jewish and Christian Visions of Hell', in *Louis Ginzberg Jubilee Volume* (Hebrew Section) (New York: Jewish Publication Society, 1946), pp. 249-70.

Gipspen, W.H., 'Azazel', in *Orientalia Neerlandica* (Leiden: A.W. Sijthoff, 1948), pp. 156-61.

—'Pharmakos, Sacrifice and Thargelia', in *Orientalia Neerlandica* (Leiden: A.W. Sijthoff, 1948), pp. 156-61.

Girard, R., *Des choses cachées depuis la fondation du monde* (Paris: Grasset, 1978).

—*La route antique des hommes pervers* (Paris: Grasset, 1985).

—*The Scapegoat* (ET; Y. Freccero [trans.]; Baltimore: The Johns Hopkins University Press, 1986 [1982]).

Girard, R., J.-M. Oughourlian, and G. Lefort, *Things Hidden Since the Foundation of the World* (Stanford: Stanford University Press, 1987).

Girard, R., *Violence and the Sacred* (P. Gregory [trans.]; Baltimore: The Johns Hopkins University Press, 1977).

Goguel, M., *Introduction au Nouveau Testament* (Paris: E. Leroux, 1925).

Goodenough, E., *Jewish Symbols in the Greco-Roman Period* (12 vols.; New York: Pantheon, 1953–1965).

Goodspeed, E.J., *An Introduction to the New Testament* (Chicago: University of Chicago Press, 1937).

Gottwald, N., 'Domain Assumptions and Societal Models in the Study of Pre-Monarchic Israel', VTSup 28 (1974), pp. 89-100.

Goudge, H.L., *The Second Epistle to the Corinthians* (London: Methuen, 1927).

Gouldner, A.W., *The Coming Crisis of Western Sociology* (New York: Basic Books, 1970).

Gow, G.S.F., 'On the Meaning of the Word ΘΥΜΕΛΗ', *JHS*, 32 (1912), pp. 213-38.

Gray, G.B., *Sacrifice in the Old Testament: Its Theory and Practice* (Oxford: Clarendon Press, 1925).

Grayston, K., 'Paul's use of objective and participatory language in speaking of the Death of Christ', *Epworth Review* 8.3 (1981), pp. 65-71.

Green, J.B., *The Death of Jesus: Tradition and Interpretation in the Passion Narrative* (WUNT, 2/33; Tübingen: Mohr [Paul Siebeck], 1988).

Grenfell, B.P. and A.S. Hunt, *Logia Iesou: Sayings of Our Lord* (London: Egypt Exploration Fund, 1897).

—*New Sayings of Jesus and Fragment of a Lost Gospel from Oxyrhynchus* (London: Egypt Exploration Fund, 1903).

—*The Oxyrhynchus Papyri, Part IV* (London: Egypt Exploration Fund, 1904).

Guenther, H., 'Gnosticism in Corinth', in B. Hudson McLean (ed.), *Origins and Method: Towards a New Understanding of Judaism and Christianity. Studies in Honour of John C. Hurd* (JSNTSup, 86; Sheffield: JSOT Press, 1993), pp. 44-81.

Gurney, O.R., *Some Aspects of Hittite Religion* (Oxford: Oxford University Press, 1977).

Guthrie, D., *Galatians* (Century Bible New Series; London: Nelson, 1969).

Haardt, R., 'Gnosis', in K. Rahner *et al.* (eds.), *Sacramentum Mundi* (6 vols.; (Montreal: Palm Publishers, 1968), II, pp. 372-79.

Hadorn, W., *Die Abfassung der Thessalonicherbriefe in der Zeit der dritten Missionsreise des Paulus* (BFCT, 24, 3/4; Gütersloh: Bertelsmann, 1919).

Haenchen, E., *Die Apostelgeschichte*, 13 (Göttingen: Vandenhoeck & Ruprecht, 1961).

Hahn, F., *Mission in the New Testament* (London: SCM Press, 1965).

Hamerton-Kelly, R.G. (ed.), *Violent Origins: Walter Burkert, René Girard, and Jonathan Z. Smith on Ritual Killing and Cultural Formation* (Stanford: Stanford University Press, 1987).

Hammer, R. (trans.), *Sifre: A Tannaitic Commentary on the Book of Deutermonomy* (New Haven: Yale University Press, 1986).

Hansen, G.W., *Abraham in Galatians: Epistolary and Rhetorical Contexts* (JSNTSup, 29; Sheffield: JSOT Press, 1989).

Haran, M., *Temples and Temple-Service in Ancient Israel: An Inquiry into Biblical Cult Phenomena and the Historical Setting of the Priestly School* (Winona Lake, IN: Eisenbrauns, 1985).

Harmon, A.M., 'The Descent into Hades' in *Lucian* (LCL; 8 vols.; London: Heinemann, 1969), IV, pp. 72-109.

Harnack, A. von, *The Sayings of Jesus: The Second Source of St Matthew and St Luke* (J.R. Wilkinson [trans.]; NTS, 3; London: Williams & Norgate, 1907–1908.

—'Die Verklärungsgeschichte Jesu, der Bericht des Paulus (1 Kor 15.3f.) und die beiden Christus-Visionen des Petrus', in *Sitzungsberichte der Preuss* (Berlin: Akademie der Wissenshaften, 1922), pp. 62-80.

Harris, M., *The Rise of Anthropological Theory* (New York: Harper & Row, 1968).

Harrison, J.E., *Epilegomena to the Study of Greek Religion* (Cambridge: Cambridge University Press, 1921).

—*Prolegomena to the Study of Greek Religion* (Cambridge: Cambridge University Press, 2nd edn, 1908).

Hauck, F., 'περικάθαρμα', *TDNT*, III, pp. 430-31.

Hausrath, A., *Der Vier-Capitelbrief des Paulus an die Korinther* (Heidelberg: Bassermann, 1870).

Hays, R.B., *Echoes of Scripture in the Letters of Paul* (New Haven: Yale University Press, 1989).

—*The Faith of Jesus Christ: An Investigation of the Narrative Substructure of Galatians 3.1–4.11* (Missoula, MT: Scholars Press, 1983).

Hecht, R.D., 'Patterns of Exegesis in Philo's Interpretation of Leviticus', *Studia Philonica* 6 (1979–1980), pp. 77-151.

—'Preliminary Issues in the Analysis of Philo's *De Specialibus Legibus*', *Studia Philonica* 5 (1978), pp. 1-55.

Helck, H.W., and O. Ebehard, *Kleines Wörterbuch der Aegyptologie* (Wiesbaden: Otto Harrassowitz, 1956).

Hemer, C., *The Book of Acts in the Setting of Hellenistic History* (WUNT, 49; Tübingen: Mohr [Paul Siebeck], 1989).

—'A Note on 2 Corinthians 1.9', *TynBul* 23 (1972), pp. 103-107

Henderson, I., *Myth in the New Testament* (SBT, 7; London: SCM Press, 1952).

Hengel, M., *The Atonement: The Origins of the Doctrine in the New Testament* (J. Bowden [trans.]; Philadelphia: Fortress Press, 1980–1981).

—'Mors Turpissima Crucis', *Justification: Pauline Texts Ilustrated in the Light of the Old and New Testaments* (trans. A.M. Woodruff III; ed. M. Barth; Grand Rapids, MI: Eerdmans, 1971), pp. 125-84.

Heninger, J., 'Menschenopfer bei den Arabern', *Anthropos* 53 (1958), pp. 721-805.

Henrichs, A., 'Human Sacrifice in Greek Religion: Three Case Studies', in *Le sacrifice dans l'antiquité* (ed. J.-P. Vernant; Geneva: Entretiens Fondation Hardt, 1981), pp. 95-242.

Henry, R. (trans.), *Photius: The Bibliotheca* (8 vols.; Paris: Société d'éditon, 1959–1977).

Henten, J.W. van, 'The Tradition-historical Background of Rom. 3.25: A Search for Pagan and Jewish Parallels', in M.C. de Boer (ed.), *Jesus to John: Esays on Jesus and the New Testament Christology in Honour of Marinus de Jonge* (JSNTSup, 84; Sheffield: JSOT Press, 1994), pp. 101-28.

Héring, J., *La Seconde Epître de Saint Paul aux Corinthiens* (ComNT, 8; Neuchatel: Delachaux & Niestlé, 1958).

Heseltine, M. (trans.), 'Fragments', in *Petronius* (LCL; London: Heinemann, 1961), pp. 322-35.

Hicks, R.D., *Diogenes Laertius: Lives of Eminent Philosophers* (LCL; 2 vols.; London: Heinemann, 1925).

—*Dionysius of Halicarnassus: The Lives of Eminent Philosphers* (LCL; 2 vols.; Cambridge, MA: Harvard University Press, 1958).

Hillers, D.R., 'Demons, Demonology,' in C. Roth (ed.), *EncJud*, V, 1523A.

Hoffman, D.Z. *The Book of Leviticus (Seper Wayyiqra')* (2 vols.; Jerusalem: Mossad Harev Kook, 1953).

Hoffmann, J.C.K. von, *Der Brief Pauli an die Galater* (HSNT, 2; Nördlingen, 1872).

—*Der zweite Brief Pauli an die Korinther* (HSNT, 3; Nördlingen, 1866).

Hooke, S.H., 'The Theory and Practice of Substitution', *VT* 2 (1952), pp. 2-17.

Hooker, M.D., 'Interchange and Atonement', *BJRL* 60/1 (1978), pp. 462-81.

—'Philippians 2.6-11', in E.E. Ellis and E. Grässer (eds.), *Jesus und Paulus: Festschrift für Werner Georg Kümmel zum 70 Geburtstag* (Göttingen: Vandenhoeck & Ruprecht, 1975), pp. 151-64.

Hughes, D., *Human Sacrifice in Ancient Greece* (London: Routledge & Kegan Paul, 1991).

Hughes, P.E., *Paul's Second Epistle to the Corinthians* (Grand Rapids: Eerdmans, 1962).

Huizinga, J., *Homo Ludens* (Boston: Beacon Press, 1950).

Humborg, F., *Kanoun*, PWSup, 4 (1924), pp. 867-75.

Hurd, J.C., 'Concerning the Authenticity of 2 Thessalonians' (unpublished paper given at the Thessalonians Seminar of the SBL Meeting, Dallas, Texas, December, 1983), pp. 19-22.

—*The Origin of 1 Corinthians* (Macon, GA: Mercer University Press, 1984; repr. London: SPCK, 1965).

—'Paul Ahead of His Time: 1 Thess. 2.13-16', in P. Richardson with D. Granskou (eds.), *Anti-Judaism in Early Christianity* (Studies in Christianity and Judaism; 2 vols.; Waterloo, ON: Wilfrid Laurier University Press, 1986), pp. 21-36.

—'Pauline Chronology and Pauline Theology', in W.R. Farmer *et al.* (eds.), *Christian History and Interpretation: Studies Presented to John Knox* (Cambridge: Cambridge University Press, 1967), pp. 225-48.

—'The Sequence of Paul's Letters', *CJT* 14/3 (1968), pp. 189-200.

—'2 Thessalonians', *IDBSup* (Nashville, TN: Abingdon, 1976), pp. 900-901.

Hyldahl, N., *Die paulinische Chronologie* (Acta Theologica Danica, 19; Leiden: Brill, 1986).

Illuminati, A. 'Mamurius Veturius', *SMSR* 32 (1961), p. 41.

Isaac, E. (trans.)., '1 (Ethiopic Apocalypse of) Enoch', in J.H. Charlesworth (ed.), *The Old Testament Pseudepigrapha*. I. *Apocalyptic Literature and Testaments* (Garden City, NY: Doubleday, 1983), pp. 5-89.

Jahnke, R. (ed.)., *P. Papinius Statius*. III. *Lactantii Placidi Qui Dicitur Commentarios in Statii Thebaida Commentarium in Achilleida* (Leipzig: Teubner, 1898).

Janowski, B., and G. Wilhelm, 'Der Bock, der die Sünden hinausträgt: zur Religiongeschichte des Azazel-Ritus Lev 16, 10, 21f', in *Religionsgeschichte Beziehungen zwischen kleinasien, Nordsyrian und dem Alten Testament* (OBO, 129; Göttingen: Vandenhoeck & Ruprecht, 1993), pp. 109-69.

Jebb, C., *Sophocles* (Cambridge: Cambridge University Press, 1883).

Jeremias, G., *Der Lehrer der Gerechtigkeit* (Göttingen: Vandenhoeck & Ruprecht, 1963).

Jeremias, J., 'The Key to Pauline Theology', *ExpTim* 76 (1964), pp. 27-30.

—'The Origin of the Typology Adam/Christ', *TDNT*, I, 142-43.

Jervis, L.A., *The Purpose of Romans: A Comparative Letter Structure Investigation* (JSNTSup 55; Sheffield: JSOT Press, 1991).

Jewett, R., 'The Agitators and the Galatian Congregation', *NTS* 17 (1971), pp. 198-212.

—*A Chronology of Paul's Life* (Philadelphia: Fortress Press, 1979).

—*Paul's Anthropological Terms: A Study of Their Use in Conflict Settings* (Leiden: Brill, 1971).

—*The Thessalonian Correspondence: Pauline Rhetoric and Millenarian Piety* (FFNT; Philadelphia: Fortress Press, 1986).

Jones, H.L. (trans.), *The Geography of Strabo* (LCL; 8 vols.; London: Heinemann, 1917).

Jonge, M. de, *Christology in Context: The Earliest Christian Response to Jesus* (Philadelphia: Westminster Press, 1988).

Junker, H., 'Die Schlacht- und Brandopfer und ihre Sybolik im Tempelkult der Spätzeit', *Zeitschrift für ägyptische Sprache und Altertumskunde* 48 (1910), pp. 69-77.

Kamal, A.B., *Stèles: Ptolemaiques et Romaines* (2 vols.; Cairo: Impr. de l'Institut français d'Archeologie orientale, 1905).

Käsemann, E., *Commentary on Romans* (Grand Rapids: Eerdmans, 1980).

—*Zeit und Geschichte: Dankesgabe an Rudolf Bultmann* (E. Dinkler [ed.]; Tübingen: Mohr [Paul Siebeck], 1964).

Kaufmann, Y., *The Religion of Israel from Its Beginnings to the Babylonian Exile* (Chicago: University of Chicago Press, 1960).

Kautzsch, E., *Biblische Theologie des Alten Testaments* (Tübingen: Mohr, 1911).

Kees, H., *Bemerkungen zum Tieropfer der Ägypter und seiner Symbolik* (Nachrichten der Akademie der Wissenschatten; Göttingen: Vandenhoeck & Ruprecht, 1942).

Kern, W., 'Die antizipierte Entideologisierung oder die "Weltelemente" des Galater- und Kolosserbriefes heute', *ZKT* 96 (1974), pp. 185-216.

Kernt, O., *Orphicorum Fragmenta* (Berlin: Weidmann, 1922).

Kertelge, K., 'Zur Deutung des Rechtfertigungsbegriffs im Galaterbrief', *BZ* 12 (1968), pp. 211-22.

Kiuchi, N., *The Purification Offering in the Priestly Literature: Its Meaning and Function* (JSOTSup, 56; Sheffield: JSOT Press, 1987).

Klein, G., *Rekonstruktion und Interpretation*, BEvT 50 (Munich: Chr. Kaiser Verlag, 1969).

Kloppenborg, J.S., '"Easter Faith" and the Sayings Gospel Q', in R. Cameron (ed.), *The Apocryphal Jesus and Christian Origins* (*Semeia*, 49; Atlanta, GA: Scholars Press, 1990), pp. 71-99.

—*The Formation of Q: Trajectories in Ancient Wisdom Collections* (Studies in Antiquity and Christianity; Philadelphia, Fortress Press, 1987).

—'The Formation of Q Revisited: A Response to R. Horsely', in D.J. Lull (ed.), *SBL 1989 Seminar Papers* (Atlanta, GA: Scholars Press, 1989), pp. 204-225.

—'Symbolic Eschatology and the Apocalypticism of Q', *HTR* 80.3 (1987), pp. 287-306.

—'Tradition and Redaction in the Synoptic Sayings Source'z*CBQ* 46 (1984), pp. 34-62.

Knox, A.D. (trans.), 'Fragments of Hipponax', in *Herodes, Cercidas and the Greek Choriambic Poets* (LCL; London: Heinemann, 1929), pp. 15-65.

Knox, J., *Chapters in a Life of Paul* (Nashville: Abingdon Press, 1950).

—'"Fourteen Years Later": A Note on Pauline Chronology', *JR* 16 (1936), pp. 341-49.

—'The Pauline Chronology', *JBL* 58 (1939), pp. 15-29.

—'On the Pauline Chronology: Buck–Taylor–Hurd Revisited', in R.T. Fortna and B.R. Gaventa (eds.), *The Conversation Continues: Studies in Paul and John in Honor of J. Louis Martyn* (Nashville: Abingdon Press, 1991), pp. 258-74.

Knox, W.L., *St Paul and the Church of the Gentiles* (Cambridge: Cambridge University Press, 1939).

Koch, D.-A., *Die Schrift als Zeuge des Evangeliums: Untersuchungen zur Verwendung und zum Verständnis der Schrift bei Paulus* (BHT, 69; Tübingen: Mohr [Paul Siebeck], 1986).

Koch, K., 'Sühne und Sündenvergebung um die Wende von der exilischenzur nachexilischen Zeit', *EvT* 26 (1966), pp. 217-39.

—*The Rediscovery of Apocalyptic: A Polemical Work on a Neglected Area of Biblical Studies and Its Damaging Effects on Theology and Philosophy* (SBT, 2.22; London: SCM Press, 1972).

Köchling, J., *De coronarum apud antiquos vi atque usu* (Giessen: Töpelmann, 1914).

Köhler, L., *Old Testament Theology* (trans. A.S. Todd; London: Lutterworth, 1936–1957).

Koester, H., *Ancient Christian Gospels: Their History and Development* (Philadelphia: Trinity Press/London: SCM Press, 1990).

—'GNOMAI DIAPHOROI: The Origin and Nature of Diversification in the History of Early Christianity', in J.M. Robinson and H. Koester (eds.), *Trajectories through Early Christianity* (Philadelphia: Fortress Press, 1971), pp. 114-57

—'One Jesus and Four Primitive Gospels', in J.M. Robinson and H. Koester (eds.), *Trajectories*, pp. 158-204.

König, E., *Theologie des Alten Testaments* (Stuttgart: Belser, 1923).

Kraft, R.A., *The Apostolic Fathers*. III. *Barnabas and the Didache* (Toronto: Thomas Nelson & Sons, 1965).

Kümmel, W.G., *Römer 7 und das Bild des Menschen im Neuen Testament* (Munich: Chr. Kaiser Verlag, 1974).

Kutsch, E., 'Sündenbock', *RGG*, VI, pp. 506-507.

Lagrange, M.-J., *St Paul, Epître aux Galates* (Paris: Librairie Lecoffre, 2nd edn, 1925 [1918]).

Lake, K., *The Earlier Epistles of St Paul: Their Motive and Origin* (London: Rivingtons, 2nd edn, 1914).

Lamb, W.R.M. (trans.), 'Against Andocides: For Impiety', in *Lysias* (LCL; London: Heinemann, 1930), pp. 112-43.

Laroche, E., *Catalogue des Textes Hittites* (Etudes et Commentaires, 75; Paris: Klinksiek, 1971).

Lattey, C., 'Vicarious Solidarity in the Old Testament', *VT* 1 (1951), pp. 267-74.

Layton, B. (ed.), 'The Gospel According to Thomas', in *Nag Hammadi Codex II,2-7 Together with XIII,2*, Brit. Lib. Or. 4926(1) and P. Oxy. 1, 654, 655*, NHS 20–21 (Leiden: Brill, 1989), pp. 38-109.

Leach, E., 'On the Founding Fathers', *Current Anthropology* 7 (1966), pp. 560-67.

Leone, P.A.M. (ed.)., *Tzetzae: Historiae* (Naples: Libreria Scientifica Editrice, 1968).

Levine, B.A., 'Leviticus', *EncJud*, XI, 138-147.

Lietzmann, H., *An Die Galater* (HNT, 10; Tübingen: Mohr, 4th edn, 1971 [1910]).

—*An die Korinther I, II* (HNT, 9; Tübingen: Mohr, 5th edn, 1969).

Lightfoot, J.B., *The Apostolic Fathers* (ed. J.R. Harmer; London: Macmillan, 1893).

—*Saint Paul's Epistle to the Galatians* (London: Macmillan, 3rd edn, 1905 [1865]).

—*Saint Paul's Epistle to the Philippians*, new edn (London: Macmillan, 1879).

Lincoln, A.T., *Paradise Now and Not Yet: Studies in the Role of the Heavenly Dimension in Paul's Thought with Special Reference to His Eschatology* (Cambridge: Cambridge University Press, 1981).

Lloyd, A.B., *Herodotus: Book 2* (2 vols.; Leiden: Brill, 1976).

Loicq, J., 'Mamurius Veturius et l'ancienne représentation de l'année', in *Hommages à Jean Bayet* (Bruxelles: Latomus, 1964), pp. 401-26.

Lüdemann, G., *Early Christianity According to the Tradtions in Acts* (Minneapolis: Fortress Press, 1989).

—*Opposition to Paul in Jewish Christianity* (trans. M.E. Boring; Minneapolis: Fortress Press, 1989 [1983]).

—*Paul, Apostle to the Gentiles: Studies in Chronology* (trans. F.S. Jones; Philadelphia: Fortress Press, 1980–1984).

—'Paul, Christ and the Problem of Death', in B. Hudson McLean (ed.), *Origins and Method: Towards a New Understanding of Judaism and Christianity. Studies in Honour of John C. Hurd* (JSNTSup, 86; Sheffield: JSOT Press, 1993), pp. 26-43.

Lührmann, D., *Der Redaktion der Logienquelle* (WMANT, 33; Neukirchen–Vluyn: Neukirchener Verlag, 1969).

Luz, U., *Das Geschichtsverständnis des Paulus* (BEvT, 50; Munich: Chr. Kaiser Verlag, 1969).

Lyonnet, S., 'L'emploi paulinien de ἐξαγοράζω au sens de "redimere" est-il attesté dans la littérature greque?' *Bib* 42 (1961), pp. 85-89.

—*Exegesis epistulae ad Romanos, Cap. V ad VIII* (Rome: Pontifical Biblical Institute, 1966).

Mack, B.F., *Mark and Christian Origins: A Myth of Innocence* (Philadelphia: Fortress Press, 1988).

Mannhardt, W., *Mythologische Forschungen* (Quellen und Forschungen zur Sprach- und Culturgeschichte der germanischen Volker, 51; Strasbourg: Trübner, 1884), pp. 124-38.

Manson, T.W., *Studies in the Gospels and Epistles* (K. Black [ed.]; Manchester: Manchester University Press, 1962).

Marshall, P., *Enmity in Corinth: Social Conventions in Paul's Relations with the Corinthians* (WUNT, 2.23; Tübingen: Mohr [Paul Siebeck], 1987).

Martha, J., *Les sacerdoces athéniens* (Paris: Leroux, 1882).

Martin, R.P., *Carmen Christi: Philippians 2.5-11 in Recent Interpretation and in the Setting of Early Christian Worship* (Grand Rapids: Eerdmans, 1967).

—*2 Corinthians* (WBC, 40; Waco, 1986).

—*Philippians* (NCB; Grand Rapids: Eerdmans, 1976).

Martion, B., *Christ and the Law in Paul* (NovTSup, 62; Leiden: Brill, 1989).

Martyn, J.L., 'A Law-Observant Mission to the Gentiles: The Background of Galatians', *SJT* 38 (1985), pp. 307-324.

—'Paul and His Jewish-Christian Interpreters', *USQR* 42 (1988), pp. 1-15.

Marx, A., 'Sacrifice pour les péchés ou rites de passage? Quelques réflexion sur la fonction du *hatta't*', *RB* 96 (1986), pp. 27-48.

Masson, C., *Les Deux Epîtres de Saint Paul aux Thessaloniciens* (Neuchâtel: Delachaux & Niestlé, 1957).

McFadyen, J.E., *The Epistles to the Corinthians* (London: Hodder & Stoughton, 1911).

McLean, B.H., 'The Absence of an Atoning Sacrifice in Paul's Soteriology', *NTS* 38/4 (1992), pp. 531-53.

—'Attic Christian Epitaph: the Curse of Judas Iscariot', *Orientalia Christiana Periodica* 58 (1993), pp. 241-44.

—'A Christian Sculpture in Old Corinth', *Orientalia Christiana Periodica* 57 (1991), pp. 199-205.

—'Galatians 2.7-9 and the Question of the Recognition of Paul's Apostolic Status at the Jerusalem Conference: A Critique of Gerd Lüdemann's Reconstruction', *NTS* 37/1 (1991), pp. 67-76.

—'The Interpretation of the Levitical Sin Offering and the Scapegoat', *SR* 20.3 (1991), pp. 345-56.

—'On the Gospel of Thomas and Q', in Ronald Piper (ed.), *Studies on Q* (Leiden: Brill, 1993).

—'On the Revision of Scapegoat Terminology', *Numen* 37.2 (1990), pp. 168-73.

Meagher, J.C., 'The Implications for Theology of a Shift from the K.L. Schmidt Hypothesis of Literary Uniqueness for the Gospels', in B. Corley (ed.), *Colloquy on New Testament Studies: A Time for Reappraisal and Fresh Approaches* (Macon, GA: Mercer University Press, 1983), pp. 203-233.

Meeks, W., *The Writings of St Paul* (Norton Critical Editions; New York: Norton, 1972).

Megas, J.A., *Greek Calendar Customs* (Athens: Press and Information Office, Prime Minister's Office, 2nd edn, 1963).

Mercer, S., *The Religion of Ancient Egypt* (London: Luzac & Co. Ltd., 1949).

Meuli, K., 'Griechische Opferbräuche', in *Phyllobolia Festschift P. Von der Mühll* (Basel: Schwabe, 1946), pp. 185-288.

Meyer, H.A.W., *Critical and Exegetical Handbook to the Epistles to the Corinthians* (W.P. Dickson [trans.]; Edinburgh: T. & T. Clark, 1870).

—*Critical and Exegetical Commentary to the Epistle to the Galatians*, (W.D. Dickson [trans.]; CECNT, 7; Edinburgh: T. & T. Clark, 1884).

Michel, C., *Recueil d'instriptions grecques* (Paris: Polleunis & Centerick, 1900).

—'Affranchissements d'esclaves', in *Revue des études grecques* (1900), pp. 922-40, nos. 1388-1426.

Milgrom, J., 'Atonement in the OT', *IDBSup*, pp. 78-82.

—*Cult and Conscience: The Asham and the Priestly Doctrine of Repentance* (Leiden: Brill, 1976).

—'The Cultic *shegagah* and its influence in Psalms and Job', *JQR* 58 (1967), pp. 115-25.

—'Day of Atonement', *EncJud*, V, 1386.

—'The Function of *Hatt'at* Sacrifice', *Tarbiz* 40 (1970), pp. 1-8.

Milgrom, J., 'Israel's Sanctuary: The Priestly "Picture of Dorian Gray"', *RB* 83 (1976), pp. 390-99.

—*Leviticus 1–16: A New Translation with Introduction and Commentary* (AB, 3; Garden City, NY: Doubleday, 1991).

—'Sacrifices and Offerings, OT', *IDBSup*, pp. 763-71.

—'Sin-offering, or Purification-offering?', *VT* 21 (1971), pp. 237-39.

—'The *Modus Operandi* of *Hatta't*: A Rejoinder', *JBL* 109/1 (1990), pp. 111-13.

Mommsen, A., *Feste der Stadt Athen im Altertum, geordnet nach attischen Kalender* (Leipzig: Teubner, 2nd edn, 1898).

Moore, G.F., *Judaism in the First Three Centuries of the Christian Era* (3 vols.; Cambridge, MA: Harvard University Press, 1927–1930).

Moulton, J.H. and G. Milligan, *The Vocabulary of the Greek New Testament Illustrated from the Papyri and Other Non-Literary Sources* (2 vols.; London: Hodder & Stoughton, 1914–1929).

Moulton, J.H., *Grammar of New Testament Greek. I. Prolegomena of A Grammar of the New Testament* (Edinburgh: T. & T. Clark, 3rd edn, 1908 [1906]).

Müller, G.H., *Zur Synopse: Untersuchung über die Arbeitsweise des Luke und Matt. und ihre Quellen* (FRLANT, 11; Göttingen: Vandenhoeck & Ruprecht, 1908).

Munck, J., 'The Judaizing Gentile Christians: Studies in Galatians', in *Paul and the Salvation of Mankind* (F. Clarke [trans.]; London: SCM Press, 1954–1959), pp. 87-134.

Murrary, J., *The Epistle to the Romans* (NICNT; Grand Rapids: Eerdmans, 1963).

Mussner, F., *Der Galaterbrief* (Herders theologischer Kommentar zum Neuen Testament, 9; Freiburg: Herder, 1974).

Naber, S.A., *Photii Patriarchae Lexicon* (Amsterdam: Adolf M. Hakkert, 1864).

Nägeli, T., *Der Wortschatz des Apostels Paulus* (dissertation; Basel: Buchdruckereizum Basler Berichthaus, 1904).

Naville, E.H., *The Temple of Deir el Bahari* (6 vols.; London: Egyptian Exploration Fund, 1895–1908).

240   *The Cursed Christ*

Neil, R.A., *The Knights of Aristophanes* (Hildesheim: Georg Olms, 1966).

Neil, W., *The Epistle of Paul to the Thessalonians* (MNTC; London: Hodder & Stoughton, 1950).

—*The Letter of Paul to the Galatians* (Cambridge: Cambridge University Press, 1967).

Neumann, K., *The Authenticity of The Pauline Epistles in the Light of Stylostatistical Analysis* (SBLDS, 120; Missoula, MT: Scholars Press, 1990).

Neusner, J., *Sifra: An Analytic Translation* (BJS, 138–140; 3 vols.; Atlanta: Scholars Press, 1988).

Nilsson, M.P., *Griechische Feste von religiöser Bedeutung mit Ausschluss derattischen* (Darmstadt: Wissenschaftliche Buchgesellschaft, 1906).

—*Opuscula selecta linguis Anglica, Francogallica, Germanica conscripta* (Svenska institutet i Athen Series altera, II; 3 vols.; Lund: Gleerup, 1951–1960).

—'Die Prozessionstypen im griechischen Kult', *Jahrbuch des Deutschen archäologischen Instituts* 31 (1916), pp. 318-21.

Noth, M., *Leviticus: A Commentary* (J.E. Anderson [trans.]; Philadelphia: Westminster Press, 1962–1965).

O'Brien, P.T., *The Epistle to the Philippians: A Commentary on the Greek Text* (Grand Rapids: Eerdmans 1991).

O'Flaherty, W.D., *Other Peoples' Myths* (London: Macmillan, 1988).

Oden, R.A., *The Bible Without Theology: The Theological Tradition and Alternatives to It* (San Francisco: Harper & Row, 1987).

Oepke, A., *Der Brief des Paulus an die Galater* (Herders theologischer Kommentar zum Neuen Testament, 9; Leipzig: Deichert, 1937).

Oesterly, W.O.E., *Sacrifices in Ancient Israel: Origin, Purposes and Development* (London: Hodder & Stoughton, 1937).

Oldfather, C.H. (trans.)., *Diodorus of Sicily* (12 vols.; London: Heinemann, 1963).

Oostendorp. D.W., *Another Jesus: A Gospel of Jewish-Christian Superiority in II Corinthians* (Kampen: Kok, 1967).

Osborne, R., 'Women and Sacrifice in Classical Greece', *CQ* 43.2 (1993), pp. 392-405.

Osten-Sacken, P. von der, *Römer 8 al Beispiel paulinischer Soteriologie* (FRLANT, 112; Göttingen: Vandenhoeck & Ruprecht, 1975).

Otto, E., *Beiträge zur Geschichte der Stierkulte in Aegypten* (Hildesheim: Georg Olms, 1964).

Pannenberg, W., *Jesus: God and Man* (Philadelphia: Westminster Press, 2nd edn, 1977).

Pape, W., *Wörterbuch der griechischen Eigennamen* (2 vols.; Braunschweig: F. Vieweg, 1884).

Parker, R., *Miasma: Pollution and Purification in Early Greek Religion* (Oxford: Clarendon Press, 1983).

Passow, F.L.C.F., *Wörterbuch der griechischen Sprache* (Göttingen: Vandenhoeck & Ruprecht, 1874).

Paton, W.R. 'The Pharmakoi and the Story of the Fall', *RA* 9 (1907), pp. 51-55.

Paton, W.R. and E.L. Hicks, *The Inscriptions of Cos* (Oxford: Clarendon Press, 1891).

Pearson, B.A., *The Pneumatikos-Psychikos Terminology in 1 Corinthians: A Study in the Theology of the Corinthian Opponents of Paul and its Relation to Gnosticism* (Missoula, MT: Scholars Press, 1973).

Perkins, P., *Resurrection: New Testament Witness and Contemporary Reflection* (Garden City, NY: Doubleday, 1984).

Perrin, B. (trans.), *Plutarch's Lives* (LCL; 11 vols.; Cambridge, MA: Harvard University Press, 1967).

Pervo, R.I., *Profit with Delight: The Literary Genre of the Acts of the Apostles* (Philadelphia: Fortress Press, 1987).

Péter, R., 'L'imposition des mains dans l'Ancien Testament', *VT* 27 (1977), pp. 48-55.

Petzke, G., *Die Traditionen über Apollonius von Tyana und das Neue Testament* (ed. H.D. Betz, G. Delling and W.C. van Unnik; Leiden: Brill, 1970).

Petzl, G. (ed.)., *Die Inschriften von Smyrna* (Inschriften griechischer Städte aus Kleinasien, 23–24/1-2; Bonn: Rudolf Habelt, 1982–1990).

Pfeiffer, R. (ed.), *Callimachus* (2 vols.; Oxford: Clarendon Press, 1949).

Pfister, F., *Der Reliquienkult im Altertum* (2 vols.; Giessen: Töpelman, 1909–1912).

Plank, K., *Paul and the Irony of Affliction* (Atlanta: Scholars Press, 1987).

Plummer, A., *A Critical and Exegetical Commentary on the Second Epistleof St Paul to the Corinthians* (ICC; Edinburgh: T. & T. Clark, 1915).

Polag, A., *Fragmenta Q: Textheft zur Logienquelle* (Neukirchen–Vluyn: Neukirchener Verlag, 1979).

Poland, F., *Geschichte des griechischen Vereinswesens* (Leipzig: Teubner, 1909).

Poole, F.J.P., 'Metaphors and Maps: Towards Comparison in the Anthropology of Religion', *JAAR* 54 (1986), pp. 411-57.

Powell, J.E. (trans.). *Herodotus: History* (2 vols.; Oxford: Clarendon Press, 1947).

Price, S.R.F. *Rituals and Power: The Roman Imperial Cult in Asia Minor* (Cambridge: Cambridge University Press, 1984).

Prigent, P., and R.A. Kraft, *Epître de Barnabé* (Paris: Cerf, 1971).

Pritchett, W.K., *The Greek State at War III: Religion* (Berkeley, CA: University of California Press, 1979).

Räisänen, H., *Paul and the Law* (Philadelphia: Fortress Press, 1983).

—'Legalism and Salvation by the Law', in S. Pedersen (ed.), *Die paulinische Literatur und Theologie* (Aarthus: Aros, 1980), pp. 63-83.

Rensberger, D., '2 Corinthians 6.14–7.1: A Fresh Examination', *Studies Biblica et Theologica* 8 (1978), pp. 25-49.

Ridderbos, H., *Paul: An Outline of His Theology* (Grand Rapids: Eerdmans, 1975).

Riddle, D., *Paul: Man of Conflict: A Modern Biographical Sketch* (Nashville: Abingdon Press, 1940).

Riesenfeld, H., 'Paul's "Grain of Wheat" Analogy and the Argument of 1 Corinthians 15', in *Studien zum Neuen Testament und Patristik: Erich Klostermann zum 90. Geburstag dargebracht* (Berlin: Akademie Verlag, 1961), pp. 43-55.

Riesenfeld, H. 'ὑπέρ', *TDNT*, VIII, pp. 507-16.

Rigaux, B., *The Letters of St Paul* (Chicago: Franciscan Herald Press, 1968).

Robert, F., *Thymélè: Recherches sur la signification et la destination des monuments circulaires dans l'architecture réligieuse de la Grèce* (Paris: E. de Boccard, 1939).

Roberts, A., and J. Donaldson (eds.), *The Ante-Nicene Fathers*. I. *The Apostolic Fathers—Justin Martyr—Irenaeus* (Grand Rapids: Eerdmans, 1885–1903).

Robertson, A.T., *A Grammar of the Greek New Testament in the Light of Historical Research* (Nashville: Broadman, 1934).

Robinson, H.W. 'Hebrew Sacrifice and Prophetic Symbolism', *JTS* 48 (1942), pp. 129-39.

—*Suffering, Human and Divine* (New York: Macmillan, 1939).

Robinson, J.M., 'Jesus: From Easter to Valentius (or to the Apostles' Creed)', *JBL* 101 (1982), pp. 5-37.

—'LOGOI SOPHON: On the Gattung of Q', in J.M. Robinson and H. Koester (eds.), *Trajectories*, pp. 74-85.

—'On Bridging the Gulf from Q to the Gospel of Thomas (or Visa Versa)', in C.W. Hedrick and R. Hodgson, Jr (eds.), *Nag Hammadi, Gnosticism, and Early Christianity* (Peabody, MA: Hendrickson, 1986), pp. 127-75.

Robinson, J.M. and H. Koester (eds.), *Trajectories through Early Christianity* (Philadelphia: Fortress Press, 1971).

Robinson, J.M. *et al.*, 'The IQP Project: Work Sessions 12–14', *JBL* 111.3 (1992), pp. 500-508.

Roetzel, C., *The Letters of Paul: Conversations in Context* (Atlanta: John Knox, 2nd edn, 1982).

Rogers, G.M., *The Sacred Identity of Ephesos: Foundation Myths of a Roman City* (London: Routledge & Kegan Paul, 1991).

Rogers, R.W. (ed. and trans.), *Cuneiform Parallels to the Old Testament*. (New York: Easton & Mains, 1912).

Rohde, E., *Psyche: Seelencult und Unsterblichkeitsglaube der Griechen* (Tübingen: Mohr, 2nd edn, 1898 [1894]).

Rothkoff, A., 'Semikah', *EncJud*, XIV, 1140-41.

Rudhardt, J., *Notions fondamentales de la pensée religieuse et actes constitutifs du culte dans la Grèce classique* (Geneva: E. Droz, 1958).

Rudolph, K., 'War der Verfasser der *Oden Salomos* ein "Qumran Christ": Ein Beitrag zur Diskussion um die Anfänge der Gnosis', *RQ* 4 (1963), p. 525.

Rutherford, W.G (ed.), *Scholia Aristophanies* (3 vols.; London: Macmillan, 1896).

Sabourin, L., *Rédemption sacrificielle: Une enquête exégétique* (Studia, 11; Bruges: Desclée de Brouwer, 1961).

Safrai, S., 'The Temple', in S. Safrai and M. Stern (eds.), *The Jewish People in the First Century: Historical Geography, Political History, Social, Cultural and Religious Life and Institutions* (2 vols.; Assen: Van Gorcum, 1976), II, pp. 865-907.

Sanders, E.P., *Judaism: Practice and Belief 63 BCE–66 CE* (Philadelphia: Trinity Press, 1992).

—*Paul and Palestinian Judaism: A Comparison of Patterns of Religion* (Philadelphia: Fortress Press, 1977).

Sanders, J.T., *The New Testament Christological Hymns: Their Historical and Religious Background* (SNTSMS; Cambridge: Cambridge University Press. 1971).

Sandmel, S., *The First Christian Century in Judaism and Christianity: Certainties and Uncertainties* (New York: Oxford University Press, 1969).

—'Parallelomania', *JBL* 81 (1962), pp. 1-13.

—*Philo of Alexandria: An Introduction* (New York: Oxford University Press, 1979).

Saydon, P.P. 'Sin-Offering and Trespass-Offering', *CBQ* 8 (1946), pp. 393-99.

Scharlemann, M.H., 'In the Likeness of Sinful Flesh', *CTM* 32 (1961), p. 136.

Schelp, J., *Das Kanoûn: Der griechische Opferkorb* (Wurzburg: K. Triltsch, 1975).

Schenk, W., *Synopse zur Redenquelle der Evangelien: Q Synopse und Rekonstruktion in deutscher Übersetzung mit kurzen Erläuterungen* (Düsseldorf: Patmos, 1981).

Schlier, H., *Der Brief an die Galater* (Kritisch-exegetischer kommentar über das NT, 7; Göttingen: Vandenhoeck & Ruprecht, 14th edn, 1971 [1949]).

Schlier, J., *Der Römerbrief* (Freiburg: Herder, 1977).

Schmidt, M. (ed.)., *Hesychii Alexandrini: Lexicon* (Ienae: Frederici Maukii, 1863).

Schmithals, W., *Gnosticism in Corinth* (J.E. Steely [trans.]; New York: Abingdon Press, 1971).

—'The Heretics in Galatia', in *Paul and the Gnostics* (J. Steely [trans.]; Nashville: Abingdon Press, 1965–1972), pp. 13-64.

—*Paul and James* (Studies in Biblical Theology, 46; London: SCM Press, 1965).

Schneider, F., 'Kalendae Januariae und Martiae im Mittelalter', *ARW* 20 (1921), pp. 391-402.

Schneider, J. 'ὁμοίμα, *TDNT*, V, p. 196.

Schoeps, H.J., *Paul: The Theology of the Apostle in the Light of Jewish Religious History* (ET; H. Knight [trans.]; London: Lutterworth, 1961 [1959]).

Scholfield, A.F., *Aelian: On the Characteristics of Animals* (LCL; 3 vols.; London: Heinemann, 1971).

Schütz, J., *Paul and the Anatomy of Apostolic Authority* (SNTSMS, 26; Cambridge: Cambridge University Press, 1975).

Schweitzer, A., *The Mysticism of Paul the Apostle* (New York: Seabury, 1931).

Schweizer, E. 'Πνεύμ α, πνευματικό', *TDNT*, VI, pp. 332-455.

—'Slaves of the Elements and Worshippers of Angels: Gal. 4.3 and Col. 2.8, 18, 20', *JBL*, 107 (1988), pp. 455-68.

Schwenn, F., *Die Menschenopfer bei den Griechen und Römern* (RVV, 15.3; Giessen: Töpelmann, 1915).

Seeley, D., 'Jesus' Death in Q', *NTS* 38 (1992), pp. 222-34.

—*The Noble Death: Graeco–Roman Martyrology and Paul's Concept of Salvation* (JSNTSup, 28; Sheffield: JSOT Press, 1990).

Segal, A.F., *Paul the Convert: The Apostolate and Apostasy of Saul the Pharisee* (New Haven: Yale University Press, 1990).

—*Rebecca's Children: Judaism and Christianity in the Roman World* (Cambridge, MA: Harvard University Press, 1986).

Sethe, K.H., *Dramatische Texte in altaegyptischen Mysterienspielen* (Hildesheim: Georg Olms, 1964).

—*Übersetzung und Kommentar zu den Pyramidentexten* (6 vols.; Glückstadt: J.J. Augustin, 1935–1962).

—*Urkunden der 18. Dynastie* (Urkunden des ägyptischen Altertums, 6; Leipzig: J.C. Hinrichs, 1935).

Sharpe, E.J., *Comparative Religion* (New York: Charles Scribner's Sons, 1975).

Shedd, R., *Man in Community* (London: Epworth Press, 1958).

Sieffert, F., *Der Brief an die Galater* (Kritisch-exegetischer kommentar über das NT 7; Göttingen: Vandenhoeck & Ruprecht, 9th edn, 1899 [1880]).

Slingerland, D., 'Acts 18.1-17 and Lüdemann's Pauline Chronology', *JBL* 109/4 (1990), pp. 686-90.

Smith, J.Z., *Drudgery Divine: On the Comparison of Early Christianities and the Religions of Late Antiquity* (Jordan Lectures in Comparative Religion, 14; Chicago: University of Chicago Press, 1990).

—'When the Bough Breaks', *HR* 12 (1973), pp. 342-71.

Smith, W.R., *Religion of the Semites: The Fundamental Institutions* (New York: Meridian Books, 1889).

Snaith, N.H., 'Sacrifices in the Old Testament', *VT* 7 (1957), pp. 308-17.

Snyder, G., *Ante Pacem: Archaeological Evidence of Church Life Before Constantine* (Macon, GA: Mercer University Press, 1985).

Sokolowski, F., *Lois sacrées de l'Asie Mineure* (Ecole française d'Athènes; Travaux et mémoires, IX; Paris: E. de Boccard, 1955).

Spiegel, S., *The Last Trial: On the Legends and Lore of the Command to Abraham to Offer Isaac as a Sacrifice: The Akedah* (New York: Pantheon, 1967).

Stählin, G., 'περλίψημα', *TDNT*, VI, pp. 84-93.

Stanford, W.B. (ed.), *Aristophanes: The Frogs* (London: Macmillan, 1958).

Stanley, A.P., *The Epistles of St Paul to the Corinthians* (2 vols.; London: John Murray, 1855).

Stendahl, K., *Paul Among Jews and Gentiles and Other Essays* (Philadelphia: Fortress Press, 1976).

Stengel, P., *Die griechischen Kultusaltertümer* (Munich: Beck, 2nd edn, 1920).

—*Opferbräuche der Griechen* (Leipzig: Teubner, 1910).

Stern, H., 'Notes sur deux images du mois de Mars', *REL* 52 (1974), pp. 70-74.

—'Les calendriers romains illustrés', in *ANRW* II, 12 (1981), pp. 432-75.

Stevenson, W.B., 'Hebrew *'Olah* and *Zebach* Sacrifices', in W. Baumgartner (ed.), *Festschrift Alfred Bertholet* (Tübingen: Mohr, 1950), pp. 488-97.

Stocker, A.F., and A.H. Travis, *Servianorum in Vergilii Carmina Commentariorum* (3 vols.; Oxford: Oxford University Press, 1965).

Stowers, S.K., *Letter Writing in Greco-Roman Antiquity* (Library of Early Christianity, 5; Philadelphia: Westminster Press, 1986).

Strachan, R., *The Second Epistle of Paul to the Corinthians* (London: Hodder & Stoughton, 1935).

Stuhlmach, P., 'Sühne oder Versöhnung? Randbemerkungen zu Gerhard Friedrichs Studie: "Die Verkündigung des Todes Jesu im Neuen Testament"', in U. Luz and H. Weder (eds.), *Die Mitte des Neuen Testaments: Einheit und Vielfalt neutestamentlicher Theologie: Festschrift für Eduard Schweizer zum Siebzigsten Geburtstag* (Göttingen: Vandenhoeck & Ruprecht, 1983), pp. 291-99.

Suggs, M.J., 'Concerning the Date of Paul's Macedonian Ministry', *NovT* 4 (1960), pp. 60-68.

Sumney, J., *Identifying Paul's Opponents: The Question of Method in 2 Corinthians* (JSNTSup, 40; Sheffield: JSOT Press, 1990).

Tabor, J.D., *Things Unutterable: Paul's Ascent to Paradise in its Greco–Roman, Judaic, and Early Christian Contexts* (Studies in Judaism; Lanham, MD: University Press of America, 1986).

Talbert, C.C., *Literary Patterns, Theological Themes, and the Genre of Luke–Acts* (Missoula, MT: Scholars Press, 1974).

—*What is a Gospel?* (Philadelphia: Fortress Press, 1982).

Tannehill, R.C., *Dying and Rising with Christ* (BZNW, 32; Berlin: Töpelmann, 1967).

—*The Narrative Unity of Luke–Acts: A Literary Interpretation. II. The Acts of the Apostles* (Philadelphia: Fortress Press, 1990).

Tasker, R.V.G., *The Second Epistle of Paul to the Corinthians* (Grand Rapids: Eerdmans, 1958).

Taubenschlag, R., *The Law of Greco–Roman Egypt in the Light of the Papyri (332 BC–AD 640)* (Warsaw: P.W. Naukowe, 2nd rev. edn, 1955).

Tawil, H. 'Azazel The Prince of the Steepe [*sic*]: A Comparative Study', *ZAW* 92 (1980), pp. 43-59.

Thielman, F., *From Plight to Solution: A Jewish Framework for Understanding Paul's View of Law in Galatians and Romans* (NovTSup, 61; Leiden: Brill, 1989).

Thilo, G., and H. Hagen, *Servii Grammatici qui feruntur in Vergilii carmina commentarii* (3 vols.; Hildesheim: Georg Olms, 1961).

Thrall, M.E., *The Second Epistle to the Corinthians* (ICC; 2 vols.; Edinburgh: T. & T. Clark, 1994).

Thyen, H., *Studien zur Sündenvergebung im Neuen Testament und seinenalttestament-lichen und jüdischen Voraussetzungen* (FRLANT, 96; Göttingen: Vandenhoeck & Ruprecht, 1970).

Tischendorf, C., *Evangelia Apocrypha* (Hildescheim: Georg Olms, 1876–1966).

Treggiari, S., *Roman Freedmen during the Late Republic* (Oxford: Clarendon Press, 1969).

Tuilier, A. (trans.), *Grégoire de Nazianze: La Passion du Christ* (Paris: Cerf, 1969).

Turner, V., *From Ritual to Theatre: The Human Seriousness of Play* (New York: Performing Arts Journal Publications, 1982).

Vanni, U., 'Ὁμοίωμα in Paolo (Rom 1,23; 5,14; 6,15; 8,2; Fil 2,7). Un'interpretazione esegetico-teologica alla luce dell'uso dei LXX', *Greg* 58 (1977), pp. 431-70.

Vaux, R. de, *Ancient Israel: Its Life and Institutions* (J. McHugh [trans.]; New York: McGraw-Hill, 1961).

—*Studies in Old Testament Sacrifice* (Cardiff: University of Wales Press, 1964).

Vaux, R. de, and J.T. Milik, *Discoveries in the Judean Desert*. VI. *Qumran Grotte 4* (Oxford: Clarendon Press, 1977).

Vermes, G., *Scripture and Tradition in Judaism* (Leiden: Brill, 3rd edn, 1973 [1961]).

Vernant, J.P., *Tragedy and Myth in Ancient Greece* (Brighton, Sussex: Harvester Press, 1973).

Versnel, S., *Transition and Reversal in Myth and Ritual* (Inconsistencies in Greek and Roman Religion, II; Leiden: Brill, 1993).

Vokes, F.E., *The Riddle of the Didache: Facts, Fiction, Heresy or Catholicism?* (London: SPCK, 1938).

Volf, J.G., *Paul and Perseverance In and Falling Away* (WUNT, 2.37; Tübingen: Mohr [Paul Siebeck], 1990).

Vollmer, H., *Die alttestamentlichen Citate bei Paulus* (Leipzig: Metzger & Wittig, 1869).

Waddell, W.G., *Herodotus: Book II* (London: Methuen, 1939).

Wagner, G., *Pauline Baptism and the Pagan Mysteries* (Edinburgh: Oliver & Boyd, 1967).

Way, A.S., 'Bacchanals', in *Euripides* (LCL; 4 vols.; London: Heinemannn, 1912), III, pp. 1-121.

Wedderburn, A.J.M., *Baptism and Resurrection* (WUNT, 55; Tübingen: Mohr [Paul Siebeck], 1987), pp. 342-56.

—'The Problem of the Denial of the Resurrection in 1 Corinthians 15', *NovT* 23 (1981), pp. 229-41.

—*The Reasons for Romans* (Edinburgh: T. & T. Clark, 1988).

Wegenast, K., *Das Verständnis der Tradition bei Paulus und in den Deuteropaulinen*, (WMANT; Neukirchen–Vluyn: Neukirchener Verlag, 1962).

Wehnert, J., *Die Wir-Passagen Apostelgeschichte: Ein lukanisches Stilmittel aus jüdischer Tradition* (GTA, 40; Göttingen: Vandenhoeck & Ruprecht, 1989).

Weiser, A., *The Psalms: A Commentary* (OTL; Philadelphia: Westminster Press, 1962).

Weiss, B., *A Commentary on the New Testament* (G.H. Schodde and E. Wilson [trans.]; 4 vols.; New York: Funk and Wagnalls, 1906).

—*Galatians* (G.H. Schodde and E. Wilson [trans.]; Commentary on the New Testament, 3; New York: Funk and Wagnalls, 1906).

Weiss, J., *The History of Primitive Christianity* (F.C. Grant *et al.* [eds. and trans.]; 2 vols.; New York: Wilson–Erickson, 1936).

Wengst, K., *Christologische Formeln und Lieder des Urchristentums* (Gütersloh: Gerd Mohn, 1973).

West, J.C., 'The Order of 1 and 2 Thessalonians', *JTS* 15 (1914), pp. 66-74.

West, M.L., *Hesiod: Theogony, with Prolegomena and Commentary* (Oxford: Clarendon Press, 1966).

—*Iambi et Elegi Graeci ante Alexandrum Cantati* (2 vols.; Oxford: Clarendon Press, 1971-72).

Westcott, B. F., *St Paul and Justification* (London: Macmillan, 1913).

Westerholm, S., *Israel's Law and the Church's Faith: Paul and His Recent Interpreters* (Grand Rapids: Eerdmans, 1988).

Westermann, W.L., *The Slave Systems of Greek and Roman Antiquity* (Philadelphia: American Philosophical Society, 1955).

Westermarck, E.A., *The Origin and Development of Moral Ideas* (2 vols.; London: Macmillan, 1906-1908).

White, J.L., 'The Ancient Epistolography Group in Retrostect', in J.L. White (ed.), *Studies in Ancient Letter Writing* (*Semeia*, 22; Chico, CA: Scholars Press, 1982), pp. 1-14.

—'Apostolic Mission and Apostolic Message: Congruence in Paul's Epistolary Rhetoric, Structure and Imagery', in B. Hudson McLean (ed.), *Origins and Method: Towards a New Understanding of Judaism and Christianity: Studies in Honour of John C. Hurd* (JSNTSup, 86; Sheffield: JSOT Press, 1993), pp. 145-61.

—*The Form and Function of the Body of the Greek Letter: A Study of the Letter-Body in the Non-Literary Papyri and in Paul the Apostle* (SBLDS, 2; Missoula, MT: University of Montana Printing Department for SBL, 1972).

—'The Greek Documentary Letter Tradition Third Century BCE to Third Century CE', in J.L. White (ed.), *Studies in Ancient Letter Writing* (*Semeia*, 22; Chico, CA: Scholars Press, 1982), pp. 89-106.

Wiefel, W., 'Die Hauptrichtung des Wandels im eschatologischen Denkens des Paulus', *TZ* 30 (1974), pp. 65-81.

Wigan, H.W., *Sancti Irenaei Episcopi Lugdenensis* (2 vols.; Cambridge: Cambridge University Press, 1857).

Wilckens, U., 'Was heisst bei Paulus: "Aus Werken des Gesetzes wirdkein Mensch gerecht"?' in *Rechtfertigung als Freiheit: Paulusstudien* (Neukirchen–Vluyn: Neukirchener Verlag, 1974), pp. 77-109.

—*Der Brief an die Römer. 1–3* (2 vols.; EKKNT; Cologne: Benziger; Neukirchen–Vluyn: Neukirchener Verlag, 1978-1982).

Wilckens, U., 'Christologie und Anthropologie im Zusammenhang despaulinischen Gesetzesverständnisses', *ZNW* 67 (1976), pp. 64-82.

Wilkinson, G., *The Manners and Customs of the Ancient Egyptians Including Their Private Life, Government, Laws, Arts, Manufactures, Religion, Agriculture, and Early History* (5 vols.; London: John Murray, 3rd edn, 1847).

Williams, A.L. (trans.), *Justin Martyr: Dialogue with Trypho* (London: SPCK, 1930).

Williams, S., *Jesus' Death as Saving Event: the Background and Origin of a Concept* (HTR, 2; Missoula, MT: Scholars Press, 1975).

Windisch, H., *Der zweite Korintherbrief* (H.A.W. Meyer [ed.]; Kritisch-exegetischer Kommentar über das NT; Göttingen: Vandenhoeck & Ruprecht, 9th edn, 1924).

Winer, G.B., *A Grammar of the New Testament Diction* (E. Masson [trans.]; Edinburgh: T. & T. Clark, 3rd edn, 1861).

Witherington, B., *The Christology of Jesus* (Philadelphia: Fortress Press, 1990).

Woodhouse, W.J., 'The Scapegoat', in *Encyclopaedia of Religion and Ethics* (J. Hastings [ed.]; Edinburgh: T. & T. Clark, 1920), XI, pp. 218-23.

Wrede, W., *Paul* (repr.; Lexington: American Library Association Committee on Reprinting, 1962 [1908]).

Wright, D.P., *The Disposal of Impurity: Elimination Rites in the Bible and in Hittite and Mesopotamian Literature* (SBLDS, 101; Atlanta, GA: Scholars Press, 1987).

—'Gesture of Hand Placement in the Hebrew Bible and in Hittite Literature', *JAOS* 106 (1986), pp. 433-46.

Yadin, Y., 'Pesher Nahum (4QpNah) Reconsidered', *IEJ* 21 (1971), pp. 1-12.

—*The Temple Scroll* (2 vols.; Jerusalem: Ben Zvi, 1983).

Yerkes, R.K., *Sacrifice in Greek and Roman Religions and Early Judaism* (New York: Charles Scribner's Sons, 1952).

Zahn, T., *Der Brief des Paulus an die Galater* (KNT, 9; Leipzig: Deichert, 3rd edn, 1922 [1905]).

—*Der Brief des Paulus an die Römer* (Leipzig: Deichert, 3rd edn, 1925).

Zaidman, L.B., and P.S. Pantel, *Religion in the Ancient Greek City* (P. Cartledge; Cambridge: Cambridge University Press, 1989–1994).

Zerwick, M., *Biblical Greek: Illustrated by Examples* (trans. and adapted from 4th Latin edn by J. Smith; Rome: Pontifical Biblical Institute, 1963).

Zohar, N., 'Repentance and Purification: The Significance and Semantics of *hattath* in the Pentateuch', *JBL* 107 (1988), pp. 609-18.

Zorell, F., *Lexicon Hebraicum* (Rome: Pontifico Instituto Biblico, 1956).

INDEXES

INDEX OF REFERENCES

OLD TESTAMENT

APOCRYPHA

NEW TESTAMENT

INSCRIPTIONS

INDEX OF AUTHORS